OPEN MIKE

MIKE
SHEAHAN

The Slattery Media Group Pty Ltd
1 Albert St, Richmond
Victoria, Australia, 3121

Text copyright © Fox Footy 2013
Design copyright © The Slattery Media Group Pty Ltd 2013
First published by The Slattery Media Group Pty Ltd 2013

The original transcripts for the interviews of this publication were part of the Fox Sports television program, *Open Mike*; all transcripts used with permission. Interviews have been edited for the printed format.

All images used with permission. See images for credit information.

National Library of Australia Cataloguing-in-Publication entry
Author: Sheahan, Michael, 1947-
Title: Open Mike / Michael Sheahan.
ISBN: 9780987420541 (pbk.)
Subjects: Australian football.
            Sports–Australia.
            Sports personnel–Australia–Interviews.
Dewey Number: 796.336

Group Publisher: Geoff Slattery
Editors: Martin Blake and Andrew Gigacz
Cover photography: James Troi
Cover and page design: Guy Shield

Printed and bound in Australia by Griffin

slatterymedia.com

CONVERSATIONS FROM THE
GROUND-BREAKING **FOX FOOTY** PROGRAM

OPEN MIKE

MIKE
SHEAHAN

visit *slatterymedia.com*

ABOUT THE AUTHOR

Mike Sheahan has covered AFL football for more than 40 years, beginning his career with *Newsday* in Melbourne in 1969.

He has worked for *The Age, The Herald, The Sunday Age* and the *Herald Sun*. He retired from newspapers in 2011 after 18 years as chief football writer of the *Herald Sun*.

He has also worked in radio, with the ABC and 3AW, and in television, with Channels 7 and 9 and Fox Footy, where he appears on *On The Couch* and hosts *Open Mike*.

OPEN MIKE

CONTENTS

INTRODUCTION 8
Questions and Answers by Mike Sheahan

Author's note: Interviews are published in alphabetical order. Dates of broadcast are noted at the beginning of each interview.

INTRODUCTION

QUESTIONS AND ANSWERS

MY first major interview in my first job in Melbourne newspapers—in October 1969—began with a telephone call to Sam Kekovich, laid up in a Melbourne hospital bed recovering from a knee operation.

I was so nervous, I could barely manage to dial the hospital number. It was as if I had been plucked from obscurity for an audience with a head of state, an eminent public figure, a movie star, a sporting idol. The reality had frozen me.

He was 19, a boy from tobacco-growing country at Myrtleford in central Victoria; me 22, a young man from Werribee in Melbourne's west, someone who had grown up with most sportsmen and all footballers on an exalted plane.

Admittedly, the teenage Kekovich had won North Melbourne's best-and-fairest award that year and was the most explosive new talent in the game, but...

The jangling of nerves describes the impact footballers had on so many boys who grew up in the so-called football states of Australia.

No apologies from me. Forty-plus years on, I'm still in awe of the stars of this unique and wonderful way of life known as Australian football, more recently AFL.

It's why I still get nervous and excited at my age interviewing players and coaches on Fox Footy's *On the Couch* and, more recently, *Open Mike*, the program that has re-energised me after more than 40 years in newspapers, radio and television.

Kekovich and I now work frequently at functions: he the clever, articulate (I think), risqué after-dinner speaker and star of the brilliant national television campaign extolling the virtues of lamb as a staple in a healthy and tasty diet; me the straight guy treating football with a weird sense of reverence.

Yet I have to confess I still occasionally see him as larger than life—in more ways than the obvious!

For the record, I recall sharing a coffee with two of Kekovich's coaches, Keith McKenzie and Ron Barassi, late in 2012 and listening to them declare Slammin' Sam perhaps the best player in the game in his prime, a period that extended for just a couple of years.

He is high on my list of preferred interview subjects for the second season of *Open Mike* in 2013. It may well be the first edition requiring subtitles!

Everyone has a story. Everyone. Journalists have the task of drawing those stories, recalling events, be they triumphs or famous failures, and prodding memories into interviews in print or on radio or television.

Open Mike gives me that opportunity; it is my journey down Memory Lane. I have relished the task.

When I made contact with Phil Carman mid-season 2012 to invite him to join me in front of the camera, it was the Kekovich moment of 1969 revisited.

I had been friendly with Carman during his brilliant yet incident-charged career, but hadn't spoken with him for nigh on 20 years. I had no idea how he remembered my assessment of the highlights and lowlights of his playing days, how he saw a widely despised media that, in his time, had been less than glowing of his career, and how he had grown into his senior years.

'Fabulous' Phil and I picked up where we left off all those years ago. Yes, he was happy to come on the program, happy—content is probably a more appropriate word—to trawl through the incidents that made him such a prominent figure in football history; prominent for his mix of genius and capacity to cause mayhem, to himself and his club(s).

Carman, remember, was suspended from not one but two Grand Finals in 1977 on a striking charge from the second semi-final, a mindless act against Hawthorn that almost certainly cost Collingwood the premiership to be won by North Melbourne in just the second Grand Final replay in the Victorian game's history.

It was good to catch up, but I wanted to reach into Carman's soul, to take him back to the inexplicable lapses of discipline in his playing days. I did. He was uncomfortable, frustrated that all his old sins were paraded yet again. As brilliant as he was as a player—and there is a mountain of vision to support that fact—I couldn't help but feel he thought I had the balance wrong that morning at Fox Studios; too much of the negative, not enough of the positive.

It's a fine line we tread. Like all Collingwood supporters who consider themselves blessed to have seen Carman in the flesh, I could watch his 30-minute highlights package with sheer pleasure, yet marks and goals are merely an element of the Carman story. It is much deeper, far more complicated.

That's what we must do as reporters and commentators if we are to do our job properly.

We share the love of the Carmans of the world on the playing field—and more recently others of his ilk, such as Gary Ablett senior, Tony Lockett, Ben Cousins, Brendan Fevola and co.—but our primary function is to tell or elicit the complete stories of the biggest names in the game.

During my 40 years in print, I was repeatedly asked who I barracked for. My answer was as consistent as Gary Ablett junior is as a player: 'I barrack for the story.'

How lucky can one person be? A lifetime working in football, now a fresh direction interviewing, coaxing, probing, enjoying the memories of the biggest names in the game. My heroes.

I finished the 2012 *Open Mike* series chatting with Peter Hudson and Kevin 'Cowboy' Neale about their bloody battle during the 1971 Hawthorn-St Kilda Grand Final. It was like an entertainment reporter sitting in front of two Hollywood icons on set at Universal Studios. Paul Newman and Gene Hackman, perhaps.

I loved it. Good guy Hudson, villain Neale (a trait apparent only on the field in an era that glorified violence), both happy to revisit the brutal events of 40 years earlier, both respectful of each other, the on-field culture of the time, their contributions to football's rich history.

Open Mike was born of a long-standing ambition of mine to try to emulate Andrew Denton in sport, a wish accommodated by Fox Footy chief Rod Law. It was seen on an ad-hoc basis for several years until Law elevated it to weekly status in 2012.

It has featured many of the game's biggest names—a remarkably reflective Leigh Matthews, the endearingly matter-of-fact Greg Williams, the brutally honest Dermott Brereton, Glenn Archer, Mark Ricciuto, Robert Walls and Steven Baker, the unique Malcolm Blight, the giant of broadcasting Tony Charlton, Jason Akermanis (you choose the adjective), the lovable rogue Martin Pike, the controversial and intractable Don Scott, the charming Tadhg Kennelly. Those interviews—and many more—make up this book, with new chapters to come in 2013, and another series of *Open Mike*.

Mike Sheahan
February 2013

JASON AKERMANIS

In a career spanning 16 seasons and 325 games, Jason Akermanis managed to thrill, frustrate and alienate footballers, coaches, fans and even those outside the world of football. From a pure football standpoint, his record is one that stands up against almost any other player. Having joined Brisbane when in the death throes of its incarnation as the Bears, Akermanis became a driving force behind the Brisbane Lions' powerhouse that won three successive flags from 2001 to 2003 (the only team in the past 60 years to achieve that feat). With Simon Black, Nigel Lappin, Michael Voss and Luke Power, Akermanis formed the engine room of that successful era. The group were collectively dubbed the 'Fab Five'.

'Aker' became famous for his bleached hair and post-game handstands, in which he would kiss the turf after each Brisbane (and later Western Bulldogs) victory. The Lions played finals football in all but one year from 1999 to 2005. Underlining his influence during that golden period, Akermanis won a Brownlow Medal, two club best-and-fairest awards and was an All-Australian four times.

Despite of his on-field success, Akermanis at times caused headaches for fellow players, coach Leigh Matthews and the club in general with his often controversial comments on radio and television. Things came to a head in 2006 and the relationship between Akermanis, Matthews and several players deteriorated to a point where he was no longer welcome at the club. At the end of that season Akermanis became a Western Bulldog.

Remaining as flamboyant as ever, Akermanis gave the Dogs solid, and sometimes scintillating, service over three-and-a-half seasons. As a midfielder-cum-forward, he was a key element of the Bulldog teams that made it to the preliminary finals in 2008 and 2009, heading the club's goalkicking in the second of those years. Having flagged his intention to retire after 2009, Akermanis persuaded the Dogs to give him one final season and a chance at another flag in 2010. But his 'motor mouth' again landed him in hot water with the players and the public, leading to the club to sacking him mid-season.

MAY 30, 2012

Mike: Jason Akermanis the footballer was talented, exciting, audacious, compelling. He was a three-time premiership player and a Brownlow Medallist with more than 300 games to his name; the stuff of legends. He's also one of the most controversial figures of his time; a flawed genius. Jason, what we've got is a recurring theme and it's that the Brisbane Lions, the Western Bulldogs, the AFL, all have dumped you, haven't they?

Jason: Well, Brisbane wasn't a firing. It was just a parting of ways. I mean, I just said: 'Look, I need to move on.' And we just moved on.

Mike: Is that true—is that literally true? Did they not cut your commission short late in the 2006 season and say: 'That's the last time you'll play for this footy club'?

Jason: What I remember distinctly ... and the relationship that broke down wasn't really with the players. It was just me and Leigh Matthews and I have no one else to blame about that than myself. Because the year before, I'd won the best and fairest, and had a really good year and we came out in the first round against Geelong and I remember distinctly having three players rotate through me. I went on the ball, and I wasn't getting arrested; I could see that that's where the game was going.

And foolishly in one of my columns I said: 'We need to learn and get better at it.' It was a bad idea. Our relationship for so long was so good and that's the one time I just pushed the wrong button and Leigh took it personally, and he should have. There's nothing wrong with the reaction, but then in all the whole procession after that, I don't have anyone to blame.

The players were put in a position where they had great leadership for so long, and I clearly was getting stale. I just behaved badly and became a disruptive kid. Leigh and I agreed just before then that we should part at the end of the year, so we were pretty happy, Leigh and I. Then later I did an article, which is up to interpretation, but basically I said I was less than five percent chance to stay.

Mike: Have you left a bit out there though? My understanding was that Michael Voss, your captain at the time, was the one who lost faith in you when that story appeared, because you had said to the playing group: 'Look, let's put our heads down; adopt a low profile and see ... and let our actions on the field speak for themselves?'

Jason: Yes, that's right. I do remember that now. We'd just lost to Sydney and I gave away a free kick or something stupid against Jared Crouch and 'Vossy' said: 'Shut it down.' In fairness to Vossy, he and Leigh were always huge supporters and saw a great positive in everything that we did up to that point. I just reckon that it got to a point where Leigh said: 'Mate, even he's not listening to you; I think it's not working.' And that's fair enough; it wasn't.

So in the end, while the support of Michael might have been drying up ... even after that particular little five percent quote it wasn't as bad as: 'He's got to go and I don't think so.'

Mike: But it was a very sad way for someone as celebrated as yourself, a three-time premiership player, to leave a footy club.

Jason: Look, I don't regret anything but I wish I did things a lot better, and you learn as you go. I feel disappointed in many ways that I let myself get that bad. I didn't have to do it like that but you think you make the best decision at the time. I was never good at parting ways with things or people. It wasn't one of my finest hours.

Mike: This is unlike you. I think we have got a good relationship but I've always noticed that whatever you've done, no matter what the fallout, Jason Akermanis thinks that he's done the right thing. And here we are,

CAREER
Born: February 24, 1977
Clubs: *Brisbane* 1995-2006—248 games, 307 goals;
Western Bulldogs 2007-10—77 games, 114 goals
Honours: Brownlow Medal 2001; Brisbane's best and fairest 1999, 2005; All-Australian 1999, 2001, 2002, 2004; State-of-Origin (Allies) 1996-98; International Rules series 1999-2000; premiership side 2001, 2002, 2003

you're talking about how you may have done things differently; how you should've done things differently.

Jason: I'm 35 now. I've matured out of footy; I've had a couple of years where I've not had to worry about anything, the day-to-day running around a footy club and dealing with all the stuff you have to do being an athlete, and while I've enjoyed that, you get a chance to look back and think: 'If this situation happens again, can you do it better?' I think how stupid and almost immature I was at times but you get caught up in it.

Mike: So was that fabricated, or was that you?

Jason: No, I hate losing and I hate being called a maverick. It's all right to be called a maverick when I go and play golf and or go-karting. It just pisses me off because I've been in the industry 16 years and I've played since a little kid. Now, while I may look different and have my own thoughts and ideas, I cannot tell you how I always submitted to the team and I did that in all the teams I played for.

Mike: But, Jason, the blokes who played with you at both Brisbane Lions and the Bulldogs would dispute that and say that your problems were because you wouldn't conform to team ethics.

Jason: No, no, not when I was at the club and on the football field, and that's what should matter and that's why Brisbane, I think, had a really good leadership. They knew that, and they accepted that and all that other stuff. Leigh's not a big media supporter when you're in that kind of environment, he just detests it. I think even he could see that it had some great benefit for all of us. I started media in 2002, which was the year after the Brownlow, and Michael Voss, Justin Leppitsch and Alastair Lynch all came after that and were able to have great careers in the media for that period.

Mike: So you're 35 years of age; are you a bit of a lost soul?

Jason: Maybe but I don't feel lost. I'm disappointed in some ways that after 10 years, you see guys get jobs ahead of you in the media, and it's all kind of fluffy, it just makes me laugh. I spent 10 years doing TV, radio, newspaper stuff, and have all the skills that you want. I'm not necessarily everyone's cup of tea, but we're in the entertainment industry and you see guys get put in the system and they've got to get coaching to help them speak to the camera. They were employed to do and that disappoints me but you know what? But I've got no one else to blame.

Mike: I was just saying that not everyone else can be out of step. Sometimes we all have to say: 'If everyone says I'm doing the wrong thing, maybe everyone's right.'

Jason: Yes, maybe they are, and two years away is ... because there's no jobs for me in this industry and whether ... do you just smell bad sometimes and you come back in the cycle later? I don't know, but I haven't lost a great deal of sleep. I've been disappointed at times, don't get me wrong, because I think I've got a lot to give. But you know what? If you kind of just accept the inevitable, it's nothing.

There's lots of other things I can do, and I suppose you have to set yourself up to have option A and B, and while I would've loved to have still been involved in the media, that just hasn't happened.

Mike: So you've got a family; Megan and two girls. You can't do the speaking circuit for the rest of your life can you?

Jason: No, no, I can't.

Mike: So what are you going to do?

Jason: Well, this year was always to play and to speak and, the last couple of years I've been doing nearly 70 shows a year but that will start to come down, even though it's been a good business. There's not a great necessity to work every day. You just sort of do what you have to do, and my wife has picked up the slack. I think I'll just do karting and Superkarts and golf because that's just a lot of fun.

Mike: No money?

Jason: No money. I would think that after that I will seriously have a look at coaching my own team somewhere, I don't care where. I've just got to get that experience, because I've seen a few ex-teammates go straight into coaching, and I think that if you could do it this way, I think your skills may be better suited for the longer run.

Mike: When do you believe that things started turning sour for you in Brisbane? Was there a moment?

Jason: Yes. Round 2, 2006. After the column, that was it.

Mike: But my understanding was that there was a major fallout when you revealed Nigel Lappin's cracked rib in the week leading up to the 2003 Grand Final. Now, I'm guessing here, but I would've thought had Brisbane lost that game they would've sacked you.

Jason: Yes, maybe. I heard that too, and Leigh has never denied that I was in a lot of trouble. He was really pissed off.

Mike: So doesn't it date back to then?

Jason: No, I think Leigh got over it. We won, and it was 'You know what? I forgive that one; don't do it again.' That was Leigh's style and to his credit he always was able to get on with stuff. You deal with it, you say you're sorry if you are, and then you don't carry it with you.

Mike: Let me ask you this, Jason. We're back in 2003; Lappin's a critically important player to your team. What would've motivated you to tell the world that he had an injury that the opposition would immediately target and make worse?

Jason: I don't know. I'm not big on misleading the public at the best of times but it was probably the worst week to. I couldn't even justify it; I can't even understand why I'd be so silly but everyone knew he had sore ribs.

Mike: What about the Bulldogs? They were interesting times; you came to Melbourne, had finished poorly in Brisbane. You've had a fresh start here, and it started so well. But it didn't finish on a good note, did it?

Jason: It's probably the most disappointing thing I'd seen. Look, I take full responsibility for my part but at the end, there was a big difference between the Bulldogs' leadership and the Brisbane leadership, and I mean that, and there's no nice way to say it. From the top down in Brisbane, it was still strong and while I'd pushed it to the nth degree, it was just really me and Leigh. I just felt at the Bulldogs, I've never seen a group get so hysterical. I just couldn't understand it. And Brisbane and Leigh... it wouldn't worry them; just wouldn't worry them and...

Mike: Well, it did worry them; you know that's not true.

Jason: Well, to a point. I know that some things were off the charts, but little things were just not an issue. At the Bulldogs they were an issue, a big issue. They were so fanatical over stuff said in the media, I'd never seen anything like it. Really sensitive and I said: 'Look, I said those things and I take responsibility for them, but I did not ever think that you could go to that degree of lack of understanding on just the reality of what was happening.'

Mike: Did you shed tears when you were cleaning out your locker?

Jason: Yes, that was ... man, when you get told your footy career is over there's a lot of emotion building and building and building, so a little volcano burst out. I'm an emotional guy at the best of times, and I don't like crying, but I just felt everything was just shit. I had to sit in front of the group, eat shit sandwiches, it gives me no joy in talking about any of it.[1]

Mike: Well, I've got to stay with it for a moment. Was that the most demeaning thing that happened in your football career, having to sit out the front and defend yourself in front of the playing group? You've come from a club that's won three premierships and a successful club, and you've gone to a club that doesn't have a lot of silverware, and you had to answer to these blokes. How did that sit with you?

Jason: Still today it burns for a lot of reasons, because when I sat out there and had all my teammates sitting there like some kind of great judges that were going to rain down awfulness if you don't agree to what they do ... I've never seen such open bullying. I've seen blokes really put other blokes in bad spots, but this is on a big scale, and I'm sitting there and I've got this little faction over here that's caused me great grief. They're in the leadership group and they're going hysterical over this column about gays in footy, and I'm telling them the truth. I'm telling them where it's all at. We get to a point where they say: 'All right, Jason, we want you to give up your media.' I said: 'All right. Well, let me just make you understand this. I've given up over $250,000 to come back, they begged me to come back and I wanted to come back, but if I come back with this reduced wage that's fine. Just let me at least do the media.'

It's the first time ever that I've earned more money in the media than in football, which is probably a big shock to everyone in the system, but somehow that happened. So all of a sudden media was actually my main job. I distinctly remember Adam Cooney saying: 'Mate, if you give up the

---

1 Akermanis had made comments in a newspaper article about homosexuality in football, which caused a stir and drew the ire of his players. Under the 'Leading Teams' model of leadership adopted by the Bulldogs, players are often required to sit before a 'peer review' conducted by senior players, to explain certain actions.

media, you could be a four-time premiership player.' And I thought: 'These guys seriously think that this is going to matter.' And I said: 'All right, fellows, the last I looked I'd given up $250,000, and I'm going to give up the media, for which I'm earning more money in. I'm going to have to change a whole lot of loans and default on things; this is not just an easy thing.'

I said: 'The last time I looked, I've given up more to be in this group than anyone in this group, more of myself for you guys. What more do I need to do to prove this? When I come here you know, and you've seen it categorically, I'm all for you. I come and train my arse off. I'm out in the field and I work my arse off, I put my body on the line. I do those things, that is my requirement. When I get out of here, I'm sorry, fellows, I don't give a shit about you. I care about my family and friends. When I come back in, I'll do it again.'

The decision was made not long after that. It was: 'Mate, there's no trust. We can't have you like that.' Sam Newman and I had lunch and he said a great thing: 'Jason, nothing's going to change here. You do this and stop media, nothing's going to be any different. All they've done is put you in a position where they'll think they're happy, they're manipulating you, where in reality you're still going to play the same footy. You're still going to give all for the club.'

In the end, I said: 'I'm not going to give up the media because it's too important.' They said: 'No trust here.' They terminated my contract.

Mike: How much were you playing for in your last year at the Bulldogs, from the footy club?
Jason: $200,000. It's not bad money. Not terrible money.

Mike: Now, your natural father did come back into your life while you were in Brisbane, didn't he?
Jason: Yes, I instigated it. I knew that I had half-siblings, and I knew that while I had two half-sisters, the half-brother had a pretty unique name, and I would be able to find him. The siblings grew up in a family unit; they didn't realise their dad had an affair and had me and my brother. It's a little sordid and probably uneasy. His wife knew nothing about it, and it was tough for them, no doubt. But I felt like at 28 years of age, I should say that they deserved to know, and they were so thankful that I did.

Mike: Was it disruptive for you?

Jason: Probably. That emotion is pretty hard. You know that you have a dad and I had nothing except for his 23 chromosomes, that's it. There's been no influence; he never helped my mum. My mum did it tough and raised us both.

Mike: You lost your mother at a young age, too, didn't you?

Jason: Yes. I remember it was my first season, three years before I had a really bad accident and nearly died. It was a bad blood clot in my brain. It was awful, and I had depression out of that. I really wanted to finish it all off, literally commit suicide. I was 15.

It was the only time I've ever been knocked out, like properly. It happened at 4.30 in the afternoon. I was on rollerblades and at 9.30 at night I'm in a hospital room asking how that happened.

Three months goes by and I get double vision. I can't go to school, I have to sit on my back. The doctor said: 'Mate, you won't be playing sport again, don't worry about that.'

And I just was heartbroken. But I did heal quickly and it was good. I was lucky. I was pretty young, and I didn't have a lot of long-term damage. My headaches stopped and the double vision stopped. I went back to school and things started to return to normal and three years later I was good enough to get on to an AFL list, with the Brisbane Bears. I had a good under-18 carnival, I got an All-Australian jumper and the club came around.

For my first year I played 17 games and I made more money than my mum. We'd never had any money, so it was just a really good time to be alive. And then one day in the off-season, mum says: 'I don't feel so good.' She has a full fit and I had no idea what was going on. By the time two days had passed, and she'd had another couple of seizures, clearly there was something wrong.

And then we went to hospital and the doctor called us in. He said: 'We did a CAT scan. See this golf-ball-sized area inside your mum's skull? That's a tumour, and we've done a biopsy and it's a category five cancer, boys.' And he said 'Your mum's got no more than three months.'

And I said: 'Mate, you cannot be serious. She doesn't drink, didn't smoke, she walked to work every day, had vegies every night, she was as healthy as you could possibly ever imagine.'

And she didn't last very long. It was 18 months. The next month, my brother turns 18, the next year I turn 21, and then she'd passed away. I'm there trying to help my brother, we've got her house and I'm trying to play footy, and thank God I had footy. Because it was the only thing I loved that was left. I was a wreck. I thought the world owed me something. I went off the rails, drank too much and if it wasn't for footy that got me up, I was gone. But I had some structure ... enough structure to get through it.

Mike: Let's consider a few of your contributions via your columns over the journey, Jason. You threatened not to play with Wayne Carey after he left North Melbourne and there was some talk he might go to Brisbane. You accused a West Coast opponent of playing on performance-enhancing drugs; more recently, and I think most insensitively, you called Jimmy Stynes 'a nasty man in his day', two days after he died. How do they sit with you?

Jason: The Jim Stynes stuff was awful, awful timing. I've copped abuse, but never on that scale. It was honestly disgusting, the abuse that I copped. What I said was in context. He was a competitor and he was aggressive and nasty and all the things; mates were saying the same thing. But I knew straightaway, I'd done the wrong thing, wrong timing, wrong context. All I could do is say: 'I am sorry and I'm sincerely sorry.' I left it there and moved on as quickly as I could.

Mike: But were you sorry because of the outrage that you'd caused, or were you sorry because you said something intemperate?

Jason: No, I was sorry for all of those things. I'm sorry that I didn't say it well enough, that I said it then, and that it just blew up into something that was not really representative of where the hell I was going.

Mike: But this man had died two days before you said that. Now, I know we sit in judgement and things are said on radio. We've all done it, but I can't actually understand how you could say that and not think that that was going to cause uproar and hurt your reputation.

Jason: Well, I said it and I take responsibility for it, and it was a dumb day in my life, I can tell you.

Mike: You're married with two daughters. Does Megan ever say: 'Jason, what in God's name were you doing or saying?'

Jason: She lives with me so sees my context, and she knows where I'm coming from. She'll often bemoan the fact that the people can't understand where I came from. But there's many times that she's said: 'What are you ... why, why, just why, tell me why.' And I go 'Well, this is what I'm thinking.' And then she gets it and understands.

Mike: You've often said 'regrets are for fools'. Do you still believe that?

Jason: Absolutely, yes.

Mike: But you've expressed regrets today.

Jason: That word is fine. You can call it regrets but there's no doubt that I could do it better. But I can't regret what I've done; I've done what I've done.

Mike: You can regret what you've done.

Jason: Well, yes, but there's no point in learning if ... you could say 'I feel bad about that and I wish I never did it', and that's fine. Okay, call it a regret...

Mike: Isn't that a regret?

Jason: Maybe it is. I don't want to split hairs, but if you regret it and carry it with you, that's foolish. It really is. You learn your lesson and I think you should just get on with it and the next time you're in that situation, and I've been in many, 'I've done terribly I should do it better' situations. And if I don't, I'm just not learning.

GLENN ARCHER

Glenn Archer was not awarded the title 'Shinboner of the Century' by the North Melbourne Football Club without reason. In his 311 games, Archer rarely, if ever, gave his own safety a second thought in his quest for the ball or the man who had it in his possession.

Originally from Lyndale/Noble Park in Melbourne's outer east, Archer joined the Denis Pagan-coached North Melbourne's under-19 side but, despite showing great promise, was reluctant to remain a Kangaroo, preferring the fun and mateship of suburban footy. Pagan and other North officials convinced Archer to persist and he made his debut in 1992.

By the following year, Archer was a regular member of the senior team, now coached by Pagan after Wayne Schimmelbusch was sacked during the pre-season. Archer was one of several seeds planted in the first half of the 1990s that would bear premiership fruit in 1996 and 1999.

Having spent his early seasons swinging between attack and defence, Archer settled into a more or less permanent defensive role in the latter half of his career. Regardless of position, Archer's ferocious attack on the ball no matter what lay ahead, and his willingness to back into a pack to take a saving mark, were unparalleled in his time.

Playing his first Grand Final in 1996, Archer was rewarded with the Norm Smith Medal for his best-on-ground performance as the Roos broke a 19-year premiership drought. He was prominent again when North backed up for another flag three years later.

As is the case with many long-term players, Archer's twilight years were affected by injury, but he missed few games, often playing in pain or with the aid of painkillers to help him through. Throughout his 16 seasons he remained unassuming, but no one could ever doubt that Glenn Archer is one of North Melbourne's greatest heroes.

APRIL 11, 2012

Mike: He holds the most respected title of the North Melbourne Football Club, yet Glenn Archer always seems uncomfortable as the 'Shinboner of the Century'. In contrast to so many of his contemporaries, he seems to have disappeared from public view. He holds no official position at North, no television or radio roles, no newspaper column. Glenn, you've walked away from everything. Is that deliberate, or is it just the way this unfolded?

Glenn: It probably comes across like that, because I don't do any footy media but I still seem to be out there in other parts of my life, with the work and all that sort of stuff.

Mike: You're at Stride Management?

Glenn: Yes. We manage about 160 of the AFL players and I have taken on a joint general manager's role with one of my managers, Tom Petroro. So, I really enjoy that. And I've got another business called Ultimate Sports Tours, with Leigh Colbert. He's the ultimate tour guide. So we take clients all around the world, to all the big sporting events. And you've got to pinch yourself sometimes, you know? I know last year we were on a boat in the harbour in Monaco, watching the Grand Prix, sipping piña coladas, and then I nudged 'Colby', and I thought: 'Bloody hell. Noble Park one day... Monaco the next.'

Mike: You genuinely are a revered figure in football, there's no doubt about that, respected by everyone and held in a lot of affection for the way you played. But things could have been a lot different, couldn't they? Without football, I mean, where would your life have taken you, do you think?

Glenn: I don't know. I definitely got to that fork in the road when I was about 18. I was playing at Noble Park, playing some senior footy then. I'd already done a pre-season at North Melbourne, under Denis Pagan, when I was about 17. And I went from my local footy club, where basically I could do whatever I liked, to Denis, down at Kensington Park, running

400s and him screaming obscenities at me. And I thought, 'Nah, this isn't for me'.

Mike: That's when you coined the phrase, then, you thought Denis might have been a lunatic. Is that right?

Glenn: I thought he was a lunatic. And he probably proved it sometimes. Sorry, coach.

Mike: You went home with no intention of going back to North?

Glenn: I was happy to play at Noble Park, probably because in the back of my mind I didn't think I was good enough to play AFL footy. I was a short little fat bloke, playing at Noble Park in the seniors, playing full-forward. I thought I was okay, but I never thought I'd be good enough to make that next step. But I got a phone call in 1991 from Denis Pagan. It was already Round 5 of the season, and he said: 'Come down and play one game in the under 19s. We need a forward.' I was a forward back then. He said: 'If you like it, stay; if not, go back to Noble Park.' I said 'no' a couple of times and he persevered. So I said to my girlfriend [now wife]: 'I'm going to go down and play one game and get this bloke off my back.' So I went down and played. I always remember it, we played Carlton at Arden Street. We won. I kicked a couple of goals. And I thought: 'Oh, this is all right.' I really enjoyed the company of the other players. And we were playing Sydney the weekend after, so I thought: 'I might hang around.' I'd only been on a plane once, so I wanted to go to Sydney. So I did that, and enjoyed it, and I thought: 'I'll hang around for a little bit longer', and 17 years later, I was still there.

Mike: You didn't get him off your back, did you? You had him on your back for 17 years?

Glenn: Yes, and I've said a lot of times, I'm indebted to that man for the rest of my life. If it wasn't for his perseverance … I'd never had any other club speak to me, I'd never played Teal Cup, I'd never played any of that sort

---

CAREER
Born: March 24, 1973
Club: *North Melbourne* 1992-2007—311 games, 143 goals
Honours: Norm Smith Medal 1996; North Melbourne's Team of the Century; Shinboner of the Century; All-Australian 1996, 1998, 2002; State-of-Origin (Victoria) 1998; premiership side 1996, 1999; AFLPA Robert Rose Award (League's most courageous player) 1998, 1999, 2002, 2003, 2005, 2006; AFLPA Madden Medal (Community Spirit Award) 2007

of stuff. So Greg Miller[2] found me, Denis Pagan persevered in getting me down there, and the rest is history.

Mike: You were a pretty wild kid, weren't you? And I don't think that's exaggerating, is it?

Glenn: I was pretty wild. I had a really bad temper, which spilled into my AFL career at times, as well, and that haunted me for a while. We used to get up to no good when we were kids, and again, I hit that fork in the road that Denis dragged me down, the right road. There's some of the guys that I knocked around with ... one of my close friends passed away at 27 of a heroin overdose. I'm pretty sure I wouldn't have gone down that path, because I was never into that sort of stuff, but you just don't know. Maybe the peer-group pressure might've got hold of me and I could've ended up like that as well. So, again, that's why I was so indebted to Denis.

Mike: Glenn, you're the Shinboner of the Century, six times the Most Courageous Player in the competition. You're a Norm Smith medallist. But you never won a best and fairest at North. I know you're a team player— I understand that—but does it irk you that you were never acknowledged by your own footy club as the best player of any given year?

Glenn: Not at all. And this might sound clichéd, but it's an individual award, and if I wanted individual awards I would have played an individual sport. I was lucky that I played through an era where we played in 20-odd finals matches, three Grand Finals, two premierships. And the individual stuff pales into insignificance once you've achieved the team ultimate of winning the premiership. And people might think that's clichéd, but I am dead serious. I wouldn't care if I finished 20th every year.

Mike: You grew up a passionate Collingwood supporter. And why am I not surprised that Darren Millane was your hero?

Glenn: Yeah, he was my hero. He came from the same club, as well. I just loved everything about him. Obviously, when you see him make the grade and he comes from the same area, you're going to watch him a bit closer, but I just thought he was the ultimate footballer. He was tough, he could mark really well overhead, which was something that I really admired...

---

2 Miller was North Melbourne's head of recruiting. He later became football manager of the Kangaroos.

Mike: He could belt blokes.

Glenn: He could belt blokes. He was great kick. And you look back at his statistics, as well, he had some unbelievable games, having 30-odd kicks in a game, and he was a fantastic footballer.

Mike: Your present met your future in the 1980 night final at Waverley Park. That was the game in which Kerry Good kicked the winning goal after the siren for North Melbourne. Now, you were on the ground, weren't you, when Kerry Good took that kick?

Glenn: I was. I was six years old at the time, and I was a mad Collingwood supporter. I had my older brother Mark with me, who would've been 11, I suppose, and my dad was in the stands. We rushed down to the fence, as we used to always do, and jumped over the fence, and he used to cart me out there, obviously, being so young. I was one of those little blokes in the duffle coats running at Kerry Good and hoping he'd miss it.

Mike: You've got a colourful history at Waverley Park, haven't you? Are you prepared to own up to a few of the escapades out there?

Glenn: I lived across the road on Jells Road, which was 150 metres from the front gates at Waverley, for years. So I used to spend every Saturday there. We never paid once. We knew all the places to jump the fence, get into the Members' area. Somehow I worked out that my locker key from school worked for the catering elevator. So we used to get in there and go down to the rooms. At half-time of the seniors we used to get in there before the Little League and take their pies, have a couple of free pies.

Mike: You had a fear, or certainly a very, very healthy respect of players at other clubs. Did you work them over, or not?

Glenn: Oh, yes. I'd sort of worked out, probably midway through my career, that you could bluff a few. There's no doubt about it. Particularly back then, you could chop the arms. I mean, obviously the rules have changed now. And so even if the guy was going to take an easy mark in front of me, I'd always chop his arms and try and get a little bit of the side of his head at the same time. 'Next time, I'm going to do the same', sort of thing. I found that worked a bit. I found my teammates around me helped a lot, because some of these players thought that I was a bit mad. Guys like David King used to wind them up, saying: 'Oh, Archer's going to punch you in the back of the head.' And: 'He's going to kill you.' I used to say: 'Yeah, keep it going.'

Mike: You played on heaps of big names, lots of them. Were there one or two that you really looked forward to playing on, where you looked forward to the battle?

Glenn: No, not really, because I'd never really look forward to playing. I used to think about the game too much, and I used to think about the bad things too much, about what could happen. So, leading into games was quite tough, because I used to sit there and think about my man kicking 10 goals on me, and then I'd feel sick, and think: 'I'm going to lose the game for us.' It got to a stage towards the end where I had to live on sleeping tablets, just to switch myself off.

Mike: All during the week, or just night before?

Glenn: Both. It was all the time. But once I'd get out on the ground, I was fine. It was just leading into the game, which made it tough.

Mike: It was the fear of failure, wasn't it?

Glenn: Yes, absolutely. I used to speak to the psychologists. The coach used to say: 'Believe in yourself.' I found at the end, I reckon that helped me, because it made me work harder.

Mike: There's a famous moment where you and James Hird exchanged jumpers at the end of the game. Tell us what it was like playing on someone like Hird?

Glenn: It was really tough with 'Hirdy', because I used to look at him and think: 'He doesn't look like a footballer.' He would lead to certain spots where you think: 'There's no way that they're going to give him the ball.' But they used to always get him. You might be having the best game of all time, but he would always find a way of working his way through. I've found that people used to talk about my courage all the time—because my talent wasn't all that good, so they used to just focus in on that—but I found, with the really talented players, they didn't really talk about their courage that much. I think we were too busy talking about how good they were.

Wayne Carey was the same. They had amazing courage, but we just didn't really talk about it that much, because they were so good, and we talked about the games that they won.

Mike: In 1993, Glenn, you were playing at North Melbourne on $5000 a year? Correct?

Glenn: Yes, something like that.

Mike: Sydney makes you an offer of $450,000 for three years, which is a pay rise of $145,000 a year. You said 'no'. Is that loyalty or stupidity?

Glenn: It was definitely loyalty, back then. And as it turned out, it was the best decision I ever made, because I ended up playing in the premierships and they ended up looking after me at the end. I spoke about it with my girlfriend, and she gave me the advice of: 'What's your heart say?' And I said: 'My heart says 'stay at North Melbourne. They gave me the chance.' It would've looked terrible if I ran away. I loved where I was. It was my third year at the club. I had really close mates already, I could see we were going to do something, and like I said, they looked after me later on.

Mike: Your courage was legendary. It still is. Was that natural, or was it manufactured?

Glenn: Mainly instinct, it came naturally. But I think it was a Denis Pagan thing, as well. Once I did a couple of courageous things early on in my career, we'd go and watch the review of the game, and he used to make this point about: 'Oh, look how courageous that was, that's amazing.' I think mainly it was instinct, but Denis's encouragement helped a lot, as well.

Mike: I'm sure you love Jonathan Brown. I think we all do. But when you watch Brown play, with the series of injuries that he's had to his face, do you think it's reckless?

Glenn: It's just him. I've heard commentators kind of putting him down, saying: 'That's stupid courage.' But that's the way he plays. That's the way he's always played. And you think about the amount of times he's done it, compared to the amount of times he's got injured, sure, there have been freak incidents, and they've been pretty bad, but he's been doing that his whole career. I reckon he'll find it really hard to change it, because it's generally that little man in the back of your head saying: 'You've got to get there, you've got to go.'

Mike: In 1998, do you think your temper cost you the best and fairest?

Glenn: Yes, I got suspended for a couple of weeks that year. I definitely missed four games.

Mike: Yet the previous year, I thought one of probably the most unnerving moments of your career came when you missed that final. You were standing in the race at the MCG. North had been beaten by St Kilda and missed a spot in the Grand Final, and you and Wayne Schwass are there, suspended. The coach was not happy, was he?

Glenn: He wasn't happy at all. We watched the game from the race. Obviously, this is to get through to a Grand Final. I could've played the following week if we got through, and Wayne couldn't, because he got four weeks' suspension. I remember Denis coming out of the coaches' box, walking along the MCG, and I could see his eyes just burning towards us. And I said to Wayne: 'Let's get out of here.' And he goes: 'Nah, I'm staying.' I said: 'Yeah, good luck.' So I went down, hiding behind the players, away from Denis, giving them a pat on the back, and he went straight to Wayne and absolutely tore strips off him.

Mike: He did. He would've got to you, though, wouldn't he?

Glenn: He did. We went into the rooms and the boys filed into the players' room, and the door closed and Wayne and I were outside, and you hear: 'Where are Archer and Schwass?' So, he basically gave it to us, and said: 'Look at your mates, you've cost them a Grand Final.'

Mike: You tripped Garry Hocking to get the suspension?

Glenn: But I got done for kicking.

Mike: That's still a slur, isn't it, the perception that you've kicked someone? It doesn't seem like a Glenn Archer thing to me.

Glenn: And I did half kick him. There's no doubt about it. It was a wet night, the ball came in and went through my hands—it just went straight through, behind me—and it was more out of temper, I went to kick the ball. I knew halfway through that I was going kick him, but I went through with it anyway. I tried to say it was a trip, but, in hindsight, it was the temper taking over and I kicked him in the thigh.

Mike: Wow. You got better, later, about discipline on the field?

Glenn: Much better. I don't know why, maybe I was just older and wiser. I remember we got a knock on the door one day from Campbell Brown, and he was going through a bit of a bad time with his temper and getting suspended and reported, and he wanted some advice. The only advice I could give him was: 'You get better as you get older.'

Mike: Let's go back to the summer of 2001 and 2002, and the biggest event in your life, the Wayne Carey scandal that erupted at your house.[3] Are you friendly with Wayne now?

Glenn: No, we're not friends anymore. I see him at the odd footy function, or North Melbourne function—so generally once a year—and I always say 'hello' and we're always civil to each other, there's no doubt about that. But, no, we're not friends anymore.

Mike: At that time, Anthony Stevens and Wayne were your two best friends at the footy club, is that true?

Glenn: 'Stevo' was definitely my best friend, and Wayne was definitely up there. We spent a lot of time together, had a lot of fun together on footy trips, and after games and premierships. Probably the biggest emotion that comes out of it is sadness. Because when we won the premierships, one of the things that I was really looking forward to was the reunions. And the reunions, you walk in now and they're still good, because you catch up with the other guys, but there's this tension in the air that I don't like, and no one else likes. That's one of the things that comes with what happened.

Mike: Could you understand the magnitude of it? I mean, it must've taken a while to sink in. It was your wife's 30th, wasn't it? What impact did it have on you personally?

Glenn: It was getting out of control, there were people camped outside my house for days on a time, and helicopters following me and Stevo up to the bush, and it was really hard to comprehend. I'm thinking: 'This is never going to end.' It just drained the hell out of Anthony and myself in the end, to the point where I thought: 'That's it for me. I don't want to play any more.' I just couldn't see myself playing footy any more. This whole saga had just consumed your whole life. But it was Stevo, who was the one who basically told me to pull my head in, and he said: 'If I can get through it and play, I think you can play.'

So he was the one that dragged us through that, which shows how tough

3   Carey and the wife of North Melbourne vice-captain Anthony Stevens, Kelli, were found together in the toilet during a party at Archer's house. It was subsequently revealed that they were having an affair.

that bloke is. You know, to go through what he did and then become the captain and pull everyone together when everyone wanted to fall apart, he was the glue—along with Leigh Colbert and John Blakey—that held the place together.

Mike: You played for North against Adelaide in Wayne's first game with his second club. It must have been an amazing feeling on the ground that night?

Glenn: It was a terrible feeling. I'll always remember the noise of the place, because everyone was waiting for someone to do something—to hit Wayne or whatever.

Mike: It was like a fire that was ready to break out, wasn't it? There was a chance that you and Wayne could have had a fight, wasn't there? Who would have won?

Glenn: Well, put it this way, had I thrown that punch, I would've got about five on the chin pretty quickly, because he was the best that I'd ever seen in and out of the ring. He was very good at holding his hands up. But, he'd done something to Anthony on the wing. So my words, I think, when I went to him, were: 'If anyone should be doing anything to anyone, he should be doing something to you.' And then, for some reason, I pulled the fist back, but, like I said, I was getting older and wiser. I didn't throw it.

Mike: Have you ever contemplated the idea of sitting down with Wayne, of ringing him and saying: 'Mate, we need to talk. We had a good friendship. Things have happened. Is it worth, an hour's chat over a few beers?'

Glenn: I've never really thought about. I'd feel like I was betraying Anthony if I was to do that. And, personally, I don't think I really want to. Our lives have taken different paths. I know Wayne's getting himself together now, but the path that he went down amazed me.

Mike: What do you mean by that?

Glenn: Just the drugs. I just could not believe it. For a guy that preached anti-drugs more than me when he played at the footy club, I don't know what happened. But, apparently he's got through that now. It's been 10 years. Maybe in 15 years. I don't know.

Mike: I want to ask you about that Shinboner of the Century title. Does the Carey spectre hang over you? Do you think it might belong to someone else in different circumstances. Is that fair?

Glenn: Probably, even though some people get confused with the Shinboner of the Century. They think it's for the best player of the century. It's not. It's for a player who epitomised the shinboner spirit the most. And it was voted by the players. It's not just Wayne, it's all the others like Anthony Stevens, Wayne Schimmelbusch, Keith Greg, Malcolm Blight. I just look at these guys and they're revered. But, you're probably right. Had the circumstances been different, Wayne might have got the votes.

Mike: Is Carey the best footballer that you've seen?

Glenn: By a street. I was lucky, you know, I had the best seat in the house. I was on a half-back flank. I could watch the whole thing, and sometimes you'd get carried away. He'd do something and you'd go to your opposition: 'Oh, did you see that?' I don't think I'll ever see anyone like him again, and I know they try and compare current-day players to Wayne, but I don't think anyone really compares. He used to demoralise teams, not just the player that he was playing on, he'd demoralise the guy that *I* was playing on.

Mike: You were as hard as anyone that's played the game in my time, there's no question about that. Are you worried about the hardness of the modern game?

Glenn: No, I'm not. I reckon the game's as hard now as it ever is. It's just logic—they're bigger, they're stronger, they're faster, so they're going to hit harder. Again, people get confused with what hardness is. They think having a punch-on is hard. My son can go punch someone in the face. That's easy. But, put a ball down there with Jonathan Brown coming the other way and you've got to put your head over it—that's hardness. I look at the game now and I feel lucky that I was born with my body size through the '90s because I wouldn't get a game now. It's unbelievable the way they play the game.

STEVEN BAKER

There are those who would describe Steven Baker as a footballer from a bygone era, based on some of the tactics he used to intimidate and quell his opponents. However, that would be to sell short Baker's 13-year, 203-game career—one that included the Trevor Barker Award for his best-and-fairest year of 2005.

Taken by St Kilda at pick 27 in the 1998 National Draft, Baker was a product of the under-18s Geelong Falcons 'football factory'. He had a relatively slow start to his senior career, playing only nine games in his first two seasons, but established himself as a regular part of the Saints line-up with a solid year in 2001.

Baker proved to be a rock in St Kilda's lean seasons of 2001 and 2002, before becoming an integral part of the team that pushed deep into the finals in most years from 2004 until his retirement at the end of 2011. He blossomed into a fine, rugged defender under coach Grant Thomas, but gained a reputation for 'crossing the line' in his efforts to quell his opponent.

His 'living-on-the-edge' approach to tagging opposition players led Baker to visit the tribunal several times and to some long enforced periods on the sidelines. In 2007, Baker was charged with rough conduct and received a seven-match suspension after an incident that left Fremantle's Jeff Farmer with concussion. Three years later, Baker received an even longer sentence (nine matches) after a series of altercations with Steve Johnson in a match against Geelong.

Baker's career came to a sad and somewhat controversial end at the close of the 2011 season. After St Kilda had been eliminated by Sydney in the first week of the finals, coach Ross Lyon announced that Baker had retired. Baker then took to Twitter to advise that his departure was not his choice at all.

Notwithstanding its less than ideal conclusion, Baker's 203-game career will long be held in high esteem by Saints players and fans alike.

AUGUST 20, 2012

Mike: You retired immediately after the 2011 elimination final lost to the Swans. Did you know you were retiring?

Steven: Not that night. I did by the end of the night when I was told, but it was a bit of a shock at the time. We hadn't really discussed it. But I knew I was getting the flick halfway through the season. I had a meeting with Ross Lyon and he said: 'You probably won't be needed next year.'[4] That night, at the end of the Sydney game, he said that I'd retired, and we hadn't discussed that. I think he was just trying to look after me.

Mike: How is that looking after you?

Steven: Well not looking after me as such, but just giving me a good exit.

Mike: You were in your footy gear, weren't you?

Steven: Yes, I was. I think he was just trying to give me a good exit and I'm an honest guy. I think I left the ground and I think I Tweeted something. I was new on Twitter, and I said: 'I definitely haven't retired.' I still wanted to play on and I might have wanted to play somewhere else. I copped a bit of a little barrage from the club saying: 'Why did you do that?' But I didn't really care.

Mike: When Ross left St Kilda and moved to Fremantle, did you resent the fact that someone who wasn't going to be there in 2012 had actually made your decision for you?

Steven: Not really. I still don't know if it had come from him or Chris Pelchen[5]. I think he came in and then it seemed that I had a meeting with Ross a couple of days after that, so, I didn't know if it was his decision, or Ross's. I caught up with Ross at Lenny Hayes' wedding, and he said it wasn't him.

Mike: Did he?

Steven: So, I still don't really know, but I didn't resent Ross. I got along with Ross really well, and he was always upfront with me and I'd respected the

---

4 Many St Kilda supporters were angry that coach Ross Lyon spoke of Baker's 'retirement' immediately after the game, which was the club's last of the season. It had not been announced previously. In fact, Baker was being moved on, but Lyon said later he did not want to downgrade Baker's contribution by putting it that way.

5 Chris Pelchen is St Kilda's head of football.

fact that he told me mid-season. But it was just a bit of a shock that night. I don't like telling 'porky pies', so, I'd just come out and basically said: 'No, I've got the arse.'

CAREER
Born: May 22, 1980
Club: *St Kilda* 1999-2011
—203 games, 35 goals
Honours: Trevor Barker Award (St Kilda Best and Fairest) 2005; Grand Finals 2009, 2010 (2)

Mike: You played 203 games for the Saints, that's in the top 25 in the 115-year history of the footy club. I suspect you're probably as proud of that as you are of sharing the best and fairest with Luke Ball in 2005?

Steven: The games played never dawned on me. I would never aim to reach 200, but my brother pulled me aside one day and said: 'You know, this is bloody amazing.' It was pretty special and you're up there with some big names, so it was something to look back on. I'm pretty proud now.

Mike: You played three Grand Finals for one draw, two losses. Are you scarred?
Steven: Yes, you've always got something churning in the guts. I wouldn't say 'scarred'. I wasn't one to take it to heart too much, but you watch Collingwood and you watch the highlights and something turns in your guts. I get more angry than anything. Seeing Lenny after the game and the first one (in 2009), seeing your best mates cry was a hard thing to do.

Mike: Did you cry?
Steven: I did have a tear after the Geelong one in 2009. I think it might have been Lenny who set me off. I went over and saw how disappointed he was, and it set me off a bit. I think in the Collingwood one in 2010, I might have got used to the feeling, so I didn't cry.

Mike: Is there one thing in Steven Baker's heart that if he could change, it might have made a difference in that 2010 Grand Final, the drawn one? I'm talking about you personally, not the bounce of the ball with Stephen Milne but just anything that you could have done differently that might have made a difference?
Steven: I'm not sure. I think coming back after a bit of a break[6] and then playing my guts out, the next week in the replay I felt like I probably

---

6 Baker was suspended for 12 matches—reduced to nine on a guilty plea—in 2010 for a series of incidents involving Geelong's Steve Johnson, including punching Johnson's broken hand. He completed the suspension in preliminary final week, and was picked for the Grand Final and the replay.

shouldn't have played. My body was just feeling so bad. I probably should have put the hand up and said: 'No, I'm no good, coach.' I had a break in my foot. I snapped my second metatarsal.

It's still a bit of a mystery as to how that happened, but I snapped it straight through and trained the next day, then I had to get the operation. I had a plate inserted, and I've come back for the first Grand Final, but then I put a little snap through the next toe in the game. I didn't know that at the time. I felt it in the first quarter, in the second Grand Final, so I was getting jabs. I couldn't run, and I was useless to the team in the second Grand Final.

Mike: And was it general fatigue, too, about having come back after virtually three months out?
Steven: Yes. I think I was trying to chase bloody Scott Pendlebury and couldn't catch up with him, and I was blowing after two minutes of the first quarter. I remember I was going to give him a little cheap shot, and I couldn't even do that.

Mike: Not you?
Steven: I couldn't even get within five metres of the bugger so I thought: 'Shit, if I can't chase someone down in the first five minutes, I'm in for a long day.' And it was.

Mike: You missed nine games through suspension and came straight back into a Grand Final. That suspension, lengthy by anyone's standards, occurred because of your running duel with Stevie Johnson. Take us back to that day. It was virtually a free-for-all between you and 'Stevie J' for two hours wasn't it?
Steven: Yes. I think because we had a good battle in the first Grand Final in 2009, I think he held a bit of a grudge and, I wanted to get him again, and it just clashed. The better the opposition player, the dirtier I am, usually. It started off with a few little niggles. I started the niggling but he gave me a ripper punch, a big back-hander and I don't know at that time if he broke his hand in the game, but he gave me a ripping crack across the forehead and it wasn't caught on camera. There was behind-the-goals vision of it and I thought: 'Shit that's great.' I came in, the camera has zoomed in just as I was giving him an upper-cut straight after. I got done for retaliating, then he came back on with the sore hand. I started cracking into his hand

and I just didn't think much of it at the time. I thought, it was just a bit of playful fun, trying to break his hand even more, then he got me a ripper at the end. That was probably one of the best I've copped in my 12 years.

Mike: What do you think now about the morality, for want of a better word, about targeting a player's injury in a game? Have you got any qualms about that?

Steven: Well obviously, I think it's okay.

Mike: But you did at the time. I'm talking now, reflectively.

Steven: No, I think if you're on the ground, you know you're a target and you *should* be targeted if you've got an injury. It's a man's game, I've said it's been getting soft over the last four or five years. All these little rules they're changing suit the umpires, rather than the players, rather than making it a better game to watch. All these little hands-in-the-back rules make me sick, when you don't even move the player. I find it hard to watch.

Mike: I'm with you on that one, but I'm talking more about you seeing the Johnson hand, knowing it's injured or certainly sore. It's interesting: did you play in that game in Brisbane when the Brisbane boys took off after Nick Riewoldt with the broken collarbone?

Steven: No, I don't think I played that one. But I actually said the week after, I thought that was good play, targeting Nick that night. I reckon he's fair game. I think if you're on the ground with an injury ... like if someone's got a sore shoulder, you're going for a hip and shoulder, do you ease up?

Mike: I'm interested in your relationship with Stevie Johnson. I mean, he's a superbly skilled player. He's one of my favourites the way he plays. You seem to relish the task of playing on him, but there was the bad blood that occurred during games. This year, a mate of mine at Geelong suggested that you sent Steve a message and the PS to it was: 'You've always been my favourite player.' Is that true?

Steven: Yes, I think it was a Tweet. I think I said about the hit that he gave me: 'That's the best hit I've ever had.' Then at the end of that I said: 'PS: now you're my favourite player.'

Mike: But isn't it funny, you admired that in him, didn't you, the willingness to say: 'Okay, I'll cop it but you're going to get one back.'

Steven: I like the players who get back into me. He probably gave more than I gave that day. I got the 12 weeks, and he gave me a couple of ripping punches in the head and I think he was just smarter getting it off-camera.

Mike: Now you were a tough young man from a tough area in Colac. I mean you would have grown up on the wet muddy grounds up there. Then you go to the Geelong Falcons. Did you play the same sort of footy there? I presume there you were more of a free-flowing midfielder?
Steven: No.

Mike: You weren't? What role did you play at the Falcons?
Steven: I was on the bench most of the time. For the first half of the season I wasn't really getting a game and I nearly quit. I talked to the old man and he talked me out of quitting, around 14, 15.

Mike: You wanted to give footy away?
Steven: Yes, I wanted to give footy away. I was only playing just for the sake of it really. I didn't really enjoy footy that much; I was a basketballer, and then the coach came up to me and said: 'Mate, your skills are shit. What can you do?' And I said: 'I don't know.'

He said: 'You're a good fighter. What if we put you on this player? Do you reckon you'd be able to stop him?' Some peanut that was averaging 40 touches. I went on him and just beat the shit out of him and he came off the ground very sore. Had one or two kicks and came off. The coach said if I beat him, I'd get the game ball. I don't think I could even afford a footy at the time, so I was pumped; I got this footy and then that was when I got my role as a tagger. I came up and I played three good games in the finals. I think I just scraped into the Falcons. I think I would have just scraped in getting into St Kilda too, but it's worked out all right.

Mike: Steve, Tim Watson was your first coach at St Kilda. Rumour has it that it was close to the point of where Tim was just going to say: 'Look, on your bike, go home. You're not serious, you're not committed to football.' Is that true?
Steven: Yes, he was nearly my first and last coach. The first training session was the problem. I missed it, so I nearly got the flick. I went out drinking. I was star-struck with big Barry Hall and [Austinn] Aussie Jones and they were feeding me a few shots, and we had a training session, I think at 7am,

meet the coach and what-not and all I can remember was being at the bar with the boys and then waking up and I was just wet as a shag and in bed. I didn't know where I was and I was in the nude. I thought: 'What have I done here?' I walked into another room, and there was a girl screaming at me.

'I'm sorry, I don't know where I am.' She says: 'I'm Barry's girlfriend. He threw a bucket of water on you about three hours ago.'

I was late by a few hours, so I got put through a rigorous training for three or four hours and I was throwing my guts up. Tim nearly sent me home the next day. It wasn't a good start. I remember him saying: 'You're nearly on the first train back to Colac.'

Mike: Everyone who's had any experience with Malcolm Blight has a story about him. What are your memories?
Steven: I remember him yelling at me because I couldn't baulk. He says: 'You pick up the ball. You're allowed to dodge players, you know, 'Bakes'. You don't have to run head-first into them and get tackled every time.' He belittled me in front of the group, got me out the front and made me try and baulk around him, made fun of me a bit, so I wasn't a big fan of 'Blighty' at the time.

Mike: When you heard the club had sacked him[7], do you remember what your gut reaction was?
Steven: Just, 'yippee', I suppose.

Mike: When do you think the penny dropped with you that if you wanted to be a League footballer you had to change your ways?
Steven: Probably, just hanging out with Lenny Hayes, seeing his professionalism and getting through training. The older I got, the sorer I got and if I didn't do the things that you had to do to be a footballer, I couldn't get through a game, so it sort of was a slow progression. I might have dragged Lenny down a few pegs and he bought me up a few.

Mike: We need to finish the coaches: your memories of Grant Thomas?
Steven: They were all good memories. He's a positive person, just inspiring. I'm still good mates with him to this day, so we still catch up for a quiet beer occasionally. I was sad to see him leave.

---

7 St Kilda sacked Blight in 2001, just a few months into his tenure.

Mike: You went out with his daughter for some time, didn't you? Did the relationship change when he was the prospective father-in-law?

Steven: Yes, the relationship dwindled a little bit for six months there. I said: 'Thommo, I really like your daughter.' And he stared right through me and we didn't talk for a while, and I was too gutless to face him again, so me and his daughter we had a little bit of a relationship outside of his knowing for a few months.

Mike: Your Wikipedia entry says: 'He used a variety of tactics to prevent his opponent from getting the ball, including standing on their feet and repeated hits to the arm.' What was your preferred tactic? You played on lots of big names in your role.

Steven: Well the punch in the back of the arm, I love. I remember I got hit there one day and it gave me a dead arm for the rest of the game, and I couldn't move properly, so that was one I used to work on. I used to hit them just above the elbow and just constantly in the same spot. I got a few players that actually went off because their arm was too sore. When they're kicking and marking they seem to drop marks when you do that.

I had my stops sharpened a couple of times. The boys still laugh about that. We used to file them a bit sharper and then stand on their ankles. Also, I used to know the good spot to hit them in the guts. Just as the ball was getting close, just give them a little one in the sternum and that takes the wind out of them. And I had the old backwards head-butt when I knew they were behind.

Mike: My memory says that you actually got into Chris Judd's head when he was at West Coast, and he got reported for smacking you?

Steven: Yes, he got me a ripper, a bit of a backwards elbow and I think I was being a bit annoying. I would have whacked me too that day!

Mike: Did that change your view of him?

Steven: Yes, he was my favourite player for a while until Steve Johnson.

Mike: You played on some big guns during your time. Scott West, Brad Johnson, Stevie Johnson, Chris Judd, Jeff Farmer, Kane Johnson, Gary Ablett junior. Who was the most difficult opponent?

Steven: Gary Ablett and Judd. With Gary, I used to have the wood over him in the early days, but then if I played him the last couple of years he would have sliced me to pieces. 'Juddy' was just a machine, aerobically I couldn't keep up. I'd have to do every tactic under the sun to stop him, with the little punches and getting in his road and trying to stop his run. If he got a metre on me he was out of there, so, it was just the concentration on those players.

Mike: Is there anything that you wouldn't do in your role to try to win a game of football? Anything?

Steven: Obviously there are a lot of things I wouldn't do. I never really king-hit. I'd try and get away with what I could inside the rules when the umpire wasn't watching. I remember I used to have a thing that I used to drop players after they'd handballed. I used to grab them and drop them and I think they changed that rule; now it's a 50-metre penalty. I'd like to think I changed a few rules in my time. I left my mark on the game a little bit.

Mike: Jeff Farmer cost you seven weeks once. And there was no vision. What happened?

Steven: It was an incidental, accidental, deliberate, yes it was a bit of a head-butt. I was just running down the wing and found myself in front, there was a bit of stop-and-prop and I tried to stop him. But I didn't think I'd get him that good.

Mike: How did they rub you out without film?

Steven: I think it was bad legal advice. I told them what happened. I said: 'Look, I stopped-and-propped.' The conclusion was, I caused the contact and it was high, so it was points, and it was severe because he broke his face pretty badly. I think even if I didn't say that, they would have found a way to get me anyway. They would have, you know, found someone in the crowd that said they saw it. I don't think it would have mattered what I said. I could have gone in there in the nude and threw bloody pies at them and it wouldn't have mattered, it would have been the same outcome.

Mike: Of the 40 most-reported players in the history of the game, you are the only one with a 100 percent guilty record. Fifteen charges, 15 suspensions. Is that because it was S. Baker each time?

Steven: I've come to that opinion. I think I got two weeks for attempted striking and another time, I had a bloke standing on my foot, and I've kicked his foot off and got three weeks for a 110kg guy standing on my ankle. I think it was Steve Alessio. I always felt like I was doomed before I even went in there. I could go into meetings and I'd sit in there for five hours listening to some QC. I'm going: 'This is a waste of time.' You know, I'd rather be home bloody sitting on the couch because I know the outcome before I go in there. People are probably thinking: 'Poor Stevie Baker.' But that's the way I felt. I felt like I was going in there and I'd get the script and it was the same result every time.

Mike: The script; do you think things were pre-determined or not?
Steven: I felt like it was... whoever was on the bench, I think I Tweeted something, and they were just like puppets.

Mike: Puppets for whom? Who was pulling the strings?
Steven: I think I said: 'The AFL.'

Mike: Consider this, because it's a fairly big claim. Do you think that there's interference from the AFL in the determinations of the match review panel and the tribunal?
Steven: I felt there was, I felt there would have been for sure. I thought: 'Let's rub this little bugger out and let's see our good players play.'

Mike: Because you are a despised race aren't you, the run-with players, the taggers, whatever term we want to use. I think the media and the authorities all say: 'Well the game is better without them.' Do you agree with that?
Steven: Definitely. I think the AFL likes to see their good players on the park and getting 30 or 40 touches. When they get five or 10 touches it's a massive talking point: 'Taggers should be scrapped.' And: 'Get taggers out of the game.' I remember there being headlines many a time about it. When you do a good job on someone, they've got to think that we've got a job, and we get told to do that.

Mike: I mentioned some of your regular opponents before, one of whom was Kane Johnson. I was at Etihad one day. Do you know where I'm going with this? It was a break, wasn't it? And you just took off after him as if he'd stolen your wallet or something?

Steven: Yes, I remember that incident. I think I was just at a stoppage and he come up, and I was tagging someone else and he elbowed me in the back of the neck. I went to my knees and looked up and just saw his number, and I saw red and chased him down. I just went up to remonstrate and ended up throwing the fist.

Mike: You've paid your dues, there's no doubt about that. How do you look back on what Steven Baker did in his footy career?
Steven: I suppose I'm in one word, 'proud' when I look back at what I've done. The more you're out of the game, the more you think: 'Oh shit that's actually pretty special.'

Mike: Now, you lost your father recently?
Steven: Yes.

Mike: It reminded me when I heard that news of your father at Footy Park in Adelaide one year. I don't know whether it's fact or fiction, but Fraser Gehrig was on fire, kicked his 100th goal in a final at Footy Park and the St Kilda boys invaded the field, led by your father. Is that true?
Steven: It's a true story. I think the whole crowd was going over to Fraser, then I got a pat on the arse. Lenny was near me and the old man said: 'Get a f'ing kick boys.' He had a big smile on his face; I think he had a few whiskies on the way to the ground and then he drove back all through the night and got back to my sister's netball Grand Final the next day. He got in the leotard and did a run at half-time on the old netball court, so he was a character.

Mike: The apple hasn't fallen far from the tree, has it?
Steven: No, I think that's how I got that trait. He didn't really think about consequences and stuff too much, so that's something he's handed down.

Mike: Your father has gone from Melbourne to Adelaide to watch a game of footy. Obviously there was a pretty strong relationship between the two of you?
Steven: Very strong, he used to come to every game and give us a hug after every game.

KEVIN BARTLETT

Known simply as 'KB', Kevin Bartlett is a true legend of the Australian indigenous game. Although he barracked for Footscray as a kid, he grew up in the heart of Tigerland and was always destined to play for Richmond.

Bartlett joined the Tigers as a youngster and worked his way through their under 17s, under 19s and reserves teams (winning junior best and fairest awards along the way), before making his senior debut in 1965. He played 14 of a possible 18 games in each of his first two seasons before embarking on a run of 17 seasons in which he barely missed a game.

Along the way, Bartlett collected five premierships, four under legendary coach Tom Hafey, with whom he became a life-long friend, and one in 1980 under Tony Jewell. Bartlett was rampant in that 1980 Grand Final, kicking seven goals and winning the Norm Smith Medal.

As a rover and small forward, Bartlett developed a reputation for always having a shot at goal rather than handballing to a teammate in a better position. This earned him the unflattering nickname of 'Hungry', one that Bartlett always accepted with good humour.

Bartlett's speed and agility were such that he seemed to always evade tackles, and he often gave the impression of running rings around his opponent.

Having had no serious injury during his entire senior career for the yellow and black, Bartlett's game total when he hung up the boots in 1983 was 403, a VFL record at the time, and since bettered by only Hawthorn's Michael Tuck.

Bartlett later coached Richmond for four seasons, but this was during an era of financial crises for the Tigers and, with extremely limited resources, he was unable to take the club to finals in any of those years. He was removed as coach after the 1991 season, and the manner of his dismissal led him to shun the club for many years before he finally made his peace with the Tigers in 2007.

SEPTEMBER 5, 2011

Mike: It's a magnificent career, mate. You should be proud of it.

Kevin: Well, I'm very contented with my playing career. I enjoyed playing. I played with great players at a great time of the Richmond Football Club, and had a great coach. In fact, I had several great coaches. And it was nice to be a premiership player and to do something that you loved all of your life.

Mike: Lots of great memories, obviously, over such a long period. Five premierships; best and fairest in three of those. Team success obviously takes precedence, but it must be nice to know that you were best player in the best team.

Kevin: Well, I think when you win a club best and fairest, it's always nice, because that's your club and you hope that you're doing things on the playing field that the coach likes, or the selectors like. But at the same time, I think the main thing is, you want to be the best you can, whenever you played. And there was never a game I went out and played that I didn't have a vision of being the best player on the ground. Even in my last game when I was absolutely stuffed, I was going to go out, be the best player on the ground, and maybe kick five or six goals.

Mike: In fact, did you hurt your knee in your last game?

Kevin: No, I actually tore my thigh muscle at training a couple of days before my last game, which was a bit unusual. I did ask the club doctor to give me a jab to get through training. So I was able to just get through training, and I had a jab on the last day; and right about half-time, when the first jab wore off, so did I. I was playing on a young Richard Osborne, blond hair and about six foot [180cm], and ran like the wind, and jumped over tall buildings in a single bound. And I'm trying to keep up with him...

Mike: They say reputations are made in September. Did you ever get nervous? Do you remember being nervous before, say, your first final or your first Grand Final?

Kevin: I wasn't a nervous footballer. I never felt nervous prior to a game. I liked to be calm all the time, particularly when I was playing. I never tried to get into too much hype before the game. A lot of players are yelling and screaming and frothing at the mouth, doing exercises, and running up and down, and punching balls in the air, and crashing into everyone. I didn't like that. I liked to just sit down. I used to like to try and play the game over in my mind all the time, just thinking about from the centre bounce, taking the tap, beating an opponent, running with the ball. I suppose it was a bit of imagery. It's amazing the number of times that you went out on the field, and it actually happened that way.

Mike: Perhaps it was those fish and chips on Friday nights, was it?

Kevin: Fish and chips were beautiful on Friday night.

Mike: Is that fact or fiction that you had fish and chips every Friday night before you played?

Kevin: That's fact. Every Friday night. One, it was cheap—I couldn't afford too much more than that. And you didn't have to wash the dishes, of course. And the leftovers could go to the dog at the same time.

Mike: When you arrived at Richmond, you were only young, I think 16 or 17. What were your physical dimensions?

CAREER
Born: March 6, 1947
THE PLAYER
Club: *Richmond*
1965-83—403 games, 778 goals
Honours: Australian Football Hall of Fame Legend; Norm Smith Medal 1980; Brownlow Medal—2nd 1977, 3rd 1974; Represented Australian Galahs 1968; Victorian captain 1980; Richmond Hall of Fame; Richmond 'Immortal'; Richmond Team of the Century; Richmond best and fairest 1967, 1968, 1973, 1974, 1977; Richmond captain 1979; Richmond premiership side 1967, 1969, 1973, 1974, 1980; Richmond leading goalkicker 1974, 1975, 1977, 1983
THE COACH
Club: *Richmond*
1988-91—88 games, 27 wins, 61 losses, 31 percent winning percentage

Kevin: Well when I first arrived, that was 1962, to play in the fourths, which was the under 17s, I was about 14 at the time. I was about jockey-size then, probably nine stone [about 57kg].

By the time I got into the under 19s, I was 15 or so, I was probably nine-seven or something like that. And by the time I played in my first game, I reckon I would've been about 10 stone. So that's probably in the 60kg range.

Mike: Did you ever venture into the gym, or in fact, did Richmond have a gym?
Kevin: I didn't. Well, someone told me they did, but I don't remember ever seeing a gym down at Richmond. No, in actual fact, football clubs in those days were pretty amateurish. And while Richmond may have had a few odd weights, that's about it. They didn't have a gymnasium to speak of. But I did go to the gym a lot, particularly at lunchtimes; I used to work with PMG[8] in those days, and Telecom and Telstra—they've changed their names over the years. Our head trainer at Richmond used to run the police gymnasium up in Russell Street, and I used to go up there at lunchtimes. Also, Stan Nicholls ran a big gymnasium in town as well, and a number of young Richmond players—myself and Royce Hart, Kevin Sheedy—used to go down to the Stan Nicholls gym and train a lot during the off-season as well.

Mike: Kevin Sheedy wrote in your book, *KB: A Life in Football*[9], that you had calves the size of rockmelons. You never had hamstring problems but you couldn't touch your toes either, could you? So explain that to us.
Kevin: Well, I don't know about hamstrings; they're a mystery to everyone. But I can remember teammates of mine, they'd put their leg up on top of the old wire fence there at Punt Road, and then they'd bring their head down and touch themselves on the knee. Now, I couldn't even actually get my leg up on to the wire fence. And I couldn't get within about 18 inches [45cm] of touching my toes.

So I don't know about hamstrings in terms of flexibility; I think it's probably the strength of the hamstrings. I never had a soft tissue injury

---

8 PMG: Post Master General
9 Kevin Bartlett as told to Rhett Bartlett, *KB: A Life in Football*, The Slattery Media Group, 2011

really in my life, or probably until the last week of my life, when I actually tore a thigh muscle.

Mike: But you did have explosive pace. And now the conventional wisdom is that for someone who's so quick off the mark, you're vulnerable in the calves, and the thighs and the hamstrings. Never occurred to you?
Kevin: Never, no. I never used to do a lot of the exercises that the players did. I used to hate that stuff before a game, when they'd get all the players, as they say, frothing at the mouth. When the side used to warm up doing that, I used to just sit in the corner or run on the spot a lot, do a bit of skipping and things of that nature. To me, that was warming up.

Mike: You were a very good runner in your own right. Did you win on the professional sprinting circuit?
Kevin: I won the double at the Portland, and also one at Broadford.

Mike: You played with lots of football immortals, and they are genuine stars of the game: Royce Hart, Francis Bourke, Billy Barrott, Dick Clay, Ian Stewart, lots more. Who was the best of them, Kevin?
Kevin: Royce Hart is probably the best player I've ever seen. Royce was a magnificent player for Richmond. And I played with him week-in, week-out. Our style of play was: 'Kick it long to Royce and get out of his way.' That's all we had to do. And you know, we won four premierships with that very, very simple game plan.

But he was a magnificent mark, and he used to float across in front of the packs. He was very, very quick for his size. He was only about six foot one and a half [186cm], too, Royce. He wasn't like the big centre half-forwards of today. But he was a great chaser, a great tackler, he was tremendous on the ground, he never fumbled, he was a beautiful kick, and he was a great competitor.

Mike: Let's compare Royce at his best, in the late-'60s, early-'70s. Compare him with Wayne Carey at his best.
Kevin: I think Royce is the greatest centre half-forward of all time. You know, the others will come and go, but I still think he's the best. I think it was fitting that when they picked the AFL's Team of the Century,

they picked Royce as centre half-forward, and Teddy Whitten, Mr Football who was a champion centre half-forward and the greatest player of all time to many people, was named at centre half-back. If you can knock Teddy Whitten out of the centre half-forward spot, you have to be pretty damned good.

Mike: Yes, I agree with that. You were finally made captain at the age of 32, and yet you lasted only 12 months. Why so late, and why so short?

Kevin: Well, that's an interesting one. I'd won the best and fairest in 1973 and 1974, in back-to-back premiership wins. In '75, I had just a reasonable season; I may have finished top four in the best and fairest, or something like that, but not as good as the previous two years. And we lost in the preliminary final that year to North Melbourne.

I'd captained the side a lot over that period of time between '73 and '74, because Royce, who was the captain, had some knee problems, and I was the vice-captain for four years or so. And I just actually expected to be captain in 1976, when Royce had his injuries, and the club decided that Royce was not going to be fit enough to be captain.

But not only did they *not* name me as captain, they didn't even name me as vice-captain, which was something that made me grow up a lot, too. In those periods of time there are a lot of people wandering around, patting you on the back all the time.

So it sort of matured me a little bit. Maybe it was my first understanding that there's double-speak in football, and there's a lot of bullshitting in football.

Mike: Did it prompt you to consider an offer from Essendon?

Kevin: Not then, no. Definitely not then. I just gritted my teeth and didn't say anything to anyone at that particular point in time. No one said to me why I wasn't appointed captain; there was no explanation given. Francis Bourke was appointed captain, a great player, and deservedly captain as well, and Neil Balme was appointed as vice-captain. But there was no reason given to me whatsoever, as that was probably what took place in those days. I mean, you just turned up and played, and boards and coaches and the chairman selectors made decisions.

Mike: Now despite your genial appearance, you can get stubborn and you can get offended by decisions made around you. Did you think then perhaps that you might try to engineer a way out of Punt Road?

Kevin: Not then, no. Because I just accepted that as a kick in the backside. It didn't stop me from focussing on what I loved doing, and that was playing. In 1979, I was appointed captain, and Tony Jewell took over as coach. We changed captains pretty regularly, too, by the way.

Mike: And coaches.

Kevin: And coaches. Kevin Sheedy had been captain, and then Kevin was stood down as captain, and then I was asked if I would I take over the captaincy. Barry Richardson, when he took over as coach in 1977, came to me and asked would I accept the vice-captaincy role again. He probably knew there was a bit of angst or heartburn from several years prior. And I said 'yes, I would'; I was happy to be vice-captain under Kevin Sheedy, because he's a great friend and a great player, and he's a great Richmond person. I took it as an honour.

Then when they decided Kevin Sheedy was finished, they asked me to be the captain, so I captained in 1979. At the end of 1979, I'd been roving right up to that period of time, so for 15 years I'd just been roving. Then out of the blue I was told that I was no longer roving. No explanation given, but just: 'You're no longer roving, and you'll be played on the half-forward flank.'

Mike: That was Tony Jewell's call as coach?

Kevin: Well, Tony was coach at the time, yes. But I don't know. No one even said whose call it was.

Mike: The funny thing about that was, I think at the time I remember that you were probably a bit miffed that the great rover had been told that his future, at 33 years of age, lay on a half-forward flank...

Kevin: Yes.

Mike: Yet in the finals in 1980, you kicked 21 goals in three finals, won the Norm Smith Medal.

Kevin: In 1979, when that first took place, a lot of things were different back then, as you know. If you got named in the paper at full-back, you played at full-back; you're named at centre half-back, you played at centre half-back; if you were first rover, you were first rover; in the centre, you were centreman.

So there was a bit of kudos and prestige, and players tried to be the best they could in those particular positions. The half-forward flank in those days was a little bit different than these days, where everyone's on the ball. It was sort of like, 'there's your little spot of ground over there, you stand there and don't get in the way'. The *graveyard*, I think they used to call it, half-forward flank.

I remember going out to Waverley and Rob Astbury, the TV reporter, he collared me as I was walking into the ground, and he said to me: 'It's going to be a big day for you today.' I said: 'Why's that?' He said: 'It's your last game. I've been told that this is going to be your last game.' I gritted my teeth. That got me a bit fired up.

Mike: In your book, *KB*, you talked about a senior journalist who was being fed stuff from Punt Road to virtually to undermine you. Is that a fair assessment?

Kevin: That's true, yes.

Mike: So are you suggesting someone like Graeme Richmond[10] was telling someone like Rob Astbury this sort of stuff?

Kevin: That's my take on it, yes. I mean, that's what I thought was taking place at that stage, that the club wanted me out. People just come to decisions. They make decisions, what they believe are best for the club at that particular point in time. Rightly or wrongly, if you've got enough power, it happens. Francis Bourke finished up before the end of the season. Royce Hart finished up before the end of the season. Dick Clay finished up before the end of the season. Kevin Sheedy finished up before the end of the season.

So there's no problems with Kevin Bartlett finishing up before the end of the season as well. But because he's told me that as I walked into the ground, that got me fired up. And I kicked four goals that day, playing on the half-forward flank, so it was probably a bit hard to drop me the following week.

---

10 Graeme Richmond was a longtime Richmond committeeman and powerbroker.

I was able to see out the season. I thought: 'Look, if I'm not required, I've had a great time here, I've enjoyed it immensely, then I'll move on.' Because I still wanted to play, because I loved playing. I didn't want to be one of those players that they just shoved out when they felt they wanted to shove you out the door. And I felt that was the case, so as a result, I decided I would just resign.

So I went to them and I said: 'Look, I'm resigning, I'm leaving, because I genuinely believe that the hierarchy at the Richmond Football Club don't want me here, and I can accept that.' I said: 'So if *I* can accept it, then obviously *you* can accept it; and therefore I will go. I'd like to play elsewhere.'

Of course they said: 'Well, that's not the case, *no, no, no.* We think very highly of you.' But I didn't believe them, because I've seen other things take place in the past, I just felt that I could see the signs were there.

I actually wanted to go and play at Collingwood, because Tommy Hafey had gone to coach Collingwood, and I loved Tommy. I had a lot of meetings with Tommy, and also Ronnie Richards, who was Collingwood's chairman of selectors at the time, about going to Collingwood and playing at Collingwood.

Ronnie was really keen, and I was keen. Tommy was the sticking stone; he was a bit concerned about taking me away from Richmond, whether or not if we looked back in years to come, whether we'd both regret it; that I should be a one-team player, how it was going to look in the eyes of people with Tommy pinching me and taking me to Collingwood.

Mike: You were going into your 33rd year at the time, right?
Kevin: Yes, I was really fired up, and Ian Stewart, who was at South Melbourne, rang me and he was keen for me to go too. I met with Carl Ditterich, who was coaching Melbourne at the time. He was keen for me still to come and play. I just wanted to play. Barry Davis was coach of Essendon at the time, and I spoke to Barry. And I warmed to Essendon because Tommy didn't want me to go to Collingwood.

So I said: 'Look, I'll sign a heads of agreement.' I suppose, in the back of my mind I really wanted to go to Collingwood, but with that shutting, I did the heads of agreement.

Mike: So what reconciled you with Richmond?

Kevin: Tommy said: 'I still think you may regret that if you look back in time and leave the Tigers. Whereas I think if you stay at Richmond, put your head down, forget about everyone else that's there, do what you like doing, play the best you can, and see if you can get the best out of yourself.'

So Michael Green, who was my great friend and a great ruckman, a premiership ruckman, I got him to broker it. And at one stage there they said to me that they would have me back and I'd be captain, but I told them I did not want to be captain of the club, because I didn't think they respected the captain of the Richmond Football Club.

Mike: Grand Final day, 1980. Probably the high point of your career, was it?

Kevin: Well, it was one of the great moments, because we won the premiership. Look, it was a terrific finals series. We played Carlton in the first final and it was my 337th game; I broke the League record at Waverley. And I kicked six goals that day, three in the first quarter, which sort of gave me a great buzz at that particular point in time. And then we played Geelong in the second semi-final, and I was able to kick eight goals that day. That led us into the Grand Final against Collingwood, which Tommy was coaching.

And it was a great day for the club.[11] It was a great day for Tony Jewell, who did a magnificent job in coaching the Tigers, who should never have been sacked. But that's another story.

Mike: Tom Hafey is probably your best mate. He coached the Tigers for 11 years, won four premierships, contested seven finals series, never finished lower than seventh, and got the flick. What was going on at that place at that time?

Kevin: Tommy of course lasted one more year after 1975, and the end of 1976, he was appointed as coach, but he resigned a couple of weeks later. He knew he didn't have the backing of Graeme Richmond, and therefore he felt that there was no point in continuing as being coach of Richmond if Graeme wanted him out.

---

11 Richmond won by a League record 81 points.

Graeme had been trying to get Tommy out. He'd been going around to close friends and confidantes of Tommy's, particularly his brothers, and telling them that they should have a chat to Tommy about giving it away. Tommy thought there was no point coaching Richmond if you didn't have the support of Graeme, so he resigned.

That was a pretty sad day. I can remember Tommy ringing me at home and telling me that he was going to resign the next day, and I was really shocked. I tried to talk him out of it at that stage, saying: 'Listen, the players love you, Tommy. We play for you.' But Tommy's pretty dogged and single-minded himself, and when he felt that he didn't have the full support, particularly of Graeme, then he felt he would move away. That shocked us all.

Mike: He was an amazingly powerful figure, Graeme Richmond. And my understanding of the Hafey decision was that 'GR' allowed Hafey to win the vote, but actually voted against him so that the word would get out that he didn't have 'GR's' support. Is that correct?

Kevin: I don't know the workings of it. But all I do know is that he didn't support Tommy to be the coach of the Richmond Football Club. I suppose that's where I became very wary of Graeme myself. My relationship with Graeme was always a bit icy. We were friendly to each other and we would talk to each other, and when he was ill in hospital, I went and saw him in hospital, because I respected him enormously. But I was very, very wary of him.

And as a result, he realised that, and I told him that in meetings we had in 1979. I said: 'A lot of things are appearing in the paper that 'Kevin Bartlett's had it', and 'He should be gone or should be retired', and things of that nature.' I remember Graeme saying to me: 'Where do you think all that's coming from?' I said: 'It's coming from you. That's where it's coming from, Graeme.' Because no one else at the club had the power to do that. And Graeme knew all the journalists in those days. He worked the media magnificently.

Mike: Four hundred and three games, 778 goals, one known hand pass. You didn't enjoy it much, did you, the handball?

Kevin: No, no. It was a fad, it was a craze. It was never going to last. And Tommy told me that once. He said: 'Whatever you do, don't get involved in this handball craze. It'll never last.' And I always did as the coach told me, Michael. When I was a kid growing up, following the Bulldogs, if anyone handballed on the back line, they used to get booed. In fact, it was an absolute no-no if anyone handballed on the back line. So it's amazing how football has changed over the years from handball being a last resort, and now it's nearly the first option.

Mike: Yet in your book, every footy card has got you handballing. Who taught you how to do that?

Kevin: But you never saw the fist actually touch the leather!

Mike: Now a serious note about the handball, I know it's become a bit of a myth, but did any of your teammates think that you were selfish? Did they think that you were prepared to take a handpass but you were never prepared to give one?

Kevin: I don't think so, to be quite honest. I like to think I got on pretty well with all my teammates. I think we had a pretty good relationship. I never thought about it, to be perfectly honest. But they had a bit of fun with me over the years and ribbed me from time to time. But I only just tried to do my best, and the coach was pretty adamant in those days... Tommy had Alan 'Bull' Richardson, Matthew's father, handballing out to people. Well, he probably had 10 handballs a game, so he was a 'handballing genius'. When we won Grand Finals in '67 or '69, there were probably 30 handballs for the game. So while I was having no handballs, most of my teammates were having one or two.

Because the idea was to kick the ball long to an advantage, to either of the key forwards. Tommy built the Richmond style on Norm Smith; he loved Norm Smith as a coach. He loved the way Melbourne played.

Mike: Kevin, you seemed born to coach. You had a spell in the media, then you took the Richmond coaching job in 1988. You took over a wooden spoon team, one that finished behind the Brisbane Bears in their first year, and then it ended in tears, didn't it?

Kevin: It was a very difficult time. I'd had opportunities to coach a couple of other clubs and I went and spoke to a couple of clubs. And there was a couple of teams that indicated that all I had to do was sign on the dotted line and I'd be their coach.

There was Fitzroy; Melbourne was another club. I know the Bulldogs spoke to me at one stage. But I suppose, Michael, I've always been a Richmond person, apart from when I barracked for the Bulldogs as a kid. And Richmond was my club. If I was going to coach, I suppose my heart had to be in it. And therefore the opportunity came. I got a phone call from Richard Doggett[12], and he said to me that Tony Jewell was going to retire, he wanted to give up coaching, and he wanted to move into another aspect of football. I said I would be interested in coaching the Tigers.

So I went down and had a chat to the Richmond Football Club. It was a few weeks before the end of the season, and I said: 'Look, the club's not on the bottom because Tony Jewell can't coach. Tony Jewell is a premiership coach. I mean, you can't get a better recommendation than that.'

So I said: 'Under no circumstances am I going to put my hand up and try and undermine Tony Jewell as coach. I don't want to do that. If Tony doesn't want to coach, then come and see me; but if he wants to coach and he finishes the season off well, fantastic. Don't worry about it.'

Anyway, they came back and said: 'No, no, no, Tony definitely doesn't want to coach.' So I was appointed coach of the Tigers. I remember saying to them: 'We're not on the bottom because the coach is no good; we're on the bottom because obviously we haven't got enough good players.' I'm smart enough to know that you need good players to win games. And if you want to win premierships, you might need some great players as well.

I wanted them to go out like Richmond once did, recruiting. And they said: 'Yes, yes, that's not a problem.' By the time I started coaching, here I am being told that we're over $1 million in debt, and it never got any better. So I had to go out with my own money, I went out to Buffalo Sports and I bought punching bags, and I bought the punching balls, and I put them up myself. Phil Grant[13] was great, he had a bit of a sports business going and he'd bring down some gloves. He hunted around, got some weights for me, and you know, the club was obviously absolutely broke. David Cloke had left, and Geoff Raines left, and Bryan Wood left, and Brian Taylor left.

---

12 Doggett was chief executive of the Tigers.
13 Phil Grant was the brother of Peter Grant, Richmond's runner in the premiership year of 1980.

Mike: Twenty-seven wins from that four-year period. I think you invested so much time and so much emotion that there was no question you got bitter when you got the sack.

Kevin: Well I was disappointed, because we all knew how tough it was. They were dishonest with me in the first place by telling me that we probably had a future, and we had the ability to go out and get players. We'd go along to the draft, and I was told we weren't allowed to draft players. I remember I spoke to Russell Morris, who loved Richmond as a kid. His dad was a great Richmond supporter, and Russell was. But St Kilda offered him four times more than what we could offer.

We just couldn't attract anybody. We had no money to attract anybody; we were not successful. I knew that everyone understood the difficulties that I was facing, and I understood the difficulties that they were facing. People would come to me and say: 'Listen, who can we drop off the list? Who can we get dropped? The banks are knocking on our door.'

Mike: You did harbour the grudge for a long time, did you not?

Kevin: Well, I was disappointed, yes 16 years. Look, I never, ever went to any other club, or begged for another club. I never caused a club any trouble. I never tried to join any board to unseat anybody. I got approached by a lot of people. 'Can you join us? We can move in, we can do a better job.' Over the years, that happened to me on several occasions. I even got offered jobs down at the club, football manager, or general manager. I mean people made enquiries. And I said: 'I don't want to have anything to do with it.' Because I had completely walked away from the club.

My disappointment was that after I'd been at the club for some 26-and-a-half years, and four years as coach that I felt were really, really tough, that Richmond had a reputation of just sacking coaches, and then we'd all start again. We'd all have a big smile on our face invite them down to the first game, give them a free lunch, get them up, say a few words, pat them on the head, 'all is forgotten'. Richmond thought making tough decisions was sacking the coach. Tommy Hafey had to resign because he didn't have the support. Now how could you *not* have the support, if you're Tommy Hafey?

Barry Richardson takes over, coaches for two years, makes the finals, and gets sacked. He's replaced by Tony Jewell, *he* coaches three years, wins a premiership, gets sacked. Taken over by Francis Bourke, coaches two years, makes the Grand Final, gets sacked. Replaced by Mike Patterson, who lasts one year and gets the sack. Paul Sproule comes in, and even Barry Richardson, as president of the club, had to sack himself, because he gave Paul Sproule his word that he'd coach for two years, and after one year the board said: 'No, we're going to sack him.'

Mike: Wouldn't they love that problem now? Sacking blokes who have taken them to the finals.
Kevin: It's unbelievable.

MALCOLM BLIGHT

As a highly talented, dual premiership player and dual premiership coach who pushed the boundaries, Malcolm Blight qualifies as a footballing genius.

Blight's senior football journey began in 1968 when he joined Woodville in the SANFL. Blessed with uncanny skills, he made an immediate impact and was a fine player over the next six seasons, winning the 1972 Magarey Medal.

In 1974, North Melbourne convinced Blight to join the Kangaroos. He made a relatively quiet debut against Footscray in Round 2, but soon established himself as a regular player.

Over the next nine seasons, Blight delighted fans, North Melbourne and otherwise, with his mix of brilliance and football nous. As a player (and later as coach), Blight was always prepared to try something different and while he was successful when doing so far more often than not, this would at times infuriate coach Ron Barassi, and the pair's relationship was at times tumultuous.

Blight was a solid contributor when North Melbourne won its first flag in 1975 and was one of the Kangaroos' best when they won the 1977 Grand Final replay.

A first attempt at coaching while still playing at North in 1981 was unsuccessful, with Blight soon falling to the pressures of the dual role of captain-coach.

After finishing at North Melbourne in 1982, Blight took on a coaching role at his old club Woodville, where he obtained a solid leadership grounding, which stood him in good stead when he became Geelong coach in 1989. In his six-year tenure at the Cats, Blight took Geelong to within a kick of a flag in his first season, and was losing Grand Final coach again in 1992 and 1994.

Blight was lured back to coaching by the Adelaide Crows in 1997 and achieved immediate success, with the Crows taking the 1997 and 1998 flags. The Crows failed to make September in 1999 and Blight again gave coaching away.

A final coaching attempt with St Kilda in 2001 was short-lived. Blight moved to Queensland in 2012 where he held a directorship at the Gold Coast Suns and was mentor to coach Guy McKenna.

JUNE 13, 2012

Mike: Now, you know it's 17 years since we first shared the couch on *Talking Footy* with Bruce McAvaney at Channel 7.
Malcolm: And we haven't changed a bit.

Mike: I think you bullied me a bit back then, but you were always interesting and provocative. What are your memories of this concept? It was an original concept then, wasn't it?
Malcolm: We were going to sit around a bar, remember? Just like three blokes talking over a bar. I thought you bullied me, to be honest. We had differences of opinion, which is fine, isn't it?

Mike: Now, despite your achievements, I've always suspected there's been a degree of frustration with you about your footy career. Is that accurate?
Malcolm: I think I wanted to be better. That's true.

Mike: In all phases, we're talking about?
Malcolm: I did. A lot of people said I was pretty relaxed, and I was probably, but there's a lot of things I did away from the ground and personally to try and motivate myself to play better. And when I played poorly I was not good company. I was fairly harsh on myself.

Mike: You're an original member of the Australian Football Hall of Fame from 1996. You're not a legend. My own view is that you should be. Are you ever so slightly miffed that you don't have that official legend status?
Malcolm: I didn't really think about it, Mick. I mean, I was pleased to get the first one, really. A lot of blokes don't get that. And one of the things is, having been a coach, I reckon you actually understand that you're the

selector and you've got to make decisions. And people make decisions, so it's a bit like the umpire; you can't change their mind. So I never really think about it.

Mike: Let's go back to the start, all the way to Woodville in Adelaide. Tell us about your first footy and how you acquired it.

Malcolm: Well, I used to go down to Woodville Oval, four streets from home, and they were my team after following Port Adelaide initially. But they got into the League, and when someone got a mark in the goal square and kicked over the fence, I saw these kids back behind the fence at Woodville Oval, and you'd see the scramble for the ball. Well, after watching this for about six or eight weeks I decided that my turn was out there. One finally came over about the second time I was out there and I can't remember how I got it, I just remember running. I was pretty small, but geez, I could go quickly. And I ran through every backyard I knew and got home and buried it in the big wheat tin about six feet [180cm] down.

Mike: What were you doing with a wheat tin?

Malcolm: To feed the chooks. We had chooks at home. So I hid it for

CAREER
Born: February 16, 1950
THE PLAYER
Clubs: *Woodville* (SANFL) 1968-73, 1983-85—163 games, 359 goals; *North Melbourne* 1974-82 —178 games, 444 goals
Honours: Member, Australian Football Hall of Fame; Brownlow Medal 1978; Magarey Medal 1972; North Melbourne Team of the Century; North Melbourne best and fairest 1978; Woodville best and fairest 1972, 1983; All-Australian 1972, 1982, 1985; Coleman Medal 1982; SANFL leading goalkicker 1985; North Melbourne premiership side 1975, 1977; North Melbourne leading goalkicker 1978, 1979, 1981, 1982; Woodville leading goalkicker 1983, 1985
THE COACH
Clubs: *North Melbourne* 1981—16 games, 6 wins, 10 losses, 38 percent winning percentage; *Woodville* (SANFL) 1983-87—Night premiership 1983; Geelong 1989-94—145 games, 89 wins, 56 losses, 61 percent winning percentage; *Adelaide* 1997-99—74 games, 41 wins, 33 losses, 55 percent winning percentage, premierships 1997, 1998; *St Kilda* 2001—15 games, 3 wins, 12 losses, 20 percent winning percentage
Total (AFL): 250 games, 139 wins, 111 losses, 56 percent winning percentage

six weeks in the wheat tin, a brand new Faulkner, I was about nine or 10, I reckon, and that was my first ever footy.

Mike: I was doing a bit of research, and I actually was at Arden Street the day you arrived. And you were 24 years of age. It's late for someone to come from interstate and start in what was then the VFL, isn't it?

Malcolm: It probably wasn't that unusual, really. You tended to establish yourself in either Western Australia, Tasmania and South Australia. And there were only about four or five South Australians playing in the competition at that time. And I really did want to play 100 games for my home club, Woodville, who I dreamed about playing for. And I did that, so I was really pleased I did.

Mike: You played in two North Melbourne premiership teams, won a best and fairest, won a Brownlow Medal, won a Magarey Medal and captained Victoria and South Australia. Why the insecurities?

Malcolm: In a sense it's like, that was so quick. How do you answer that? I think I was like anyone—you really wanted to play well. When you're doing it, you actually don't give it any thought. It's only when you look in the rear-vision mirror, you actually say: 'Oh, did I do that?'

Mike: 1977 was the year that North Melbourne and Collingwood played in two Grand Finals, North triumphed in the end. Is it fact or fiction that Ron Barassi was keen early in the week of the replay to leave you out of the team?

Malcolm: Yes, I think that's pretty right. There were three of us, I think Brent Crosswell, John Cassin and myself. And the reason being, in the first final, Mike, I actually went back on the ball ruck-roving, and I remember kicking one across the front of the goals, centreing the ball. It was a silly thing to do, I reckon, when no one's there. Anyhow, I kicked it too far and I've kicked it straight to a Collingwood player, and they've gone bang, bang, bang, got a goal. I got some sprays in my life, and I've seen some players sprayed, but Barassi has given me the biggest spray about that kick, about that one kick, and then banished me to the forward pocket. So for the next half of the game we didn't kick a goal. I hardly went to the ball. I was as fresh as a daisy, and at three-quarter time he said: 'Johnny Byrne, you're off. 'Blighty', you go back on the ball.' And I thought: 'Oh, poor John, but beaut for me.' He walked away from the huddle and he said: 'No, Blighty, you're off.' So I sat out the last quarter of the drawn Grand Final.

So I thought I was a bit hardly done by, but once again, what could I do about it? The coach is going to make his decision. But thankfully I played okay in the replay.

Mike: Barass marked his good players hard, didn't he?
Malcolm: He did.

Mike: And I think later in life, you probably did the same things with yours. But certainly with yourself, Keith Greig, players of that ilk, he was a hard taskmaster, wasn't he?
Malcolm: Hard is a very, very kind word, Michael. Harsh, sometimes. But now you can say it in hindsight, I don't think 'Barass' ever thought that he wasn't trying to help. He wasn't doing it for reasons other than to get better, to make you get better.

Mike: So the lasting effect of that, the Barassi iron fist, the high expectations—did that influence your later life?
Malcolm: It did, yes. I actually coached fairly hard, you know. Because you'd seen success at North Melbourne, and that was passed on from Norm Smith to Ron Barassi and then perhaps on to me—and Robert Walls, you know—we came from a similar type area, that you coach fairly hard. When I tried to be the playing coach at North Melbourne[14], which didn't work, and when I went back to Adelaide I was fairly tough on the Woodville players, because they needed some help. But I think each year I probably got better.

Mike: One of your more famous altercations with Barassi was when you kicked a goal from the boundary, which you loved doing, I think in about 1980. The team ethic was that it had to be the more conservative course of kicking it to a teammate in a better position, or to the top of the goal square. How did you feel about that?
Malcolm: No one was in the goal square. And the funny thing about it was that in the 1977 Grand Final, I tried to do that, slightly miskicked it, and they got a goal from it. I reckon you're better off having a shot if no one's there. If someone was there, I would have kicked it to them.

---

14 Blight was playing-coach at North Melbourne in 1981, but the arrangement did not last the season out.

Mike: Particularly if you can put it through.
Malcolm: Yes. He actually did a little test. It was left-foot check-side, and, yes, it went through.

Mike: And tell me about that test. I know about this story.
Malcolm: Barass was writing for *The Truth* in those days and said: 'Oh, that was just a low percentage kick. He wouldn't get one out of 20. So come out next Thursday night at training and I'll put it through the test.' Barass made me do 20 kicks. He's bowled me over every time. So he was right up my ginger. I think I kicked five or six goals, hit the post twice and never not scored in 10. He said: 'Oh, that's rubbish and just get back to training.'

Mike: That's it. No apology?
Malcolm: No, no nothing.

Mike: Tim Watson wrote a book about you in 2011 titled *Malcolm Blight: Player, Coach, Legend*[15]. The blurb at the time said it was an authorised biography of you. My understanding from you is that's not the case.
Malcolm: No. Tim rang me up a number of times and I said: 'Why waste your time?' And he was persistent, and then I said: 'Well, Tim, if you're going to do it, how can I stop it?' So in the end, he did it. I've never read it, never seen it, by the way. Never got a copy of it.

Mike: But didn't Tim come to Queensland with the journalist, James Weston?
Malcolm: Yes, he did. I spent a few hours with James Weston with him, and they were terrific, by the way. But in the end I just sensed that the book was Tim's, not mine. It was his assessment of what people were saying.

Mike: Aren't you interested in this 350 pages about you?
Malcolm: Yes, but can I tell you something? It's probably unusual what I'm about to say, but if every word in there is true—and I've never seen it, Mike, and that's God's honour—I don't need to read it.

Mike: Because you know it.
Malcolm: Yes.

Mike: Coaching seems to have caused you recurring pain—Geelong with the three Grand Final losses, Adelaide, even though you won two flags

---

15 Tim Watson with James Weston, *Malcolm Blight: Player, Coach, Legend*, Hardie Grant, 2012

there, and dare I say it, St Kilda. Now, you were born to coach, and you were a great coach, there's no doubt about that, with five Grand Finals, two flags. What was it that just sort of drained you so much?

Malcolm: Well, to be perfectly honest I reckon I went too hard. And my family, my kids and wife, could tell you the stories. As soon as we lost a game I would go home, get hold of the video or DVD, and I wouldn't go to bed until I found out the reason why we lost. And it's not always player-related, by the way. Do you know what I mean? So ... and sadly, Mick, I have to say that I'd sit there with my cigarettes and maybe a bottle of port occasionally, and I would—I just couldn't let it go.

Mike: Well, you walked away from coaching Adelaide after only three years. You had one year off, and then you took that fateful decision to join St Kilda in 2001. Was it a mistake?

Malcolm: I don't think so. One of the things everyone forgets is they only won two games the year before. I mean, they weren't a very good football team. They were going to take two, three, four years anyhow. And after I got the flick, they lost the next six games anyhow. I mean, it wasn't going to happen overnight, and I think—I call it the magic wand I had—getting Geelong into a Grand Final in their first year, Adelaide into a Grand Final in their first year, it just disappeared.

Mike: Did they seduce you with the offer of a million bucks for each of two years? It's a very seductive figure.

Malcolm: Yeah, it is, it is. But that's not the truth, by the way.

Mike: Well, why don't you share the truth with us?

Malcolm: Maybe it could have been for the first year. A second year, it was nowhere near that.

Mike: Okay. So we're all seduced ... we can all be seduced by money. How much did the money influence your decision, compared with the challenge of taking a basket case as a footy club and making a success of it?

Malcolm: I think both. To be honest I think it's probably both. I mean, it was the challenge of doing it again I'd had a year off, and I half freshened up, and the money was attractive, no doubt about it.

Mike: The popular view was that you didn't really want to coach, and you didn't have much respect for St Kilda, and you didn't rate their players. Now, if that's true, that's a recipe for disaster, is it not?

Malcolm: So you want to go there and coach and not win?

Mike: No, no, no.

Malcolm: That logic, Mick, if you think about it, is just stupid. It is a stupid logic. If you go there, you make the decision to go there. You move your family. I mean the whole thing. You move back to Melbourne, and you take it on. Now, this is me, whether you think I was good, bad or indifferent, I was me. I didn't change, do you know?

Mike: I accept that only you know the answer to that. But it seemed like when you go there the reality of coaching through a season and standing out there in the middle of the ground on wet nights with a bunch of blokes, most of whom weren't much good, didn't appeal to you a lot.

Malcolm: No, that wasn't true. I was actually really enjoying it—Lenny Hayes, and Nick Riewoldt had played his first game, Justin Koschitske looked like a real talent, Jason Blake was there, Stephen Milne we played in the first game. So I was actually really starting to get into the young group. And you knew more were coming, because you're going to finish down near the bottom again.

Mike: I want to remind you of a comment which was, I think, an astute comment, but it shocked us at the time, where you said of Robert Harvey, the dual Brownlow medallist, that he ran to the wrong spots on the footy field.

Malcolm: No, I said that a couple of years earlier when we played them in Adelaide. They were down, and he ran forward, and I made a comment on that. Robert Harvey is one of my favourite all-time players. He was a great player. But trying to help him get better is not a bad thing from a coach.

Mike: I remember writing a story on the seventh anniversary of your sacking from St Kilda, quoting the president at the time, Rod Butterss, and it was his administration that appointed you in 2000 to replace Tim Watson. That night on Channel 10, Stephen Quartermain interviewed you. You were offended, you were angry, and occasionally you were vindictive. Why did that hurt you so much?

Malcolm: I think you wrote ... and I think that was said, it was a naïve decision by St Kilda.

Mike: What, to appoint you or sack you?
Malcolm: No, sack me. I agree.

Mike: Yes. But you were so angry towards certainly Rod Butterss, who I was quoting in that story.
Malcolm: Yes, I'd have to think about ... was I? Yes, I probably was. But I didn't say anything for seven years.

Mike: That's true, I understand that. And you're not used to failing, are you? I mean, if it's perceived to be a failure.
Malcolm: It was a failure—I didn't finish. But sometimes your legs are taken out from underneath you and it's a free kick. Do you know what I mean? Some things, you can't control.

Mike: Sure. Why did you keep your peace for so long?
Malcolm: I didn't think it achieved anything. What was I going to do about it? You know, once again the selectors have made their decision, move on.

Mike: The one thing that clearly cut you was the assertion that you weren't committed to the footy club.
Malcolm: Oh, well, that's just absolute rubbish.

Mike: I have one example: I want to ask you about this. There might be a totally plausible explanation for this. But St Kilda played in Brisbane, things hadn't gone well, and you and the coaching staff stayed up there and played golf the next day when the club wanted you back in Melbourne. Is that true?
Malcolm: No, not true. I think I played golf. But I actually answered that. I reckon there are coach-free zones. Barass did that, you know, and it was one of those things that you build up for a week, you play your game, and then the day after, recovery day, I just reckon sometimes you both need space, the playing group and the coaching group. I'd do all sorts of things, including go through the tape again, do you know what I mean? There's a whole host of things—go for a walk, go for a swim. It was really as much to freshen me up and the players. I'd done that for the last 15 years, 20 years.

Mike: You were gone after 15 rounds and three wins. Now, the night of the sacking I called around to your place in Brighton. There was your wife Patsy, yourself, me and Kate, my daughter, who'd been at the footy, and we went down from the MCG. We were in the kitchen, there was no television, no radio. It was like a morgue. It was as if someone had said to you: 'Blighty, you're going to be deported tomorrow.' Had you ever been affected psychologically like you were that day, that night?

Malcolm: Yes, probably, the day I finished at North Melbourne as coach, and Barry Cable came in to coach us. And that was Round 16. I had a few bad Julys. If I got through July I was okay. But back then I said: 'Can I just go? Can I just go home?' They wanted me to warm up and join the rest of the group. Well, I had every cameraman in my face as I did my two warm-up laps, right round Arden Street in those days, and I'm telling you, that was as bad as I've ever been.

Mike: And a couple of days later, from memory, you played with North Melbourne under the new coach. You kicked 11 goals at the Whitten Oval against the Bulldogs. This is the part that I'm interested in, and did you then grab your gear out of your locker and jump straight in the car in your footy gear and go home?

Malcolm: No, not quite. There were council elections on...

Mike: So it is true.

Malcolm: I had a shower, obviously. I said: 'Look, I haven't voted, and I've got to get home by six for the council elections.' You know, I'm a civic-minded person, Michael.

Mike: Were you bitter, or was it just hurt?

Malcolm: Yes. Disappointed, probably. Severe disappointment.

Mike: Blighty, you were what we might gently call 'unorthodox'. Some would say slightly eccentric, some would say bizarre in elements of your behaviour as coach. What was the most radical ploy you called upon in your coaching career?

Malcolm: Apparently so, mate. Most of it wasn't planned. Some of it was. But I always figured if you were getting beaten—and it always happened when there was a loss. When you had a win, you wouldn't have heard boo from me; I just let the players play. I was very big on that. But when you have a loss, I reckon that you're duty-bound to try to do something about it. Now, sometimes I thought a little bit differently to other people. That may have been the case. But it was only ever to try and avoid that loss again. So as I said, I think I was the easiest bloke in the world when we won but I probably did think: what do you do? Do you say to the players: 'Oh, that's not good enough'? I mean, sometimes you paint a picture. Sometimes you take them to a different environment. Sometimes you put them through a whole different action. So it was really just to try and get players to think a bit more outside the square themselves.

Mike: I understand that. But what I wanted to ask you about, and I've always been meaning to ask you this—I mean, how would banishing Austin McCrabb from the three quarter-time huddle and having him stand alone at Waverley, how would that help him or the team?[16]

Malcolm: Probably to make a point.

Mike: And the point being?

Malcolm: The point being we were kicking into the breeze against Hawthorn. We'd played one side of the ground. So I don't care if you've got the ball on this side, we kick it back over that side. And I did that a lot in my career, you know. I mean, these are the rules for the day, make sure you stick by them. Austin, for some unknown reason, kicked it to the other side. I couldn't wait to get him and throttle him. But he's a fantastic fellow too, Austin, and tried hard, but at three-quarter time I just said to him: 'Look, you're not part of us. For you to do that, you're not part of us. Get over there.'

Mike: And now all these years on, are you happy that that was the right tactic for the moment?

Malcolm: For the moment, yes. I wouldn't have changed it, actually. Maybe I would have grabbed him aside and given him a fair little voice over.

Mike: Because you didn't like being ... I mean, it didn't happen to you much, and you were a different level to Austin McCrabb, but you didn't like being humiliated.

Malcolm: No. But I tell you what it did—it livened me up.

---

16 In a game against Hawthorn in 1990, Blight sent McCrabb away from the team huddle because a kick across goal had cost his team a goal. McCrabb was made to stand alone.

Mike: Did it?

Malcolm: Yes. I didn't like it. No one does. I reckon sometimes if we don't have red traffic lights, it's mayhem on the streets. And there are some things that you've got to do, and I reckon in team sport and football there are some things that won't change. And if the person in charge says: 'That's it,' I reckon that's got to be it. There's got to be some common ground for the whole team to understand.

Mike: What about the bloke now officially known as David 'Pathetic' Pittman?[17]

Malcolm: David played a poor quarter of footy. We only had one tall at the time, and, we got beaten. I did say it was pathetic. I did say it about the quarter. When I did the press interviews after, I omitted the word 'quarter', so it sounded like his whole career was like that. And that was never intended. I made a mistake, and I told him so.

Mike: Now in the 1994 semi-final against Carlton, at Waverley Park, your three late withdrawals were Paul Couch, Mark Bairstow, Garry Hocking and Michael Mansfield. You were given no chance. Those who should know say it was probably the most inspirational address you gave in your time at Geelong. What was the theme? What was the message?

Malcolm: Now, the fact that it was a final, wasn't a Grand Final, but you can actually talk about this game for the rest of your life. That was the theme, you know. If you get over this hurdle... Don't forget, the week before we'd beaten Footscray by a kick after the siren by Billy Brownless. We had that great win against Carlton, who had that great team, and they went on to win the next year almost undefeated, and the following week was the Leigh Tudor kick to Gary Ablett to win by a kick after the siren. So we actually made a Grand Final with three—I'm telling you—of the great finals wins of all time.

Mike: And that's the belief thing, is it?

Malcolm: Sadly, the petrol tickets ran out the following weekend with the West Coast Eagles just flogging us.

---

17 After coaching Adelaide in a game at the MCG in 1998, a furious Blight labelled his ruckman, David Pittman, 'the most pathetic ruckman I have ever seen in my life in footy'.

Mike: The other story from Geelong, the public view was that you sat them all around a swimming pool and they exchanged a peace pipe. Is that right?

Malcolm: Yes. Billy Brownless has messed that up a bit. It's changed. It was actually two different stories. There was once around the swimming pool, and once when I asked them to bring a blanket to the MCG. And the reason being, we sat down like we were Indians, and we're going out to attack the natives and all that sort of stuff. So it was just a symbolic thing, because we were playing poorly and you do something different.

Mike: Were they spontaneous things, or did you learn them from people in other sports and what had gone before?

Malcolm: I'd love to say all of those were copied from somewhere, but I don't think they were. You know there's a little fellow up here that talks to me a fair bit.

Mike: Now, one of your many fans at Geelong was Billy Brownless. I mean, he loves what you brought to the footy club and he loves the interaction and the friendship that you had with him, yet he's a bit different. I wouldn't have picked him as one of your favourites.

Malcolm: He was. He's a really likeable guy, you know. I reckon you've got to be careful. It's all right to move people in and out, but some players just *are* the club. And I felt that Bill was always that.

Mike: Yep. How good a player would he have been, Malcolm, had you not had a bloke called Gary Ablett playing in his vicinity?

Malcolm: Actually, I did an interview one day, and they said: 'What do you reckon is the best move you've ever made?' It was actually Billy Brownless who asked me that question. And I said: 'It was probably moving you out of full-forward and putting Ablett there.'

Mike: I mean, unfortunately Ashley McIntosh probably got him in a couple of Grand Finals, but he was a very good player, Billy, wasn't he?

Malcolm: If you had your time again you might have put the great Barry Stoneham at the backline, because we never had enough talls, and Billy could have handled centre half-forward or full-forward with Ablett. You know, hindsight's fantastic.

Mike: Now, Gary Ablett senior. His best years probably came under you, and I think there's a bit of Blighty in Ablett. Did you have an empathy with him that brought the best out of him?

Malcolm: I think so, yes. I've said it, he changed more games than any other player I'd seen. I mean, he could really turn it on, you know. When he was in his bubbly mood, and best mood, he'd kick a lot of goals, or even get the ball a lot, and so he was really great to watch.

Mike: So how did you tap into him? What was your message to him that made him ... free him up and made him play the way he can play?

Malcolm: Good question. I think you'd have to ask Gary that. But I enjoyed talking to him and trying to help him with his footy, as I did most players.

Mike: You saw yourself as a teacher, didn't you?

Malcolm: Yes, I did. Look, coaching's about painting a picture. You know, I'm convinced more of that now. You paint a picture so the boys can fit themselves in there. Now, for a coach to win games, I've never ever thought that. I think what you can do is make a move to be a catalyst for a player to change the game, but winning games—you might get lucky a couple of times a year. You know, just everything falls into place? But I actually enjoyed the teaching side of it.

Mike: You were very strict with all your players at all the clubs you had. Did you bend the rules for Gary Ablett?

Malcolm: I did, in regard to a religious belief he had at the time. He avoided Sunday training a fair bit. So in the end you make him do a little bit extra training.

Mike: You're not being cynical about that excuse, are you? Do you accept the religious belief?

Malcolm: Well, I was at training. I mean, I presume he was doing his stuff. And I think that perhaps it was the start of the accommodating players and other things that players did. But I just said to the senior group: 'Well, look, I've got this issue. He's not turning up Sundays. This is what he's doing. He'll either go back to the seconds, or we'll dismiss him from the club.' He'd just kicked 10 that weekend, or 12 or something. So the older blokes said: 'Oh, no. Well, if that's his belief, that's okay.' So I sort of squared it off with the rest of the playing group.

Mike: When he gave it away for half a season[18].

Malcolm: Yes, he did.

Mike: Did you try to coerce him back, or did you give him his space?

Malcolm: I gave him his space. Other people at the club did try, because they were genuinely interested in his wellbeing, the president Ron Hovey, those sort of blokes. They were just really kind to him, and they really wanted to look after him. But from a playing point of view, I didn't think it was right for me to talk someone into playing. It's a hard enough game to play as it is without having to talk someone into it. So, I was pleased when he came back. And he did play seconds, by the way.

Mike: What was the explanation, Blighty?

Malcolm: I'll tell you what it is. Sometimes you just get sick of being yourself.

Mike: More information?

Malcolm: Sometimes the hardest thing in the world is to be you, with the expectations on you. And I think perhaps I'd been through that a little bit, and I think I could see that in Gary.

Mike: Did you think he was gone?

Malcolm: No, I didn't think he was gone as a player. Mentally he was not there. You know the thing I was pleased about? He was actually honest about it. 'I am really struggling with this.' So instead of going through the charade of just doing it, he opted out for a while.

Mike: Have you seen a more gifted player, a more naturally gifted player?

Malcolm: I'm on the board of the Gold Coast Suns now. We've got one there who's pretty good.

Mike: Yes. His name happens to be the same, doesn't it?

Malcolm: Same name, yes. Young Gary's got some genius in him, too. I mean, it's amazing.

Mike: I want to ask you about the two of them. We know they're totally different in the way they play the game, but as a spectator, I suspect that we prefer to watch Gary Ablett senior, but I'm guessing if I were a coach, I might prefer to coach Gary Ablett junior.

---

18 Ablett departed Geelong in 1991, saying he had retired. But he returned later in the season.

Malcolm: I'd like them both. But in answer to that question, Gary's played just over 200 games now. His dad played nearly 250, and missed a bit of footy. Young Gary's knocking on Dad's door, don't worry about that. They are completely different players. Gary senior changed more games, as I said before, than any other player. But young Gary, he could have found the footy in the wheat drum, you know?

Mike: Tell me the story about you and one of your many chats with Gary Ablett senior at the bridge.

Malcolm: The bridge at the sanctuary. Well, it was when I first went to Geelong and Gary had missed a few training sessions. And once again it was like: 'We've got to set some rules here, boys.' They'd sort of been that team that was just below, had just missed out for 10 years. So, I said to Gary: 'Look, I've got to meet you.' And we met at Balyang Sanctuary in Geelong. It's become pretty famous. I think there might be a plaque there, Mike.

But, I said to him: 'Look, Gary, this has got to stop. Either you walk across the bridge with me, go and get your footy gear and come to training, or I'll symbolically push you into the creek and you're out. You may as well not turn up here again.' I had to be strong. The football world was changing, nearly professional. So after the discussion, Gary went home and got his gear.

Mike: Were you confident?

Malcolm: No, no, no. I was hoping. I mean, you knew he had talent, good heavens. But it's no good if the talent's not used.

Mike: Did you feel at that time that fate had dealt you a rough hand? I think on reflection that your performance at Geelong was amazingly good. I think we were deluded by the stars at the top, and we didn't see the bottom end of your group. A bit like St Kilda under Ross Lyon.

Malcolm: I agree with that.

Mike: You ran into Hawthorn in 1989.

Malcolm: Yes. Great team.

Mike: I don't mean to bring back these nightmares, Blighty.

Malcolm: That's actually not a nightmare. In '89 someone has to run second, and it was such a legendary game, and it was such a great year.

I've had this debate with you before, probably on the couch in the old days, but running second sometimes is not a bad thing. It takes two to tango. I think the second team gets dealt a harsh blow, and that was before I coached seconds, or runners-up.

Mike: No, I totally agree with that. That's why I reckon you're better running third than second in the AFL.
Malcolm: Exactly. And as I said, preliminary finals, they're like dancing with your sister. You're nowhere. It's a terrible feeling, losing preliminary finals.

Mike: In '92 and '94 you lost to West Coast, who were a great team, no question about that. Is there one of the three Grand Finals you should have got?
Malcolm: '92, I thought. We led at half-time by a couple of goals, but we also led by four and a bit goals with four or five minutes to go to half-time, and I think someone kicked a couple of goals late, and momentum just shifted.

Mike: When you got to Adelaide in 1997 you made some big decisions there. From memory, you sacked Chris McDermott, Andrew Jarman, Tony McGuinness and Greg Anderson. No one else would have got away with that.
Malcolm: Yes, but each of them for different reasons, Mike. They weren't sacked. I thought Chris had finished. Greg had sort of pulled the pin. Andrew didn't turn up for duty one day and so the club was not very happy with him. It's since been resolved, which is good. Tony was the hard one. He probably had another year in him but you make those calls.

Mike: Were you trying to make a statement? Was this to say that 'the culture that's been at this footy club is no longer applicable, nor is it good enough and I'm going to change it'?
Malcolm: Tony was a fantastic bloke, and I had a lot of conversations with him after. And he coached, and I guess they all understand now that 'hey, I've had decisions made on me, and you're paid to make them on other people'. It's the hardest part in footy. So it's not as though you go out there with a dartboard and say: 'He's going because of this.' And it wasn't because they weren't good people. You're making an assessment and it's not even personal.

Mike: But it is personal.

Malcolm: Oh, personal to them. Yes, of course.

Mike: Mark Ricciuto told me recently that he thought you'd almost had enough of coaching after the 1997 flag. You could have walked away then satisfied with what you'd done. You'd got the flag that you so desperately wanted. Did you contemplate giving it away after the '97 premiership?

Malcolm: Yes, to be totally honest, it was the Wednesday after the Grand Final, in the euphoria of it all, and the camaraderie of the team, the whole club, and the whole state. At the Wednesday meeting to decide who we're going to finish up at the football club, because the rules say you've got to turn three over and then, there's injuries and you've got to make decisions on people. You've gone from this unbelievably euphoric state, to making decisions on people's lives again two days, three days later. Spare me. I just think it's not right.

Mike: So did you contemplate it?

Malcolm: Yes. And the following year, too. I can't believe you can be so high and then be so low. 'Who are we going to get rid of?' I mean, hard stuff.

Mike: How difficult was 1999, your last year in Adelaide, for you? You've coached the footy club in your home town to two flags in a row, and you clearly exuded the body language then that you'd had enough, and you couldn't wait for the season to finish.

Malcolm: Yes, that was true. About halfway through the year I could just feel myself slipping. What do you do? Just charade it through? So I went to John Reid and Bob Hammond[19] and I said: 'Look, I am in "strugglesville".' I don't know if that's weak or being honest or being stupid, but I was. I was flat as a tack. We had a lot of injuries, but the team still played flat. As a club, I reckon we'd done four finals in a row, five interstate trips in a row for the second one. No one's done it tougher than what Adelaide Football Club has, and I don't think Victorians and some of the football population understands. They were two of the most remarkable Septembers you've ever seen. And I think it took its toll on everyone.

---

19 John Reid was football manager of Adelaide and a confidante of Blight's. Don Hammond was chairman of the club.

Mike: What did the first flag as a coach in '97 mean to you personally? Was it validation?

Malcolm: I tell you what, the night before, I'm telling you, I was worried. I could have said another word.

Mike: Say you were nervous.

Malcolm: A four-time loser. And that's what it would have been. Mate, I'm telling you, it was the worst night of footy I've ever had. I don't reckon I slept a wink. I've never said that before, that Friday night before the '97 Grand Final was probably the worst night I spent in football. Forget the St Kilda sacking, forget the North Melbourne sacking. Mate, I was petrified.

Mike: Were you lucky to be in that Grand Final?

Malcolm: We were lucky to be anywhere. Thirteen wins twice, and you end up with premierships. It's a remarkable September. And that's why if I could get every clipping out now, there is not one expert—and rightly so—would have picked Adelaide to get within five or six goals of St Kilda.

Mike: I want to remind you about a bloke called Darren Jarman, who was another one I would have thought that you'd have a very, very rich appreciation of for his footy skills. He was critical of you, wasn't he?

Malcolm: Andrew McLeod and Darren Jarman are probably the most equally gifted players we had in the team at the time. For them to play well twice in a row on that last Saturday in September was a gift from the gods. And they had gifts of the gods.

Mike: After the St Kilda fiasco, you almost went to Queensland in self-imposed exile, didn't you? Then you came back to the industry as a commentator on Channel 10. A lot of us saw you as sort of angry, even bitter at that point, that the game wasn't what it was, the players weren't as good as they should have been. Is that a fair assessment or not?

Malcolm: I'd hope not. There might have been the odd time, but generally speaking, I still go to the footy. I watch every game now still, because I love watching good players.

Mike: When you came back with Channel 10 I didn't get the impression that you'd embraced the game again, that it was like a chore with you, and you didn't like what you were seeing.

Malcolm: If I was like that, Mick, I would have given it away. I still don't like some of the things that happen in the game now, but that's only an opinion. You know, if you're inside coaching the team, you do those things to try and make them win.

Mike: You were in an unusual situation when you took a position on the Gold Coast board. You were still working for Channel 10. You were the football man. One night, there was sort of heavily implied criticism of Guy McKenna, the coach. Do you accept that?
Malcolm: I would have ... yes.

Mike: Did anything come of that?
Malcolm: No, not really. It would have been done for the betterment of the telecast and betterment of the game, and if it was what I thought, I would have said it.

Mike: Do you mentor McKenna?
Malcolm: I talk to him infrequently, you know.

Mike: Well, why don't you do it frequently?
Malcolm: I don't want to be in his pocket. He's got to be his own man. But certainly if I see something I think I can help him with I'll certainly ring him up or he'll ring me. And he's the coach, he's learning, he's seriously getting better daily.

Mike: When do you think that the Suns can play finals?
Malcolm: I thought: 'Maybe year three.' There are signs that our team is slowly maturing—and I say slowly. And there's going to be some more pain, Mike. There's got to be.

Mike: Your problem from a long way away, seems to me to be can you retain these kids that you've brought from all over Australia? Will you be able to keep them as the group that you assembled?
Malcolm: I think that's a fair assessment. We hope we can. We hope we've got an environment of learning and improvement. And it's actually a really good place. It's actually quite a fun place to be at. You know, it's a real bubble still. We'll get better.

Mike: I can't interview you without asking you about that torpedo goal at Princes Park in 1976. You kicked a 'torp' after the siren at Princes

Park, to win the game. It certainly went through post-high. I was at the ground at the time.

Malcolm: And you're the 438-thousandth person who was at that game.

Mike: What's the current yardage of that kick?

Malcolm: It's nearly 100 metres, but I've left it at 98.

Mike: And what do you reckon it actually was?

Malcolm: They measured it for a story in the paper the following day. Kids from the University of Melbourne went out there and they tried the projectile angle, let's just say, and they measured it at 83 yards. So about 77-78 metres. There was one I kicked that same year at the other end from the centre circle that hit the back fence. The commentator said: 'Oh, he'll have to kick this 100 metres.' Or 100 yards. I think I did. It just must have got caught in a whirligig up the top there, and off it went.

Mike: Blighty, over your footy career looking back the past 40 years now, are there any regrets? Any that you'll take to the grave?

Malcolm: Oh, the obvious thing is to say I wish I got a few more kicks, but that's a fair way back.

Mike: Nothing that occurred ... like, the St Kilda situation?

Malcolm: It happened. It's part of my tapestry of life. I mean, what can I do about it? You know, I couldn't do anything on the day. Even the North Melbourne bit. I mean, I'd love to still be coaching North Melbourne deep down, if I had my chance. But you know what? I played for Woodville. That was my boyhood dream. Woodville in Adelaide was my team.

Mike: We change our dreams though, as we go along. If you walked out the front now and ran into Rod Butterss and Grant Thomas, which is unlikely in itself, but if you ran into them would there be any dialogue?

Malcolm: Yes, I'd say hello.

Mike: And you wouldn't want to take it any further?

Malcolm: No, not really, no. Just hello. I mean, have a look at us. Look at our age. There are cobwebs on us, so taking something like that or not enjoying what you do today, it's just not in my nature.

DERMOTT BRERETON

From his first game, the 1982 first semi-final, Dermott Brereton personified flamboyance and flair. After kicking five goals in that match against North Melbourne, the man who came to be known as 'The Kid' went on to forge a 211-game career (189 of those for Hawthorn) as the star centre half-forward of his time.

Brereton used his shortish (186cm, 92kg) frame to perfection as a big-marking, hard-leading target, and he combined with Hawk teammate Jason Dunstall to form one of the most potent forward line duos in the game's history. A proven big-game player, he was a pivotal member of the Hawks' 1983, 1986, 1988, 1989 and 1991 premiership teams. Brereton also played in the losing Grand Finals of 1984, 1985 and 1987 and kicked a then-record eight goals in Hawthorn's 1985 Grand Final loss to Essendon.

As talented as Brereton was, he will also be remembered as one of the game's tough men. He was always willing to put his body on the line (an attitude that almost certainly curtailed his career) and never shirked an issue. After being flattened at the opening bounce of the 1989 Grand Final, he famously lifted himself from the 'carpet'—a moment immortalised in vision as he vomited his way to the goal square, only to mark and goal minutes later—inspiring the Hawks to premiership glory. Injury, in particular a chronic hip complaint, cut short the latter part of his career and he managed just seven games in 1992, before missing the entire 1993 season.

Brereton made two attempts to rekindle his career, in 1994 with Sydney and the following year with Collingwood. However, despite some handy performances for both clubs (especially the Magpies) he was forced into retirement at just 31 years of age after a glittering 14-season career.

Brereton later established himself as a radio and television commentator, with his analysis of player and game held in high regard.

APRIL 4, 2012

Mike: Tell me the origin of the nickname, 'The Kid'.

Dermott: It happened very early on. I think I might've been 16, definitely no more than that, and I played in a reserve game. Des Meagher was the coach, and at halftime he said to this guy: 'Smithy, get a kick or we're going to put on…' He pointed at me and went: 'That kid!'

Mike: You always look happy to me. Are you?

Dermott: I wake up every morning without any precedents, and I smile. I'm just happy to be there, get up, get into life, have a bit of fun and spread it around a bit.

Mike: But there's a period in your life when you must have been unhappy and I would suspect, confused. I mean, your father, Dermott, and your brother, Paul, both took their own lives at young ages. What sort of impact did that have on you?

Dermott: It had a massive impact. I mean, my father, incredibly so. I know a lot of people say: 'Why don't you coach? Why are you always late?' And the reality was, I was so self-centred as a footballer, while I was playing, everything was football to me. My dad was getting sicker and sicker mentally.

And I couldn't see it happening, because I was just so into my own world. So when I retired, you have responsibilities in various areas of life. I won't say shirked, but I've evaded serious responsibility since then.

Mike: Does that guilt sit on your shoulders still?

Dermott: A little bit, in that regard, yes. I don't want to take things too seriously. It's pretty hard to wake up and see that: 'Hey, I could have done something about that.' That hurts a bit.

Mike: Let's talk about your football. It was a great career, there's no doubt about that, by any definition. But it prompts a few questions in review, I reckon. I mean, your best year was 1985; you won the best and

fairest, you won the goalkicking, you kicked eight goals in a losing Grand Final, and you're All-Australian, and you were 21 years of age. I can't remember you having a better year than that.

Dermott: I reckon I did. I reckon I played better in '87, '88, '89…

Mike: Allan 'Yabby' Jeans was your coach. He's an exalted figure in your mind, isn't he, in your life?

Dermott: Yes.

Mike: Tell us why. He was more than a coach to you, wasn't he?

Dermott: I was 14 and somebody came and knocked on my door. 'Want to train at Hawthorn?' Dad said: 'No, not until he's 15.' Done.

By 15, later in that year, I'm invited to play with the seniors. You train Monday night, Tuesday night, a light run Wednesday and Thursday night. My dad was working at nights.

> **CAREER**
> **Born:** August 19, 1964
> **Clubs:** *Hawthorn* 1982-1992—189 games, 427 goals; *Sydney* 1994— 7 games, 7 goals; *Collingwood* 1995— 15 games, 30 goals
> **Honours:** Member, Australian Football Hall of Fame (inducted 1999); Hawthorn Football Club Team of the Century; Hawthorn's best and fairest and leading goalkicker 1985; All-Australian 1985; International Rules series coach 1999; premiership sides 1983, 1986, 1988, 1989, 1991

I'm listening to Allan Jeans more than I had my own father. When you look back at your life and you say: 'Right, what was the period that really mattered?' That's what you took in. Everyone that you listened to at that stage, they tend to mean the most.

So then, from 17, when I'm on the verge of seniors, through to when Yabby leaves when I'm about 28, I heard him every day.

Mike: Did you cry when he died?

Dermott: Yes. I still struggle not to cry when I think about him.

Mike: When your own father died in 1993, you were 27? What was your relationship like with him?

Dermott: I had a great relationship with him until the last few weeks.

Mike: What happened then?

Dermott: He'd run into some trouble with the law. He had a dark past that had resurfaced.

Mike: Can you talk about that?
Dermott: Family members probably don't really want me to. But I said something to him that he never recovered from.

Mike: Really? How does that sit with you now?
Dermott: They were the last words I said to him.

Mike: Is that right? So you hadn't spoken to him for a month before he died?
Dermott: Yes, about that.

Mike: And you don't want to share that exchange with your father?
Dermott: No.

Mike: And your brother was living with you, wasn't he?
Dermott: Yes, he came and lived with me for a few weeks. And I'd seen the writing, on reflection, knowing what had happened with my dad, then to see what was happening with my brother, you recognise some signs. I thought he loved life too much to do it, though. But obviously it got the better of him.

Mike: You were reported 17 times during your career and suspended nine times for a total of 39 games. Were you irresponsible, or was that just the Irish temper taking over?
Dermott: Temper. Very combative.

Mike: Acceptable levels of temper, or not?
Dermott: No. Sometimes, no. I was very combative, very protective over other players. You've got to be honest. I felt I had a great sense of justice.

Mike: You were the judge, though, of that justice.
Dermott: Unfortunately, yes, and that's what society can't afford, people to take the judgement into their own hands. But on the footy field, I thought I did, and I probably shouldn't have. If I saw something that I thought was unfair or unjust, I'd act on it. Very, very seldom was I the true instigator, very seldom.

Mike: We'll get back to a couple of those incidents. While we're talking about your heritage and that Irish temper, was the story right that you sent money back to the IRA[20] during your playing days?

Dermott: I'm glad you've asked that. I didn't think you'd ask it, but I'm glad you've asked that, because, no, I didn't. I am a prolific donator of money— we're not talking thousands of it, we're talking about 100 here, 100 there—to people who I believe … once again, it's that sense of justice. I've sent it to the retired English soldiers who served in Northern Ireland and come out of it disfigured and they have their charity. I've sent money to them.

What I did send to was a national Irish group who look after under-privileged people. Now somewhere along the line, that gets blurred into being a direct amount of money to the IRA.

Mike: So there was nothing from you directly to the IRA?

Dermott: Never has, never will be.

Mike: Okay. Let's go to a couple of those on-field incidents we talked about before. One that we're particularly interested in involved Danny Frawley. I've got a feeling that ended a friendship.

Dermott: I liked 'Spud', and I like him again now but it created some animosity for a few years. I was very good friends with Trevor Barker, and he was having a testimonial night that night. Spud was an exceptionally good player. Spud grabbed me. You do it, you don't do it, back in those days, it was kind of an unwritten law that you could do it. And then it was kind of an unwritten law back in those days, with two umpires only in vogue, that if you did it too much, you were warned.

Mike: You're talking about hanging on here?

Dermott: Yes. And I warned Spud, and he called my bluff. And I thought: 'Well, I've got to do something.' I backhanded him, he's whacked me back, I've lurched forward, and then much to my regret, I lurched back, and the back of my arm lifted him under the chin. And, unfortunately, I just knew there was no coming back from him from that.

Mike: Dermott, you said earlier that you were never the instigator.

Dermott: Rarely.

---

20 IRA: Irish Republican Army.

Mike: I want to remind you about an incident involving a bloke who'd been a teammate of yours, Rayden Tallis. What did Rayden Tallis do to you that day in 1994 to make you stand on his head?

Dermott: Nothing. There was some of the worst sledging by blokes who'd never played a senior game for Hawthorn in the two or three minutes before, in a lonely end of the ground when the ball was up the other end.

Mike: Was Tallis one of those? Was he getting into you?

Dermott: I don't think Rayden was; he just happened to be holding the ball some minutes later.

Mike: Now, I don't know if you've ever admitted that you actually did wilfully, intentionally, and perhaps maliciously stand on his head. Did you?

Dermott: I'll give it to you. I wilfully wanted to stand on him. I wilfully wanted to hurt him. I was that outraged by some of the comments that the young guys...

Mike: Because you were wearing the Swans colours at the time, were you not?[21]

Dermott: Yes. I slam-tackled him as well. He's one tough unit. I really slam-tackled him, put him down, put my hand on him, the ball went that way, and I looked up and thought: 'I'm going to go for the ball, and it'll be a disguise, and I'm just going to step on anything.'

Mike: It just strikes me that you were worried. You had your insecurities yourself, then, about where you were at.

Dermott: Absolutely. You also understand that I'd come from a club that I felt I'd given ... you're a paid employee as a footballer. But there are times when, as a paid employee, you go above the call, and I'd felt I'd done that at Hawthorn. I understand why they'd made the decision they did back in that era, but I felt pretty unjustly dealt with. And it rankled with me.

Mike: So it flowed over from when Hawthorn came to you and offered you what was a pitiful amount of money...

Dermott: Yes.

---

21 Brereton left Hawthorn at the end of 1992 after a contract dispute. He returned as a Sydney player in 1994, and later played for Collingwood.

Mike: That resentment stayed with you for a long time?

Dermott: Yes, it did. I remember, I was on good money. It was $175,000, which was top dollar in the League in those days.

Mike: That was your money in your last year at Hawthorn, was it?

Dermott: Second-last year. Then Peter Hudson was brought on to the board, and he was brought on as someone who had to help cut costs and the likes. So I went from $175,000 to getting an offer of $7000 base, $1500 a game, and bonuses that could take me up to $175,000.

And those bonuses came at 18-game milestone, 20-game milestone, and 22-game milestone. And I said to Peter and John Hook[22], who was in on the meeting: 'What, have you blokes been promoted, or am I less important?' Which didn't go down well with them. I said: 'This is great that you're giving me the opportunity to earn the same money, but you do know that next year there's only 20 games in the season. It's going to be pretty tough to get to 22 in a 20-game season.'

So I came back to them and said: 'Look, a base of $30,000 to have me at work for 48 weeks a year—four weeks off—$1500 a game, and give me bonuses on eight, 12 and 16 games. And if I play 16 games, that's a pretty good year.' And they said no. They stuck to the $7000 base.

Mike: You understood, though, that they had money problems, but obviously you clearly felt insulted by the offer.

Dermott: Yes.

Mike: Staying at Hawthorn, talking about one of your teammates, a famous teammate and a bloke you seemed to be so close to during your playing career, Jason Dunstall. Are you matey with Jason?

Dermott: I love having the banter with him. He's a ripping bloke. I like his company. But he's an ordinary bloke, too. He's just this weird sense of humour, like Oscar the Grouch in *Sesame Street*. That's what he's like. But he's hilarious. He's highly intelligent. He goes through life thinking: 'I've got enough friends at the moment, and unless they're going to add something exceptional, I have no need to meet anyone else.' So he gives nobody any time.

---

22 Hook was football manager at Hawthorn.

Mike: Are you one of those friends?

Dermott: If he needed me for anything, he wanted me to do anything, yes, I would.

Mike: Did you once say of Jason, he's the most self-centred, unselfish footballer you've ever seen?

Dermott: Yes, I did. Did you hear that? Yes, he is. He's an amazing contradiction. As a player, he was completely team-orientated; as a human, he's completely 'self-centric'. But he's hilarious.

Mike: Where does he sit among the great players? I know your reverence for Leigh Matthews. Where does Dunstall sit?

Dermott: He's right up there. People ask me: 'All right, pick the full-forwards, how good are they?' If you wanted to play in a team and look back over your head at the goal square and just applaud, you'd have Gary Ablett. If you wanted a bloke one-off to win one game—they're all playing at their best, I might add—you go for 'Plugger' Lockett. You want a bloke to play for your season, to actually get to where you want to go and professionally do the job, that's Dunstall.

Mike: Dermott, your first game, we all remember that you kicked five goals in your first game at a final at the MCG against North Melbourne. I think there's another enduring memory for you from that game, isn't there?

Dermott: I've seen Andrew Demetriou, CEO of the League, run this way, and I knew that Leigh was following me. And I heard a crunch, and the best analogy I can use is, if you got a hessian sack and you filled it up with brisket bones, a little bit of flesh still on them and you hit it with a baseball bat, the dull thud and the sound, that's what it sounded like. And I'm playing my first game, I've just turned 18, and I thought to myself: 'This is a different world up here. If you don't do something, you're going to get killed. If you allow them to do it, they are going to kill you, and it's going to happen quickly.'

Mike: So you adopted Leigh Matthews as your mentor from that moment, did you?

Dermott: Funnily enough, until I played AFL, I had never been reported or sent off.

Mike: It's a different game these days, there's no doubt about that, far less physical. Do you like it?

Dermott: I do. You know what, I would love to play it in this era, too.

Mike: Who do you like watching, Dermott?

Dermott: I'm a Jonathan Brown fan. But there's only one bloke I've ever seen who was the hardest bloke to tackle, and I have never watched a player and giggled and laughed because of how good they are and what they do. I do it with Cyril Rioli. When I was playing as a young man in Hawthorn, the hardest man ever to lay a glove on and tackle in League football, in my 30 years, was Maurice Rioli. You couldn't tackle him.

Mike: Now, we can't do an interview without talking about the 1989 Grand Final and Mark Yeates. He owed you one, didn't he?

Dermott: Yes, he sure did.

Mike: Earlier that season, was there something that you might have done to him that...

Dermott: Yes, absolutely. As I say, I felt aggrieved. I'd been, I thought, infringed against. And a lot of the time, because of my noticeable appearance and that, I felt that the umpires gave me a fairly hard time. I felt a bit victimised.

Mike: Probably because you whacked every other bloke in the opposition.

Dermott: Well, it eventually ended up being a whack. But I felt like they'd turned a blind eye to stuff that they wouldn't have if I had've committed that act. The ball went out of bounds after I felt one of these acts. I screamed at the umpire. I looked up and Paul Dear, the substitute ruckman, had locked arms with 'Yeatesy' on a boundary line throw-in. The ball went up over the head, I charged him, went to go for the ball but not really go for the ball, just put a knee into Yeatesy, just drive one into him. He went down pretty hard. And as he was getting carted off, I had a few words to him just for good measure.

Mike: I know you're friends now; I understand that.

Dermott: He's a great guy. And then when he got me in that Grand Final, in the opening quarter, I remember just strolling past him at quarter-time and looking at him. And we're even. People say: 'Why don't you dislike him?'

We're even. And I went past him, I'd looked at him and I winked and I went: 'I'm still here.'

Mike: The 'Line in the Sand' game[23], there's been some confusion about your role in that. You were on the Hawthorn board at the time. You allegedly had an exchange with your captain Richie Vandenberg at half-time. Is that true, and what did you say to him?

Dermott: Well, that's true. Actually, it's not going to look that good for me. He got reported that day. He and Campbell Brown got the most at the tribunal.

Mike: Essendon was seen to intimidate Hawthorn at the time.

Dermott: Essendon had belted up Hawthorn for years. Hawthorn had not got within a bull's roar of them. And they were a better team. But they emotionally belted up Hawthorn as well. They scared them into submission before the first bounce.

I'm a big believer that actions speak volumes of what you want to do, what you want to achieve. You make an action, you have to live up to that action. I think that day, Hawthorn broke the mould. There's a ripping bloke, too, from Essendon, Mark Johnson, he slam-tackled Robert Campbell. Whistle went, because the ball was pinned to him. So play went dead. Inexperienced young Robbie then went limp, relaxed, and Johnno slam-tackled him. I went down at half-time, and they were geeing themselves up; they were well on the way to a frenzy. And I went into the toilet and it just happened at the one time, Richie and Campbell Brown were there, and my words without the adjectives in it was: 'Don't let Mark Johnson walk off...'

Mike: So the average losing margin for Hawthorn, the previous 12 encounters, was 10 goals plus. But next time they played Essendon, Essendon won by three points.

Dermott: Hawthorn won the next 10.

Mike: You were a massive big game player. I mean, you're noted for that, and it's true. But in the '87 Grand Final, Carlton played David Rhys-Jones on you, at centre half-back. He won the Norm Smith Medal.

---

23 The Line in the Sand Game refers to an Essendon-Hawthorn match in 2004, when 18 players were reported.

Now I know you're not into alibis, but did he just outpoint you, or did you have broken ribs that day?

Dermott: That's not right. I had a crack in my ankle, which got operated on several weeks later. And I had a back brace on … I mean, I couldn't touch my knees. Dunstall had gone down. His ankle had blown up to the size of a pumpkin. So we had no key forward. Paul Dear played, and he was in about his third or fourth game, so I had to play. Rhys's strength was my weakness. I thought I had him covered, with my marking mobility, but I lost my mobility, I lost my co-ordination because of various elements. And when the ball hit the deck, he was like a cat, Rhys. He could just gather it in, and I couldn't chase him.

Mike: Dermott, you were coaching your son Devlin's under-13 footy team. Surely they're not going to play like Dermott Brereton played his footy? I mean, what are the priorities for you with your boys' footy team?
Dermott: To see their skills improve.

PHIL CARMAN

He played only 100 games over eight seasons but few players have left such an indelible mark on the game of Australian football as 'Fabulous' Phil Carman.

From Edenhope in western Victoria, Carman was tied to Collingwood in the VFL but when he decided to play 'big-time' football it was with Norwood in the SANFL. His prodigious talent was obvious during his years at Norwood and Collingwood eventually persuaded him to join the VFL after the 1974 season.

A sensation with Collingwood from his very first game, Carman set the VFL alight with some brilliant performances in his debut year with the Magpies (1975). In Round 20 against St Kilda he kicked an amazing 11 goals and he also collected two other bags of six in that season.

Collingwood had a poor year in 1976 and Carman's form also waned. But with four-time Richmond premiership coach Tom Hafey taking over the reins in 1977, Collingwood and Carman ascended new heights. Carman was superb in the second semi-final against Hawthorn, kicking four goals and sending Collingwood into the Grand Final. But his fiery temper, long a feature of his game, cost him dearly that day. He was later suspended for two matches for striking the Hawks' Michael Tuck, missing the Grand Final—which Collingwood drew with North Melbourne—and the Grand Final replay. There are few who don't believe Collingwood would have won the flag had Carman been available for that first Grand Final.

After a comparatively mediocre 1978 season, the Magpies and Carman parted ways and he became something of a footballing nomad, playing for Melbourne, Essendon and North Melbourne over the following four seasons.

Although he played some excellent games during this period, his infamous legacy of the time was to be remembered for head-butting boundary umpire Graham Carbery when playing for Essendon in a match against St Kilda in early 1980, for which he received a 20-match suspension.

Carman later captain-coached Eastlake in Canberra and Sturt in the SANFL, lifting the club to within a whisker of a flag in 1988.

AUGUST 13, 2012

Mike: It's been an interesting journey, hasn't it? Did we see the best out of what Phil Carman had to offer?

Phil: Oh, look I'm often asked that. Obviously not. A hundred League games of footy, it's nothing, is it? I look back and I'm actually envious of guys that have played 200-plus games. But there are a lot of situations or incidents that occurred that sort of stopped me from playing more.

Mike: When you left, there were the four clubs. There was Collingwood, Melbourne, Essendon and North Melbourne. Did you feel unfulfilled or look back on what you might have been?

Phil: Well people are always saying: 'Do you have any regrets?' And obviously you do. I would love to have been a one-club player. I would love to have stayed at Collingwood because I just enjoy that environment. But circumstances had it that I switched clubs every year or two.

Mike: Let's talk about those circumstances at Collingwood. It was inconceivable in your first three years at Collingwood that you would ever part. I mean you were a star; they were a good club, playing finals. What went wrong in 1978?

Phil: I came across from South Australia and I was with a club, Norwood, that seemed to have a very professional attitude. And when I got to Melbourne, I imagined that in the VFL it would be a far more professional club, but it wasn't. In the first two years, actually, there was a lot of turmoil. There was a lot of in-fighting and all I wanted to do was play footy and I didn't want to be associated with things off the field. And therefore I just lost a fair bit of interest, I think. When Tommy Hafey arrived as coach in my third year, I'd already got into a pattern of misbehaviour that he didn't like. And that continued into my fourth year and his second year as coach.

And at the end of that year, he parted company with myself, Len Thompson, Max and Wayne Richardson and probably another two or three players as well. I'm just so disappointed, in hindsight. I would loved to have stayed there. And I think, in a way, Tommy did the wrong thing by himself. Had he kept me there and spent some time one-on-one, well ... they played in a few Grand Finals after that.

Mike: I was just thinking that, 1979 through 1981 they played Grand Finals.

Phil: And those few years, I'm thinking: 'Gee, you know, I'd love to be there.' He probably did himself, in a way, a disservice. He probably thought he did the right thing but he could have kept myself and probably one or two others he let go.

Mike: When you mention misbehaviour, I mean my memory is not that you misbehaved. I think you were sort of a free spirit in a lot of ways. But what do you mean by misbehaviour?

CAREER
Born: September 4, 1960
Clubs: *Norwood* 1970-74—58 games; *Collingwood* 1975-78 —66 games, 142 goals; *Melbourne* 1979—11 games, 23 goals; *Essendon* 1980-81—10 games, 12 goals; *North Melbourne*—13 games, 27 goals
AFL total: 100 games, 204 goals
Honours: Copeland Trophy (Collingwood best and fairest) 1975; Collingwood leading goalkicker 1975, 1976

Phil: Well I love training. At that time I was employed as Collingwood's development officer, so really I wasn't working as such. I would train in the morning and train in the evening. But I always felt that training should be pretty specific. And I trained hard in the morning and the other guys would get to training, start at 5.30 and training would go until 7.00 and I felt that I'd done enough in the morning, that I didn't need to do that much training as well. So I would tend to leave the track early on lots of occasions. And that happened when Murray Weideman was there. It happened again when Tommy was there. I recall one night Tommy coming into the change rooms and he said: 'You'd better come out on the track.' And I said, 'No, look I'm not.'

Mike: Is that the complete story? My understanding of that story was that you left the track because you had done what you considered a reasonable amount.

Phil: Yes.

Mike: Tommy came looking for you and ordered you back out from the shower.
Phil: Right, and I didn't go, go back out. That's right.

Mike: No wonder the relationship soured. But Phil, this is stating the obvious to you, but in a team game, can an individual, no matter how good he is, can he set the rules?
Phil: No, absolutely not, but it's just that I enjoyed playing. I didn't enjoy the environment of a club situation that much. And so I just got into a habit of doing things my way and I got away with it to a certain extent. I wasn't held to account often enough. I think once they may have called me into a meeting and explained to me that 'you can't do it' but, as I said, I just got away with it and it just happened too often.

Mike: Let's go to 1977 and the second semi-final against Hawthorn. You, for reasons best known to yourself, whacked Michael Tuck in the middle of the MCG. You were suspended for two games. There's no question Collingwood at the time believed that the incident cost them the flag. Do you subscribe to that?
Phil: Yes, well looking back, I do. But it's interesting, you know… if we can talk about that for a moment? It was a second semi-final, playing in front of 80,000 people, I'd kicked the first goal of the match and I'd handballed to Len Thompson, so he kicked the second. And the adrenaline was really, really pumping, and it was still early in the first quarter. The ball had been knocked away from our centre half-forward and I chased the ball down. I had to make a split decision. I didn't know who it was and I just ran through, hit him with a forearm. I didn't think there was much in it until after the game. I was shown a replay of the incident and I knew then that I was in a bit of strife.

Mike: Has Tommy ever forgiven you for that?
Phil: I've only spoken to Tommy on a few occasions since. We haven't discussed it but I certainly wouldn't think he has. It's hard because he was quite a sensational coach at Collingwood. He took us from the bottom to play off in a Grand Final in '77.

Mike: Given your importance to that footy team, was the action irresponsible?

Phil: Well it obviously was, but when you're playing these things happen on the spur of the moment, you know? It wasn't premeditated. As I said, I just saw him there and I thought: 'Bang, I'll knock him over.' Which I did. It was a stupid thing to do but a lot of people have made similar errors.

Mike: Sure, but at finals time? I mean the stakes are so much higher. And in that case, the year of 1977, when there was a draw in the first Grand Final, it was amazing. I mean the fact the two games you missed were both Grand Finals, were they not?

Phil: That's right.

Mike: Did you appeal after the draw? Did Collingwood and you go back to the VFL to see if, given that the second match was going to be another Grand Final, that they might have relented?

Phil: Yes, when I was suspended, they actually said that they were suspending me for one week this year and the first match of the following season. So we felt we had a case to go to appeal. We went in there and they just threw it out and said: 'No, look, you're suspended for the replay as well.'

Mike: What about the reaction from your teammates and from the supporters too, to events that unfolded? And I understand your point about not planning to hit Tuck. Was there resentment?

Phil: Oh look, I would think so because even though I've caught up with a lot of Collingwood players since and we don't discuss it, you'd be annoyed, wouldn't you, if one of your teammates had let you down and you'd played in two Grand Finals and had a draw and a lost one, and the player who would have made a difference is not there. So they'd be a bit dirty on you, for sure.

Mike: When you left Collingwood after four seasons and a spectacular stay, you went to Melbourne and took Ron Barassi's number 31 jumper. Did you not have enough baggage without loading that on to your back?

Phil: I think they thought that I was going to be an impact player for them, and they wanted some sales, or something happening with marketing stuff.

Mike: Why Melbourne, Phil? I mean, they weren't a great side at that time, were they?

Phil: I'd actually agreed to play with South Melbourne. Graeme John, the president of the club, Ian Stewart and a few other people came out to my farm at Lilydale, and we sat out in the back garden with a box of beer and at the end of the night I shook hands and I'd agreed to play with them. And I actually went on an end-of-season trip to the Gold Coast with them at the end of '78. But then when I got back, Melbourne had been talking to me, and Collingwood had had approaches from other clubs too. But Collingwood would only clear me to a club that wasn't near the top of the ladder.

Mike: You only had the one year at Melbourne. What prompted another change?

Phil: Well Carl Ditterich was coach and there were a couple of incidents that occurred at training. I wasn't playing well and normally the selectors tell you the team, but this particular Thursday evening they had the reserve side and the senior side up on the wall and when I walked in, a few blokes said: 'Did you see the teams?' And I said: 'No.' I was in the reserves. We weren't training particularly well that night, and Carl called us in and said: 'Leave the footys there. Jog a lap and I'll see you inside.'

Anyway, when I ran past the footys, I picked one up and kicked it directly at Carl. I had to yell out to him: 'You'd better duck, Carl.' And he said: 'I'll see you inside.' And I whispered, I said: 'No you won't.' So I grabbed my bag and went home. I was called into the club. The next day they fined me $1000 and Ray Manley from the club said: 'The club's not big enough for both you and Carl.'

Mike: Have you always been a law unto yourself, do you think?

Phil: No, well I've always been an individual, but not a law unto myself. But as it's turned out and as we're discussing, yes it would appear so.

Mike: Let's go back to the start. You came across from Adelaide in 1975. I understand in your third game… I know Collingwood was playing Fitzroy. You kicked six goals in the first half, an amazing start for someone to step into the elite competition in this country and have that sort of impact. Were you surprised? Did you think you could come over and take it by storm?

Phil: That's why I left it so late, because I think I was pretty comfortable in Adelaide and I was only 24. I thought I'd give it a shot. I thought it was going to be a lot more difficult, the competition. But it wasn't. And to me it was just like playing back in Adelaide. It wasn't nearly as good as I thought it was going to be.

Mike: You played the first 10 games straight, averaging 21 possessions. Then you break a foot representing Victoria. You miss eight games of football, you come back and you kick six and 11 goals in successive weeks. I mean you were a phenomenon, there's no doubt about that.
Phil: Yes, that was the best year of footy I've played. There's no doubt about that. I would love to have played more footy like it but situations just didn't allow it.

Mike: Moorabbin's big in your football life.
Phil: For a couple of reasons, isn't it?

Mike: For more than one reason, yes. One of them was the game you played at Moorabbin and kicked 11 goals in the white boots when white boots were taboo. Just explain to me. This is not a criticism but why the white boots?
Phil: Maurie Plant, representative for Adidas, came out to training and I'm sitting there with a few other players and he sat down alongside me and gave me a box of boots. And he said: 'Have a look at these.' I opened them up and they were white and he said: 'What do you think?' And I said: 'You're kidding, mate. Nobody would wear those.' And so he handed me an envelope and I opened the envelope and there was a cheque there and I said: 'Yeah, I'll wear them, yes.'

Mike: Do you remember the numbers on the cheque?
Phil: It might have been $1000 or something. Not much.

Mike: April 19, 1980. You're playing at Moorabbin for Essendon, against St Kilda. It was a fairly momentous day in your life, wasn't it? That was the head-butt with Graham Carbery, the boundary umpire. And the report for striking Gary Sidebottom. Can you explain the rationale for events that happened that day?
Phil: It was in the second quarter. I contested a ball against Sidebottom and we both went to ground near the boundary. For some reason or other

I looked to my right. I could see the boundary umpire just squatting down near the point post and for some reason I just gave Sidebottom a bit of whack with my left. And unbeknown to me the field umpire was behind me. He ran in and said: 'Look, I'm reporting you for striking.' And then moments later Carbery, the boundary umpire, came up to me, and, and he said he was reporting me. And I asked 'why'.

Anyway, he didn't answer but it seemed like an eternity. He was chesting me. And you couldn't touch umpires. You couldn't put your hand on them. And he had his chest right up against mine. I'd never done anything like it before. I just dropped the forehead and ... it wasn't terribly hard or anything. And he felt a bit of an impact and played it up a great deal, I think.

Mike: He made it look like it was forceful contact, didn't he?
Phil: Yes. I think if you watch the incident, you can see that it was just sort of: 'Get out of my space.' It wasn't very vicious, I wouldn't think.

Mike: But all these years on, 30 years on, do you admit that you headbutted him?
Phil: Oh yes, for sure.

Mike: Did you think it warranted the penalty you got, 20 weeks' suspension?
Phil: Well of course.

Mike: Because it's an umpire?
Phil: Yes. I was probably fortunate it was only 20.

Mike: How did you feel when the dust settled on that? Because in our sport, the umpires are sacred, aren't they?
Phil: Yes. Well on the way home to Lilydale in the car, I think I was pretty close to tears. You know, realising ... I'm thinking: 'Shit, what have you done?' And then subsequently you had the tribunal and it was a pretty ordinary time.

Mike: Did you resent Graham Carbery's evidence and his reaction to the incident, or you took that as that's what happened?
Phil: That's it.

Mike: Have you seen him since?

Phil: No I have not, no. He umpired a game in Sydney, and we were on the plane together after the game.

Mike: Did you say anything to him?
Phil: Yes, just said, 'G'day.' Something like that.

Mike: Didn't you end up sitting near him?
Phil: I did but I wouldn't say what I said to him. But I did swear at him. But I can't say what.

Mike: Was there a second head-butting incident in your footy career in Canberra?
Phil: No, it was a push. I got suspended for pushing an umpire, not head-butting an umpire.

Mike: Where do you think this sort of behaviour came from? When you were growing up, were you a wild kid in terms of behaviour?
Phil: I think I can tell you why it happened. As a 17-year-old playing for Edenhope against Apsley, I was playing full-forward. I took a mark early in the game and kicked what I thought was a goal and the goal umpire sort of just put up his finger and said: 'A point.' Anyway, minutes later I took another mark, kicked the goal and he put the two fingers up and so I walked up and I said: 'Oh, about time you got that one right.' And as I walked away up the ground, next minute, bang, I hit the ground. He came out and hit me across the head with the flags.

Mike: The goal umpire did?
Phil: The goal umpire. I look back now and I think: 'That's one defining moment, that…'

Mike: That Canberra incident—why were you angry with the umpire then?
Phil: Well look, when you've got the name that I had, umpires weren't your best friend and I think they always gave you a hard time. They wouldn't award you the kicks that other players would receive. I can't recall what happened, but I know that he came out to talk to me about something and I actually just put a hand on and he said: 'No, keep away.' I didn't want anything to happen. Subsequently I got reported for manhandling the umpire but there was certainly no head-butt in that.

Mike: Was it like the Greg Williams incident?[24] **Do you remember that one?**

Phil: Yes, exactly. 'Just keep out of my space', sort of thing.

Mike: You say the umpires didn't like you. They liked you enough to vote you third best in the Brownlow in your first year in the AFL, didn't they?

Phil: I was squeaky clean then. But there were certain guys like myself and Dermott Brereton and others who didn't get what other players did.

Mike: Let's go to coaching. You got the job at Sturt in the SANFL in 1995. They were on their bones, weren't they? This great footy club was down the bottom?

Phil: Correct. I had seven years as senior coach. I was two years as an assistant coach when Haydn Bunton junior was coaching.

Mike: Did you have a different perspective on players as a coach?

Phil: Absolutely. I'm glad you brought that up… this is something positive, actually. This was probably the highlight of my footy career, I think. I enjoyed playing but I enjoyed so much more than I got out of Sturt. They'd been on the bottom six years prior to me getting there. They hadn't won more than four games in a year. My first season, Mike, we didn't win a game and then we won four, then I think we won 12 and then we finished up in my third or fourth year as minor premiers. Port Adelaide beat us. They had eight players that represented Port Power through the season. They beat us by eight points, but coaching Sturt was just a wonderful thing.

Mike: I know one thing; you would have had them fit. In the time that you were playing here, I think you were probably the fittest player in the competition. Your off-season regime was intense, wasn't it? You made sure you came back to football as fit as you could be.

Phil: When I was in Adelaide, or even as a kid in Edenhope, I just ran all the time I used to run 10 miles [16km], once or twice a month, that sort of thing.

Mike: How do you look back on your career? I mean, I sense that you think that I'm focussing on the negative stuff now, but how does Phil Carman see his life in football?

Phil: Well… disappointing. People often say: 'Have you got regrets?'

---

24 Williams was suspended for nine matches in 1997 for pushing field umpire Andrew Coates.

And of course you do. I'd love to have played 200 games. I'd loved to have played in a premiership and those sorts of things. But unfortunately what's happened, happened. You can't get it back.

Mike: Do you take any pride out of the highs in your playing career?
Phil: It's interesting. We've been discussing all the negative stuff, and not many people say: 'Geez, you can play.' It's always this incident or that incident, type of thing. But yes, I should be pretty pleased with what I've done.

Mike: It's your life, I understand, but I suppose it's us looking at you and we see this immense talent in front of us and probably think: 'There could have been more.' I'm sorry if you think that I'm just hammering you about the dark side of your career, but I'm just probably thinking, in an envious sort of way, I would love to have had your talent and seen where it took me.
Phil: Well that's why when I was coaching, if I saw a guy … I used to say to them all the time: 'You just can't afford to waste your time, energy on other things. Just do the correct thing.'

Mike: What's your one favourite footy memory?
Phil: I would say my favourite one was when Sturt actually won our first game. It was Adelaide Oval, sensational, yes.

Mike: That was better than the Copeland Trophy?
Phil: I probably think so, because you're with a group of guys that have been through so much and so many people around the club, we've all been wanting the success and we've just been waiting for it and bang, it happened.

TONY CHARLTON

I n today's non-stop world of football broadcasting, names such as Eddie McGuire, Dennis Cometti and Bruce McAvaney are writ large. Some of the not-so-young followers of football will also know the names Lou Richards, Bob Davis and Jack Dyer. But preceding all of those TV stars was the original doyen of football broadcasting, Tony Charlton.

Coming from a broadcasting family (his father Conrad spoke the first words on ABC radio and his brother Michael became the first announcer on ABC television), Charlton began his career in radio in 1952 when he was invited to join the legendary caller of the time, Norman Banks, as his partner on 3AW, after Banks had joined the station from 3KZ.

Charlton quickly established himself as an authoritative broadcaster, with an encyclopedic knowledge of the game and its players. He spent eight years at 3AW. He also hosted the radio sports shows, *The Kia-Ora Sports Parade* and the *London Stores Football Show* on 3UZ and 3KZ.

In 1960, Channel 9 convinced him to join the network as chief football caller and as host of a Sunday sports show. In later years he also chaired *Tony Charlton's Football Show*.

It was on *Tony Charlton's Football Show* that perhaps one of the most emotionally explosive pieces of football drama ever seen was played out. Two days after being sensationally sacked as Melbourne coach, Norm Smith agreed to be interviewed on Charlton's show to air his side of the story. Even today that broadcast is seen as one of football's most significant media moments.

Charlton continued to call football on Channel 9 until 1970, when Australian Rules became predominantly the domain of Channel 7 and the

ABC. Charlton was also highly respected as a commentator of other sports, and he covered five Olympic Games and two Commonwealth Games. He paved the way for football broadcasting stars and was inducted into the media category of the Australian Football Hall of Fame in 2011. He died on December 17, 2012, aged 2013.

JULY 16, 2012

Mike: There's not much you haven't seen and done since you joined forces with the legendary Norman Banks at 3AW in 1952. It's been a great journey, hasn't it?

Tony: Well, it has, and I feel privileged and I think providence was at work there. Yes, a seismic shift occurred in radio at that time. There was no television. Norman Banks left 3KZ and came to 3AW.

Mike: So there was poaching even back then, was there?

Tony: Yes. 3AW, in those days, was a music and racing station. Ever since Norman Banks arrived it's been a talk and football station.

Mike: What did Norman Banks say to you when he decided to take you on as his—I suppose—lieutenant, almost?

Tony: Well, what a privilege. I had no idea. He just took to me, and to celebrate his arrival at 3AW, a football match was covered. It happened to be the Essendon-Richmond game with fearsome rain. Where? Under lights, if you could call it that, at the showgrounds. The showgrounds was lit as a trotting track and that's where they played the game. It was a sort of dull sepia. And I didn't appreciate then that Norman Banks had eyesight problems. When the play came close to him, he took over the call. When they disappeared into the gloom, he handed over to the kid. Death by a thousand cuts. I nearly died that night.

Mike: So Banks had called football at KZ, had he not?

Tony: That's right.

Mike: But it was your first game?

Tony: My first game.

Mike: There wouldn't have been any broadcast booths like we've got now. I mean were you in the open air?

Tony: It was primitive, right up through early television years. I mean when I see what the facilities are today for broadcasters, I'm green with envy.

Mike: It was 60 years ago. Now you're a member of the Sport Australia, MCG and Australian Football halls of fame. Why don't you simply sit back in state at the MCG and nod to your subjects on big match days?

Tony: I like being involved and have the energy to do it and I hope it continues for a few more years.

Mike: I love your description of the fundamental role of a commentator: 'To produce words, like bubbles in champagne.' Literally, I do. I think it's a beautiful description of what we try to do. Is that your own?

CAREER
Born: March 28, 1929
Died: December 17, 2012
RADIO
3KZ 1952-59: Match commentator, host of *The Kia-Ora Sports Parade* and the *London Stores Football Show*
TELEVISION
Channel 9 1960-70: Match commentator, host of *The Tony Charlton Football Show*
Honours: Australian Football Hall of Fame inductee—media

Tony: It is an art form, I trust it is. I didn't know I'd said that but you've picked up on it. I trust that's what it is, and the art of a pause. I think I learnt that from Stewart MacPherson, that marvellous Canadian sports commentator who made a fortune at the BBC in the early days calling empire title fights like: 'Sam's on the ropes and gets off quick.' I really was attracted to his style and that was a point that he made: 'Learn the art of a pause.'

Mike: You called multiple Olympic Games and 12 Grand Finals. Where does football rank with track and field and the Olympics in your view?

Tony: Oh, very highly. It's such a religion here, isn't it? It's marvellous to be a part of it, to have the privilege of being mixed up in it to whatever degree. I've never forgotten the feeling, having arrived as a youth from Perth, going to the MCG for the first time, totally absorbed by the sounds and the size of the crowd and the reactions of the crowd. I mean Greg Baum was right when he so beautifully wrote, 'the theatre of the great and grand', and that's what it is. So I've loved my football association.

Mike: One of your many experiences makes me both curious and envious. You watched the great John Coleman play. You've said to me many times

that he's the best footballer you've seen and you don't even consider it a contest. Is that true?

Tony: That is true and I'd have many who would support me in that. Unfortunately many of us are falling off the twig but Bill Jacobs, for example, a marvellous sports caller and into sport, dyed-in-the-wool Fitzroy man. He joined the Essendon Football Club specifically so that he could watch Coleman. Coleman would move from end-to-end, and I can fully understand that. He was magical. I mean he was the first League player to kick 100 goals in his first year. He made the state team in his first year. He averaged 5.5 goals every match.

Mike: But Tony Lockett, and Jason Dunstall and Peter Hudson have those sort of figures in terms of kicking big goals in games. I asked you once to prove to me, or tell me why Coleman was better than Wayne Carey, who's the best player I've seen. And you almost sort of treated it with contempt. You've always been a modernist, I mean you always think that the sport of the day is probably better than it's ever been played. Why then does he stand supreme in the field?

Tony: Simply because he was. The things he was able to do. He was a very good ground player. He used to tell Ted Leehane who was full-forward in the 1942 premiership side, centre half-forward in the '49 premiership side: 'Just kick it in front of me. Just kick it in front of me.' But the acrobatic leap was just extraordinary. Gary Ablett senior was wonderful, and I don't wish to degrade any of these great players...

Mike: Are you saying he went higher than Ablett?

Tony: But Coleman ... oh God, he'd jump over that roof.

Mike: Is there a romantic notion about things that happened 50 years ago? Or are you happy with your recall about all the things that he did?

Tony: Yes I am and thank you for the challenge of that. I sought the opinion of John Kennedy: tall, angular, good ruckman, awkward to play against. And, of course, he had a marvellous reputation as both coach and a servant of the game through being chairman of the League commissioners. He told me: 'Tony, if you wanted to win a game, I think I would choose Leigh Matthews.' He was one of the four football icons at the MCG. 'But if you wanted the most spectacular player I ever saw by far, it was John Coleman.'

And he went on to tell me that he had never experienced before, something that happened at Glenferrie Oval one day. He said Coleman came from behind the pack, went straight over him—he was tall and, as I say, angular—took the ball cleanly and landed in front of the pack on his feet. I referred that to Geoff Leek, who got into commentary through me and served 25 years calling the games. Dear Geoff is with us no longer. He said Coleman did that every night at training at Essendon.

Mike: Okay, I defer. I bow to you on that. I mean I never saw Coleman. You actually called his last game. It was John Coleman's 98th game of football. He was a legend, a heart-throb. He fell over and hurt his knee and never played again.

Tony: Jock McCorkell was the full-back for North Melbourne. It was at Windy Hill. They were racing out, Coleman in the lead. There was a tumble. He grabbed his knee. Never played again. But then I had the experience of introducing him in his first public appearance after that tragedy. For the whole community, the football community, it was like there was a death in the family. And this was pre-television days. A very big thing in radio was *Kia-Ora Sports Parade*.

And I used to MC that, following Norman Banks and then Doug Elliot. Nobody could have anticipated the reaction of the crowd. It was at the Melbourne Town Hall. It was Essendon's night. The place was absolutely packed to the rafters. And on introduction, he stood there, this Adonis on crutches—knee heavily bandaged, which was the way of it then—and they stomped and hollered and applauded and shouted and cried for seven minutes before we could get the show going again. That was the power of Coleman. He was magic.

Mike: So he was a rock star?
Tony: Absolutely.

Mike: He's 24 or something when he finished. Were you aware of the story, Tony, that Coleman's knee wasn't sufficiently serious to end a career; that he just chose to give it away after that injury?
Tony: No, I don't think medical science was up to the standards that we take for granted today. I think he would have played again in a year's time. I can give you another indication of his magnificence. This was told to me

recently at Don McKenzie's place. John Birt, twice best-afield in Grand Finals for Essendon, marvellous player, number 11. Little Johnny, he said that Coleman hadn't played for six years, was coaching Essendon and teaching the new full-forward some of the tricks of the trade. There were 10 kick-outs by the full-back; Coleman marked eight of them.

Mike: Malcom Blight would say that he did the same sort of thing when he coached, but do you see any of John Coleman in James Hird? I mean I do, and I'm only dealing from the memories that I have of Coleman and what I've heard. But this sort of outstanding player, born to be a coach, a bit reluctant to come back, finally does and makes a success of it.

Tony: Yes, a marvellous figure of the time. You make me think of the more bizarre side of football because he fits into that category for me. There were 78 chances for clubs to get him before Essendon did. That was how it played out in those times.[25]

Mike: Now you even had your own sports program on Channel 9 in the '60s. Head-to-head with *World of Sport* and Ron Casey?

Tony: Yes, with Ron Casey, they were the willing encounters. I only had two days off in three years, I think. The application was pretty intense and we hardly ever saw each other except at sports occasions.

Mike: Was there a competitive edge?

Tony: Yes, there was. And I think you'd have to say that he had a stellar career.

Mike: I want to ask you about Norm Smith. Obviously we can't have an interview with Tony Charlton and not raise the name of Norm Smith. You did a one-on-one interview with him in 1965, which is probably the most dramatic football news event in the history of television, I suspect. Melbourne is 9-3 after 12 rounds, having won its first eight games. Melbourne was the defending premier from 1964, and Melbourne had won six premierships in 10 years. Norm Smith gets the sack. Take up the story from there...

Tony: Oh, it was unbelievable. Just an extraordinary thing. I mean it was impossible. I mean people were in shock about that. They were, 'What?

---

25 Hird was pick 79 for Essendon in the 1990 National Draft.

Norm Smith sacked? Just couldn't be.' But it was and the president of the club at the time, Doctor Don Duffy, said this had been brewing for some time. Norm could be very autocratic, I understood that side of it, and he wanted things his way. In running a club, not always can that be though. But he was on a matter of principle, as far as this was concerned.

Mike: The principle being?
Tony: Well I'm trying to remember his quote and I think I can: 'They went to a public school; I went to a state school. I was brought up that way, Len[26] was brought up that way. And if you haven't got principle, you haven't got anything. And I've got principle and I'll fight for this principle till the day I day.'

Mike: It was an amazingly powerful interview that you had with him.
Tony: Well it was amazing *because* of him.

Mike: Did you need to coerce him into doing that?
Tony: No, he was true to his word. I mean he had offers for substantial money of the time to give his story elsewhere. But as he was part of the channel I was with and our football show, he was man of principle. He resisted that and saved it for the Sunday in the sports show.

Mike: Were you nervous doing that interview with Norm Smith?
Tony: Yes I was because the tension was extremely high and his wife, Marge—she was a wonderful, wonderful support to him—she was just off-camera in tears as this developed, and that upset me greatly.

Mike: Your discussion with him was as friend-to-friend...
Tony: Yes.

Mike: ...and a dramatic event, no doubt about that. But did you see the sort of the commercial reality in it, that you had the interview that everyone wanted?
Tony: Yes I did. And of course I was extremely grateful to him for resisting the opportunities that he had to—for far greater money—to give an interview elsewhere. It certainly was a very dramatic time. Just a marvellous man and the sport lost a hero when he passed on.

---

26 Len Smith, Norm's brother, played and coached VFL football.

Mike: We're talking about this man, again, six premierships in 10 years. What sort of impact did it have on the community?

Tony: Well you're a noted sports journalist. You would appreciate this more than most. But it was reported and took the first four news pages of *The Sun News Pictorial* on the Monday morning.

Mike: Do you give any credence to the theory that the Norm Smith curse has been imposed upon the Melbourne Football Club because of events back in the '60s? They haven't won a premiership since, and so many people now believe that it's how they treated Norm Smith that's caused the fate.

Tony: No, I don't subscribe to that view.

Mike: What do you think's gone wrong with your football club?

Tony: It was a totally different era. The complexities of it and the critical nature of getting the talent, the recruiting of the right people, just doesn't happen overnight. And it certainly hasn't happened for Melbourne for a far too long period.

Mike: He died at 57. It must have been a huge shock. I mean blokes are still coaching post-57. What happened?

Tony: I think it was heart failure. I visited him out at Moreland, at Sacred Heart Hospital out there, a couple of times. But the family were pretty tight-lipped about that. You didn't talk about those things in those days. I'm sure it was his heart. Subsequently it might be proved that that's not accurate, but I think that is right.

Mike: Do you think he was heartbroken, Tony?
Tony: Yes…

Mike: He ended up at South Melbourne[27].
Tony: …it broke his heart.

Mike: It did, did it?
Tony: Yes. We got them back together; I played a small part in that, we got him back to Melbourne but the twain never met. It was never the same again. The trust was gone.

---

27 Smith was reinstated within a week. He left Melbourne at the end of 1967, and coached South Melbourne from 1969 to 1972.

Mike: You broadcast 12 Grand Finals for Channels 7 and 9. They included St Kilda's only premiership win in 1966 and Carlton's amazing fight-back in 1970. Does one stand out for you?
Tony: Yes, that Carlton one.

Mike: When did you sense that things had changed? I mean 44 points should be an insurmountable lead at half-time in a Grand Final. Do you remember sort of standing there and thinking: 'The momentum's swung here.'
Tony: Well it swung dramatically, right from the bounce of the ball for the second half. That's where they made up the leeway.

Mike: There must have been a massive outpouring of emotion then, when the Saints finally broke through in '66.
Tony: Yes, there was. Extraordinary, just extraordinary. Marvellous relationships within that side, and you've got to have those. All successful sides, I believe, have that element. They were a close-knit unit and boy, they fought it out till the last and it was nip and tuck, as the result proved.

Mike: Tell us about the footy back then. What's your memory of how the game was played?
Tony: Oh, totally different. Everything's changed, from the size of the goalposts to the size of the ball, the configuration of the centre circle, coaches coaching from benches on the ground. Just amazing changes. The strips, everything else. The boots.

Mike: Which is the better game, the current game or the game played in the '60s and '70s?
Tony: Oh, when you get to this age you tend to look in the rear-vision mirror rather than through the windscreen. I've loved the game for the magnificent attractions it had in those days: stab passing, drop-kicking, torpedo punts. We spoke of Coleman before, those fantastic 60-yarders [55m].

Mike: Oh don't start there again. He was the best kicker of his time too, was he?
Tony: But the hand-passing today is just as miraculous. I mean they're just geniuses the way they get the ball out and into the hands of players running past or at close range.

Mike: You called seven Olympics? I can remember first-hand your call of Betty Cuthbert in Tokyo in '64 when she won the medal, I think eight years after she'd won her earlier gold medals.

Tony: That's right, and she was wiped off as having no chance because she was injured, right up til the last, and they forced her to give a trial, which she wanted to avoid because she knew she was suspect. She wanted the extra time. What a brave girl; marvellous lady.

Mike: What were you like at the track?

Tony: I was very nervous about it and she was just terrific.

Mike: You've interviewed some big names, haven't you? I mean not just sport. Did you interview Harold Wilson when he was prime minister of England?

Tony: Yes, yes I did.

Mike: How did that come about?

Tony: ... and Bobby Kennedy and ... oh, well just by direct approach. It was an interview program, after the movie on a Sunday night. That was the best thing I did, I think, in the media.

I was very fortunate. It sounds boastful and I would hate it to be taken that way, but it was a sort of *Parkinson* show. So anybody who came here was sort of on that show.

Mike: So where did you get Bobby Kennedy?

Tony: By rolling up to Capitol Hill in Washington and sitting there all day in the portico. Yes. And the Vietnam debate was on and he's in the house all day and they said: 'Well wait here.' And I wait and wait and wait. I must have waited seven or eight hours. Out he came; grabbed him.

Mike: So what did you say? 'I'm Tony Charlton, from Australia'?

Tony: Americans are very polite people. Yes, he was gracious, yes. And I fired off a couple of difficult questions for him to answer, but he handled them.

Mike: Did he ask for a DVD? Gregory Peck, the famous actor. He was part of your stable?

Tony: Well, yes but just by the chance of me working with the film unit. Wonderful bloke. Had a bit to do with him here. Sat in his caravan with him while he was reading books for his next film assignment and whatever else.

And then dined I with him at his home, he and Veronique in Brentwood, one of the upper-class suburbs of Hollywood, yes.

Mike: Tell me the art of interviewing, Tony.

Tony: Well I think you've got it.

Mike: No, I'm just learning it.

Tony: Keep the questions short and listen to the answers.

Mike: I remember in an interview you did some years ago, you talked about the TV rights in the '60s. And you were aghast at the VFL's request for, I think, £2000 a year. Is that correct?

Tony: You have done your research and that's absolutely right. And Keith Cairns—who came out of *The Herald* in Flinders Street and was managing Channel 7, it was the early years—started to get very agitated about this at Harrison House, where the deal was done. Sir Kenneth Luke[28] is chairing the meeting, Eric McCutcheon taking over and saying: 'This is how it will be.' Saying: 'We can't possibly afford that,' to Keith Cairns. 'We can't possibly afford that.'

Mike: That's four thousand bucks, in today's terms. We talked about the commentators before, and your tip for how to do an interview and to be a commentator. Who are the ones that you like most? If you're watching a game of football who do you think does it best?

Tony: I think as the game has grown, commentary has grown with it. I mean Dennis Cometti is a marvellous caller, so is Tim Lane. Bruce McAvaney, just without question, marvellous fellow. I mean he lifted Olympic Games coverage to a degree, internationally, that had not been known before. What a gifted man. And so on it goes.

Mike: To borrow from your vernacular, what's been your finest hour in 60 years in this business?

Tony: Surviving it, I think.

Mike: No, but there must be some special moments that you cherish, we all do. There are certain things that we do that we think, 'That's as good as we can do it'.

---

28 Luke was president of the VFL.

Tony: Well I've enjoyed doing the Prime Minister's Olympic Dinner over the years, since its formation in 1980. They've been big nights, we've raised a lot of money for the Olympic movement, in which I believe. And I hope I've played a role there.

I think probably most of all the Dawn Service is important to me. My father was in the forces in World War I; I've accounted for that. I have strong memories, during war time in Perth, when we were sure we were going to be invaded and we were scared out of our wits. I was a kid in short pants and I remember going to my first Dawn Service in Kings Park and feeling the atmosphere of that, surrounded by guys in duffel coats and slouch hats and heavens knows what happened to them in the course of the war. The Dawn Service is a very important thing and it's very stimulating to see the crowds now drawn to it at the Shrine in Melbourne, up to 40,000, hail, rain or shine.

Mike: Tony, let's talk technology for a moment. Fox Footy has 20 cameras at most games. How many cameras were you working with back in 1957?
Tony: Great, cumbersome things. Yes, two for a major game; one for the secondary game. And we had one zoom lens in the entire place. Look at it today. It's an absolute wonderment and I'm uplifted by it, just the capacity of the technology today is amazing.

Mike: Your bucket list—we've all got one. I'm not hastening your departure from this planet, but are there things that you want to do that you've still got on your list?
Tony: Yes, to continue flying. Flying's been a great interest of mine and to fly around this country, which I've done many, many times, is a constant joy. It's just such a marvellous place and aren't we lucky to have it?

Mike: There was one flight that you didn't enjoy particular much. You went to the Northern Territory.
Tony: Yes, I got these symptoms and didn't know what in the hell had happened because I was full of energy and eating well and regular and all of those things, no bleeding, no nothing. I got back here—made a good decision there, one of my few—and said: 'There's something wrong with me.' I left the plane there for somebody from here to get it, take it back to Moorabbin, and went into hospital and was told I had bowel cancer and

given not much hope of existing more than a couple of months. Well, I seem to have dodged the bullet. Leaves you wondering why. Why would I dodge a bullet, if that's in fact what happens? When Jim Stynes who did just such good work in the community, half my age, goes out the backdoor. I don't understand that.

Mike: Regrets?
Tony: None.

Mike: There's not one thing that you would do different in your life?
Tony: Oh, I'd like to look like Gregory Peck. Look at me. I look like Methuselah.

ROBERT DIPIERDOMENICO

O ne of football's larger-than-life characters, Robert 'Dipper' DiPierdomenico will always be a favourite son at Hawthorn, where he played 240 games in the Hawks' golden era and won five premierships.

Although he went on to establish himself as one of the competition's high-profile players, DiPierdomenico, recruited from North Kew, struggled to get a senior game when he arrived at Glenferrie Oval. After making his debut in Round 18, 1975, DiPierdomenico did not taste football at the highest level again until the opening round of the 1978 season.

From then, DiPierdomenico did not look back. He played almost every game in that season, including a best-on-ground performance in the Hawks' Grand Final win over North Melbourne. As a wingman, DiPierdomenico was bigger and stronger than his contemporary opponents.

In an era where players tended to play in a fixed position, DiPierdomenico developed fierce rivalries with other wingmen of his time and his one-one-one battles with players such as Melbourne's Robert Flower and Footscray's Doug Hawkins became the stuff of legend.

DiPierdomenico had an aggressive streak that occasionally landed him in hot water and saw him awarded several 'holidays' courtesy of the VFL Tribunal. But when this streak was kept in check, he could be a breathtaking player, a fact confirmed by his 1976 Brownlow Medal win (which he shared with Sydney's Greg Williams).

No one ever doubted DiPierdomenico's courage and willingness to put his body on the line. This was acutely exemplified in the 1989 Grand Final when he played out the match (which Hawthorn hung on to win by just six points) after having absorbed a painful blow to the ribs. After the match he collapsed and was rushed to hospital where it was discovered that he had punctured his lung.

DiPierdomenico later went on to become a popular commentator and ambassador for the AFL's Auskick program.

MAY 31, 2010

Mike: You were the biggest name in football 10 years ago. Where have you been recently?

Robert: I've still been around. I'm still working in football, which I love doing. I'm involved with the Auskick program, which I became the face of about six years ago. I think at the time we had about 46,000 juniors between five and 12 years of age in our program, but obviously it's a national game now, we've got 185,000. I travel four days a week when it's Auskick season and really love it, and just like being involved with the game at that level, because the kids haven't seen me play before but I'm a cartoon character for these young kids and they just hang off of you.

Mike: We go a long way back 'Dipper', way back to the mid-'70s. It's been some journey for you, hasn't it?

Robert: It has, it's been a great journey; it's been a wonderful journey. I think 1975 was the first time that we met. It was one of your best stories of all time. I've got the front page of *The Age*.

Mike: Tell us about life growing up in inner-suburban Melbourne in the 1960s as the son of Italian immigrants?

Robert: Well it was tough in a way because obviously, it's changed with regard to racism. Obviously my mum and father came from Italy, dad came in '54; mum came to Australia in '56. They were married by proxy over the phone. Basically, my grandfather sent my dad and two other brothers across the world. He said to dad: 'You're packing your bags up, you're going to Australia.' Dad really didn't know much about it, so, he jumped on the boat and landed in Melbourne, and shacked up in Richmond with a few of the boys and became a bricklayer and a hard-working man that way. And then mum came over in '56 while dad established some sort of home here, and they were married. When I was growing up in school, a few of those Anglo-Saxon boys used to call me some names and in a way I took up sport to override that.

Mike: Did it hurt?

Robert: At the time you're not quite sure if it hurts or not, but the fact is you wanted to be a part of the system, and at the age of 11, 12, 13 years-of-age, the Anglo-Saxon boys called me so many names. It really helped me become who I am today.

I used to have a really bad stutter back in those days. I was very hyperactive. These days they call it ADD[29], I mean there's tablets these days, but back in those days I was really stuttering, I was really not confident, but, I took up sport. Running, jumping, skipping, hopping, playing footy, anything for the school, cross-country runs, all of that sort of stuff. And because I could run all day and I was very hyperactive, I had plenty of energy, so it really helped me mix in with the Anglo-Saxons.

CAREER
Born: May 5, 1958
Club: *Hawthorn*—240 games, 130 goals
Honours: Australian Football Hall of Fame inductee (2007); Brownlow Medal—1986; VFL/AFL Italian Team of the Century; Six times Victorian interstate representative; Hawthorn Team of the Century; Hawthorn Hall of Fame inductee (2008); Hawthorn premiership side 1978, 1983, 1986, 1988, 1989

Mike: You started with Hawthorn in 1975 and then didn't play a game in '76 or '77. What happened?

Robert: No, I didn't, and it was quite interesting. I don't know why, but obviously, when I first came to Hawthorn I came four or five rounds into the season. I came from Kew Amateurs, it was coached by John Fisher, an ex-Hawthorn person, and at the time I was 17 or 18 years of age or so and, when I first came here I played some under-19 games and then I played some reserve games and next thing I find myself—courtesy of you, on the front page of *The Age*—playing against Fitzroy at Junction Oval. And, I was 19th man that day and I came on and did what I did, and I think that gave me a taste of what it could be.

---

29 ADD: Attention deficit disorder.

But then, two years following that I languished in the reserves and also some under-19 games as well. It was about learning the game and growing my body in a way, because I wasn't always this big you know.

Mike: Now the modern player would be staggered by this, but is it true that you played 99 games in the seconds? That's an amazing apprenticeship, to think that you've had five full seasons playing in the seconds. I mean it just wouldn't happen today.

Robert: I think that's the word: 'apprenticeship'. At Hawthorn at the time, it was hard to get into that side, because back in the early days, I was a half-back flanker, I didn't have much skill. Ian Bremner was on the half-bank flank, and a guy like Peter Welsh. On a Tuesday night it was mouthguards-in, it was one-hour round the ground, and if I was a young, coming-up type of player, like I was, Ian Bremner would say: 'Well what jumper have you got on? You're against me.' He used to punch the crap out of you. Which taught me a lot about the club and how hungry you have to be for your position.

Mike: Early in your career there was a perception that you were a bit of a scrubber. Is that fair?

Robert: Absolutely.

Mike: And then you made yourself into a high-quality player. Is that a fair assessment?

Robert: Well I wouldn't say high-quality player. Look, I was a scrubber. I was just a very hyperactive young man just trying to play football, I found myself at Hawthorn, and head over the ball was the one thing I could do. I wasn't scared to put my head over the ball. I remember Don Scott having a go at me, I remember Leigh Matthews having a go. Even at training, I could not kick the ball from 20, 30 metres to hit someone on the chest.

I remember 'Scotty' screaming at me and then Allan Jeans came in as coach and really said: 'Don't worry about your courage, it's your skill level.' We worked and worked on our skill level and at the end there, I think I could pass the ball.

Mike: The encyclopaedia of AFL footballers lists you at 88kgs. I'm saying that's under.

Robert: Yes, very much under. In my first game I would have been around about 76 or 78kgs, and obviously I grew that to about 103kgs. In the '83 Grand Final I played at 103kgs, but then the dieticians came in. We were eating steaks and chips and eggs before a game, then there were bananas and muffins. I mean there was Dermott Brereton, Jason Dunstall and myself, 'The Fat Club' they'd call us. We used to put it on pretty quickly. I ended up playing around about 94kgs and I was stronger, faster and it was just amazing how football turned around.

Mike: You and Greg Williams tied for the Brownlow Medal in 1986, but you didn't win the Hawthorn best and fairest that year.

Robert: No, I never won any best and fairest.

Mike: Did the Brownlow surprise you?

Robert: It surprised all of us, I was 50-1, I didn't have a dollar on it. I remember going that night, it was quite funny. We were training at the MCG before the Grand Final in '86. Of course, Essendon had beaten us in '84 and '85 and 'Jeansy' said just before we finished up on that Monday: 'Boys from now on, tuck in, no media. No media from this moment on. All we need to do is concentrate. You guys have got to focus. Don't worry about your tickets; don't worry about your families and whatever. From now on we've told the club we'll answer all the questions on your behalf, just concentrate on the game.' I said: 'Okay, that's great.'

And back in those days I was living in Boronia, so I drove all the way to pick up my wife Cheryl. I was thinking: 'I couldn't be bothered going in anyway, because it's going to be a long drive in anyway.' We finally get in, entrée had been served and I'm sitting around. And all of a sudden it came down to the end and I knew that Paul Roos and Greg Williams had played against each other. I thought: 'Well I'm even with Greg Williams here.' And he was looking at me and I'm looking at him thinking: 'I don't know.' But I was shit scared, if I can say that, because all I was thinking about was that the media and the cameras were all over me and I'm trying to hide. I remember going up there and John Elliott, the great Carlton president, was also involved with Fosters at the time, and we were playing Carlton at the time in '86 about five days, and he offered me a can of beer and I said: 'Get it out the way.'

And then, Peter Landy invited me to go up and I gave the line that 'I only came here for the free meal'. But I think I handled it pretty well.

Mike: You played much of the 1989 Grand Final with a punctured lung. It was courtesy of Gary Ablett wasn't it? It just wouldn't happen these days. I mean, did you actually put your life in danger?

Robert: Who knows? I mean I'd do anything to win a Grand Final. It was our seventh Grand Final in a row and no Hawthorn side had ever won back-to-back.

Mike: There's no doubt in anyone's definition it was a serious injury.

Robert: Look at the time, when you hear these words: 'It's yours, Dipper.' You stand under that ball and it's the only game in the world where someone can come from behind you and do what they do. In the '80s it was like that, you stood under that ball and whether it was my turn, you've got to do what you've got to do. I knew what was coming behind me. Gary, was telling me he's coming. I went back and copped what I did.

Mike: Did he literally tell you he was coming?

Robert: 'I'm coming big fella', you know. I could hear him and I'm thinking: 'Oh hurry up, hurry up' because there's no place to hide on the MCG. Even in today's football when that ball is in the air, it's what you're there for. Forget all the skills and forget all the training you've done or whatever, it's something that you've got to do for your teammates and that's what the game is about. He had eyes on the ball only and if you look at that footage, it's just what football is about.

Mike: Now you spent Grand Final night in hospital. How ill were you?

Robert: I was quite ill. I know you won't believe this, but I really haven't sat down and watched that Grand Final or any of the Grand Finals I've played in. I know that we've lost and I know that we've won some. I know the '89 Grand Final, certain parts of the game. I know the fact that I ended up in hospital and I know that I was very lucky to survive the day but, I remember also, sitting there knowing that we'd won a premiership and that was the main thing. I can go on and talk about the '89 Grand Final, but knowing that we won and being a part of that Hawthorn's first back-to-back has really helped me overcome that day.

I remember a lot of players got injured that day. Johnny Platten got knocked out in the first quarter. Dermott[30] did what he did in the first couple of minutes. It was arrogant, it was fantastic. That's what a Grand Final is about.

Mike: But that was the most brutal Grand Final I've ever seen.
Robert: I've played in a few and Geelong had a few blokes too, a couple of broken jaws here and there.

Mike: Steven Hocking and Garry Hocking were hurt.
Robert: You know I ended up fixing him up.

Mike: You did. You fixed a lot of blokes up in your playing career, didn't you?
Robert: Well, you're there to protect yourself in a way. I mean I got cleaned up a few times, too. Make no mistake about it, it was great footy. It was great one-on-one. It was me versus you, and other guys trying to pin you all the time and vice-versa.

Mike: There was the celebrated on-field clash with Alan Stoneham[31] and his twisted face and Rod Austin and his jaw. I mean are there any pangs of remorse about those two?
Robert: Absolutely. There was remorse about it because we're all playing the same game. But there were times when, it's hard to explain to the people, that you don't go out deliberately trying to hurt people. Yes, there were times that you can fix someone up, off the ball and whatever.

I mean I got cleaned up a few times off the ball as well but with Alan Stoneham, I still remember, Glenn Hawker getting the ball out of the middle at Princes Park. He handballed the ball over his head as I'm coming off the wing, and the siren goes for half-time. Everyone slows down and I looked to my left and there's Alan coming at a hundred miles an hour at me. I've taken one step, put my elbow up and next thing you know... I mean the first thing I did was go down and see if he was all right and

---

30 Brereton was pole-axed by Geelong's Mark Yeates soon after the first bounce. He went to a deep forward position soon afterward, marked and converted.

31 DiPierdomenico was reported for elbowing Footscray's Alan Stoneham. The footage of Stoneham leaving the field with his nose twisted across his face has been replayed many times. Austin was smashed by DiPierdomenico in the 1984 qualifying final against Carlton.

then I got pushed out of the way. And then, I ran towards the rooms and I looked back and there was a big fight.

Mike: There was. Do you have conversation with Alan Stoneham?
Robert: I've spoken with Alan a thousand times. I've apologised and we've spoken about other things. And 'Curly' Austin is exactly the same.

I remember him and Leigh Matthews had the best contests you'd ever see. It was at Waverley, it was a final and I was coming off the wing, thinking that I would read the ball. But the ball actually bounced into their faces and I ran past and I gave Curly one, not sort of meaning to do it but I, as I'm running past, I've given him one. Next thing I find out he's got a broken jaw.

Mike: Were you ever scared on the football field?
Robert: At times. There was one game against Essendon I was pretty scared. Cameron Clayton gave me an absolute beauty, put my nose all over my face, but I had to go back out there unfortunately. I just wanted to stay in the shed.

Mike: That was the payback for Stoneham, wasn't it?
Robert: It was one of the paybacks for Stoneham, yes. I got cleaned up that day a few times.

Mike: You played in five premierships teams. Is there one that's your favourite?
Robert: It's hard to split them. I mean the first one in '78, who would have thought, three years after I'd joined the club, that I'm playing against North Melbourne and I remember making the side on the bench? Back in those days we used to go to Myer and have a chicken sandwich and a cup of tea at the Grand Final parade, and we used to be introduced to the crowd on the podium and wave in front of the people. Ron Barassi was coaching North, and he came up to me and he said: 'What's your name?' Stupidly, I just said: 'You'll find out tomorrow.' And I suppose '89 was great because it was the first ever back-to-back, it was a great game to be involved with, people talk about that game.

And I love it when people talk about the ins and outs of that game. Not just what happened to me and Dermott and a few of the other guys, but what the game meant to both sides and how both sides approached it. I mean Mark Yeates, to have the balls to do what he did, I think that's great.

Mike: Tell us about your relationship with Allan 'Yabby' Jeans?
Robert: He was a father figure to me but also, he really laid the law down to me, he made me grow up. He got stuck into me a few times and abused me a few times, loved me a few times, hugged me a few times, but that was Jeansy.

The best thing about Allan Jeans is this: he knew how to handle personalities. He didn't hit every player over the head with the same stick; he knew how to get to me and Dermott up. He knew how to get Gary Buckenara up, he knew how to get to Johnny Platten, but in different words, because if you use the same stick to all of us, we all get sick of it.

Mike: Did Jeansy ever break you down? I know he was a comfort for you and he encouraged you, but he did have a caustic tongue at times.
Robert: Oh he broke me down a few times. Don't worry about that. There was one time I was quite stupid, I was quite naïve, I was quite angry, I was quite arrogant in thinking I should have been playing in the seniors and not somebody else. I made him know that, after I had a few Scotches at the club. And it became quite a significant time in my life at Hawthorn.

Thursday nights was obviously trainers' night, every club has them and our trainers, Bobby Yeomans and all the guys used to cook up a feast for us, some fish and some chips and some dim sims and a glass of Coke. I used to have a dash of Scotch. Bobby Yeomans said to me: 'Listen, I've just been into the coach's room, and you've been dropped this week.' I said: 'Well you'd better give me another glass of that.' I didn't realise that Jeansy was going to come out in about an hour-and -a-half later and I've had a couple. All of a sudden he walks in and it was just me and him. And he says: 'What are you doing?' I said: 'What am I doing? What about you? You're dropping me, hey. What right have you got to drop me?'

He said: 'Why don't we discuss it in the coaches room?' We walked in and Jeansy's gone 'bang' up against the wall. I don't know what's going on. His elbow is up against my throat. He says: 'How dare you, how dare you. You treat the Hawthorn Football Club the way you are tonight.' I still get a little bit emotional about it because I was this arrogant, one-time premiership player at the time. He said: 'You've embarrassed the football club who made you. From now on, as far as I'm concerned you're out of this club.' And I've just gone: 'Waaaaah.'

Mike: Who was your toughest opponent? And if you don't say Doug Hawkins, I reckon your fibbing.

Robert: Well I will say Dougy Hawkins, no doubt about it. We played against them 11 times, we've got the same birthday, of all the things, I'm a couple of years older than him. I remember, I loved playing against him because he was a smooth mover around the ground. Left foot, right foot, he was half my size but we had these battles. In '85 he was one of the best players in Australia, in the '85 final series, he absolutely tore me apart, right. And they kept kicking it out to me and he kept sticking his bum out and taking marks.

Mike: There have been some well documented problems with the taxation department of recent times. Did that embarrass you?

Robert: Well it embarrassed me at the time because I knew nothing about it. I just received a phone call from a journalist saying to me that: 'Hey, tomorrow we're printing this article.' I could not believe it. But as soon as I found out the ins and outs of it I just rang up and it's done and dusted.

Mike: But there was a debt of several hundred thousands dollars. Is that correct?

Robert: Well apparently there was a debt of a few hundred thousand dollars. It was from a business situation but it had nothing to do with me. I'd sold the business but anyway, I can understand where it was coming from. I went through a hard time because I tried to keep my name pretty clean because of the work that I do in football, especially with kids and families and things like that.

Mike: You're living down on the Mornington Peninsula these days. Did you have to sell your house as a result of the taxation department investigation?

Robert: No.

Mike: When the taxation episode hit the papers, did that shake your confidence and your self esteem?

Robert: Well it does shake your confidence because nobody likes to be front page because of something that you don't know about. It did shake me a little bit but it's just like anything, if you put the cards on the table, I've always said to my kids: 'Put the cards on the table. Let's have a look at where we are, and then we'll deal with it.'

Mike: What are you most proud of?

Robert: I don't know. I don't think I'm finished. I don't know what I'm searching for. I don't know sometimes what I'm doing. I just love promoting the game that I enjoyed. Being involved with Hawthorn for 18 years of my life, when I first walked in and I was 17 or so years of age and Peter Knights shook my hand and said: 'If you embrace Hawthorn, Hawthorn will embrace you and I think you're going to be here for a long time.' He said to me: 'Would you like a pair of boots?' He was the state manager of Puma at the time and he went to his car and gave me a couple of pairs of boots and said: 'Look, enjoy the ride here.' I mean and who's to know, 18 years later I'm at that one club.

JASON DUNSTALL

Perhaps the greatest footballer to come out of Queensland, Jason Dunstall was one of football's finest full-forwards.

Recruited from Coorparoo, Dunstall made his debut for Hawthorn in 1985, kicking 36 goals. Although inconsistent in that season, an eight-goal haul against Richmond in Round 16 served as a portent of what was to come.

Dunstall's break-out season was 1986. He played 22 games, kicking 77 goals, including six matches of six goals or more. He topped it off by kicking six in the Hawks' Grand Final win against Carlton.

In subsequent seasons, Dunstall became even more prolific in front of goal. A 94-goal season in 1987 (including 11 in a match against Brisbane) was followed by an amazing 132-goal tally in 1988, another Hawthorn premiership season. Dunstall kicked seven goals in the Hawks' obliteration of Melbourne in the Grand Final and also bagged nine other totals of seven goals or more that year.

In 1989 the Hawks won another flag, with Dunstall kicking 138 goals for the season, including two 11-goal hauls. In 1990 Dunstall suffered a horrific injury, when an accidental knee from Melbourne's Earl Spalding fractured his skull. Dunstall returned to the field just five weeks later, wearing a helmet.

Ankle ligament damage hindered Dunstall's 1991 season, although he still kicked 82 goals (six in the Grand Final), as Hawthorn chalked up yet another flag. Then, in 1992, Dunstall had his most prolific season: he kicked 145 goals, falling just shy of the record of 150 goals. In Round 7 against Richmond, Dunstall kicked an amazing 17 goals, and would surely have broken Fred Fanning's game record of 18 goals had he not been so unselfish in giving goals away to his teammates.

In 1993, 1994 and 1996, Dunstall again topped the 100-goal mark and, although less prolific in his final years, he finished his 269-game career with 1254 goals. Only Tony Lockett and Gordon Coventry kicked more.

Dunstall embarked on a successful media career after retiring, one that continues to this day.

AUGUST 30, 2010

Mike: It seems that greatness sits uneasily with you. I mean, you're always into the future. Your recollection about the past is sketchy. Are you a bit embarrassed about how good you were?

Jason: No, I never quite thought of it like that. I don't remember great specifics of the past, that's fair to say. Maybe I copped a couple too many knocks to the head, I'm not sure. I had a fantastic time playing, and I'm thrilled with what I achieved as part of a great team, but I never think about being a great player, or that it sits easily or uneasily with me. It's just the way it is.

Mike: It's been an interesting 12 years since you retired. You're the most influential man at Hawthorn as the director of football. And you're the face of Fox Sports. You're the head man at Triple M, and you're often seen on the golf course and the tennis court. Now, you've fashioned a very, very interesting life for yourself.

Jason: Very enjoyable. You know, after spending 14 years at a footy club, the game is such an important part of your life. It's a wonderful privilege to be able to actually continue in the same vein and do something associated with the game as a means of going forward. And, you know, as you say, I've had 12 fantastic years staying involved in the game.

Mike: You do love footy? You love it in the pure sense?

Jason: I'm passionate about it, absolutely. I love watching the game and it's funny, you do three or four games a weekend at times and halfway through the season you start thinking: 'Gee, I'm a little bit sick of the footy.' And you see a few ordinary games, but every time you see a great one it just brings you back to saying: 'This is a fantastic game.' And then the season gets to the stage when you get excited about the finals rolling around.

Mike: Do you enjoy the modern game?

Jason: I love it. It's brilliant to watch. I get a little concerned when the officials who make the rules start suggesting they want to tinker with the game a little more, and capping interchanges and goals rebounding off the post. Those sorts of things tend to raise my eyebrows a little bit. But the people in charge have done a good job bringing the game to the point that it is now. I think it's a great time just to let it settle and let's enjoy the game.

Mike: Lots of people say that it's not the game it was because of the physicality: 'They've turned it into netball or basketball and sanitised it.' It's still pretty tough, isn't it?

Jason: You speak to the current-day players, and they wouldn't have a clue what you're talking about, because they go hell for leather. They bang heads, they smash into each other. It is a taxing game. You only have to see the amount of time they spend on the training track. You look at what they do pre-season and I mean, what they do during the course of a week to get themselves up for a game. It is incredibly taxing on the players.

> **CAREER**
> **Born:** August 14, 1964
> **Club:** *Hawthorn*—269 games, 1254 goals
> **Honours:** Australian Football Hall of Fame inductee (2002); Coleman Medal—1988, 1989, 1992; Brownlow Medal—2nd 1988, 1992, 3rd 1989; Eight times state representative; Hawthorn Team of the Century; Hawthorn Hall of Fame inductee (2005); Hawthorn premiership side 1986, 1988, 1989, 1991; Peter Crimmins Medal (club champion) 1988, 1989, 1992, 1993; Hawthorn leading goalkicker 1986, 1987, 1988, 1989, 1990, 1991, 1992, 1993, 1994, 1995, 1996, 1998

Maybe there's no behind the ball incidents like there used to be. That was a fear playing back in the old days when tough blokes or mean blokes just decided there was one way to fix things, and that was to give you one in the back of the head, side of the jaw, whatever. That doesn't happen anymore. But that doesn't mean it's any less tough.

Mike: Hawthorn recruited you from Queensland where you played with Coorparoo. What was your Australian football background?

Jason: I starting playing when I was five in the under 7s at Coorparoo, and then played under 7s, under 9s, 11s, 13s, 15s, didn't play 17s for some reason. I think school might have got in the way of that, and then played 19s and seniors. So the way I got into it: My father was a rugby union man, he played rugby union at private school in Brisbane, and he would have loved me to have played rugby union. He wasn't overly thrilled when I gave it away. But when I was five, the only game you were allowed to play as a five-year-old was Australian Rules. So they took me down to Coorparoo and I was just having a run around there.

Mike: Would have been a big culture shock, Jason, coming from Queensland to the madhouse of Melbourne with its football. What are your recollections of that time?

Jason: Oh, it was a massive culture shock, absolutely massive. I was like a deer in the headlights when I came down. Queensland was so laidback compared to Melbourne. And the importance that the footy culture plays in people's lives in Victoria was extraordinary. I mean, people's working week depends on how their team goes on the weekend, or a lot of it did for some people. And I'd never experienced anything as intense as that, so that took a lot to adapt to. And I grew up as a kid barracking for Carlton. I used to love Carlton. We played in the same jumpers at Coorparoo, and I used to idolise blokes like Bruce Doull and Wayne Harmes and Wayne Johnston and all these sort of guys. I learned to hate Carlton pretty quickly when I got down here though. But the cold winters—I mean, I'd never experienced anything like it. But it was also a wonderful experience, like going to the Big Apple, you know?

Mike: I remember interviewing you late in your career, and my recollection is that you said Darren Jarman was the best player that you played with.

Jason: The best player I've ever played with *on his day*. His day didn't happen as often as some of the most consistent players we've seen play the game, some of the great ones, but on his day he was the most magical player I'd ever seen, because I played with the guy for years and I didn't know if he was a left- or right-footer. It made no difference. He'd kick it 50 across his body on either foot and he wouldn't break stride. He didn't look quick, yet he could dance out of four or five players and make them look like they're standing still. He could take the big mark. He never fumbled the ball. He could pick it up at ground level. He was a genius.

Mike: When you gave 'Jars' that accolade, I remember it caused a lot of discussion in the footy community. Where did that leave you with Dermott Brereton, Robert DiPierdomenico, and even the great Leigh Matthews?

Jason: Oh, look, people think that because I said he's the best player I've seen on his day that he's the best player I've played with. They're two different things, if that makes sense. I mean, I played with guys like Gary Ayres and Michael Tuck and Chris Langford, Dermott, 'Dipper', Johnny Platten was a superstar, I mean, a little bloke that just relentlessly ran all day. In the later years I played with Shane Crawford. They were great players. All I'm talking about was a bloke that on his day was the best that I'd seen.

Mike: Over the journey who was the best Hawthorn player that you played with?

Jason: I only played one year with Leigh Matthews so it's unfair to judge. I mean, he's regarded as arguably the best that's ever played the game, and I saw him on TV. He was winding down as I was just coming into it, so while it would be easy to say 'Leigh Matthews is the greatest I've ever played with', I never saw him at his best.

It's too hard to narrow down. I played at a fantastic club that just had stars all over the ground.

Mike: You played a lot of football with Dermott. You were an outstanding combination as key forwards. Why did you two fall out?

Jason: I understand it's a serious question, and most people believe that to be the case. And ... you know what? There's a lot of role-playing in the media, and this is all that's happened. There's two very big healthy egos there, Dermott and myself. And, look, we got on brilliantly on-field, and we were again part of that successful team. I played longer than he did. His body probably gave up and he had to drop out a little bit earlier, and then we'd had this friendly banter on and off, and it's just grown and grown and grown.

Mike: I've got to say I don't believe you about that.

Jason: Okay. So you're calling me a liar.

Mike: I think there's a clear level of animosity between Dunstall and Brereton.

Jason: There's no animosity whatsoever. There's a lot of one-upmanship. And I've always loved sledging, and I always love to niggle blokes. Dermott's exactly the same.

Mike: If you assembled a group of eight or 10 blokes to go away on a golfing weekend, would Dermott be one of them?

Jason: No, absolutely not; (a) he doesn't like golf, but (b) he's not in the group that I hang with. That's the other thing from footy clubs—there are cliques within footy clubs, and you get on better with some players than others. Dermott was always a little bit removed because he was such a visible superstar. I mean, he lived the typical rock star life, driving the Ferraris, he had the model girlfriends. He had the Harley Davidson, he had the coloured boots, the bleached hair, the big diamond earring. This is back when very little of that actually happened. So he was a rock star playing football.

Mike: I've got a thing about conflict of interest in this business. How do you rationalise your roles as a commentator, a very prominent media performer, and the man in charge of the football department at Hawthorn?

Jason: I can't do anything about that conflict, first and foremost.

Mike: Do you acknowledge that a conflict exists?

Jason: In most people's eyes, yes. Having said that, a large proportion of the people that work in the media have conflicts. It's how you manage that conflict I think. I don't think I've ever favoured Hawthorn in any of the work that I've done in the media. In fact, I've been criticised for being too hard on Hawthorn when I've called Hawthorn games. I mean, you can never win because people see things differently. But I always try to call it as I see it. I would do anything for the footy club; I'm still involved, because as I said it was such a big part of my life, I'd give anything back to that club that they needed me to do, and I will continue to do so. But I also need to make a living, and the job that I enjoy doing the most is working in the media and following the game. Now, sometimes I'm going to call Hawthorn games—so be it. I don't think it's an unmanageable conflict.

Mike: Now Jeffrey Kennett, Jason—I remember alerting you to the former chairman's outburst at the coach, Al Clarkson.[32]

Jason: Which I didn't know about at the time.

Mike: You were extremely angry that the president had gone public with his comments.

Jason: No, I wasn't. No I wasn't.

Mike: Well, you were.

Jason: We've had this discussion a lot of times. Jeff is Jeff and will always be Jeff. It's the way he was when he was Premier of Victoria. He has a unique style. He's been very good for the footy club. He comes warts and all. Would I do it the way he does it? Absolutely not. In fact, most people wouldn't. But he believes in this inalienable right to communicate to the members and to be brutally honest with them.

Mike: Did you counsel him after that?

Jason: We've had discussions over the years about how he does things, how I would do things, how I think perhaps it's best for the footy club. But that doesn't mean that I'm right, and it doesn't mean that he's wrong.

Mike: In 2009, Jason, Hawthorn missed the finals after winning a flag in 2008. It looked like you had built a platform. Is there a genuine explanation for that, or did they just get ahead of themselves?

Jason: I don't think they got ahead of themselves at all. I thought Geelong were clearly the best side in 2008, but we were the best side in September. And I think we introduced a style of play that Alastair Clarkson brought to the club and worked on for three or four years that won us a premiership. I thought the coaching was equally responsible for the premiership, as was the playing group.

But all the opposition sides started to work out how to combat the zone[33], how to manipulate the zone, and the game's progressed enormously from a couple of years ago. So all of a sudden we had to go from playing largely uncontested footy back to contested footy, and I think we found out—and this is a pretty brutal assessment of our list as well—that we had a number

---

32 After a bad loss in 2010, Hawthorn president Jeff Kennett said the club's coaching staff were 'on notice'.
33 Hawthorn played a rolling defensive zone in 2008 that was credited with improving their performance dramatically.

of blokes that weren't that comfortable winning contested footy. And we've had to educate them to get back to winning contested footy, and I think that's taken the best part of 18 months.

Mike: I think it's fair to say your fingerprints are all over that premiership win in terms of assembling the coaching group and maybe even the player group.

Jason: I don't like the way you phrase that. I was very responsible for getting Alastair Clarkson to the club, but that was my job at the time. I don't like saying 'my fingerprints were over the premiership'. That's the coaching staff and the playing group. The football department worked enormously hard for four years. That's their premiership, mate.

Mike: I was going to say, compare the sense of pride and satisfaction that ... you got out of that with the premierships that you played in— you played in four as a player. I know they're different; I understand that. But you must have extracted a lot of pride from the 2008 success.

Jason: Absolutely. You're right, it's a very different feeling, but I was over the moon. I was so chuffed inside sitting in the Southern Stand watching the 2008 Grand Final. It was almost a surreal feeling, thinking: 'This can't be happening. We're actually going to win this.'

And I guess the most special moment for me, and I'll forever remember this day, because I had family and friends down from interstate, so I was just having a barbecue at my place that night rather than attending the club function. And we were sitting there after it had all quietened down and we'd all enjoyed the game, and it was fantastic and we were thrilled. It must have been 7.30, and coming down the hallway was Alastair Clarkson, Ian Robson and Mark Evans[34] with the premiership cup. And that to me was just such a special moment to share that. I just hugged 'Clarko' and said: 'Oh, mate, how good was this? It was brilliant.' They just stopped in on the way to the official function. And I'm very grateful for that.

Mike: You kicked 1260 goals in your career.

Jason: It was 1254, mate. Don't credit me with six I didn't kick please.

Mike: What was your kicking routine?

---

34 Ian Robson was chief executive of Hawthorn in 2008. Mark Evans remains football operations manager.

Jason: I developed it from the early days, when I didn't have much of a routine at all. I just used to try and kick the cover off the footy and the ball kept coming down so much I didn't perhaps value or understand the value of missing shots for goal.

But as you get older and you get to the latter stages of the career and the ball's not coming down as frequently, and you're not as good and you're not getting as much of it, you think: 'I've got to make every kick count.' So my kicking in the back half of my career was much better than in the front half. But that's something you get from countless hours of repetition on the training track.

Mike: Did you have a certain number of steps?

Jason: I didn't count steps. I had a couple of basic principles, obviously. If you could imagine a lane on a running track was my run-up, and couldn't go out of that in any way, shape or form. And also with the follow-through leg—everything had to be in line with the target. Now, if there's a breeze blowing you adjust it to however far you need to adjust it from the centre of the goals to allow for the breeze. But, essentially it's the same kick every time you go, and I didn't stab at the ball. I kicked through it all the time. And then it was just trying to make sure that the drop of the footy was as good as I could make it. I didn't have a great style. I dropped the ball from pretty high, so I had to work hard at it.

Mike: Have you ever bothered to try to help Lance Franklin and Jarryd Roughead with their kicking?

Jason: It's a fallacy, this. It's a fallacy that people think that because you've done something so well you can make others do it just as well. I spent time working with the guys on goalkicking two or three years ago, maybe four years ago, did a few sessions with them. But we've now got so many full-time staff at the footy club whose job it is to do that, they don't need me poking my head in once a week and doing something like that. You need a consistent message.

But the difference is also, they don't have the time to practice the way we used to. Because we trained part-time when I first started out, you could spend extra hours doing it. They're at the club all day every day. Now, they *do* have goalkicking sessions. They have a number of goalkicking sessions, and they've got people working on it. They review the videos all the time. They look at the things they're doing right, they look at the things they're doing wrong. It's going to take time and practice.

Franklin's a unique case. Buddy's unfixable. He is that far away from what you would say is a textbook way of kicking for goal. Look, we tried a couple of times to put poles down and have him run in a straight line and kick it, and he nearly fell over. He can't do it. And then he'd nearly miss the ball at the end because it felt so uncomfortable for him.

So you've got to allow him to kick the way he's going to kick and accept the fact that he's probably going to be marginally better than a 50-50 chance.

Jarryd Roughead is an exceptional kick when you watch him on the training track. And I've watched him in pre-game warm-ups where he's just slotted goal after goal. But it's a mental battle for him. It's getting that confidence and being able to do it and expecting to being able to do it in match situations, and it hasn't come for him yet. But I have no doubt that whether it's 12 months or 24 months down the track he'll develop into a very good kick for goal.

Mike: There's a perception about you of being a grump. Is that fair?
Jason: Again, this comes from the role-playing that I was speaking about, you know, from *The Footy Show* in the early days. I was the grumpy one that'd always take on Sam Newman. I'm very good at playing a grump, mind you. But I think we know each other well enough, and you've seen me in other circumstances, and I'm a pretty happy-go-lucky person that loves to have fun away from things as well.

I mean, I've got to be serious when the time's right to be serious, whether it's on camera or working in my role at the footy club, but I love having fun as much as the next bloke does.

Mike: You work a lot with Danny Frawley. What was your view of Frawley when he was your regular opponent when you played against the Saints?
Jason: He was a hard man, 'Spud'. He loved to punch on. That was back in the days where if you took a mark and they couldn't spoil it, they'd punch the back of your head. Spud would do that as well as anyone. He was a fierce competitor. He's a bloke that got the most out of himself, and we had some great battles.

But the great thing about working with people that you thought were like that—Glen Jakovich is another. Glen Jakovich, I used to think, was the most serious bloke with no personality when he played, and I admired him as a footballer because that was back when we had a fantastic rivalry with West Coast as well. But having worked with him now, he's a ripper, 'Jako'. I love going out and having a beer with him after we've done a game interstate. We have a ball just having a chat and having a laugh.

Mike: You worked with a lot of famous names. I reckon your rapport with Wayne Carey on *Saturday Central* was as good as I've seen. I mean, there's clearly a mutual respect between you and 'The Duck'.
Jason: We always got on great. And I think there was that respect, no doubt about that. And he's the guy that I will always say was the best footballer I've seen, period. Consistency, skill, ability to impact a game throughout his entire career—he was peerless.

Mike: Both you and Wayne have expressed reservations publicly about the tactics of Stephen Silvagni, who was a regular opponent for both of you. Did he play within the rules or did he break them?
Jason: Let's clarify that. He got away with whatever he could get away with, and was entitled to, as every full-back was back in that era. These days, we laugh because these days you can't do half the things that you used to be able to do back then. And the reason we probably moan about it is because he was so bloody good, 'SOS', and he was so hard to beat. I never kicked a huge bag on him, and it annoyed and frustrated the hell out of me, because you'd think you had him beaten and he'd find a way to get that arm in.

I get on great with SOS when I see him. There's no dramas there. There's a fantastic respect there as well. But if you actually did beat him in a contest he'd then whinge to the umpire saying: 'Oh, he pushed me.' Or: 'He grabbed me.' And then we'd sit there going: 'Are you kidding me? It just can't be like that.'

Mike: There were lots of superstars at Hawthorn in your day, Jason, and several players who were underrated by the broader community, players like Chris Langford, Chris Mew, Gary Ayres, Darrin Pritchard, those sort of guys.
Jason: I think most of them got the respect they deserved. I reckon Chris Mew was a vastly underrated player. 'Mewie' never said boo, you never saw

him after a game—straight back to Rosebud with the family. He was a very quiet sort of a guy, but an unbelievable player. I mean, he played against the best centre half-forwards in the game, and I can't remember him getting towelled up on any day.

Mike: You played with the worst item of headgear[35] that we've seen in world sport since Tony Greig's days with World Series Cricket. Were you embarrassed running around with that whatever it was?

Jason: Why I should be embarrassed? Here's me thinking I'm making a gutsy effort to get back on the playing field, because I was only allowed to play by the surgeon if I wore this helmet that he specifically designed to cover the fractured skull that I had. And all I did was get ridicule and laughter from all and sundry. I thought: 'Oh, gee. No pity here, is there?'

Mike: How long before you played after the accident?

Jason: It was a depressed fracture of the skull, just above the eye. There's two layers of bone, and I only broke the first one. If you break both of them you're in all sorts of trouble, so I was very lucky there. So I had a plate and screws put in there, where they cut you across the top of the head, they pull your face down, put it all in then staple you back up. So I was in hospital for a week or so, and I reckon I missed seven games and then came back, and was only allowed to play with a helmet if I was to come back.

And it wasn't until I probably got a couple of whacks to the head that I actually felt comfortable and confident again that it was all okay.

Mike: In 1992 you kicked 145 goals with an average of 6.3 a game, and finished second in the Brownlow Medal. Surely that was your best year as an individual sense, was it?

Jason: Yes, it was. The disappointing thing I guess that year was I also kicked, I think, 84 points. So if I had have been a little bit more accurate, I could have kicked 150-plus, which would have been nice. Not that I'm interested in records, but it's just disappointing to kick that many points.

But that shows you how much ball was coming down, and the fact that I did get a lot of the footy. So from an individual perspective, it certainly wasn't our best team year, but individually my best year, yes.

---

35 Dunstall wore a helmet for a period in the 1990 season after suffering a head injury.

Mike: You talked about records, and I understand they're not important to you. But you kicked 17 goals against Richmond at Waverley Park in 1992. Now, my recollection is you almost seemed to run away from the opportunity to get the shot to kick the 18th and equal the League record held since 1947 by Fred Fanning. Is that fair?

Jason: I didn't even know what the record was. Because again, I didn't grow up with the game, so I wasn't aware of what all the records in place were. And I think the scoreboard started flashing up when I kicked 16 that it was a Waverley Park record, and then 17 was a Hawthorn record. A couple of teammates then came and told me: 'Got to get another one.' But—call me mad—but it didn't change the way I played the game. So when my opponent ran up the ground, I ran up with him. And this was late in the game. And I'd had a pretty big game. I'd had 29 possessions. I was tired. I didn't have a lot of energy in the tank at the best of times. I was knackered. I reckon I walked back to position in the last couple of minutes and perhaps missed an opportunity to kick 18. But, you know, that was just a fantastic day for me where everything went right and I've got great memories of it.

Mike: Would you have liked a share of the record, retrospectively?

Jason: In hindsight yes, it'd be great, but I kicked 17.5. I spoke to Fred at some stage after that but before he passed away [in 1993], and he said: 'Jeez, if you weren't so inaccurate you would have had the record.' Because he kicked 18.1, I think it was.

I'm thinking: '17.5 is very accurate over the journey. I mean, you're kicking more than three goals for every point, which would be a brilliant conversion rate over your career.' But he called it 'inaccurate'. I thought: 'Jeez, I thought it was okay.'

ROBERT FLOWER

Recognised by all and sundry as one of the game's gentlemen, Robert Flower is one of the Melbourne Football Club's favourite sons, and one of the finest wingmen ever to pull on a boot.

The Demons recruited him from Murrumbeena and he made his debut for the club in Round 10, 1973. Such was the impression he created, Flower immediately became a fixture in the team, and remained so until his retirement at the end of 1987.

Flower was placed on a wing by first coach Ian Ridley and remained there for most of his career. With Stan Alves and Greg Wells, he formed one of the best centre-lines of the '70s. However, unlike Alves and Wells, who moved to other clubs in search of (and finding) premiership success, Flower remained true to Melbourne for his entire playing career.

When Ron Barassi returned to Melbourne as coach in 1981, he moved Flower to a half-back flank, a move seen by many as tactical madness. But, if anything, Flower—despite even his own doubts about the move—became an even more accomplished player, setting up countless counter-attacks for the Demons.

Despite Barassi's return, success continued to elude Melbourne and Flower, and it wasn't until his final season, 1987, that Flower played in a final. During that finals series, with Melbourne trouncing North Melbourne and then Sydney, it appeared that Flower's swan-song season would have a fairytale finish. But the Demons, after leading Hawthorn for almost the entire 1987 preliminary final, fell short of a Grand Final berth when Gary Buckenara kicked a post-final siren goal to give the Hawks victory. It was a heartbreaking end to a magnificent career.

MAY 23, 2011

Mike: On behalf of your legion of fans, it's great to see you so fit and well in your mid-50s, but it's nearly 24 years since that fateful day at VFL Park, Waverley, when Melbourne lost a preliminary final on a kick after the siren. Have you moved on?

Robert: I think I was over it on day one, to be honest. I live a life of no regrets. Sure, the pain was there straight after the game. A reflection of everything that happens in life and football, but I tend to think that there's always tomorrow and move on, and my motto always has been: 'Life goes on, so get over it and get on with it.' So I don't look back at it with any regrets.

Mike: You finished the '87 preliminary final with a popped collarbone. Would you have tried to play in the Grand Final?

Robert: Yes, well, Robert DiPierdomenico popped it in the second quarter, to be honest, so I went off for injections and tapings and so on, which happened in those days. You'd try and get back out on the field as quick as you could. To play the next week would have taken a lot of work, probably genius work by the medical staff. They would have really needed to put some painkiller in there, make sure that it wouldn't drop out.

Mike: How did you blokes feel, looking back when you realised that Jimmy Stynes running through the Gary Buckenara mark[36] had probably cost you a chance to play for the premiership?

Robert: Jimmy was the unfortunate end result of a day that probably looked as if we could have won it at any time. And the first quarter I took a mark 15 metres out, if that, on a slight angle, had a shot for goal and hit the guy on the mark, so it goes through for a point. Put that back on the score line and where do we sit? So you never look at isolated moments within a game and, while it was frustrating, the siren had actually gone before the ball arrived with Buckenara. The umpire never heard it, the crowd all heard it and there was a tremendous roar, but the game should have been over before the mark.

---

36 Stynes, Melbourne's ruckman, conceded a 15-metre penalty immediately after Buckenara marked, by running across the mark. Buckenara's goal from 45 metres put Hawthorn into the Grand Final.

Mike: Is that right? I wasn't aware of this. So the ball was in the air when the siren sounded?

Robert: Yes, and the umpires hadn't heard it, and it's still over when Jimmy ran across the mark. So, really, there was no need for him to go and pick up an extra man. If the umpire had heard the siren, there wouldn't have been a 15-metre penalty.

So all those things culminated into an incident that I think became pretty famous, particularly in my life. Melbourne supporters would still come up me and talk about the '87 prelim. It was my last game of football ever, missing out on making the Grand Final for the first time since 1964, so there were a lot of things adding up to that.

> **CAREER**
> **Born:** August 5, 1955
> **Club:** *Melbourne*—272 games, 315 goals
> **Honours:** Australian Football Hall of Fame inductee (1996); All-Australian 1980, 1982, 1983, 1984; Brownlow Medal—3rd 1979, 1984; 15 times state representative; Melbourne Team of the Century; Melbourne Hall of Fame inductee (2001); Melbourne best and fairest 1977; Melbourne leading goalkicker 1979, 1983

Mike: We saw the fury from John Northey, the coach, after the game with that famous picture where he pointed his finger at Jimmy. And I was in the crowd with Melbourne supporters who just couldn't control their emotions. I was surprised that you were able to move on so quickly after that.

Robert: When I look back on my career, my ambition was to play for the Melbourne Football Club. That was my ambition in life. I used to sit there in school and dream about it. Then to play for the football club, getting a game the next week, once you cement that, it becomes about making the finals. So I played a career from 1973 to '87 without playing one final. And it was the ultimate, but there was nothing I could do about it once you didn't. I couldn't change it, I couldn't go back. So all you have in your mind is bitterness if you're going to live like that. And you look forward to the next challenge and what you need to do. I was probably a little bit saddened by it, but I wasn't bitter about it.

Mike: In your 15 years at Melbourne, you won 105 of 333 games. That's a rate of less than one in three. That's a very, very lean period in a footy club history.

Robert: It was. But I can honestly say that in the years I played, I always would think that we were going to win the game of football. I'd arrive at the ground, regardless of who we're playing, thinking that we were going to win the game. I'd go there preparing myself to be victors of the day. And that was me mentally preparing to play well but also hoping that the other guys within the team would be doing the same to actually win the game of football.

Mike: Your first game must have been an interesting experience. You're still at school, you're playing football for the club that you grew up barracking for, and you didn't know any of the players. Tell us about that.

Robert: Well, I was only 17 and still at school and I remember we were at home of a Thursday night, we used to wait for the League teams to come across on the radio. And Noel McMahon, Melbourne's chairman of selectors, actually rang my place and got dad on the phone. I was in the lounge room; dad's in the kitchen. Dad's going: 'Look, Noel, he's thin. You know, I don't think he's ready for this. I don't know if I'm going to give permission for him to actually play.' But finally he was convinced and I was going to play in the senior side for the first time in my life. I'd trained with the under 19s, played with the under 19s, got promoted for three games, one as an interchange then two full games in the reserves and, all of a sudden, I'm thrust into the senior side. I hadn't met the players. I knew who they were, I barracked for them, I loved them. So to walk in the rooms was a dream, to actually walk in and be among them in the first place and let alone play with them.

Mike: So you came to the ground with your parents?

Robert: Yes, I came with mum and dad and we arrived at the gate, just outside the change rooms. I hadn't trained with the side, so I hadn't been to the club since I'd been to under 19s training during the week. So I didn't have any tickets to get in. I only had under 19 tickets. So we paid our way in and got into the rooms and Barry Bourke[37] grabbed me, took me around and introduced me to all the players.

---

37 Bourke was a 1964 Melbourne premiership player.

Mike: Who was your hero? You ended up playing with lots of heroes, I suppose.

Robert: When I was a kid, I grew up with number four on my back and number four in the '60s was John Lord, big John Lord, who was a bald-headed ruckman. I do remember the story, and 'Lordy' will probably hate me for this, but he had to change his strides out on the ground one day because they got ripped, and he had more hair on his bum than he did his head. But I became good mates with Lordy, he's been fantastic. Then Tony Sullivan had number four after that.

Mike: Tell us about your relationship with Ron Barassi.

Robert: Good, very good. Barassi was fantastic for the football club because he turned our football club around from being an amateur organisation under the auspices of the Melbourne Cricket Club. He went back to grassroots with teaching us how to kick, how to handball left-hand and right-hand. We'd have to do drills—100 left-hand handball, 100 right-hand handball, left-foot kick, right-foot kick—before we actually went out and did our work. You had to be prepared right in a lot of things, little things in football, things when you haven't got the ball, prepped you for life, your time management and the way you went about things with people in life. So in the package of life and football, he was fantastic for me and I appreciate it. He was very harsh, though, too, in the same breath, in that the expectation of success was enormous. So he was teaching us to do it right and that was the expectation that you had to do. If you didn't do it right, then he'd be down on your like a tonne of bricks.

Mike: Why did he move you from a wing, which was your province, to the half-back flank?

Robert: I loved the wing. I thought the wing was a great position because it was a tactical position, you had to read the play and understand where the ball was going and make a judgement on whether you went forward or back, whether you could be attacking or be defensive, whether you moved across the other side of the ground or stay on your own side of the ground. And it was in an era a lot different from today's football. And there were a lot of great wingers around. But what was happening, I was getting tagged frequently, almost every week. So Barassi decided he'd change that and make me tag someone else for a period. So I would mind someone, their thought processes as a half-forward would be attacking, which would allow me, when the time was right, to be an attacking half-back flanker. And the logic was quite sound. And I played half-back flank in 1984 and ended up third in the Brownlow Medal in that year.

Mike: You went back to the half-back flank and you went further back at one point, didn't you? You went back to full-back and played on Malcolm Blight, an interesting experience?
Robert: Did you *have* to say that?

Mike: Just take us through that minute-by-minute, would you?
Robert: Look, there was only two minutes of it because in the side at the time was Brent Crosswell who was at full-forward, and Barassi put me at full-back on Malcolm Blight. And my job was actually to play on him and stop him kicking goals. Well, the first three minutes, Jimmy Krakouer and Phil Krakouer got the ball out of the centre and hit him on the chest three times and he kicked three goals. All I remember was Barassi sending the runner out, 'Tiger' Crosswell going to full-back and me to full-forward. So I slunk around the boundary line as Tiger came charging down the middle of the ground to take up the position of full-back. It was very short-lived.

Mike: Now I know you came into football as a strapping 69kg player. What was your weight when you matured and played probably in the last five years of your career?
Robert: From 73 to 75kg. Look, our facilities here were quite dismal. We had our changing rooms at the MCG and they were very small, antiquated. We had a four-way rotational piece of equipment that was our gym and a few heavy weights, and I wasn't big on the weights. At times, we had to train around the cricket pitch and, at times, actually train in the car park. So for a club that's at the pinnacle or the top of the tree as far as the sport goes, to have those facilities was quite dismal.

Mike: One of your ex-teammates, Greg Wells, described you as a 'pull-through' when you arrived at the Melbourne Footy Club. It was a tough era at the time, how did you stay out of trouble?

Robert: Look, I got knocks, there's no question, but I think awareness was a strength of mine, being aware of what's around you. But I put it down to being respected... that no one really came the crunch on me.

Mike: Take us back to Whitten Oval, Round 22, 1987. Tell us about that.
Robert: Absolutely, it's my favourite memory of my career because it was the culmination of everything, to actually make the finals and it was that game that got us into the finals. And it was touch-and-go, because there were five teams going to make the finals, and three teams were still vying for that fifth spot. And one of them was Footscray who we were playing, the other one was Geelong who were playing Hawthorn, the top side. So the results at the end of the day were going to determine who made it. So I went there knowing that it was going to be my last game of football if we lost. So driving out there I had very mixed emotions of where it was going to end up. And at half-time, I'm in the room thinking 'this is going to be the worst day', because I hadn't had a touch of the football. I may have touched the ball twice in a half of football.

Greg Eppelstun was my opponent, who'd had the better of me throughout the year, a very tough, dogged player. I've spoken to him since that game, and he's a lovely guy by the way, but we were enemies on the football field. I came out, I remember, after half-time, really angry, and in the third quarter I kicked a couple of goals that put us into a position to win the game. At three-quarter time, we wanted to know the results down at Geelong but the team manager, John Sell, said: 'Don't worry about this result. All you need to do is win, because down at Geelong, they're getting thumped.' When we were so far in front, we thought we were in. But towards the end of the last quarter, the crowd erupted and we thought the game was over, and it was actually Jason Dunstall, he'd kicked a goal to put Hawthorn in front.

Mike: One of the most amazing statistics in the Melbourne history is that a chap named R. Flower topped the goalkicking three times and won just one best and fairest. I mean, I still find that hard to comprehend.
Robert: I wasn't a good goalkicker.

Mike: But the fact that you won only one best and fairest. Is there any resentment?

Robert: No resentment. Again, life goes on and you can't do anything about it. I think I was runner-up a lot of times. But we had some really good players going through. Laurie Fowler won three and he was tough, tenacious. I think there was maybe one season where I only played the full 22 rounds of matches.

So you miss a game, a couple of games, and it's costly whereas in a Brownlow Medal, that type of award, you can only poll in 10 or 11 games and win. In saying that, we really did have some good players; you know, Stephen Smith and Gary Baker and Steven Icke and Alan Johnson, all great players and I've got no qualms about finishing behind any of those players.

Mike: What did you think was amiss at the place at the time?
Robert: There's certainly something to say about being prepared. The facilities that we had to prepare in didn't put us in the best light. I don't think we were badly coached by any means.

Mike: Carl Ditterich, the coach, Robert, it seemed to me that every time he was on the ground, you blokes stood a lot taller.
Robert: Definitely. If you had a look at your stats on the winning-losing record, if Carl Ditterich is actually playing, we had a better chance of winning, and if he wasn't playing, Melbourne hardly ever won a game. So he did make people stand taller. He cast a shadow, and his nickname is Shadow.

Mike: You finished third in two Brownlows—1979 and 1984—both times behind Peter Moore. Should you have won a medal?
Robert: I look back and the second year, I was only a bee's knee away from winning a Brownlow but I remember two games where I probably shouldn't have got votes. I'm probably miles away. I shouldn't have got votes. So it's all conjecture and life goes on. I've got no regrets with that.

Mike: The other thing about your statistical background that surprised me, is that you've kicked more than 300 goals. I mean, that's a good return from a bloke who played primarily on a wing and even half-back.
Robert: Yes, I think one of the joys of football is actually kicking goals. The culmination of what you're trying to do, as a team, is kick goals. And I had the freedom—and coaches gave me the freedom—to actually slot down into

the forward line when I did. So the ball's tracking down the other side of the ground, to actually float in, take a short pass or a mark down the goal square or even kick from outside 50.

Mike: You played 15 state games. You were a sensational state player. They must have been like your Grand Finals, were they?

Robert: They were great moments in my life in that I got to play a game. While coming to Melbourne, playing with the guys I admired, playing in state football was the next level up again with the guys that you admire. So to be alongside Wayne Schimmelbusch and Bruce Doull and Gary Dempsey, these guys were legends of the game and I was humbled by being in the same room with them. All you had to do was be in the right position because you knew Bruce Doull on the half-back flank was going to get it to you somehow, or Geoff Southby or Kelvin Moore in the full-back line, all you had to do was read the play and be in the right spots. I made lots of great friends out of state football that I continue to see; I play golf with Bernie Quinlan, and all these guys that you just loved being with in that time.

Mike: A lot of great wingers played when you were playing. Was there one that you had sort of an ongoing battle with?

Robert: Wayne Schimmelbusch was a tough opponent because he was unusual. He wasn't just a skilled, gifted footballer, he was dour and tough and rugged and would never give in, regardless of where the result of the game may well be, whether it was the first quarter or the last quarter, North miles in front, North miles behind, he was there doing what he had to do. And that was a trait of his that I admired.

Mike: I want to ask you about a couple of teammates of yours. One is Gerard Healy, a best and fairest winner at Melbourne and suddenly he's gone to Sydney where he won three best and fairests. How did he get away from the footy club?

Robert: Gerard did leave the club to go to Sydney and I was unsure of the circumstances, but I could see ourselves on the cusp of going somewhere and felt that it was important, so I wasn't happy that he left. When we made the finals in '87, we played Sydney and knocked them out of the finals and his younger brother Greg was playing with us, and I think we were secretly happy, not only to beat Sydney but Gerard actually missed the rest of the finals. But he was a great footballer and very much innovative in his own way. I used to take clinics, go to football clinics where we'd go to schools and clubs and take drills, and that was part of the culture of the VFL or AFL in those days. When Gerard came along, they were fantastic sessions to run, because he'd think of things to do that were not just handball and kicking.

Mike: Mark Jackson was another interesting player that you played with at Melbourne. Did you have an altercation with him at any point?

Robert: I knew 'Jacko', he lived in the local area and I had sporting good stores out at Forest Hill and he'd come in the shops and interact with the kids and do all those things. And then he came to Melbourne, and one practice match, Ray Jordon[38] and Ron Barassi were coaching, took us over to the old Scotch grounds. Well, Barassi had me at full-back on Jacko, the ball came down, I punched the ball away, the ball came down, I'd knock it around him and take off. Then the ball came down and Mark turned around and clocked me. So, with that, there was nearly every player on the field in a melee with me holding the ball and Jacko taking on everyone else. So it became a famous incident. Barassi said to Jacko: 'Jacko, this isn't what we're about, playing footy here. It's a practice match.' And Jacko's response was: 'Well, I'm practising how I play.'

Mike: Let's talk about your health. You're in your mid-40s and suddenly you learn that you've got a prostate problem, a serious prostate problem. Tell us about that.

Robert: Well, you know very well what happened there, Michael, because you're the one that instigated the test. At my age, I was very naïve to any type of illness and the male ego says that you can actually beat any type of illness. And you suggested after a golf day that cancer in men over 40, the possibility of prostate cancer was quite high. And I didn't even know I had a prostate, let alone that I had the cancer. So two weeks later, I was just getting my cholesterol checked and I suggested to the doctor that I be checked for prostate cancer. Lo-and-behold, I've got cancer. The options that were given to me by my urologist was that I could get the prostate taken out and hopefully take the cancer with it, or you could leave it, take pot

---

38 Ray 'Slug' Jordon coached Melbourne under 19s at the time.

luck and see if it grows any further. The danger of having prostate cancer is it moves to other parts of the body—your bladder, your bowel, other areas associated—and it becomes your death sentence basically. The other option was having radiation therapy. We went down, got it out and you live to see your kids grow up.

Mike: Now tell me about your love affair with football. You started as a kid, it probably came on you much quicker than you would have thought. Is it still a passion for you?

Robert: I love watching it and being there, but I don't think it's the passion of having to be at every Melbourne game. I think when you grow out of football and your family comes along, I like watching my kids play their sport. I love watching my kids play their sport. So I like having the option. So that's taken away from the full-on commitment of being there every week and every second of a game of footy.

PETER HUDSON

One of several champions to come out of Tasmania in the 1960s, Peter Hudson can lay legitimate claim to being the greatest full-forward seen at VFL/AFL level. Although he sits 17th on the list of all-time goalkickers, it is his goals-per-game average that supports this claim. In 129 games, Hudson kicked 727 goals, an average of 5.64. Of the players who have kicked 400 or more League goals, only the legendary John Coleman's average (5.48) comes close to this.

Hudson's senior career began in 1963 with New Norfolk in Tasmania, where he kicked 378 goals in just 78 games. He joined Hawthorn in 1967, where he kicked 57 goals in 17 games in his first season, a relatively low return by his standards. But he hit his straps the following year, opening the 1968 season with a 10-goal haul against Essendon. It was the first of three double-figure bags for Hudson that season, as he accumulated 125 goals in just 19 games.

Hudson produced a similar return in 1969, with 19 games producing 120 goals, including hauls of 16 and 13. In 1970, Hudson scaled even greater heights, kicking 146 goals in 22 games, including three double-figure bags.

Despite Hudson's success, Hawthorn had not tasted finals football during his time there. This changed in 1971, as the Hawks reached the Grand Final, defeating St Kilda to take out the flag. Hudson kicked three in that match to equal Bob Pratt's all-time season record of 150 goals.

Hudson kicked eight goals before half-time in Hawthorn's 1972 opening match before tragedy struck. He did not play again that year, and played only three further games before he returned to Tasmania to play with

Glenorchy in 1975. The Hawks convinced him to give the VFL one more try in 1977 and, although not as agile as he had been, Hudson still managed to kick 110 goals for the year.

Hudson returned to Glenorchy in 1978, finally retiring from football after the 1981 season.

SEPTEMBER 26, 2012

Mike: What are your memories of that fateful day in 1971, when you needed four goals in the Grand Final against St Kilda to break Bob Pratt's record of 150 in a season, and of Kevin 'Cowboy' Neale's crude tackle?

Peter: Not very good.

Mike: You kicked the first goal that day. You looked like you were headed for another bag. You ended up with three, and probably squandered about four or five opportunities.

Peter: The first one, looking back on it from the footage I have seen, was probably one of the best goals I've ever kicked. So, I felt that I was on a high and anything was possible. We were in a Grand Final, over 100,000 people there, I felt a million dollars. But then unfortunately the lights went out and that's all there was to it. The rest of it's just what I have virtually seen on film.

Mike: So 'Cowboy' miscued. He hits you in the ear, lacerates the ear and concusses you. Why didn't you go off?

Peter: Well, we'd lost Les Hawken in the first quarter with a hamstring and Ken Beck came on, and those were the days when you didn't have interchange. You went off, you stayed off. So Les is gone, he's finished. And Robert Day had been knocked out and one of the things I can remember on that day was Robert Day in the rooms at half-time after he'd been knocked out and I'd been knocked out, and they were sewing my ear back together, and I can remember them saying to him: 'Are you all right?' He said: 'Yeah, which way are we kicking?' He didn't even know he was in the room. So I thought, 'Well...', and they couldn't take us both off, because we would have been down to 17.

Mike: Everyone who talks about this game uses the same term, that it was a 'brutal' game.

Peter: Well I don't know what other word you can use, Mike, because there were lots of people got knocked out on that day and there was a lot of carnage. And I just thank my lucky stars as football people, that that doesn't happen these days like it did back in those days, because it wasn't good.

Mike: You finished level with Bob Pratt on 150 goals, and it's still the record. It will probably never be broken the way football has trended. Do you feel cheated that you were robbed of the opportunity to hold the record in your own right?

Peter: No I don't, because for starters Bob Pratt played less games than I did[39]. I'm not sure how many less than me, but I think it was a substantial number, and he deserved to have that record. I was delighted to share it with him. But the one thing I feel robbed of is the memory of that Grand Final. That is what I would have loved to have had, but football karma delivered, and we won the game.

> **CAREER**
> **Born:** February 19, 1946
> **Club:** *Hawthorn*—129 games, 727 goals
> **Honours:** Australian Football Hall of Fame Legend (1999); Coleman Medal—1968, 1970, 1971; Brownlow Medal—3rd 1971; eight times state representative; Hawthorn Team of the Century; Hawthorn Hall of Fame Legend (2010); Hawthorn premiership side 1971; best and fairest 1968, 1970; Hawthorn leading goalkicker 1967, 1968, 1969, 1970, 1971, 1977

Every year that has gone by I still feel the same about that situation. I went to Bob Pratt's funeral and it was a beautiful funeral and I stood there and it was like somebody flicked a switch and I know I said to myself at the time: 'Gee, I am really glad I didn't break his record because he has gone to his grave with that record.'

Mike: Twenty-four games for 150 goals; you finished equal second in the Brownlow Medal to Ian Stewart. You don't win Hawthorn's best and fairest. Explain.

Peter: I wish I could. But I mean Leigh Matthews had a fabulous year. The one thing I am certain of with full-forwards, you make a rod for

---

39 Pratt, who kicked 150 goals for South Melbourne in 1934, played only 21 games. Hudson played 24 games in 1971.

your own back. And when you first come into footy, if you kick five or six goals, the chances are that you will get three votes and as you go on, you are expected to kick seven, eight nine, 10, and it goes on. And I know that one day, I kicked 12 and never got a vote. That's gone on as long as I can remember and it will go on forever.

Mike: I want you to explain the Hudson phenomenon to me. You weren't overly quick. In your own words, you didn't fly a lot, you weren't physically intimidating but you just kept racking up goals.

Peter: Well, two things Mike. I think one is judgement and the other one is anticipation, and people would say to me: 'How do you get out on your own?' And people would say to me: 'You're quick over the first 10 metres', but it wasn't physically quick as in Usain Bolt. I think it was quick because I was concentrating so much. I was anticipating, I would watch the ball at the other end of the ground because I worked on the theory that if I kept concentrating all that time, when the ball came back into play I might get that much of an advantage over the full-back, and that's what it was.

Mike: Your coach, John Kennedy, cleared the forward half of the ground, almost literally. Everyone played up. It was Hudson versus his opponent in the square and you worked your magic from there. Whose idea was that?

Peter: It evolved. It was John Kennedy's idea but I don't think it happened overnight. I think it evolved and I think John worked out that my best method was to out-position my opponent with my body. And I did that and the more I played, the better I got at it, and I think what he looked at was that if I can be one-out with the full-back, the chances are that I can kick enough goals for us to win the game. I think that was as simple as the theory was.

Mike: Knowing what you know now and looking back retrospectively, that theory that, 'put all your eggs in the Hudson basket', did it work? I mean you only played in one Grand Final in your time at Hawthorn.

Peter: Well that's true, and I mean there would be people who would argue that you need multiple goalkickers. But the fact of the matter was that we went from a very young side in 1967, we progressively got better using this methodology or this system, and we played in the 1971 Grand Final. I went there to Hawthorn because I felt that there was enough there to potentially win a Grand Final in the not-too-distant future. From 1967, with a brand new team from the one that won the premiership in 1961, it got better and better and better, and we won it. From 1967 to 1971 is not bad, most people would settle for that.

Mike: Let's go to 1972. It's Round 1, Hawthorn's playing Melbourne at Glenferrie Oval, and about five minutes before half-time you've got eight goals to your name. You take a mark, you're pulled to the ground, you hurt your knee. What were you going to end up with that day?

Peter: Well you talk about regrets, and there is a song about it, isn't there? 'Regrets, I have a few.'

Mike: Too few to mention.

Peter: But the only regret I've got in footy is I couldn't have played that game out. I have often said to people, if I'd done both my knees at the end of that game, if I could have played it out, I would have settled for that, because I reckon I was a chance to have a crack at that record of 18. Because I had eight, marked dead in front for nine, and there was still plenty of time to go to half-time, and as a team we were so far on top it didn't matter. I knew that I could play another half of footy, and the great people that we had in that side such as Peter Crimmins and the Bob Keddies and these sort of people I would think ... I truly believe they would almost kick it backwards to me to give me a chance to break that record.

Mike: Let's fast-forward 18 months. You've used the expression you had 'publicanitis', the weight had blown up by about 10 or 12kg. You hadn't played football for 18 months and you hadn't trained for that entire time. John Kennedy rings you and says he wants you to come out of retirement. It is an amazing story—and you did. There are two rounds to go in the competition and Kennedy coaxes you back into playing, and you come over on the plane from Hobart to Melbourne and then a helicopter from Melbourne airport to Waverley.

Peter: I mean it couldn't happen today. Let's face it. It just couldn't happen. But the irony of it was, John flew to Hobart, which was a big deal in those days in itself, to see how I was and I ran the length of the ground, goalpost to goalpost, and I was blowing like a draught horse.

And he said to me ... I can remember, he went: 'Whoa, probably a bit worse than I thought. Look, train for a couple of weeks and then we will reassess it.' I trained every day for two weeks, which was my pre-season, and then the decision was made to fly over. But that was full of drama because the Saturday morning that I was to fly over, my plane wasn't going to get into Hobart to take me to Melbourne.

Mike: You had the perfect preparation though. You had only been up until midnight the night before in the pub, looking after Norman Gunston[40].

Peter: They said: 'We will fly you over on Friday'. I said: 'I can't come.' They knew I had to be back in the pub on the Saturday night. They said: 'Why?' I said: 'I've got Norman Gunston appearing at my hotel on the Friday night.' Not to be deterred, they said: 'Well we'll fly you over on the Saturday morning and we'll have a helicopter to make sure you get out to Waverley on time.' And that's what happened.

Mike: I was at that game. I saw you flown in. It was a huge story in sport in Melbourne at the time. You fly in, you're unfit, a few kilos over the scale, Hawthorn is playing Collingwood, the top team on the ladder and you kick eight goals. You had a lot of big days, but where does that sit among them?

Peter: Well it's the most freakish day in my footy career ... when I say 'freakish', I mean the things that happened that day were freakish. Like my opponent, Lee Adamson, was standing facing me and the ball came over his head and landed in my arms. And thank heavens I kicked very straight that day, and I often say: 'Whatever possessed me to do it?'

Mike: 'Huddo' I have a memory of you putting your hand up to the bench early in the game, indicating that you had hurt your bad knee. Is that true?

Peter: Yes. I tore the cartilage. When they operated, the cartilage was repaired, not taken out. So the minute the real pressure got put on it, I just tore it, and it didn't tear to the extent that I had to be carried off, it tore it to the extent that it was terribly painful.

---

40 Gunston, aka Garry McDonald, was a popular comedic act.

And after the game my knee blew up. I can remember I thought my trousers were going to split, and then once I had the cartilage done, I went on and played for years after that. One year at Hawthorn and five in Tassie.

Mike: The most fascinating part of your career to me is that you played one game in 1972, one game in 1973, and I think in the space of three years you played four games You come back to Hawthorn in 1977 and kick 110 goals. I mean that is just staggering to me that you can be out of football effectively for five years, and then come back and kick 100 goals.

Peter: I can't fathom that, what happened that day in '72. The thing I can fathom is how I did it in 1977. I trained hard. Even for me. I dropped three stone. I ran the Elwick Racecourse in Hobart. And David Parkin, who'd taken over as coach, was in a state of shock because he didn't think I was capable of that, and I didn't either, to be honest.

Mike: So that's how keen you were to get back and have another crack at it?

Peter: I was keen. Once we had made the decision to come back, I'd had a good year in 1975 and 1976 in Tassie at Glenorchy, and then when the decision was made for me to come back, I gave it everything. And at the end of that year I was totally physically and mentally exhausted, and hence the fact that I didn't come back again in 1978 and 1979. I played in Tassie.

Mike: What sort of pressure was on you? You've kicked 100 goals, almost at your prime, and you just walk away from it.

Peter: Well, the reason I could do that Mike, in a simple way, was that my livelihood, my family's livelihood was the hotel and that's where my future was going to be, and I knew that. My financial future above all was in that hotel. So when I was able to get to the end of 1977, after flying over every weekend and back we played the night games, flying in on Friday and back at the pub by Saturday.

Mike: You're famous for your conversion, and even now I know the one thing that frustrates you about the modern game is the way people kicking for goal with set-shots squander their opportunities. What is it? Is it mental or is it technique, or what?

Peter: Well I think it is technique but some people, mentally, I don't think could ever be good goalkickers. Physically I believe anybody could be, but some guys just cannot get over the fact that they have got to kick that ball through those two big posts.

But the two things that do frustrate me: one is that so many players never use the same routine twice and yet the great goalkickers, if you watch them on film, you could almost count the steps.

You could almost watch their eyes watching the ball, watching the target, watching ball. You can see it all if you really examine it. The second thing that really grates on me these days is when you see a player coming in flipping the ball round his fingers.

To me that's the equivalent of having a golf ball on a bit of elastic, swinging backward and forwards. It's hard enough to hit it off the tee, let alone when it's swinging, and that's how I see guys running and flipping the ball around their fingers.

Mike: I've heard you talk before about how good Tony Lockett might have been. He is the greatest goalkicker in the history of the game anyway, but you think he was almost unfulfilled don't you?

Peter: Well, probably to say that he was unfulfilled is a bit of an exaggeration, but the one thing that I do believe, he is the one player I have seen in my lifetime that I think was capable of kicking nine or 10 goals a game, and I think he could have done that any game that he wanted to do it in. Now obviously you can't do that. You can't kick 10 goals every game. But he was the one player that I saw that I thought genuinely had the ability to do that.

Mike: To kick 180 in a season.

Peter: Yes. And he could do it anytime he almost wanted to because he was fearful of nothing. He had the strength, he had the height, he had the silky smooth kick. You know, his skills were perfect, and the fact that he didn't do that is not a criticism. I love Jason Dunstall because I thought Dunstall got every ounce out of himself he possibly could, and he was almost a perfect full-forward because he maximised every opportunity.

Mike: One of the things that fascinates me about you is that you get so much more joy and you are so much more nervous when someone in the

family is doing something. When you are watching your son Paul play I know how involved you were emotionally, and there's great memories of you in the rooms after the 1991 Grand Final when Hawthorn won the flag, and Paul played in it.

Peter: Well, I am very proud of Paul and I am very proud of Perry, too, my daughter, but what I admire about Paul is the fact that it is a hard act to follow. Paul came along in those early days of sons following their fathers into footy, and what I liked about it was the way he approached his footy. He said: 'Well I'm not my old man, I'm not six foot three, I'm a half-forward flanker with an occasional run on the ball and that's my game.' And I thought he did pretty well.

When he won that premiership, I can tell you, heart on sleeve, that I was so thrilled and the first thing is said to him: 'They can't take that off you.' And when he made the All-Australian side I was just as thrilled and I said the same thing.

Mike: Huddo, let's go back to that 1971 Grand Final, the one that we all thought would be the record breaking shot at goal. Barry Lawrence was on the mark. You run in, your routine is as it normally is and you kick it into him.

Peter: And I reckon if ever I did kick into the man-on-the-mark before that … it probably happened once, I just didn't do that. I used to get so far back deliberately so that I didn't kick into the man-on-the-mark. At that stage of course it was all about sealing the game. I mean the game was still in the balance right up until the end, and I think from the little bit that I can remember of it, and when I look at it on the replays now that's the thing that I feel, is that I could have sealed that game by kicking that ball anywhere other than into the man-on-the-mark.

TADHG KENNELLY

Tadhg Kennelly's AFL football journey is a remarkable story of travel, tragedy and triumph. Born in Listowel in Ireland in 1981, Kennelly was the son of Tim Kennelly, a Gaelic football star who had won an All-Ireland Senior Football Championship with Kerry.

Kennelly grew up playing the Gaelic game and was seen as a future champion of the sport in his teens. But Sydney turned that career path on its head when it came calling on Kennelly's family in 1999. The Swans convinced him to make the long journey to Australia and he was added to their rookie list for the 2000 season.

Although he struggled early on with the gruelling fitness regime, Kennelly adapted his natural skills quickly to the oval ball game and impressed coaching staff to the point that he was upgraded to the senior list in 2001. He debuted for Sydney in Round 14 of that year and played in all but two of the remaining games that season, including the Swans' elimination final loss to Hawthorn.

Over the ensuing seasons, Kennelly went from strength to strength, establishing himself as one of the competition's premier defenders. His career reached its pinnacle when Sydney won the 2005 Grand Final, breaking a 72-year premiership drought. Kennelly famously danced an Irish jig on the dais after receiving his premiership medallion.

Kennelly continued to play good football until the end of the 2008 season when he announced that he was returning to Ireland to play for Kerry in the Gaelic Athletic Association. Kennelly explained that it was his ambition to win an All-Ireland title with Kerry, just as his father (who died in December 2005) had.

Remarkably, Kennelly achieved that dream in his first season at Kerry in 2009. He then returned to Australia to play two more seasons with the Swans, retiring at the end of 2011.

SEPTEMBER 19, 2012

Mike: How does a boy growing up in a pub in a little town in Kerry [in the south west of Ireland] become an Australian sporting hero?

Tadhg: It's a long journey. I suppose it started off when I was 16, 17. I played for Ireland against Australia as a young fellow, and then I got a call from Danny Frawley, who was the assistant coach at Collingwood at the time, and he came and met my father and I, and talked about coming over, and that kind of petered out a small bit. And then Ricky Barham from the Swans called up one day and said did I want to come for a trial up in Dublin at a race track. And up I went and two weeks later I got an opportunity to go to Australia on a rookie-listed contract for two years. I was never going to let it pass by. There are a lot of young fellows who grow up desperate to play a professional sport, and I was no different. You know, Gaelic football was an amateur sport.

Mike: But your father, Tim, was an icon of Gaelic football. Did you not want to emulate his feat? In fact you were to do that later on.

Tadhg: I certainly did. I idolised my father. I grew up wanting to do what he did. The only problem is my father had won five premierships.[41] So I had a lot to live up to. But, I did. I certainly wanted to do that. But also in my head, growing up you had that dream of putting on your boots, and getting paid for it as a professional, it was something that rang home an awful lot. And when I got the opportunity, I took it. It wasn't easy. But, look, I made the decision. It was a lot of banging doors and arguing with my mum, especially. You know, my dad had said: 'Do it,' in front of me. But in front of my mum he was like: 'No, no, don't do it.'

Mike: There were a lot of phone calls from Australia, too, by Ricky Barham, the Swans' recruiting manager and the former Collingwood winger. He called the pub a lot, didn't he?

---

41 Tim Kennelly is a legend of Irish football, having captained Kerry to five All-Ireland titles. Tadhg Kennelly's brother was also an All-Ireland champion.

Tadhg: Yes, Ricky used to call the pub in the afternoons and we'd be upstairs having dinner, but the bloke that would be running the pub downstairs would answer the phone. He'd run up to the bottom of the stairs and he'd shout up to my mum, Nuala, saying: 'Nuala, *the bloke from Australia who wants to take your kid away* is on the phone.' So, that's how Ricky is known as now in the Kennelly household.

> **CAREER**
> **Born:** July 1, 1981
> **Club:** *Sydney*—197 games, 30 goals
> **Honours:** AFL Rising Star nominee (2002); Six times International Rules representative (Ireland); Sydney premiership side 2005, Sydney Grand Final side 2006

Mike: So he finally won?

Tadhg: He finally got his way.

Mike: It's a massive move for you, though. I mean this town, Listowel, has got 2500 people. I presume when you were a kid a trip to Dublin was a big experiment.

Tadhg: Well, I'd never been on a plane. I'd only been to Dublin once, and that was to an all-round football final and I knew nothing about the game, Aussie Rules, I'd never seen a game. I'd heard a bit about Jimmy Stynes, but that was about it. And here I was, 18 years of age, flying around the world to play a game I knew nothing about.

Mike: The oval ball, now we'll come to some interesting stories about that, but when did you first see, or touch a Sherrin?

Tadhg: I touched it when I was 18. The clinic up in Dublin was the first time I'd held it, and it was just such a foreign object to me. It was just such a pain in the butt really for me even at that early stage. And it was in the latter part of my career as well, Mike.

Mike: So people in Australia are just amazed how quickly some of the Irish boys have adapted to this game. George Stone[42], who is still on the Swans' staff, you were his project player, were you not?

Tadhg: Yes, look, you've got to remember back then the football department and the football club wasn't there, the welfare wasn't there

---

42 George Stone, a former VFA player, has been on the coaching staff of Sydney for many years after being an assistant at Hawthorn.

in football clubs. And it was really 'Georgie' who put me under his wing and said: 'Right, I'll be your father figure out here and I'll show you everything to do with the game.' You know, back then you had the head coach and you had forwards, backs and midfielders' assistant coaches, or line coaches, and that was it. And Georgie had no obligation to do it, really, but he said he was going to take the project on, and he put me under his wing and taught me everything. And one thing that really struck home to me a lot was that if you can't kick, you won't play AFL football, and that's the same today. And that was Georgie's attitude towards AFL football and that's why I worked so hard at my kicking. It's something that I'm trying to say all around the world to people, that you're dealing with a blank canvas. You're not dealing with the young fellows coming in with bad habits. You know, he can teach a young fellow at 18 with no bad habits.

Mike: So in that period you're doing the normal training with the Swans squad, and then you and Georgie Stone are doing how many hours a week on top of that?

Tadhg: Oh, I can only imagine. Three days a week, three times a day. And I remember my hand being covered in blood from the handballing. George is very good in keeping it very basic and simple for me and understanding exactly, I suppose, what was going to go on. And understanding the football knowledge and the football terminology was extremely different for me. I couldn't understand … it's true, I couldn't understand what they were saying to me. So there was a lot of smiling and joking for six months inside there, and people nodding their heads and looking at each other inside the rooms.

Mike: Did you get close to saying: 'I'm not going to make this work, I'm going to go home'?

Tadhg: I certainly did. I vividly remember a couple of times. There's a shopping centre where I lived and I used to go past a travel agent and on it was 'return flight to London'. And numerous times, I thought: 'Let's just go in, take the ticket and go home. Just stuff it. Just go and forget about it. You can go home. You've got comfort at home. You can play Gaelic football. You'll be fine.'

Mike: So what got you through it? Was it your inner commitment to make this work, or did your parents say to stay?

Tadhg: No. I really blocked myself out of that, and I tried not to contact home an awful lot. It just made me feel really bad, and I was homesick and I'd block it out and I'd say: 'Look, I'm here on my own and I'm going to do it.' It was a lot of that fear of failure, like I said, I wanted to do it because growing up as a young fellow I could play a game of Gaelic football. I was coming up and getting better and better, and you're going to be the next big thing, the son of a legend, and I knew that. Then all of a sudden I came out here and I was bottom of the pile. No one knew anything about me. I had to learn a new game. I was at the back of the line trying to get a game in an AFL football club and, I suppose, I had to work extremely hard to get myself back up the ladder and. That was that fear of failure of not going back to my small country town where people would be saying to me for the rest of my life: 'Well, you couldn't make it in Australia.' And that's what drove me an awful lot to tell you the truth.

Mike: Tell me about the ball and your relationship with this weird and wonderful object.

Tadhg: I just remember having the ball in my hands constantly, like flat out. I used to take it everywhere. I use to walk on the street and the shopping centres and just at home in front of the TV. But I remember referring to it at one stage, and I'd go for it here, and I'd go for it there, and I referred to it as a 'fucking rabbit'.

Mike: So the Swans have rookie-listed you, the first to win the Ron Barassi scholarship, funded by Basil Sellers. What was that worth, Tadhg, and how did that influence you to travel halfway across the world?

Tadhg: There was big money involved back then, Mike, it was $30,000 a year for two years. At the time, look, I was very green. It was such a rude awakening after six weeks. You know, I was getting physically and mentally challenged for the first time in my life, in a game that I knew absolutely nothing about. My body was like a twig. I was 70kg, six-foot [180cm] tall, there was just nothing of me. You could break me in a minute. But I was lucky that George was there and really took me under his wing. I truly believe if George wasn't there, I would have gone back home.

Mike: In that period, 2002 to 2006, you played in two Grand Finals; win a premiership; and averaged 23 games a year. Now it is a staggering story for someone to make such an impression.

Tadhg: Yes, I had a really good run. Obviously I had a fantastic coach in Paul Roos and a great coaching staff, but I think also what 'Roosy' gave me was a belief in what I was good at and that I could do it and play the game. He backed me into being an aggressive, free-flowing, attacking-style half-back.

Mike: One of the amazing things about your story is that Roosy and the Swans had sufficient faith in you, a kid from Ireland, to actually kick in from full-back.

Tadhg: I draw it back to George Stone saying in the early days that if you can't kick an AFL football, you're not going to play a game. And those words rang home with me every day, and I learnt to kick that ball. And I kicked it, kicked it to the death, really.

Mike: This is a hazy memory, but were you not involved in a racial vilification issue, as the victim?

Tadhg: Yes, I was. Look, it's a hot topic at the moment, and it's something you can't excuse footballers for saying it, because we're so well educated that you just shouldn't say it. I don't care what's going on emotionally, in the heat of the moment, you just can't say it. And you've got to understand that, and something that you might think doesn't affect your feelings can affect the person you're saying it to. And that's something you've got to think about and in a lot of things in life, not just racial vilification, but other things in life as well.

Mike: But it's interesting from you because historically it's been a colour issue in Australian sport, hasn't it? I mean it's been people calling someone a black so-and-so. In your case, obviously the colour is not an issue. What was said to you?

Tadhg: Well, you could be anything from an Irish 'c', or you can be anything, go back to Ireland you… whatever, you know what I mean. So, that's my heritage, and I'm an indigenous Irish man and I'm very, very proud of that. And you're coming out to a game where I think some people forget about the Irish people and the footballers that are here.

They fit in obviously with the Australian culture and the Australian way of life, but, also you know what? Hang on a second. They're still Irishmen at the end of the day, and that's part of who they are and what their make-up is.

Mike: On 2005 Grand Final day, I mean it must be an enormous thrill for you? You're this far away from home, you played in a premiership team—your club's first premiership in more than 70 years. Two things I remember: you kicked a really important goal in a low scoring game late, and the Irish jig on the platform when you got your medal.

Tadhg: It was an unbelievable week. I'd never really experienced anything like it, you know. Here I was playing in a Grand Final. My parents were coming out, half of Ireland were coming out. And I do remember my father telling me to 'soak up the whole thing and not let it pass you by, and enjoy the week and enjoy the game'. And that experience of playing in the Grand Final, the parade and everything that goes with it, it's just a moment that you want to tell footballers to remember and enjoy and not let it pass you by. Football clubs try and protect players, which is okay, but some players want to soak that up and enjoy the whole occasion and I certainly was one of them.

Mike: No nerves?

Tadhg: No, very little. I was quite surprised with it. I do get nervous before games, but before the '05 Grand Final I was quite relaxed and I remember looking up into the crowd and I saw my parents were sitting there with an Irish flag, and I just felt quite relaxed about it.

Mike: 2006, I thought, was your better Grand Final. I thought you were playing an outstanding game in that return match against West Coast. Do you share that view?

Tadhg: Yes, I think so. It's funny, you try and block out memories of the game and stuff and you try and block out that game itself, but I definitely played a better game in the 2006 Grand Final. And, look, we nearly got there. But that game, it was a pivotal moment in the Swans' culture as well, I think. We were down four or five goals and there was a lot of finger-pointing and there was a lot of blokes just being brutally honest with each other. And I won't forget the moment because from that moment on, we really came out of our shells and we nearly got there. But that, at half-time, blokes being able to voice their opinion in a Grand Final was enormous and to be able to come out and suck that out ourselves, it's great. We've got coaches and high-calibre coaches but that just showed, I suppose, a maturity of that group at that time.

Mike: Given that you'd won one and given that enormous weight that's lifted off the shoulders of the entire footy club, did that burn deeply, the 2006 loss?

Tadhg: Yes, it did. You know, a lot of people say, 'Well, you won one that you could have lost easily', but it does. I often still think how good it would have been to win two premierships. To a certain degree it helps that you've won one, yes, but it's difficult to deal with it. You've lost a Grand Final. It's not something that you're going to get to every day of the week.

Mike: Talking about moments, let's go back to 2005, the final 60 seconds. You were central, you played a pivotal role in that last minute. Tell us about it.

Tadhg: Yes, a long ball actually came in and it's gone over the top and Mark Nicoski was running on to it, and I just found an extra bit and I've got there and I've rushed the ball through that fucking rabbit. I didn't know which way it was going to go, but it bounced up perfectly for me and it just fell into my lap and I've rushed it through. And I remember rushing it through going: 'We've won it. I got the ball and I kicked it to Leo Barry into the pocket and Leo actually had a chance to kick the ball to Adam Goodes, a little short kick, but didn't. He went long and he kicked it to Darren Jolly, but 'Jolls' got whopped underneath the ball and Dean Cox got it and he's turned around and kicked it long. I actually saw Ashley Sampi there, and all in my head was Ashley Sampi had won 'mark of the year', and I could see him. 'Oh, no, here we go, he's going to win the flag for West Coast.' So I've just bee-lined for him and I just saw him and I've just held on to him for dear life. I held on to his badge and Leo's come over the top and taken a great, great mark.

Mike: You could have been penalised...

Tadhg: I should have been, yes. I should have been. It was a definite free kick.

Mike: You had a handful of jumper.

Tadhg: I had a handful of jumper and I actually met Ashley Sampi after that game and the players in a Grand Final, they get a Grand Final badge. So with Grand Final 2005 I actually had ripped it off his jumper at the time, and he told me that.

You'd be a brave, brave umpire to make that call. Leo's taken a mark and actually fell on top of me. I didn't know who marked it and I've kind of turned around and Leo's got the ball and then the siren's gone. I've just jumped on his back and I said: 'Oh, Leo, I love you, I love you.'

I kissed him in the forehead and we were just hugging each other and loving it. Just that raw emotion of 'we'd finally done it' was unbelievable. And you could feel that emotion all over the place. It wasn't just the 22 that had played. There was fierce emotion in that win.

Mike: It's actually the most memorable sporting moment for me. Just given the history that you weren't acquainted with because it was South Melbourne, but just the emotion, the outpouring of emotion that day.

Tadhg: When I got to the club it was kind of a bit soulless, and in early 2000s we understood, and we went back to where we'd come from. And we went back to the history and understanding South Melbourne and the Bloods culture and we ended up calling ourselves 'The Bloods'. Now any player that comes into the club is given an induction of where the Swans have come from, the hard stories of relocating to Sydney. Everything that South Melbourne went through to become the Swans and it gives you more pride in what you're wearing and understanding that it's not just a jumper. There's people before you that have worn it, and it's understanding the actual feeling of what you're playing for.

Mike: There's a lot of mystique attached to this Bloods culture. In a sense, describe it for us.

Tadhg: Well, there's nothing magical about it. When you come to the football club we've got a set of behaviours and we've got a blueprint of how to play AFL football. And if you come into the club and you follow this blueprint, you'll make your debut for the Swans. It's as simple as that. And that's the Bloods culture.

Mike: In December 2005, you're probably still celebrating the premiership win. You had a fateful call in the middle of the night in Sydney, from home.

Tadhg: I'll never forget the call. My brother called me and I just knew, he didn't have to say anything.

Mike: Your brother's rung you and told you that your father's died.

Tadhg: My father's just died. And for the first time ever I realised how far Australia was away from Ireland. Up to then I always thought: 'Well, it's a day trip. It's not that bad.' But I wanted to get back so bad. I couldn't get home. And it's funny, when difficult things happen in your life, I just wanted to get to the football field. All I wanted to do is block it out. And I was very good at being able to do that when things were difficult in my life, and that's what I wanted to do. I heard the news; I wanted to go to the football field.

Mike: Which football field?

Tadhg: Back home in Ireland. I just wanted to kick the ball…

Mike: By yourself?

Tadhg: By myself. And forget about what happened. And, look, I felt an awful lot of hatred towards Australia following that.

Mike: What do you mean?

Tadhg: I'd felt that Australia had taken away six, seven years of getting to know my father. I broke up with my girlfriend. I almost became a little bit of a deviant, I just hated Australia, that as an 18-year-old I was taken away from my father and I missed six years of his life, where you really get to know the stories about your father over a pint. And I had a lot of stuff going on that year in 2006 to deal with.

Mike: But it was your choice, though, to come to Australia, wasn't it?

Tadhg: Oh, it certainly was my choice. But trying to rationalise that and grieving the loss of a father was extremely difficult to do.

Mike: So was it out of the blue? Your father, Tim, was 51, wasn't he? And you're 24, marooned in this foreign country.

Tadhg: That's probably the saddest thing of the lot… 2006 will never be a great year. I mean it's the saddest year for me—I can feel my own heart ticking now just talking about it—but it's life, I suppose. For the first time ever in my life I had to deal with something that was tragic and so difficult to deal with and it made me grow up very, very quickly. The biggest thing that happened was when I arrived in Shannon airport, my father always picked me up, and he's not there. I got to the door and I was like: 'I don't want to go in.' I knew what was inside the door and it wasn't my father that was alive. So it was very difficult and I got there and we hugged; my brother and my sister and my mum, and we just said, 'let's stick together', and that's what we've done since.

Mike: You talked about the pain and the anger, did it prompt you to say: 'That's it in Australia. I'm going to go home.'
Tadhg: I remember going to the airport coming back, and I rang the club and I said: 'I can't do it.' So they changed my flight. I rang them again and said: 'I can't do it.' I went twice to go to the airport and I couldn't do it. I couldn't leave my mother. That was the hardest part, was leaving my mum and I just couldn't do it. And, eventually they sent over my partner, Nicole.

The Swans at the time were playing the Kangaroos in 2006 in Los Angeles in the middle of January. So I flew to LA and met the team, which actually helped, because we're brothers. It was my mother who really pushed me out the door, to tell you the truth. She said: 'Just go. You've got to go. You've got to go.' I think she could see that I wasn't finished with Australia and what I was doing. I'm sure if she was selfish she would have said: 'Stay by my side.' Which she didn't.

Mike: Are you an Irishman living in Australia, or are you an Australian who used to live in Ireland?
Tadhg: I call myself an Irish-Australian. Look, I was in Ireland for 18 years; I've been in Australia 13 years. I've been in Australia nearly half my life already, so I'm very much an Irish-Australian. I very much understand what the game has given me, and what the Australian people have meant to me and how good they've been to me.

Mike: You suffered injuries, shoulder injuries, knee injuries, an assortment of other problems. I remember one game watching you and it looked like Tutankhamen had run on to the ground. But then some amazing

sights followed. I mean you relocated your own dislocated kneecap in one game. You put your own dislocated shoulder back.

Tadhg: Look, I had a great run up until then, I really did. I dislocated my right knee in a game and it was a moment that I kind of went, I thought it would be okay, and two weeks later, I'd absolutely destroyed my medial ligament, grade three. I should have missed two months. But two weeks later the Swans had lost four games in a row and I trained on the ground without a medial. And certainly it was a difficult time. Looking back, those injuries finished me.

Mike: Can you divide your sporting loves, Gaelic football and Australian football?

Tadhg: I don't think so.

Mike: You went home in 2009?

Tadhg: I think 2007 and '08, with the injuries that I had, it cemented in my head that if I didn't go back then, I'm not going to be able to contribute to Kerry football and try and win our round. And that sped up the process. And I remember at the time I decided, and Roosy was actually on holidays at the time, and I'd come back to the club and I called him. He was away, and I waited a few more weeks to sit down face-to-face and talk to him about it. I knew myself I was done, but it was a difficult thing to do, to back away from the club.

I had a year left on my contract, and I copped a bit of negative gossip or criticism about leaving the club at that time, but I just knew I had to do it, no matter what anyone said to me.

Mike: That was because of your father?

Tadhg: Yes, it was plain and simple. I grew up idolising my old man and I wanted to do what he did, and it was trying to win an All-Ireland medal. It was an extremely difficult thing to do. It was probably the worst financial decision I ever made in my life.

Mike: Well, this is the All-Ireland final at Croke Park, for Kerry?

Tadhg: In front of 85,000 people and not one person getting paid for it. Look now, I suppose, I can appreciate what I've done, looking back on it. But at the time, you know, I was just ... I used to get an obsession for what

I wanted to do. If I wanted to do something, I'd get it and I'd do anything to get it. Almost in a bad way, if you know what I mean? I was obsessed with getting it. And at that final, I copped a bit of criticism from people back home saying I hit someone to start with.

Mike: You did.

Tadhg: Yes, I hit someone at the start of the game, but I was so emotionally charged. I was 28 years of age. I thought I'd have four or five All-Ireland medals in my arse pocket by then. You know, I didn't. We'd played Cork twice that year and they physically dominated us, and I came into the game saying: 'Well, I'm going to be physically hard for the first 10 minutes of the game.' But I got an opportunity in the first 10 seconds of the game. The ball was thrown in and I basically came in off the line. Looking back on it, I was very, very lucky to stay on the park. But I certainly didn't go into the game saying I'm going to intentionally hurt Nicholas Murphy, or intentionally hurt someone. You just can't plan that kind of stuff.

Mike: So you could have been out of the game for the duration?

Tadhg: I could have been sent off. Red card. That's what happens at home.

Mike: I want to ask you about the 2011 AFL Grand Final luncheon. You were the keynote speaker, and Brett Kirk had been there the year before. You spoke. My partner had said that she was crying and so many others in the room were the same. Your words were: 'It's the game of Aussie Rules that has really defined me as a person. It's made me who I am today. It's taught me to respect elders. It's taught me to respect women. It's taught me to always be honest and true to myself. Always display my passion and love. And most importantly it's taught me to be a human being, with the utmost respect for other human beings. Football, I owe you my life, as you've given me mine.'

Tadhg: For me, it was an occasion to thank a lot of people and thank the game itself, and to remember my father and to remember everything that I had been. It was like I was wrapping up my book and my story as an AFL footballer in 20 minutes.

Mike: I saw footage of that. You looked down at the prime minister, Julia Gillard, at one point. You had a message for her, didn't you? This is what you said: 'It's not about the individual, it is all about the club, and we're all just passing through and no one's ever going to be there forever. It's a bit of a 'no-dickhead policy'[43] and, I suppose, you could probably bring it to parliament maybe, Julia. It might work all right.'

Mike: You would have won that, they would have liked that.

Tadhg: It worked well. Look, they loved it. The opposition people, they were in the room and they loved that.

Mike: You're working with the AFL now. In what capacity, and does that link into sort of any ambitions to coach at an AFL club?

Tadhg: Yes, it's great. Look, I'm an international footballer. I'm from Ireland and I've been doing a lot of work with international recruiting. I was in America, I was in Europe you know, we've been to New Zealand, we've been to China trying to recruit players from all over the world. And basically my job is to try and get international players. I'm coaching the New South Wales under 16s and 18s, and I'm involved in the AIS[44] squad, which is something that's tickled me a bit. I understood the game very early when I came out here. I love watching football. That's the line I'm going. Because I like the challenge of it and it got me going a bit. It got the adrenaline going.

Mike: Why was Roosy such a good coach?

Tadhg: Roosy was a great coach because he understood people and he was very good at getting the best out of individuals and footballers, and he understood every footballer that was on the list. Now he didn't get enough credit for being a tactically great coach. He changed the game of AFL football by becoming a one-on-one team. The game had gone back to flooding. And Roosy's gone: 'Well, hang on a second. When we turn the ball over we're getting it back as quick as you can. So you get a man.'

---

43 The Swans were said to have a 'no-dickhead policy' in the Paul Roos era. In reality, it was merely one of the phrases scrawled on a wall during a team meeting. But it came to symbolise the way the club operated.

44 AIS: Australian Institute of Sport.

Mike: He won't coach in 2013, but I've got a growing suspicion that he will coach in 2014. Do you share that view, and would you like to be part of his team?

Tadhg: Who wouldn't want to be part of Paul Roos team? Look, he's a fantastic coach and been a fantastic friend of mine. I think he'll coach again, but who knows. He's a very, very competitive person.

BRETT KIRK

Brett Kirk is the antithesis of the stereotypical profile of an AFL footballer. Relatively small in stature and quietly spoken, Kirk's footballing journey reflects the qualities of a man who repudiates the 'brainless bulky boofhead' mould. Recruited by Sydney from North Albury, Kirk was promoted from the Swans' rookie list before the 1999 season but had little impact in his first two seasons.

He gained a place in 2001 as a regular midfielder and over the next few seasons he established himself as one of the competition's pre-eminent taggers. A change of coach from Rodney Eade to Paul Roos in late 2002 appeared to act as a catalyst for Kirk to take his game to another level. He had a stellar season in 2004, polling 20 votes in the Brownlow Medal to finish equal fourth (with the Bulldogs' Scott West) behind winner Chris Judd.

In 2005, when captain Stuart Maxfield was forced into early retirement through injury, Kirk stepped up to take a leadership role. With that year's semi-final against Geelong in the balance at three-quarter time, he famously took aside Nick Davis, whose efforts to that point had been considered less than acceptable, and told him that he owed the Swans a huge last quarter. An inspired Davis kicked four final-term goals to lift the Swans to a three-point win. Sydney went on to win the 2005 flag, and Kirk took out the Swans' best-and-fairest award in that season. He won a second best-and-fairest award in 2007.

He was rewarded with the co-captaincy in 2006, a post he held until his retirement after the 2010 season. Kirk's on-field persona was one of a scrupulously fair but tough and uncompromising player, steely of mind, and willing to put his body on the line in every contest.

Kirk's 241-game career will go down as one of the finest in the history of the red and white.

AUGUST 31, 2009

Mike: You've been the most reliable team in the comp, I'd say, for six or seven years. Is that good luck, good management, or a combination of both?
Brett: I think it's a combination. I don't think you can put it down to one thing. The greatest thing a footy club has is the people and what they bring in their character. And I think what we're able to instil in our players— from our coach, from our footy manager, from everyone down—that we're on the same page. There has been a united strength, really committed, for a period of time.

Mike: It's been an interesting journey for you. It started way back in 1996 when you were a rookie from Albury, but it didn't go all that swimmingly at the start, did it?
Brett: No. I remember growing up as a kid back in Albury at about 10, telling my Nan that I was going to play AFL football before she died. So I went along, didn't have a huge amount of talent, but yeah, tried my guts out. In '96 I was going to uni and flying into Sydney to play; finished a year there and nothing came about. And then I went back and really thought about my footy, how I needed to change in terms of working on weaknesses. Got another crack at it in '98, got on the rookie list, and then sort of slowly worked my way forward.

But yeah, it's been a really windy road; lots of roadblocks, lots of challenges. But I've really never in my mind accepted failure; it was always, okay, there's the challenge, there's defeat, but I was always going, 'Okay, well how do I work around this?' I look at other people in life—it's what they have inside and how they get through challenges that brings them out the other side. And there was no point in my mind ever that I never thought I was going to make AFL.

Mike: Well, blokes from your area—Paul Kelly's one—who have come from the country and gone to Sydney and been almost overwhelmed by the big city. Did that ever affect you?

Brett: Yeah, it did. I actually went through four years of full-time university before I came to stay in Sydney. I'd developed a way of life for myself and I was a bit out there at uni. I got tagged the nickname 'Hippy' when I first came, because at that point I didn't really care what people thought of me and the way I dressed. I found it a little bit hard to fit in early on; and being right on the fringe, you don't know where you sit. I did lose a bit of direction. There's no doubt my parents really, really helped me through it, and I owe a lot to them.

Mike: [St Kilda player] Lenny Hayes must dread playing on you because your record on him is so good. When you come up with people who have got like qualities, and some would say have more natural talent, how do you prevail?

CAREER
Born: October 25, 1976
Club: *Sydney* 1999-2010—241 games, 96 goals.
Honours: Sydney's best and fairest 2005, 2007; All-Australian 2004; International Rules series 2004, 2005; premiership side 2005; captain 2006-2010; AFLPA Robert Rose Award (League's most courageous player) 2006; AFLPA Madden Medal (Community Spirit Award) 2010; AFLPA Best Captain award 2010

Brett: I think it's about never accepting defeat. I know there's going to be games where a player might get a hold of me for a five-minute period or a 10-minute but I know that the longer the game goes, I'm going to wear you down. It might come down to the last one minute of the game, but I know that with my strength of mind, I'm going to get there, I'm going to get you in the end.

Mike: I can believe that. Was that born in you?

Brett: I think my parents instilled all the core values in me and what I stand for. Obviously I'll learn and develop my own way. But my dad lost his hand in a farming accident at the age of four. Growing up, he was my hero and still is my hero. I used to love watching him go and play footy. And I just looked at how hard and resilient he is and his work ethic. The greatest quality that my dad has, and that's something that's been bred in me, is that persistence, that never-give-up attitude.

And my mum's given me the hard-as-nails approach, I guess. She was the one who was on the phone when I was in Sydney thinking, 'Can I do it? Can't I do it?' She was the one that would say, 'You show those bastards'. And my dad would get on the phone and he'd choke up because he's quite an emotional character. He would struggle to find the words, where Mum was, 'Here's my shoulder, cry on it, but you bloody show them.'

Mike: Did you grow up in a religious household?
Brett: No, not at all. Mum and Dad sent my brother and I to Sunday School a couple of times. But religion was never really something that featured very heavily in our lives.

It probably wasn't until I lost one of my great mates from back home, back in the end of 2002—that's when I really started to look for meaning in life—why am I here, why do good people die? I was about 17 or 18, starting senior footy in the Ovens and Murray, and he had just come to that club as a 32-year-old at the end of his career, and he took me under his wing. He was like a mentor, a teacher, a friend, brother, father, whatever it was. He was a guy who really gave something to me then, and we became great mates. He died at the end of 2002. And death was not something we spoke about in our family, it was quite taboo, so I really struggled with it. So I started to read more about different things, and Buddhism sort of found me. It was sort of a way of life; it was like a path of transformation from the inside out.

Mike: I know you met the Dalai Lama. It must've been a huge moment in your life. Tell us about what happened then.
Brett: Yeah, the Dalai Lama came out to Australia, and just out of the blue someone rang me and said, 'Would you like to MC the event, to be on stage with the Dalai Lama?" I was like, 'Why me?' And I said, 'For sure, I'd love to.'

So I presented him with the Swans guernsey, which he had over his shoulder, draped over his shoulder for his whole hour speech. And I was lucky enough that he wanted me to stay with him up on stage.

He radiated such a warmth and an energy that it looked like he was glowing, and I actually felt like I was glowing up on stage with him. And something that really stands out to me from that day was, at the end of his speech, they asked me whether I wanted to ask any questions to him. And I asked him, 'What's the greatest thing I can give my children?' And he leant across and grabbed my hand and said, 'The greatest thing you can give your children is affection'. And talked about his childhood and getting taken away from his mother. And yeah, it was just a wonderful day. It really stands out for me.

Mike: The meditation—how often do you do it, and what do you get out of it?
Brett: I have a morning ritual that I go through. It's a routine, and I think it's really important that people have routines in their life. And I get up early in the morning, go down to my local baths, do some yoga, some meditation, some Buddhist chants, affirmations about the type of person I want to be, the footballer, the father, the husband; what I'm grateful for in life, how I want to live it; and then jump in the ocean.

It's how I start every day. I feel it not only gets me ready for the day, but it sets me up to really wanting to get the best out of myself in everything I do. I find it really helps.

Mike: Tell me about your dad. I mean, he's obviously a key figure in your life and an inspiration to you. Tell us about your dad as a footballer.
Brett: He started off in the Ovens and Murray League, and then North Albury, which was where I played all my junior and senior footy before I came to the AFL. And then at a pretty early age, he had some differences with his coaches, and he ended up moving out to the Junior League and played for the Burrumbuttock Swans. And that's where I spent a lot of my younger days, going to the footy, climbing trees, hanging out at a pub on the pool tables afterwards. I loved that time.

Things I remember from my dad and that people tell me, he played on a half-back flank, he was tough as nails; used to spoil the ball with his right hand, and give you one in the back of the ear with his left stump. And I think he won something like seven runners-up in best and fairests out there. I really admire him.

Mike: Let's talk about Barry Hall and his exit from the Swans[45]. It seemed to pain you somewhat. Were you pretty close to 'Hally'?

---

45 Barry Hall was Sydney's captain when the club won the 2006 premiership. The latter part of his time at Sydney was marred by breaches of discipline on-field, most notably his suspension in 2008 for striking West Coast's Brent Staker. In 2009 he was again suspended for striking, and was pressured by Sydney's coaching staff to leave the club. He called a press conference in July 2009 announced he would be leaving Sydney. He moved to the Western Bulldogs, where he played 39 games in seasons 2010-11.

Brett: Yeah, I am. In my footy life, it's been the toughest thing I've ever had to deal with. When it all happened, I had to give Barry some tough love, I guess. While I wanted to give him a cuddle and say, 'Mate, everything's going to be all right', we really needed to get him to stand up and take responsibility. And I think the courage he was able to show to be able to do that, to stand up and say, 'Yeah, I've done the wrong thing, I need to do something about it,' is going to hold him in good stead for the rest of his life. And there's no doubt, seeing him afterwards, that he has got some real inner peace about him, which is good. I didn't think it was going to affect me as much as it probably did. I think it really did hurt me emotionally. It sort of ... it crushed me a bit.

Mike: I know this is a taboo for you guys, but are you able to tell ... take us into the the Bloods Syndrome?
Brett: I'm not going to tell you that.

Mike: I asked nicely, didn't I?
Brett: I guess it was when Paul [Roos] took over[46], we felt that we'd probably lost a bit of that [old South Melbourne culture], coming from where we've come from, and actually learning about our history. So we wanted to get back in touch with that, because I'm a big believer that you shouldn't forget where you've come from.

We went back into history, looked at where we'd come from and the struggles that the club had been through at South Melbourne, and the players who went before us. We wanted to really get in tune with that. We wanted to teach our new players coming into the system that it hasn't always been rosy; we haven't always had these facilities. There are people who have really struggled to get where we are. It's something we really held dear— some traits that the Bloods of old had that we wanted to instil in our players. It was about standing for something.

---

46 Paul Roos played 87 games for Sydney (1995-98), after 13 seasons (269 games) with Fitzroy. He became an assistant coach to Rodney Eade, before taking the interim coaching job after Round 12, 2002. He was appointed senior coach after the Swans won six of the 10 games under Roos' leadership, finishing the season with four straight victories.

And I think the greatest thing for me was the Hall of Fame for the Swans, when you hear Peter Bedford and Bobby Skilton[47] get up on stage and say how proud they are of their footy club, and how much respect we have now, and for us to really pay homage to the players who have gone before us.

Mike: Three-quarter time, Grand Final day, 2005. You've grabbed the players at the last change, and spoke to them. It looked inspirational from where I sat. What did you say to them?

Brett: I don't know exactly the words. But I'm really passionate. I guess at that point we needed to think about where we'd come from and what we needed to do. And I guess you really want to empower the players around you, and I think that's what a really good leader does. I was just trying to do that.

Mike: Was that off your own bat, or did Roosey say he wanted you to talk to them?

Brett: No. It's just something that I feel. I lead from my heart. And I think your heart takes a risk, your heart is the gambler. Your mind can be a bit more cunning; you can actually think about things and maybe work things your own way, because you can get controlled by your ego. But my heart's really pure, and that's the way I live my life, that's the way I play my footy, and that's the way I want to lead the footy club.

Mike: I want to take you back to immediately after the Grand Final, that premiership win in 2005. You would have known what it meant to the South Melbourne people here and how important it was commercially in Sydney. What are your memories of that night? Siren time and then the hours that followed?

Brett: When the siren goes, it's not all about the exhilaration of winning. I think there's obviously a bit of relief there as well. Obviously it felt really good. I think I fell to the ground after Leo [Barry] had taken the mark, and I was about 20 metres away. Adam Goodes was right next to me; he picked

---

47 Peter Bedford (186 games for South Melbourne [1968-78]) won the 1970 Brownlow Medal; Bob Skilton (237 games for South Melbourne [1956-71]) won the Brownlow Medal in 1959, 1963 and 1968. On July 18, 2009, 23 players—including three Legends were inducted in the Sydney Swans Hall Of Fame, at a function entitled *It's in the Blood*. Skilton, Bob Pratt and Paul Kelly were named Legends. Bedford was elevated to Legend status in 2011.

me up, we embraced. You put in so much hard work with each other. And I fiercely cared about—still care about those guys. And to be able to actually get through it and to win something like that is just the ultimate in footy.

But I think the greatest thing for me was then going into the rooms after the game, where you're surrounded by your family. But then we go into the meeting room, and you've just got the players in there and the coach, and a couple of people who had been really instrumental in us getting there. And to actually just savour that moment. It's one of those moments where you want to get a bottle and just put it in and screw the top on, and just put it on the mantelpiece, and occasionally just take a swig of it. There's a real sense of happiness and contentment, it was just awesome. I don't think I had too many beers for a while because I just felt like I was floating. And then to go over to Punt Road and just to see the people's faces, and then back to South Melbourne the next day.

I remember a young kid of 11 or 12 coming up to me and he said, 'Mate, I've been waiting 72 years for that'. Then you look at some of the older people standing there waiting for us, who have been around that long, just waiting for the club to be successful again, it was such a great feeling. And then to go down George Street [Sydney], with thousands upon thousands of people in the street. It was just something that just blew me away.

Mike: You've got four kids. What are you like as a father?
Brett: I try to be the best father I can be. Kids teach you so much. I think we try to teach kids, but we can learn so much from our children. It's the greatest thing I'll ever do in my life—to be a father and to help guide them. Not to actually push them anywhere or to teach them, just to guide them along their path. They need to fall over, find their way. Kids are just so in the moment; and that's how I want to try to live my life, to be right in that moment.

Mike: So that consumes you; whatever your task at that moment is, you can be totally absorbed by that.
Brett: Yeah. Well one thing that I really try to have as a person and as a footballer is to have a really concentrated mind. I think meditation really gives me a focus, it gives me some clarity in my own head, it gives me some calm, so I'm not controlled by other things or thoughts.

Obviously things do come up, and sometimes I do get troubled by things; you get that monkey mind sometimes, where you get a thought and it just keeps jumping across in your head.

So it's actually trying to have some still in your mind so you can actually have total focus on what you're doing.

Mike: Brett, Micky O'Loughlin's[48] contribution to the Sydney Football Club, tell us about it.

Brett: He'll go down as one of the greatest players who ever played at our footy club. And the thing for me is, not only is he a great player, he'll be one of the greatest people I'll ever meet in my life. He'll be one of my most loyal friends. I know if I'm ever down on my luck or struggling, that Mick would always be there to help pick you up. He just has an aura about him that people feed off; he's always smiling. As a player, he's able to do absolutely everything. He can turn a game on his own boot. I just admire him. But ... then also to see him now as a father with his kids, with my kids, to see him, how he interacts with people. He just gives so much of himself. I love him. I tell him he's my brother from another mother.

Mike: Life after footy—have you addressed it yet?

Brett: Not really. As we talked about before, I'm someone who's really in the moment and about getting the best out of myself. And I don't want to be putting anything in place where it might take my mental focus off my footy. There's no doubt I'll have to think of it. I've got a big family, so I need to support them. Coaching is something that I've thought about. I really like communicating and getting the best out of individuals, but I know it's a big emotional and mental investment, especially on your family. My family's going to be the biggest thing, I don't want to miss anything of their lives, in their early part of their lives, because it's really when they develop.

---

48 Michael O'Loughlin played 303 games for Sydney (1995-2009), and was a member of the 2005 premiership team. He was inducted into the Sydney Swans Hall Of Fame in 2011.

ALASTAIR LYNCH

A 286-game career spanning 16 seasons with the Lions, the Bears and then the Lions again is testament to the determination and skills of Tasmanian Football Hall of Fame Legend Alastair Lynch. From Wynyard in Tasmania, Lynch came to Fitzroy in 1988 as an athletic key-position player. He kicked two goals on debut against Footscray in Round 3, 1988, and steadily forged his way forward.

Lynch spent his early years mainly in key defensive posts but a permanent move to the forward line in 1993 brought immediate success, with Lynch kicking 68 goals to top the Lions' goalkicking in that season.

After that successful season Lynch was offered an unprecedented 10-year contract with the Brisbane Bears, which he accepted. In 1994 he had an injury-interrupted season that saw him play just 13 games. The following season he played only a solitary game as he suffered a debilitating bout of Chronic Fatigue Syndrome.

Lynch learned to manage his illness and was able to return to regular football in 1996. He was appointed co-captain (with Michael Voss) in 1997 and between then and 1999 he was used as both a key forward and defender. In 2000, coach Leigh Matthews made the decision to play Lynch as a virtually permanent full-forward. It was a move that paid handsome dividends as Lynch became a potent focal point during Brisbane's most successful era.

Having made the finals in 1999 and 2000, Brisbane dominated the competition from 2001 to 2003, winning three successive flags. In each of the Lions' three winning Grand Finals, Lynch was named in their best players, kicking two goals in the 2001 decider and four goals in both 2002 and 2003.

Lynch struggled with injury in 2004 and retired after the Lions' Grand Final loss to Port Adelaide. He went on to forge a successful career in the media and as a player manager.

AUGUST 8, 2011

Mike: It's been an eventful journey for a boy from Wynyard, via Hobart, taken at number 50 in the 1986 draft.

Alastair: Yeah, it has been; it went extremely quickly, and in some ways with the ups and downs, I suppose it seemed to go for a fair while.

Mike: Your last year in Hobart you played for the Hobart Football Club in the Tasmanian Football League and your coach was the great Peter Hudson. What did you learn from Hudson?

Alastair: 'Huddo' was fantastic for me. I made the move from Wynyard down to Hobart as a bit of a change. I wasn't a great footy talent at the time and they knew 'Huddo' so I gave him a call. I worked at his pub and played footy with him and he just had that vested interest in me, so he put a lot of time into me. And I remember on numerous occasions sitting up at the TCA ground and I'd be the last one on the track, and 'Huddo' would be pounding the ball at me or I'd have to pick it up off the deck 10 times or 100 times before I'd go in.

Mike: That was the period in your life though when you were harbouring ambitions about being a Test cricketer wasn't there, a tearaway fast bowler?

Alastair: Yes, I don't know about Test cricketer, but certainly, I wanted to play first-class cricket and I was playing first-grade cricket up on the coast. I suppose the choice back then was made for you really. Once I was drafted, there was no consideration to pursue cricket at all but, for a few years, I used to just run in, try to bowl short and fast.

Mike: In 1988, your first year under David Parkin's coaching at Fitzroy, you played 18 games. Did you earn all of those?

Alastair: Probably not. I think I started in the reserves, and didn't get off to a good start because I was the only guy at our house who was playing reserves that day, and so I drove to Princes Park and got lost. I got to the game 45 minutes after I was supposed to, and the boys were about to run out on the ground. So I remember my reserves coach, Garry Wilson, told me in no uncertain terms that I was starting on the bench, so the first few games were in the reserves. I played a few at a reasonable level early and then it's fair to say I had a bit of a patch where I wasn't getting a lot of the ball.

> **CAREER**
> **Born:** June 19, 1968
> **Clubs:** *Fitzroy*—120 games, 173 goals; *Brisbane*—186 games, 460 goals
> **Honours:** Tasmanian Team of the Century; All-Australian 1993; Brisbane premiership side 2001, 2002, 2003; Brisbane captain 1997-2000; Fitzroy leading goalkicker 1993; Brisbane leading goalkicker 2000-03

Mike: I know you were athletic. You were pretty thin and you were playing half-forward early on?
Alastair: Yes, early I started at half-forward, the first couple of games in the reserves, I think, I was at centre half-forward, but yes.

Mike: I remember the famous stories out of Brisbane had you at 100kgs-plus and bench-pressing 155kgs. What was your weight when you arrived on the mainland?
Alastair: I don't think I was 90kgs, probably 89 or 88kgs I would've thought. I was probably more of an athlete than a footy talent and I could run pretty well, I was reasonably strong, and I always felt I just needed to get quicker and stronger and work pretty hard at that. I suppose to finish my career at full-forward and at a much heavier weight was mainly due to about eight years of restricted training as far as the aerobic capacity.

Mike: So was the weight natural, or was it out of the gym?
Alastair: I'm one of those guys that loses weight if I stop in the gym so it's something I worked extremely hard at.

Mike: That would have been pretty handy when you would come out against blokes like Jason Dunstall, Tony Lockett and Gary Ablett, wouldn't it?
Alastair: Yes, I suppose when I was playing on those guys, that was at Fitzroy mainly. I played a little bit of full-back when I went to Brisbane,

but Fitzroy weren't exactly flying at the time and playing full-back was a busy position. I think every team seemed to have the superstar full forward Lockett and Dunstall, Tony Modra, Ablett, Peter Sumich, Stephen Kernahan, the list went on and on, and so you could say Friday nights you weren't too relaxed. You didn't sleep too well and yes, the strength was a handy component, but I think my greatest asset back in those days was that I had very good speed over the first 20 metres and I think I used that.

Mike: The switch to full-back was the making of you, wasn't it? You played on the good players and learned from them, and that's where you established yourself at Fitzroy?

Alastair: We were at Waverley one day playing against the Saints and Tony Lockett was having an absolute day out on Gary Pert, who was one of the really great full-backs of the time. I think he was an All-Australian player, he was our vice-captain and I think 'Plugger' kicked his 10th at some stage early in the third quarter. 'Perty' didn't get taken off; I got shifted. I think I've had two or three goals off from the half-forward flank and got a message that the coach wanted to speak to me so jumped on the phone. I was told that I'm going to full-back on Lockett.

And I nearly threw up. I mean, I was *that* nervous, and obviously he's a superstar and to go there and play on him. There was a little bit of fright in that as well. I played him from three or four metres behind, one for self-preservation and two, I just thought 'that's the only way I'm going to be able to compete', because if I get side-by-side with a guy like Lockett he'd just push me out of the road. So I played him from a few yards behind and my closing speed helped me out.

Mike: So was the fear factor based on the fact that Lockett was a superstar, or that Lockett was such an imposing physical specimen?

Alastair: I think it was just his size and mass and what you'd seen in the news over the times and he was just an intimidating figure. Once I got through that particular day I used to love playing full-back. I really enjoyed it. I wasn't worried about losing the contest because all those names I mentioned before, they'd kicked bags of goals on heaps of different full-backs.

Mike: In November 1993, the news broke that you were heading north to Brisbane on a massive offer, and lots of people saw that as the last straw for Fitzroy. Do you feel any guilt about that?

Alastair: I think after I made the decision, or while I was trying to make the decision, that certainly did weigh heavily on my mind. It was something that I was concerned about, but for a few years we'd stumbled from year to year. In 1989 we had actually merged with the Western Bulldogs or Footscray[49], and I think a few of us woke up at our house and saw the news that we'd merged, so there were these things going on for a number of years. It was a really tough decision to make, but with the offer, it was almost made for me. A 10-year offer, guaranteed money...

Mike: You can say the figure.

Alastair: It was $185,000.

Mike: So, $185,000 a year for 10 years, unconditional, as I understand it.

Alastair: Yes, and a job on top of that, with Coca-Cola. I didn't quite understand it at the time; I thought well, at 25 or 26, there is no way I'm going to play for 10 years, but if I played for four years or five years, it would still guarantee that I'd get paid for the 10, so that made it really difficult to knock back. At Fitzroy, we still didn't know what was going to happen in the future, and I think at the time the guys that were running the club—Dyson Hore-Lacy[50] was heading it up—they were doing a fantastic job, working extremely hard, putting in a lot of time and effort to make sure that the club could pay its bills. I ended up making the decision; a few others went that year and a number went the year after as well.

Mike: It's interesting that Paul Roos was your captain at the time, but he urged you to go, did he not?

Alastair: Well, I spoke to 'Roosy' at the time. 'Roosy' was certainly one of my good mates at the time and our captain and someone that I spoke to enormously. I ran the offer past him and spoke to him about

---

49 Fitzroy had sought mergers with several clubs in the 1980s, but the 1989 union with Footscray was approved by both club boards. It was scuttled several weeks later when one Footscray member, Irene Chatfield, extracted an injunction to stall it, and the emboldened Bulldogs fans raised the necessary funds to continue as a stand-alone club.

50 Dyson Hore-Lacy, a lawyer and senior counsel, was chairman of Fitzroy through its darkest years from 1991.

the pros and the cons and I think he agreed that it would be very difficult for me to stay. I'm not sure whether he actually pushed me out the door to go to Queensland, but he certainly understood where I was coming from.

Mike: Robert Walls was coaching Brisbane at the time and famously likened you to Ted Whitten at one period of your career, which is—as you know—high praise indeed. How did 'Wallsy' cope when you were injured in your first year and then Chronic Fatigue Syndrome set in after that? Your start in Brisbane was very stuttery, wasn't it?

Alastair: It was. I think in my first practice match I broke my collarbone, and I missed about eight weeks and then played the season. I broke my collarbone again and needed the knee operation at the end of the season, and I think for me that was a battle because the first time I really struggled with injury. For a number of people at the club, they were disappointed I'd had the couple of breaks, but you can't do much about that. Then to have the chronic fatigue ... to go away for a weekend with the guys to Cairns and I came back and I was a little dusty from probably having a few too many drinks on the weekend. But by the Wednesday I couldn't lift myself out of bed. That was literally. I was a fit, healthy 26-year-old, and couldn't get out of bed and I had bad pains in the stomach, bad headache, I was passing blood and then from that time on I was struggling to get to training at different times. I certainly didn't understand what was going on.

I think the initial thoughts were 'I've got some sort of viral infection; stay in bed for two or three weeks and you should be right'. Now, that two or three weeks turned into two or three months. Certainly I understand for Wallsy and the coaching staff and some players, they couldn't understand or couldn't appreciate what was going on. I'd imagine that Wallsy was trying to get his team to a stage where they could compete in the finals, and his so-called big recruit was sleeping 18 hours a day.

Mike: Did you know anything about Chronic Fatigue at that point?

Alastair: No, I'd never heard of it before at all. I did hear the phrase 'Post-Viral Syndrome'. That's how it was also described to me, but there was no protocol of medication that was accepted that was going to make me right; there was no plaster to put on an arm or a brace to put on a knee and it wasn't just taking me out of football, it was taking me out of everything. To move to Queensland to try to mix in with a new group of players, a new group of friends, that became very difficult because for 24 hours a day I was just pulled out of that.

Mike: What about the psychological impact? It must have depressed you, being in a relatively new environment, knowing you were costing the club a lot of money? The expectations that you were not able to deliver on...
Alastair: Yes, the psychological component was a factor. I mean, I was told at different times: 'It's just in your head, you're just depressed.' My reply to that was 'bloody oath I was depressed'. I was depressed because I was stuck in bed and couldn't do what I love, can't mix with the people I want to mix with. That's why I was depressed. That wasn't why I was stuck in bed. So with that, it became very hard to actually get better.

Mike: Weren't you on dozens and dozens of pills a day?
Alastair: Yes, vitamin supplements. I think I was rattling by the time I walked around but the theory in the end was I needed to give my body everything, and it needed to fix itself.

Mike: What do the letters DHEA[51] mean to you?
Alastair: At one stage, they meant 'hope that this might be a medication that can help me', but certainly in the end they became a real strain and caused a lot of stress. DHEA is a precursor hormone that a lot of Chronic Fatigue patients were using around the world at the time.

Mike: As I understand it, it was picked up by ASDA[52], the drug agency that was working with the AFL, correct?
Alastair: Yes, I'd spoken to ASDA [as it was called at the time] and actually the guy that I'd spoken to and continually spoke to in Queensland, his wife struggled with Chronic Fatigue and was on the same medication. So we'd discussed it on numerous occasions.

---

51 DHEA or Dehydroepiandrosterone is a steroid that also appears naturally in the body. It is on the World Anti-Doping Authority's list of banned substances. In 1998, Lynch was charged with breeching the AFL's drug code, but he was cleared. The tribunal found he acted on advice from ASDA and that finding him guilty would be contrary to the spirit and objectives of the drug code.
52 ASDA: Australian Sports Drug Agency; now known as the Australian Sports Anti-Doping Authority.

Mike: But did it not end up on the banned list?
Alastair: Yes. After taking the medication for about two years, I was told it had been placed on the banned list, so with that instantly I rang the guy at ASDA and I said: 'Well, what do you suggest I do?' He said: 'Well, speak with the club then apply to get the exemption from the AFL to use it.' As a lot of people can do with health issues, they can take banned substances if they have the right approval from the medical board.

Mike: And then was there not an AFL investigation into the whole issue? I mean, that was a troubling time for you, I remember?
Alastair: Yes. After making the call to ASDA I went and spoke to Scott Clayton, who was our footy manager at the time, and he was fantastic about it. He sort of said: 'Well, what we should do is we'll ring the AFL and speak to them and try to go through the process of seeking authorisation to use it.'

Mike: So how did you feel when the authorities got involved? I mean, did you think there was an implication that they thought you were doing the wrong thing?
Alastair: Yes, I think at one stage I think they did think I was doing the wrong thing, and because once again, there are so many people who didn't know anything about this. It's something that I had discussed with a number of doctors and I was confident that once I had spoken to ASDA as well and this guy's wife was using the same medication and it was all fine, there was no issue. But once I had to stop taking the medication, my health didn't drop away at all. So did it work? I'm not sure, but it coincided with me improving over that two-year period. So that was a stressful time to actually go up to the tribunal and basically talk about medication and sport and banned substances.

Mike: Back to the footy. You were a three-time premiership full-forward yet some of us regard you as probably superior as a full-back. How do you see yourself?
Alastair: I think I was a full-back who found a way to go okay at full-forward. That was more by having to find a role that I could actually cope with while I was going through that unhealthy period, and I played a little bit up forward at Fitzroy, but I felt more comfortable at full-back. I enjoyed full-back I just loved the challenge of taking on the gun forwards every week.

Mike: How did you feel the day in at North Hobart Oval in 1991? Fitzroy's playing Hawthorn, and the Hawks finished with 36 goals and you were playing on the pre-eminent full forward in the competition, Jason Dunstall; how did he go? You kept him to four goals, right?

Alastair: Yes, I think nearly everyone kicked six that day, so I suppose keeping him to four was pretty good. I think he had one in the first minute so you thought: 'This is going to be a long day.' It was a tough day at the office but, playing on Jason was always one of those great challenges.

Mike: Who was the best of the gun full-forwards? Not the scariest, because I think there's only one answer there. Who was the best?

Alastair: I find it hard to split Dunstall and Lockett. Both guys were very quick off the mark, they had incredible hands in the marking contest, and that was back in the days where you could hit their arms as hard as you possibly could, and the back of the head sometimes as well. I suppose you'd probably rather play on Jason than 'Plugger', but it's hard to separate those two guys. You knew you were always going to be in for a very tough day.

Mike: Well, Paul Roos said to me recently that at the end of the 1993 season, he wouldn't have swapped Wayne Carey for you. Did you see that as probably the height of your prowess, even though you were playing with Fitzroy and not the Brisbane Lions?

Alastair: I think that was probably the peak of my athletic ability, and I think my football skills were refined over the coming years as far as playing full-forward. But as far as playing mainly down back with a few bits and pieces up forward, I think '92 and '93 were my best athletic years.

Mike: Let's talk about the golden era in Brisbane from 2001 to 2004. Only two goals in the premiership year of 2001 against the Bombers, but it was two goals four and you occupied Dustin Fletcher for the day and created an enormous amount of spillage. You finished with the ball that day, didn't you?

Alastair: I did. I think I kicked about three or four points in that first quarter; I might have had 2.4 at half-time. I didn't finish my good work off but, that was the most enjoyable game I've ever been a part of.

Mike: I hate to do this to you, but we've got to go to 2004, and your Grand Final stoush with Darryl Wakelin...

Alastair: I don't think that happened.

Mike: When you did your audition for *TV Ringside* you threw more punches than Anthony Mundine's thrown in his career, although he's probably had a better rate of hitting the target, has he not?
Alastair: Thank goodness.

Mike: What actually possessed you, that day against Port Adelaide?
Alastair: Actually going into the game I'd torn a quad or hamstring so I missed the first final or two, then came back against Geelong in the preliminary final. I actually remember thinking 'this is the best I've felt for a long time', because I'd carried a couple of back issues into the previous Grand Finals. Then I suppose to tear my quad in the first five minutes of the game was frustrating and some silly fool in the back of my head sort of went out swinging. So it's undoubtedly the most regrettable time in my career.

Mike: And it was out of character for you, wasn't it? I mean, you weren't a fighter on the football field?
Alastair: No, not really. Luckily I had no idea what I was doing but that still irks at me now. I mean, I might be just sitting somewhere quietly and it will just pop up again on television. I'm very regretful of that incident and certainly really disappointed in myself because it impacted on so many people that don't like to see that sort of stuff, people close to me don't like to see it. My opponent on the day, he didn't need those sort of distractions on a Grand Final day and it's just very, very regrettable.

Mike: Do you remember what sparked it? Was there one thing that actually set you off?
Alastair: I suppose walking back to the goal square and the constant niggle that you get from a defender. That wasn't the time that I needed the niggle I suppose and I just snapped. It was a subconscious thing and very regrettable.

Mike: Tell us about the influence of Leigh Matthews.
Alastair: Leigh Matthews is an amazing man in what he did with the football club when he came to Brisbane. At the time, we would finish last on the ladder, and there was a fair bit of factional in-fighting at the club. He came and he united the group and Leigh Matthews can make the very

complicated sound so simple. I think that's his greatest asset, so he could explain to us a very basic game plan, explain it very clearly and he'd get everyone in the room and everyone in the club to embrace it and follow his lead. I think that's why we were such a great team.

He got everyone to buy into his philosophy. Right or wrong, he had everyone going into the right direction. We were such a good team because we were predictable to each other.

Mike: Have you forgiven him for 2002? You kicked 70-odd goals including 16 in the finals. It was a premiership year and you created another 50 goals with the spillage that you caused, but you finished 17th in the best and fairest. Actually, I know for a fact that you didn't like that. You were offended by that, weren't you?

Alastair: At the time I was disappointed. Actually, I've never spoke to him about it. We had a super side. I thought maybe 17th was a little low down. That means I was only just on the ground, but at the time I was disappointed.

LEIGH MATTHEWS

The achievements of Leigh Matthews in football cannot be overstated. Four-time premiership player, four-time premiership coach, Australian Football Hall of Fame Legend, Matthews' contribution to the indigenous game is virtually unparalleled.

The man universally known as 'Lethal' joined Hawthorn in 1969, making his debut in Round 16 as a 17 year old. Short but solid, Matthews quickly established a reputation as an aggressive and skilful rover and a devastatingly effective small forward.

By his second season, Matthews was an automatic selection in the Hawks team and in 1971, still only 19, he played an integral role in a premiership season for Hawthorn, kicking 43 goals in 23 games.

Over the next few seasons, Matthews was consistently dominant as both a rover and forward. He was capable of kicking large swags of goals that were usually the domain of key forwards. In one scintillating performance against Essendon in 1973 he kicked 11 goals.

In 1975, Matthews won the Coleman Medal, kicking 68 goals. He remains the only rover/small forward to have done so. The Hawks lost that season's Grand Final to North Melbourne, but attained revenge a year later, with Matthews among his side's best.

Matthews added premiership medallions to his collection in 1978 and 1983 before retiring after Hawthorn's Grand Final loss to Essendon in 1985. He won his club's best-and-fairest award a record eight times. He then succeeded Magpie legend Bob Rose as Collingwood coach in 1986.

At the helm of the Magpies, Matthews achieved what many deemed the 'impossible'—taking Collingwood to the 1990 flag, breaking a 32-year premiership drought. He coached the Pies until the end of 1995, and then spent three years in a media role.

Brisbane appointed him coach in 1999 and he transformed the club from 'cellar dweller' into the dominant force in the first half of the 2000s. The Lions won three consecutive premierships (2001-03) under Matthews' astute guidance. He remained Brisbane coach until 2008 before returning to a media role. He has also made important contributions to the game as an All-Australian selector and a member of the AFL rules committee.

MARCH 28, 2011

Mike: There's a great Australian book titled _A Fortunate Life_. I reckon it could be the story of your life, actually.
Leigh: Yes, well, I've sort of worked at my hobby my whole life really, and I guess I've had a reasonable amount of fame and fortune out of my footy life.

Mike: You won eight premierships, four as a player, four as a coach. You're now a highly respected commentator, contented husband and grandfather. I mean, it looks like everything's in place for you?
Leigh: Well, it is but I'd like to be 20 again.

Mike: Would you really?
Leigh: Yes, because for me the memories I've got from some nice sporting achievements and all those kind of things, it's when it's just happened is when it's the best. I'd often think you'd like to be going into it again, rather than to a large degree having that part of your life come and gone.

Mike: So you'd take the risk in replicating all that you've done, to have another crack at it?
Leigh: Yes, I would.

Mike: Interesting. Are you a good grandfather?
Leigh: I try to be, yes. When I look back on myself as a father, I was so focused on what I wanted to do with my footy. So when you become a grandparent and you've got the next generation you say: 'Well, I don't want to waste my offspring's offspring being young again.'

Mike: Now, I suspect all premierships have their own appeal; does one of your eight stand out for any particular reason?

Leigh: It's funny, the premierships as a player are kind of a combination of your role within the game and the team performance, like they're all being melded around at the same time. For me the footy joys came more out of playing and coaching, but on Grand Final day if you win the premiership, coaching is even better, because the team's the only thing you've really got as a coach. So I think the memory of the siren time, or when you think you've won the game on the four that I've coached are almost more sharp and more memorable than the playing ones.

Mike: Certainly there was an extra dimension at Collingwood wasn't there? It had been so long... 32 years between premierships there, and it was as if you'd delivered them to the 'Promised Land'?

Leigh: Yes, but that's kind of a supporter's view. I mean, at the time you're just wanting to have that fantastic feeling of joy that happens if you can win a Grand Final and get through that year's campaign. So the post-Grand Final in 1990, when all the masses ... tens of thousands of Collingwood supporters joined in the joy and celebration, you appreciate that and you're glad for them, but that's not part of what you're doing, I don't think, until the game is won.

Mike: But there was a huge release of emotion from you that day. You came down and hugged Graeme Allan[53], and you were pumping the air.

CAREER
Born: March 1, 1952
PLAYER
Club: *Hawthorn—*
332 games, 915 goals
Honours: Australian Football Hall of Fame legend (1996); Brownlow Medal 3rd—1973, 1982; 14 times Victorian state representative (captain 1980); Hawthorn Team of the Century; Hawthorn Hall of Fame Legend of the Club (2003); Hawthorn best and fairest 1971, 1972, 1974, 1976, 1977, 1978, 1980, 1982; All-Australian 1972; Coleman Medal 1975; Hawthorn premiership side 1971, 1976, 1983; Hawthorn captain 1981-85; Hawthorn leading goalkicker 1975
COACH
Clubs: *Collingwood—*
24 games, 125 wins, 94 losses, 5 draws. 57 percent winning percentage, premiership 1990; *Brisbane—* 237 games, 142 wins, 92 losses, 3 draws. 61 percent winning percentage, premierships 2001, 2002, 2003

---

53 Graeme 'Gubby' Allan was football manager of Collingwood.

Leigh: I might've been involved in eight premierships but that's over 37 years, so it's like eight days and 37 years if you want to do those mathematics. That venting of emotions late in the 1990 Grand Final came because it's the moment when you know you're going to win, it's just such a special moment and the adrenaline flow is just massive.

Mike: The *Herald Sun* football writers voted you the player of the 20th century. What does that tag mean to you?
Leigh: Well, I like that tag. I mean, my ambition as a young man, young player, was to be the best player ever. I've always been lucky. I always had high ambitions and a short memory so you can never achieve that ambition but you can never feel you've made it either. It's a lovely tag to have.

Mike: Now, you talked about wanting to be the best player ever; what age of your life are you talking about?
Leigh: From the time I can remember. I grew up in a footy family and so footy was always the big sport, so there was never a time where I didn't want to play. I can't remember a time when I didn't want to go and play it when I got old enough.

Mike: My memory is that you were a North Melbourne supporter? And your hero was Allen Aylett, is that correct?
Leigh: That's right, number 17, yes.

Mike: Hawthorn went into a golden era, and you dominated the best and fairests. Did you ever feel sorry for Peter Knights and Michael Tuck and Kelvin Moore and blokes of that ilk?
Leigh: No, I remember one year, for instance 'Knightsy' and I tied for the best and fairest but at that point of time there was a count-back system. I think I won it on the count-back. I think they've since sort of gone back and made both myself and Peter Knights the winner in that year. It's nice at the end of the year to get that recognition from within your match committees, which is the group of people who are judging you the most harshly, I think.

Mike: You must have had a fair year in 1971; Peter Hudson kicked 150 goals and you won the best and fairest.
Leigh: I guess that was a breakout year. It was the first year that I became a regular senior player. It was my third year and I got a berth in the Victorian

team but I was still only 19. I think the peak of my career was more like the later '70s but we had a fantastic year as a team, of course, in '71.

Mike: Tell me about the Brownlow Medal. You were placed twice. Should you have won a Brownlow Medal, and did you want to win one?
Leigh: No, there's no such thing as *should*. Yes, I would've loved to have won the Brownlow Medal because that's the League's official award. But, clearly to win it you've got to get the most votes in any one year and I never did that, so I went to the Brownlow two or three times thinking: 'Maybe I'm a good chance tonight.' But as we know there's no form guide to the Brownlow, and it just never worked out.

Mike: Which year did you think you had a really good chance?
Leigh: I think '77, it was the best year I played, I'm pretty sure. I think I won the majority of the media awards that year but was third or fourth in the Brownlow, but certainly a long way from winning.

Mike: In 300-plus games is there one that stands out for you in terms of pure excellence?
Leigh: The best game I played was Easter Monday of '73 when I kicked the 11 goals and had a lot of the footy against Essendon at Waverley.

Mike: You did kick 11 goals and you had 38 disposals. Now, Lou Richards christened you 'Lethal' Leigh. I'm not sure how it sat with you, but your mother Lorna wasn't particularly taken by it, was she?
Leigh: No, I don't think she particularly did. I don't know whether I liked it that much, it never really grew on me as a player. My mum was never that keen on it for some reason; thought it was denigrating her little boy, I think.

Mike: A lot of your contemporaries still call you 'Lethal', don't they?
Leigh: Yes, not too many people I know do. The Hawthorn people always called me 'Barney'. That's been my nickname at Hawthorn so there's not many people who actually call me Lethal to be honest. It's more been the public nickname as opposed to what people call me in general.

Mike: Now, I presume 'Barney' is derived from Barney Rubble[54] and it was given to you by Peter Hudson?

---

54 Barney Rubble was a character in the cartoon *The Flintstones*.

Leigh: It was, yes, when I was playing reserves and in the pre-game the senior players were watching. Peter Hudson apparently said one day: 'Geez, he runs like Barney Rubble.'

Mike: In your book, *Lethal*[55], you said you played the game aggressively and physically. A lot of football followers would add 'dirty' to that. Is that fair or not?

Leigh: Yes, I think that's fair. As you mentioned at the start of this, I'm a 58-year-old mild-mannered grandfather now, but I had a fire in my belly when I was young. I can hardly remember it, you know, I was pretty cool and callous. It all happened on the spur of the moment my urge to win and succeed to a degree overwhelmed what you'd say is my competitive morality, if you want to boil it down.

So therefore the tags that were put on you in the physicality in the way you played, it's hard for me to argue with a lot of that because it was probably true.

Mike: Do you know the origin of this? Is this just the competitive spirit?

Leigh: No, there's no origin. Again, nothing was every premeditated with me, but on the spur of the moment the old rush of blood to the head happened quite a bit.

Mike: There's been lots of celebrated incidents involving you. Is there one that causes you more distress than any other?

Leigh: Well, the one that happened in 1985 with Neville Bruns was difficult. I mean, I did the wrong thing, but the wrong things are on vivid pictures, so everyone else knows you did the wrong thing as well. Of course, the police got involved and I had to go to court over it, so that was really nasty and it was very difficult and very hard to defend yourself when you knew that you had done the wrong thing.[56]

Mike: Did that hurt you? It certainly hurt your reputation for a period but did it hurt you personally?

Leigh: Yes. Well, it did at the time, yes.

Mike: In what sense?

---

55 Leigh Matthews with Michael Sheahan, *Lethal*, Caribou Publications, 1986.

56 Matthews was charged and convicted of assault after having 'king-hit' Bruns in a behind-the-play incident. He was given a good behaviour bond and the conviction was eventually lifted. He retired at the end of that season.

Leigh: Guilt, really. But I probably feel fortunate in a way that that happened in the last year of my career. I often wonder if it's something that was just as traumatic for me, even though I was the aggressor. But it happened in my 17th and final year and I also think it happened partly, too, because I was a crotchety old 33 year old.

Mike: Have you crossed paths with Neville Bruns since that day?
Leigh: Don't think so, no, don't think so.

Mike: You were quite pointed in your book about the Bruns reaction. I know there was an interview with Bruns a day or two after the incident and he said some things that seemed to upset you.
Leigh: Well, I guess it's a bit like 'what happens on the field, stays on the field', and that went past that. I think his reaction was part of the reason the police got involved, partly because the victim was aggrieved, and if I'd been the victim it would've just come and gone, if you know what I mean. But anyway, that's a long time ago now.

Mike: Did it prompt you to actually think about quitting the game immediately?
Leigh: Well, yes. On the Sunday afterward, I remember thinking to myself: 'I'm never going to play again.' I remember Allan Jeans came around on the Sunday afternoon or Sunday night and he might've said something along the lines of: 'Don't let this be the last memory of your playing days.' It was a difficult emotional time at that point.

Mike: You nearly caused Western Australia to secede from the Commonwealth in an incident involving...
Leigh: Now, this is going to be a long interview if you're going to just keep marking these things up, Mike.

Mike: But the Barry Cable incident[57] is one I think that also caused you some angst, didn't it?
Leigh: Not the angst of the whole Bruns situation. I know it happened, but remember that was about 1971. What was expected, normal, frowned upon was different even in '70 to '85 and much more if it happened in 2011, as you

---

57 Matthews knocked Cable out in state match in 1971.

could imagine. So again I'm the aggressor. I kind of did the wrong thing but I don't think it caused an enormous amount of angst thereafter.

Mike: It did in Western Australia, didn't it?
Leigh: Probably, but I lived in Victoria.

Mike: Now, one more and I'll leave the thuggery. The Grant Simmons one[58]. I do remember you telling me this story, about the Footscray player at Waverley that you hit. But you actually thought that you might've almost killed him.
Leigh: It was so much more physical or the violence you could inflict was so much more. Now we know that can't happen, but I was coming in one direction, he was coming back from a mark and he looked like he was unconscious and he was shaking. You almost think: 'Geez, have I killed him?' I mean, it was a terrible thought to have, that's a nasty memory.

Mike: Didn't you send someone from Hawthorn into the Footscray rooms at half-time to check?
Leigh: I don't know. I heard at half-time he was awake and he was okay, which was a nice thing to know when you're not sure what had transpired. Because you do things on the spur of the moment but then the aftermath... you've got to wear the aftermath because you've done the action. But when you do the action, you're not thinking of the aftermath.

Mike: Norm Goss[59], who grew up in Port Melbourne, said: 'There are sheilas in Port Melbourne who throw punches better than Lethal.' Yet the blokes that you hit, they all stayed hit didn't they?
Leigh: Well, it was quite funny, my kids used to say: 'Dad, you're not that tough.' I said: 'Tell as many people as you like. They won't believe you.'

Mike: You started as a rover and you kicked 915 goals. How would you describe yourself as a footballer?
Leigh: I often joke that in my playing time they didn't have the 50-metre lines and if they did, I would've have known where not to go. Obviously I was an on-ball forward and because I was second rover as the position designation was back in that period of time, with Peter Crimmins early

---

58 Simmons spent more than four hours in hospital after a collision with Matthews in 1975.
59 Norm Goss played and was on the coaching staff at Hawthorn.

on, 'Crimmo' would've done two-thirds of the roving. I finished my career playing as a permanent forward for two or three years.

Mike: Rovers don't actually play on each other so let me ask you about the rover you most respected from the opposition, and the player you found most difficult when you were playing forward.

Leigh: The rovers in that era in the main, while we were playing the same position you might not even touch your opponent, like when it was Kevin Bartlett or Garry Wilson or Barry Cable It's funny, I look at the extremities and I think: 'Who are the hardest opponents?" Everyone I played on in 1985 seemed to be pretty hard in my last year, and very early on Barry Lawrence used to play on me a little bit; that was almost unfair. John Rantall in that era where Hawthorn were playing the Kangaroos regularly in the finals, I never seemed to do terribly well on him; they're the main names.

Mike: You played with a bevy of great players at Hawthorn, heaps of them. It was a great era. Is there one that you enjoyed watching playing alongside more than any other?

Leigh: Well, I always think Peter Knights because Peter and I played for 17 years. We're, I think, about 20 days difference in age and we turned up at Hawthorn in January of 1969 and we left after the Grand Final of 1985. Peter was a tall, blond-haired athlete. I'd often joke that we're like twins but really it's like Darth Vader and Luke Skywalker, you know what I mean, Knightsy was always just the glamour boy but I loved Knightsy because he was a ball player, and he's spectacular and we just shared the whole era. He was a wonderful player.

Mike: You talked about arriving at Hawthorn. What sort of kid were you, because you were only 16, were you not?

Leigh: I guess sometimes now, in this part of your life, maybe you've got a little bit more self-assuredness, I suppose. But I don't think I ever felt confident ever, even in my prime as a player. So when I was a kid, you just try to make your way. Like I'm the little kid from Chelsea trying to make my way and to a degree you still felt that's been what you've been most of your life.

Mike: Much has been made of your relationship with another bloke you've played a lot of years with—Don Scott who was your captain.

What was the relationship? I mean, from the outside looking in, it was as if you two never spoke to each other.

Leigh: No, it wasn't that bad; it was teammates and acquaintances. It's just that some people think that just because you played football with people, you're all best friends and best mates; it's just not the case, never has been. Don Scott was ruckman, Michael Tuck was the ruck-rover and I was the rover for about a decade, but we just used to go to training and play footy together. All I'm saying is we weren't close friends but we weren't enemies. A lot is made of Don Scott and myself; we certainly weren't enemies but we just weren't very close. I certainly respected his desire and the way he went about his footy; I hope he did the same.

Mike: So it wasn't a situation that needed John Kennedy's intervention as coach?

Leigh: No, no, no, no, it was never anything that was going to be detrimental.

Mike: John Kennedy, your coach and obviously a huge influence on your career and life, said in your book: 'More than any other footballer, Leigh has demonstrated the capacity to remain cool under extreme pressure.' He's painting that as this almost outstanding trait in your football make-up. Does that surprise you?

Leigh: It's funny, we're doing this at the MCG; the MCG's been almost the place that I feel is like home. When I was young I felt completely at home on the footy field, more at home there than anywhere else. I think I've always had something in my exterior that never really mirrors my interior, and I've always had a fairly cold exterior, which makes people think you're calm.

Mike: Did you ever cross swords with Kennedy?

Leigh: I used to have nightmares about him in the early days because he was a really hard on you, and I reckon from say 20 to 23 I used to have nightmares about him. Then when I turned 23 or 24 I figured I was wrong and he was right.

Mike: You had legendary coaches at Hawthorn, Kennedy and Allan Jeans and David Parkin. What lessons for life did you learn from those blokes?

Leigh: John just drilled into us the basic lesson in life that we don't live on an island ourselves, and it doesn't matter how driven and how ambitious you may be, the group comes before the individual. And it doesn't matter what you think, that's the way it has to be. So he kind of drilled that into you as just the way of the world; a valuable lesson I reckon. David Parkin started to do the planning and review process around the game back in the late '70s. Then Allan Jeans was just the most fantastic man-manager and he always had the fantastic ability that even though he was a disciplinarian, everyone felt he was on for their side. He was a better psychologist than any qualified psychologist I've ever met; he just knew how to get the best out of people.

Mike: Were you a bit of a loner in your early days? The story was that you would train and then jump in your car and go home and you would play and do the same thing.
Leigh: Yes, I was.

Mike: And we used to read in the papers that you didn't want to go on interstate trips, or end-of-season trips.
Leigh: I was an 18-year-old father, so I had a very different youth in a way. I was married at 18 and a father at 18 so therefore as a young man, I wasn't actually out associating with my peers. That's probably where that came from. You're just living a very different life to most other of the young footballers of the same age.

Mike: Tell us how you got to Collingwood in 1986. Were you of the mind as soon as you finished playing football that you wanted to be a coach?
Leigh: It was just a progression. I don't think I ever thought about coaching until it got to the stage that I wasn't going to be able to play anymore, and I think most of 1985 I thought this would be my last year, and no one tried to talk me out of it at Hawthorn. At some stage late in 1985, I was asked if was I interested in doing a job at Collingwood. Bob Rose was coach at the time and Allan McAlister was chairman at the time, we met with them and that was going to be the succession plan. There's nothing new in succession plans.

The idea was I'd be assistant coach for 12 months and take over from Bob at the end of 1986, and Bob Rose was the person who was pushing that. So that's how my involvement with Collingwood began.

Mike: So Bob Rose actually then withdrew after Round 3.
Leigh: Collingwood lost the first three games and as history would say they were almost bankrupt. I can still remember the phone call on the Sunday

morning after Round 3. Bob was on the phone saying: 'Leigh, I think it's time you took over.' I can still remember the sentence, but it was incredibly exciting for me because I'd been assistant coach for six months, and I still hadn't worked out what assistant coaches were supposed to do.

Mike: There was no apprehension? You were ready?
Leigh: No, I don't know about ready but I was ready to actually have a go at it.

Mike: When do you believe that you'd learnt enough about it, and been in it long enough, to have actually been at your best as a coach?
Leigh: I don't know. I coached for 20 years and what I know about that is if I had the talent we could be really good; if we didn't have the talent we weren't much good; I was no miracle worker as a coach so therefore it's hard to answer that question. All I know is in '86 we didn't have a bad year after that bad start, and just missed the finals. We had a really bad year in '87, there was a lot of changeover of players. All I know is if we hadn't had a good year in 1988, that would've been the end of my coaching career, I would've thought. As it turned out, we were top four in 1988 and obviously thereafter we got home in 1990.

Mike: You had some good players at Collingwood. One I want to ask you about is the late Darren Millane. He fascinates Collingwood supporters. They loved him; he played the finals in 1990 with a broken thumb.
Leigh: Well, he was a gigantic influence because he was a really powerful individual and you knew as coach if he wasn't on side you had no hope. Tony Shaw was the captain and he was a major influence, but Darren was too. He was basically, I think, anti-authoritarian by nature. We got to 1990 and when he broke his thumb in Round 20 he was in plaster and he was out for six weeks. He came to me 10 days later and said: 'Listen, I've been to the surgeon. Maybe we can strap it up and put the painkillers in and I can play.'

So I gave him the softest fitness test ever, because you can sometimes play with a hand that's not working properly. You could never do that with a leg injury, obviously. Anyway, we got him on the field but the magnificent thing behind the scenes is you should've seen the pain he was in post-game, because he might've been able to inject it up. So for five consecutive weeks he went through the campaign of actually knowing post-game he's just going to be in some incredible agony once the painkillers started to wear off, and they'd re-plaster it again.

When you know that's going to happen in advance and you put yourself through it, there was an incredible inspiration that he provided by just doing that and still being of value in that 1990 finals series.

Mike: There's a bloke called Peter Daicos who was a pretty good player for you that year too. It was probably a sour finish for 'Daics' at Collingwood and you were there. But at his best he must've been one of the greatest players that you saw play.

Leigh: He was a freak; he had fantastic ball skills, a low centre of gravity but, what we'll all remember about Daics is his finishing and his ability to make the 'impossible' goal, the bouncing goal that he used to do, which we see often now. He was incredibly talented and he kicked 95 goals that year.

Mike: When you finished at Collingwood do you think ... did you think you were done as a coach?

Leigh: Well, not so much done as a coach but I've got to look back on my coaching career and think that I've got five or seven years as my maximum value in a footy club. Collingwood got to its 10th year and for whatever set of circumstances, I was sacked. It's hard to actually accept it's your time, so mostly someone has to tap you on the shoulder, but it was the right thing for me to finish. I'd had my decade; it was time for someone else to come in.

Mike: What swayed you to go to Brisbane? I think at the time you were happy in the media.

Leigh: I remember speaking to Kevin Sheedy in the finals series of 1995 about that. I just wanted to stop coaching for a while but I thought I would coach again. 'Sheeds' said: 'No, I'd be coaching next year if I was you.' One year out led to two years and then after two years I thought: 'Well, it's done.' Late in 1998 Brisbane made contact and even then I was only talking to them about it out of courtesy and then over the few weeks I just slipped down the well and decided I wanted to do it again.

Mike: You weren't fulfilled in the media though were you?

Leigh: Well, you're never fulfilled in the media like you are at club level. I mean, the thing about club-level footy is your emotions are on the line; if you care about the footy club, whether you're a player or a coach or a fan, you're putting your emotions on the line when you go to the footy. You know that at the end of the day if it's a good day, I might go home feeling happy, but there's a fair chance I'm going to go home feeling miserable. So that's a cycle gets to be part of you.

Mike: Talking about emotions; Brisbane's first flag in 2001 must've been something special.
Leigh: I guess the romance of Brisbane was that at that time the frontier teams were Sydney and Brisbane. Who could be the first team to win it out of the Swans and the Lions? It was beyond my wildest dreams to think that Brisbane would win premierships in Brisbane and through a lot of sort of good fortune, a lot of good talent, a lot of things worked together, we had a unbelievable early 2000s.

Mike: Do you think had you been given a seven-day break in 2004, between the preliminary Grand Finals, could you have won four in a row?
Leigh: It would've helped but you can never guarantee yes or no. Now if you qualify, you get the home preliminary final; back then there was this deal with the MCG that one of the preliminary finals had to be at the MCG. Clearly Port Adelaide had qualified higher than us, so they'd earned the right to have it.[60] I can sort of live with that. The decision that was made to play the game on Saturday night rather than Saturday afternoon, we're talking little things here, I know, but it's much easier if we'd been back in Brisbane on Saturday night after the game.

Mike: Jason Akermanis was one of your great players and certainly one of the most exciting players at Brisbane while you were there. You two fell out badly in the finish, didn't you?
Leigh: Well, in the finish, yes. Jason won the Brownlow in 2001, and thereafter I always felt like he was starting to work on his media career. Gradually over the ensuing years his willingness to be managed at all was difficult, but by 2006, he just wasn't prepared to be managed or coached at all. I think probably the straw that broke the camel's back is when the players got involved to say: 'Listen, you know 'Aker' we need you to stop

---

60 Brisbane Lions, who had finished second, played Geelong in Melbourne and won.

publicly talking about stuff that's just putting pressure on everybody.' Then the following week he did, and that was probably the thing where the team, the leadership just said: 'It's time for you to leave our club.'

Mike: Leigh, let me ask you about coaches taking players into games with injuries. Now, in 2003 in the Grand Final Nigel Lappin played with a cracked rib, or cracked ribs. Was that your decision?

Leigh: The medical people had to say: 'Listen, we think we can get him through.' And Nigel had to agree, but it is incredible, I remember Nigel getting out of the car on the Tuesday before the Grand Final at the Gabba, and he could hardly get out of the car because anyone who's had cracked ribs knows for the first three days you feel like you're going to die. You can't breathe; it's terrible. Anyway, the pain management specialist at the Wesley Hospital thought they could deaden his whole rib. So 'what the hell, give it a try'. He's wonderful player Nigel, and it was just enormous courage.

Anyway, we got to the Friday night; you had to test him. I said: 'If you're going to break down, it's got to be tonight, not tomorrow.' So we made it really as physical as we could make it and he seemed to survive that fine. Anyway, we got to the following morning and we got about an hour before the game when the team list has to be in, and Nigel is saying to me: 'I think I'm all right, but I can't seem to take deep breaths.' And someone said to me: 'Nigel has to eventually say 'Yes, I'm okay', or, 'no, I'm not'. You've just got to wait for him to make the decision.'

Chris Scott's going to be his replacement and he's warming up. I'm thinking to myself: 'It's an hour before a Grand Final and I don't even know who's playing, it's ridiculous.' Turns out he had a punctured lung; he played the game with a punctured lung because I reckon we punctured his lung in the fitness test on the Friday night. He played and we won and everything was good, and if we'd lost, you would've been slain. You know that. You make decisions and if they work, great. But on principle it's certainly not a good decision to take injured players in.

Mike: Nathan Buckley and Michael Voss, Leigh. You saw one of them up close for a long period, and obviously you're well aware of the capabilities of the other. Can you separate them?

Leigh: I don't know about separating them but Michael Voss, because I worked with him as coach for the best part of a decade, he was a wonderful player and wonderful captain. I was so lucky. Tony Shaw was wonderful captain and a wonderful player too; 'Vossy' was probably a better player I suppose, I think it's fair to say. So 'Vossy' just his understanding of how groups worked and his understanding of his on-field role as captain and his playing talents, he was such a hard player and so skilful but so tough and hard.

Mike: Did you leave Brisbane on good terms? Was it your decision entirely?
Leigh: Yes.

Mike: When you left did you know also that it was effectively the end of your coaching career?
Leigh: I'd say so but it was more that it was another decade. I finished at Collingwood after the decade. I don't think I left the club in terribly good shape playing-wise. At the end of 2004 Alastair Lynch retired, Marcus Ashcroft retired and you knew in the next two or three years there's this fantastic team but most of them were going to retire, and I'm certain if I'd finished at 2004-2005, there'd now been another coach because it was going to be mission impossible.

Mike: You're just one year older than Mick Malthouse, who seems to be at the height of his powers at the moment. Is it feasible for you to be coached back into coaching do you think?
Leigh: No, no. I'm a bit of a chameleon. I tend to be what I need to be, where I need to be it, and when I'm coaching I've got to be that and I prefer to be what I'm not without the coaching at this stage of my life.

Mike: I've got no idea what you just told me then.
Leigh: Well, it means you act the role. When I'm coach, for instance, I do what I feel I need to do to do that role and you become that person.

And now that I'm not that person because I'm not doing that role I like. In a way I like the life and the person that is not coaching rather than the coaching persona.

Mike: Who of the modern players excites you most? You see a lot of them these days. Is there one that you just actually love the thought of going and watching them play football?

Leigh: Well, the first person is probably Buddy Franklin. I think Buddy Franklin's 2008, I don't think anyone's played a better year than that. I reckon what he did in 2008, when he had over 200 shots at goal, he was just outstanding.

Mike: In your heart when the crunch time comes, are you a Hawthorn man, or is there any sort of affection still for Collingwood or Brisbane?
Leigh: It's not so much from my point of view. The coaching, being an off-field role, it's a bit like the king is dead; long live the king. As soon as you're not coach anymore, no one can remember what you do. So therefore the club that you played for I think is the one.

Mike: Who's had the better career out of Gary Ablett senior and Gary Ablett junior?
Leigh: Well, Gary Ablett junior is a wonderful player and might've been the best player in the competition for the last three years but Gary Ablett senior was just a freak. I can't think of an analogy but Gary's had just as good a career I think probably. Wayne Carey's the best player that I've seen because he was more valuable in more games, but Gary Ablett senior was just a freak of a footballer and it's hard to compare junior even to his dad because his dad was just so special in so many areas.

Mike: Just for the record I was one of the few people that had you at number two in the best players I've seen because I had Carey at one. Carey is the best player you've seen is he?
Leigh: Yes. It's all about how much you do to help your team win and he's helped North Melbourne win more often than any other player in my time in footy, so that, I think, gives him the right to be therefore judged the most valuable player. Gary Ablett senior is the most freakishly talented, but I think Wayne just did it so often.

Mike: What's left for Leigh Matthews; is there any horizons that you need to aspire to?
Leigh: No, I guess that's a slightly sad thing; I haven't got any particular horizons that I'm aspiring to at the moment. I try to do the best I can for the jobs I do for Channel 7 and the media roles that I do, but to a degree when I stopped coaching at club level, I withdrew myself from being on that extreme emotional rollercoaster that club footy does for you.

JOHN 'SAM' NEWMAN

John 'Sammy' Newman is probably best known these days as the enigmatic, polarising television star of Channel 9's phenomenally successful *The Footy Show*. But for 17 years and 300 games he was a star of a different kind as a ruckman with Geelong.

Newman made his debut at 18 years of age in Round 3 of the 1964 season. He spent his first few seasons as an understudy to the great Graham 'Polly' Farmer, but even during that period established himself as a fine exponent of ruckwork in his own right. His athleticism and leap also made him an extremely valuable player at both ends of the field.

After Geelong's defeat at the hands of Collingwood in the 1967 first semi-final, it appeared the Cats may have lost both of their ruck stars. Farmer announced that he was returning to Perth and Newman suffered a serious knock in the semi-final, which led to part of his kidney being removed. But Newman courageously returned to the game in the opening round of 1968 and had a stellar season, which culminated in a club best-and-fairest award.

Although troubled at times by ankle injuries, Newman continued to play fine football in the ruck and at centre half-forward until his retirement in 1980. He won a second best-and-fairest award in 1975 and captained the Cats in 1974 and 1975.

After his retirement, Newman joined the football panel on Channel 7's *World of Sport*. As he grew into the role he became renowned for his acerbic wit and one-liners. When Channel 9's *The Footy Show* was conceived that talent was identified and Newman was invited to join the show. His humour has at times pushed boundaries and caused offence, but the show remains extremely popular, largely due to Newman himself.

Regardless of his post-football-playing activities, Newman's fine career for Geelong deserves to be long-remembered.

MAY 2, 2012

Mike: What do you do to enjoy your free time?
John: I enjoy boating and I play a little golf. I got back into playing golf, and just chat with the one or two friends that I have, on a regular basis.

Mike: Your golf? I mean, it troubled you for a long time.
John: It did.

Mike: I always thought that golf caused you more angst than your football.
John: It caused me more angst. It did.

Mike: Now you're playing off, what, 14 or 15?
John: Yes, one of those.

Mike: And content with that?
John: Very content, Mick, yes, I am. Very content. Ah, golf really got to me, because I thought I was better than I was, or I thought I should be better than I was. But I wasn't.

Mike: Your demeanor on the golf course has raised a few eyebrows over the years.
John: It has. It's not something I'm proud of. I used to throw clubs, and cuss.

Mike: Are friends important to you? Do you have a lot of friends, and do you cultivate them?
John: I don't have a lot … I don't. No, I don't have a lot of friends, and I certainly don't cultivate friends. I cultivate the friends that I have. I think it's worth putting the time in with friends that you have, but I don't think it's worth putting the time into people who are just acquaintances.

Mike: I get the impression from the 25 years that I've known you, that you're not a big rap for most of the inhabitants of planet Earth. Is that fair?
John: I'm not interested in what they're doing. I'm not interested in them, no. But, nor are they with me. I have no interest in what other people are doing, as long as they leave me alone. But they usually don't.

Mike: Jeff Kennett's a golf partner. He's an interesting character, isn't he?

John: He is an obscure, diverse and lateral man. And did great things for this—now, we're not getting political—but he did great things for this state. And I'm not sure how great he was at Hawthorn—and I say that without being smart, or taking any stick to him—but he's a very nice man. Good company.

Mike: What do you think about all of the do-gooders who ridicule you for your brash, even crass, comments?

John: Like what?

Mike: Ah, well, I suppose, fundamentally, the *Street Talk* segment.

> **CAREER**
> **Born:** December 22, 1945
> **Club:** *Geelong*—300 games, 110 goals
> **Honours:** Australian Football Hall of Fame inductee (2002); 8 times Victorian state representative; Geelong Team of the Century; Geelong Hall of Fame inductee; Geelong best and fairest 1968, 1975; All-Australian 1969; Geelong captain 1974-75

John: It sounds like I'm defending myself too much. I really get sick and tired, not of that question, but I get sick and tired of the vocal minority, those people out there who have no idea of what's going on, live in their own little world. I, along with a camera crew—and we've been doing this for 19 years—we go out and speak to everyday people on the street. Some of them are simple. Not as in simply stupid; they are simple folk, just wandering along the street. If they don't want to speak to us, don't speak to us. We never harass people, or ask people to speak to us, but you'd be amazed at how many of what you would call simple folk come and speak to us and can't get enough of it. Is that a crime? Is that belittling people? I never take them to task about their intellect. I have a chat to them. That speaks for itself.

Mike: I just want to ask you about the criticism of you and *The Footy Show*. Now, you always say: 'I don't mind people having a go at me, or *The Footy Show*, but they've got to know, I'm going to have a go back.' But, I'm one of many who think that you over-correct, and you don't level the score; you just obliterate the target.

John: We've been monitored and edited, or scrutinised, to within an inch of my life, because of some of the things I have said. Would I take anything I've said back? No, I wouldn't, because you don't get a chance to take it back.

It's easy to say: 'Oh, I would've taken this back.' We do it off the top of our head. We think that's what the appeal of the show is; that it's spontaneous. And there's plenty of things that I've said that have probably been borderline. Mind you, I don't think most of them are borderline at that timeslot when you see what goes on other programs and other shows. We are pretty tame, to be honest. But people love to take a rise out of me. And that's fair enough. What I have said, Mick, is: 'Criticise me if you like. I don't mind what you say about me, as long as you don't mind what I say about you.'

And you'd be amazed how that is not a two-way street. And do you know what critics are, Mick? Critics are like eunuchs in a harem—they're there every night, they see it done every night, they see how it should be done, but they can't do it themselves. They're what critics are.

Mike: Two more skits. Shane Crawford pulled your pants down. Did you know that was coming?
John: Not at all.

Mike: You didn't? Well, did it embarrass you?
John: Of course it did, Mick, for a number of reasons.

Mike: Yeah?
John: I'd like some warning if I'm going to have my pants pulled down on live television.

Mike: Did David Schwarz have any notice that he was going to get a pie in the face?
John: To an extent. To an extent. I said, 'I might have a present for you'.

Mike: People forget that you were a very good footballer, I think. Your citation in the *Australian Football Hall of Fame* is, to my view, modest. It says: 'One of Geelong's finest ruckmen, a courageous player who overcame serious injuries, and later became a media star.' Does that do you justice?
John: Mick, if you think I'm going to try and convince people that I was any other player than what they thought I was, you're wrong. I don't care what people think of me.

Mike: Oh, I don't agree with that. I think you do care.
John: I know what I was as a footballer. I know what I was, and if the perception is that, well, good on them.

Mike: Well, describe John Newman, the footballer.

John: I'm not about to tell you how I played football, or how good I was or I wasn't. I'm not about to tell you who I would be like. That is in the eye of the beholder, that is so subjective, me telling you about what sort of footballer I was. I played for 18 years with Geelong. I missed five years, in football terms, through injury, that is, I missed 100 games through injury. Kevin Bartlett and I played for 18 years—him for Richmond, me for Geelong—and he played 100 games more than me. He played 403 games. I played 303.

Mike: You're in the Hall of Fame, and in your Geelong's Team of the Century, and having seen you play, you deserve both of those accolades. You played the bulk of your career with one kidney, correct?

John: Yes.

Mike: How difficult was that in a psychological sense, coming back as a young man when you were injured?

John: I did it in the first semi-final in '67 against Collingwood, and then—when Polly Farmer left that year and went back to Perth, I took over the mantle as number one ruckman for Geelong in '68, so I had the whole summer to get ready. But it was daunting. Tom Lonergan, I know when he suffered the similar injury a couple of years ago, he found it difficult, as well. But, you couldn't keep him away from playing football now if you if you had 100 horses. He loves it.

Mike: Well, we know in graphic detail of the Lonergan situation, but my memory is that you could have died at the MCG that day that you were hurt? Is that an exaggeration or not?

John: And a lot of people wish that I had. No, it's not an exaggeration, only in as much as—now, look, let's not make this too hokey or too dramatic—but I was taken off the ground, having been collected in the knee by someone from Collingwood, and things weren't quite as advanced in those days. I was left in the rooms—this is in the first quarter—I was left in the rooms, lying on a stretcher, or a rubdown table, until half-time. They were going to come in and examine me at half-time. And my father, God love him, he walked in about 10 minutes before half-time, and I think I was the colour of a sheet of paper and I said: 'Could you help me to the urinal, I want to urinate.' And he held me up there, and—I'm sorry about this—but it was pure blood that I urinated. And he went into a bit of a state and they put me in the ambulance.

My mother and father got in the back of the ambulance with me—and I can remember this to this day—and they were taking my boots and clothes off; I was still in my football gear. And they rushed me in—I think it was to the Alfred—and they threw me on a trolley and they swung those doors through into the operating theatre, with my mother behind me. And the doctor said: 'Now, look, you can't come in here; we're going to operate on him'. And she said: 'Is he all right?' He said: 'It'll be touch and go.' I remember him saying that to her. I had my blood supply replaced twice. I was just internally bleeding. So, Mick, look, I'm here to say that it was a success. My life hasn't been a success, but physically, they managed to save me, and here I am. And it probably would've been better if they'd just let me go.

Mike: Sam, your parents... your father was a master at Geelong Grammar, correct?
John: He was.

Mike: How were they about your public persona, your TV persona? Did they live long enough to see you be the person you are on Thursday nights?
John: It's a very good question. I suppose your parents love you, whoever you are. I know my father and mother got a kick out of me playing for Geelong. They loved their football, as my two sisters do to this day. But I think, much to the chagrin of my mother and father—and probably my sisters—they wondered what in the hell they had produced. And my father, who was an elderly man when I started doing *The Footy Show*, he used to ring me up and say: 'What are you doing?' And I'd said: 'Oh, look, Pops...' He said: 'Settle down, son.'

Mike: You've always declared Graham 'Polly' Farmer as the greatest player that you've seen. Let me ask you a harder one: who of the two Abletts has been a better player, Gary senior or Gary junior?
John: And I hate to use this word again, but this is such a subjective thing. Because some people like the flair and the excitement and the unpredictability of Gary Ablett senior, and some people like the honest, real, workmanlike class of his son.

In order for Gary Ablett to take those great marks and do what he did, he has to have someone like his son, who gets the balls 50 times a day and kicks it down to him. So, I don't think you can separate them. Gary Ablett senior was more exciting, and is probably what this game's about; Gary Ablett junior, in modern terms, is what this game's about.

Mike: The 2007 Geelong premiership ended a huge drought. I always had the feeling that you weren't as happy with that premiership as I expected someone would, given your history. You're not a Mark 'Bomber' Thompson fan, are you?

John: Well, now. Mark Thompson is, I think, a very nice man. I get on very well with him.

Mike: You do get on well with him, do you?

John: Every time I'm in his company, whether he makes a special effort or not—I don't make a special effort, I don't mind if people don't like me—but if we chat, I think I get on well with Bomber. I think he's a very nice man. So, that's that. But, in a role that I had on the radio, I thought Geelong were playing a pedantic, contrived game of football. It is starting, in my opinion, to become a better game. But for a period of time there, it became a ridiculous exercise in people trying to show how smart they were, trying to reinvent a wheel that didn't need to be reinvented, bamboozling people and showing that they knew more about the game than the actual people who played it, and confused them into the bargain. And I thought Geelong did that in spades. Bomber Thompson, don't forget, is the second-longest serving coach in Geelong's history. Probably lucky to last 11 years, not because he wasn't necessarily any good, because if you don't get success in the first handful of years, you usually get turned over, but Frank Costa and Brian Cook[61] stuck by him.

Mike: You've softened, you know.

John: I ain't finished yet. Then he made some monumental errors, in my opinion, in successive finals that saw them not play in a Grand Final when they should've. And in the end, he was—in my opinion—in the end, he was just almost counterproductive to Geelong. He was paying lip service to coaching, and he had a bigger staff around him, who had more influence.

---

61 Costa and Cook were president and CEO of the Geelong Football Club, respectively.

Now, when I see him next time out in the street, he'll say: 'Thanks for that, you prick.' And I'll say: 'Mark, I still think you're a nice man, but that was my opinion of you as a coach.'

Mike: You give the impression occasionally that you're tormented by the modern game. Is that true?
John: I'm glad I give that impression, because that is an absolute certainty. I think the way Geelong played in 2011 just was a refreshing insight into the way this game can be played successfully, if you get the ball quickly down to the people who win the game for you. That is the forwards, the power forwards. And you'd be amazed at how many people that come through the portals of *The Footy Show*—the Jonathan Browns, the Nick Riewoldts, the Barry Halls—those are just the singular boys, and the first question I always like to ask is: 'Does it confuse you when they don't kick the ball to you?' They say: 'The one thing we want them to do when they get it near the centre of the ground is kick it to us first up.'

Mike: But let me ask you one thing about that. If there were a simple way to play this game and win it, why wouldn't 18 coaches be doing it?
John: Well, maybe they don't have the personnel to do it. But you've got to play to your strengths, not to your weaknesses, surely? Why would you play football like that when you've got two or three people standing up the forward end of the ground, waiting to have an opportunity to win a game for you, and you don't kick it to them?

Mike: You played with Jack Hawkins, and he was a very good player in your era...
John: A very good player.

Mike: Are you a believer, or non-believer, in his son, Tommy?
John: Well, it's easy to say we're a believer in Tom now. I'm a believer in Tom Hawkins now, because I think confidence is everything in this game, particularly when you're a youth.

And he was in the wilderness for a couple of years there, but that game, on Grand Final day in 2011—the biggest game of the year—he suddenly came of age. But I would suggest he came of age because Chris Scott changed the way those boys played football, and they did kick it down to him more often than not, and they backed him to get the ball. But I think the greatest thing I've ever seen in football—ever seen in football that changed a game, and it's very underrated and underestimated—is what Steve Johnson did when he thought: 'I will rescue this man, Tom Hawkins, who must be getting the yips, and he's getting the ball, but he can't do anything with it.'

And when he asked him to handpass the ball to him and kick a goal and take the pressure off him, that is the best piece of team football I've ever seen. Because it won the game for Geelong, won them a Grand Final. For that man, Steve Johnson, to work that out, and to do that, and put himself on the line… if he'd missed it, he would've been laughed off the ground, particularly when he was almost not fit to play.

Mike: I'm one of the few people who call you your given name these days. Who is the 'Sam' from whom you inherited your nickname?

John: Bob Davis, my first coach, gave me the name Sam Newman from *The Jackie Gleason Show*, from Sammy's Spear and His Orchestra.

Mike: Bobby Davis?

John: 'A little bit of travelling music, Sam, and away we go'. We used to watch the show, *The Jackie Gleason Show*, and I came into training one day and I said: 'A little bit of travelling music, Sam.' And Bob Davis said: 'And away we go, out to training, Sam.' That's how it stuck.

Mike: Do you have regrets?

John: I'd like to have played in a Grand Final for Geelong. That's what I'd like to have done. You can't do anything about the past. There's not much you can do about the future. The present is what we live in. I was denied the opportunity in '67[62], and that is my one regret. But it's no good worrying about things you don't have any control over, Mick. And it's no good crying over things that can't cry over you.

Mike: Very philosophical, John. I've enjoyed the chat, as always.

John: Well, put it there. And I'm glad you looked at me in the eye; a lot of people don't.

---

62 Newman was recovering from kidney surgery when Geelong met Richmond in the 1967 Grand Final.

DENIS PAGAN

Although a reliable player with North Melbourne and South Melbourne, Denis Pagan is best known for his outstanding achievements as an AFL coach.

He trained with Carlton, but Pagan was not considered by the Blues hierarchy to be of League standard. North Melbourne took him on and he debuted for the Kangaroos in 1967.

He established himself as a regular back-pocket player in the following year and played 120 games with North, including the 1974 Grand Final in which North lost to Richmond. Sadly, Pagan had been cleared to South Melbourne when the Kangaroos went one better in 1975.

After his playing career ended in 1976, Pagan became a junior coach. This path took him to the North Melbourne under-19 side, which he led to an amazing nine successive Grand Finals.

When the AFL discontinued the under-19 competition, Pagan became reserves coach at Essendon, immediately taking the Bombers to the 1992 flag. Despite his incredible run of success, no AFL club was willing to try Pagan as a senior coach until 1993, when North Melbourne sacked Wayne Schimmelbusch in the pre-season. Pagan stepped in and took charge of many of the players he had coached at under-19 level.

The combination of coach Pagan and captain Wayne Carey formed the nucleus of a side that would immediately taste finals football. The Kangaroos again played finals in 1994 and 1995 before breaking through for a flag in 1996. The Roos fell short of the Grand Final in 1997 and then 'threw away' the 1998 premiership against Adelaide with some appalling kicking at goal.

That loss burned deeply for Pagan and he was keen to atone. North Melbourne duly did so in 1999 against Carlton. Pagan continued as coach until 2002 and North missed the finals only once in his 10-year tenure.

Pagan became senior coach of Carlton in 2003, but the club had become a shadow of its former self, due largely to penalties for systemic breaches of the salary cap. After four-and-half unsuccessful seasons, the Blues replaced Pagan with Brett Ratten.

JULY 9, 2012

Mike: As a player at North Melbourne you were handy and serviceable, with 120 games in eight seasons, including a Grand Final. As a coach, you went on to become coach of North's team of the Century, ahead of the great Ron Barassi. Now, you're now Denis Pagan, real-estate agent. How's business?

Denis: Terrific. In a price-sensitive market, tough times, we're doing pretty well and I'm in partnership with my son, Ryan, and really enjoying every moment.

Mike: Are you missing the football involvement?

Denis: Look, I did a couple of years ago. I really wanted to be involved but I couldn't find an opening, so I went back to school, got my full licence. It killed me, five months of exams and assignments. I said to Ryan: 'If we're going to do it, we'll both do that.'

Mike: Denis, you played in the back pocket in North Melbourne's 1974 losing Grand Final team against Richmond. Daryl Cumming was the permanent small forward, Kevin Bartlett was the rover, occasionally going forward. They kicked one goal between them and you never played again. What happened?

Denis: Oh, look, I was an ordinary conveyance as a player. I was pretty slow. I got the most out of myself and that's just the way they see things. You understand it when you become a coach and people have preferences and thoughts on individuals, and whether they're right or whether they're wrong, I'm happy that I tried my hardest when I was a player. And I didn't achieve a hell of a lot, but I hung in there.

Mike: You started your coaching career at Yarraville in the old VFA. How did that come about? Did you always have this desire to be a coach?

Denis: Well, when you finish probably it's the next transition. You want to be involved, you love the game. I loved football, from a young boy 10 years of age. I wanted to be involved, captain and coach for a couple of years.

Mike: Did you go into coaching with someone as your model, someone you thought you'd try to emulate?

Denis: Yes, I was always a David Parkin fan, a Tommy Hafey fan. I loved the way Tommy had those Richmond sides playing in the 1970s with Royce Hart at centre half-forward, 'get it in quick to them', and that sort of stuff.

Mike: You didn't mention Barassi?

Denis: 'Barass' was a very good coach, I'm not denying that for a moment.

Mike: What did you take from Barassi, in your arsenal as a coach?

Denis: Probably the biggest lesson I probably learnt in life—and I reckon it's probably the biggest weakness in the Australian culture

> **CAREER**
> **Born:** September 24, 1947
> **THE PLAYER**
> **Clubs:** *North Melbourne*—120 games, 5 goals; *South Melbourne*—23 games, 0 goals
> **THE COACH**
> **Clubs:** *North Melbourne*—240 games, 150 wins, 90 losses, 63 percent winning percentage, premierships 1996, 1999; *Carlton*—104 games, 25 wins, 77 losses, 2 draws, 25 percent winning percentage
> **Honours:** All-Australian coach 1999; North Melbourne premiership coach 1996, 1999

at the moment—is about accepting responsibility for your own actions. No regrets, no excuses, no alibis, never point the finger, never blame anybody else, and I've lived by that and that's probably the biggest lesson I've learnt in life, not only football, and that came from Ron Barassi.

Mike: Barassi is an amazingly mellow figure now. I mean, everyone loves him but it was different to Barassi, the coach, wasn't it, particularly in his time at North Melbourne? He was pretty caustic, wasn't he?

Denis: Oh, well he was. But times have changed. You know, in those days you'd get a burst for looking sideways, and blokes didn't even worry about it. Now, you look sideways at a player and they want to go and speak to their solicitor about it.

Mike: What took you back to North, to the under-19s coaching job?

Denis: Ron Joseph[63] came and had a chat to me. John Ibrahim was coaching the under 19s at the time. Barry Cable was senior coach. They wanted me to come back and help out with the under 19s and I did that for a year, and then I really wanted to coach in my own right after having two years at Yarraville as playing coach. Then John Ibrahim, to his credit, said: 'Look, Denis is the man to be coaching the under 19s, not me.' He went and told Barry Cable and Ron Joseph— I think it was down at Albert Mantello's office[64] in West Melbourne there—and next minute I was under-19 coach. I had the job for another nine years, I think.

Mike: Do you know how many games you coached at the under-19 level?
Denis: No, I don't Michael; a lot.

Mike: It's 238 games, with an 81-percent strike rate, and nine successive Grand Finals. Amazing, isn't it? Did you get frustrated having that success year after year and not exciting an interest from any club about a senior job?
Denis: Well, they were different days then, different times. I think one person made the comment one day: 'Have you ever seen an under-19 coach become a successful AFL coach?' I can't remember who it was. And my answer to that was: 'Have you ever seen a successful under-19 coach get an opportunity as a senior coach?'

You never got the opportunity in those days, and the people who pick coaches made some amazing decisions over the journey.

Mike: When the under 19s finished, closed down, you didn't even get the North Melbourne reserves jobs, did you? You had to go to Essendon?
Denis: That's correct. Wayne Schimmelbusch was in charge of the seniors and John Law stayed on with the reserves. Look, those sorts of things happen. Oh, sure, I was disappointed at the time and disappointed the way the news was delivered.

Mike: How was the news delivered?
Denis: I think it was at the senior best and fairest. It was said that 'Denis is moving on', and I said to Cheryl, my wife: 'Well, that's good. There you are, we're moving on 'darl'. Let's get our stuff and go.'

---

63 Ron Joseph was long-time secretary of North Melbourne.
64 Albert Mantello was a board member and powerbroker at North Melbourne.

Mike: So 12 months later North goes to Adelaide, plays in a pre-season game, gets smashed, comes back to Melbourne, Wayne Schimmelbusch loses his job, and you're appointed at North. It must have been a tumultuous time for you?

Denis: Well, I can remember it like it was yesterday. I think it was the 5th of March, it was a Wednesday evening. At that stage I was working with NZI Insurance as an agency manager-inspector. I drove into my driveway, being 5.30, and the phone rang. I looked at it and I thought: 'Gee, it's been a hard day, should I answer this?' Being the conscientious insurance inspector that I was, I picked the phone up: 'Denis Pagan, NZI Insurance.' It was a director of the North Melbourne Football Club asking me if would I like to have an interview for the North senior job. I sort of tried to be nonchalant and laid back.

Mike: Did you know 'Schimma' was gone at that point?

Denis: Oh, it was pretty common knowledge. I think there were three coaches involved in the running. I think there was Dermott Brereton, who I thought was probably 6-4 favourite, and probably Rodney Eade, probably 11-2, and Denis Pagan probably 66-1.

Mike: They get up occasionally, the outsiders, don't they?

Denis: Well, they do, especially in small fields.

Mike: It was 1993, the start of eight successive years in the finals, including two flags. It was an amazing run, wasn't it?

Denis: Well, it was. You know, I don't dwell or go backwards much in my life. I was out for the end of financial year with our staff last night, and it was in a hotel across the road from our office in Essendon, and I looked up at the TV and Fox Footy was on and there was the '94 preliminary final, the first time I've ever seen it, and you think: 'Gee, it just goes so quickly, your whole life.' It passes in front of your eyes.

Mike: You probably missed a premiership in '98, do you agree with that?

Denis: Yes.

Mike: But should you have won '99? I mean, does it level out?

Denis: Oh, I think it does. We weren't the best side in '99. It was Essendon by a country mile. I can still remember the Bombers before the preliminary final was played, and people were queuing up, going right down Napier

Street[65] around the corner into Fletcher Street, and I thought to myself: 'Gee, this is amazing.' So, whether that had any impact on the players?

Mike: You said they were queuing up for Grand Final tickets?
Denis: Grand final tickets, yes. I just wonder whether that had any effect on the players. In '94 we were beaten by Geelong with the last kick of the day in a preliminary final. I reckon if we had got into the Grand Final against West Coast we could have done a pretty good job there, too.

But it wasn't meant to be. In the '98 Grand Final we kicked a lot of points. It might have been 15 points to half-time.

We came in and all the staff were excited, and I could sense this wasn't looking good for the Kangaroos, and it came to fruition in the second half.

Mike: How deeply did '98 cut, Denis?
Denis: It did. We were the best side in the competition that year but, look, the reality is that in AFL football the best side doesn't win; the best side on Grand Final day wins. And we weren't the best side on Grand Final day.

Mike: You won two flags from your coaching career. Is that just reward for the teams you had and the way you coached?
Denis: I always remember what Kevin Sheedy says: 'You just don't realise how hard they are to win.' I reckon we probably should have won one more, but we shouldn't have won '99, so that was my thought on it.

Mike: You ruled with an iron fist, Denis, didn't you? I don't think there's any doubt about that.
Denis: Yes.

Mike: All your players would be of the same view, and you've got lots of them that declare their undying love for you, but you were tough.
Denis: Well, I was, yes, I was strong. It was probably the environment we were brought up in but you can't deny the fact that we didn't have a really genuine care and interest for the people we were involved with. And the players, the Kangaroos were just an enormously resilient and tough bunch of men. They were getting results and they could see it. There was probably a lot of humour there, but look, it's a funny thing, if you had a big white wall, just been painted with your good things and someone comes in with

---

65 Napier Street is the home of Windy Hill, Essendon's headquarters at the time.

a black Texta colour and puts a dot on the wall, people remember the black dot on the wall.

But they don't remember the good things you do.

I think I was balanced. Sure, I was hard, I was tough. I'd been brought up in a very tough environment, but I reckon I was fair. But, look, that's for other people to judge, not me. If they didn't like it, they wouldn't have played for you the way they did, the Kangaroos.

Mike: When you were installed as coach at North, Denis, you turned to a 21-year-old bloke who you'd coached at under-19 level, by the name of Wayne Carey, and you made him captain. He was I think in your own words, the best player that you've seen and coached, and he's the best player I've seen, but did you have a special set of rules for Wayne? Was he allowed to almost do and come and go as he wanted?
Denis: No, he wasn't, and that's one thing that probably riled me a bit. A lot of people used to say that, and a lot of people say a lot of things about you.

Maybe not everything got out that I said to him and vice-versa, but, opinions are like noses—everyone's got one—and a lot of people say a hell of a lot of things about individuals, but what do you do? Don't explain, don't complain, just get on with the job.

Mike: So there were no exemptions for Wayne because he was such a good player?
Denis: Well, I can't remember any examples.

Mike: Well, your players, his teammates used to say you used to say to them: 'No grog.' And some might say: 'Well, the 'Duck' [Carey] can have them.' Allegedly your response was: 'Well, the Duck can do that and come out and he'll train the house down and be best on the ground next week. You blokes can't do that.'
Denis: That's so far from the truth. I'd like to know who said that.

Mike: That's not right? Didn't Wayne drink a lot when he played?
Denis: They *all* used to drink a lot. We played a lot of Friday-night games, they'd go away for the weekend, and I'm sure Wayne was a good drinker, and I could probably name you 10 others. The thing that I'd come to accept was: 'Okay, you have a good weekend; just make sure on the training track Monday morning you train well.'

I never had any queries with any of those blokes, and more importantly Wayne, because he led from the front.

He was just sensational, and you wouldn't pick it. You go out and have a couple of beers with Wayne now, and you wouldn't want to stay there too long, I tell you. You'll find yourself sitting on the floor.

Mike: Denis, do you accept any responsibility for the events that ended the relationship between Wayne Carey and North Melbourne[66]? From the outside looking in, it looked like he was the victim of a culture that he could do what he liked at the footy club.

Denis: Yes, look, people take your greatest strength and hit you over the head with it. Did I have anything to do with the situation that exploded? I suppose, it's something you don't even want to talk about. I don't think I did. It was one of those things that happen in life; it was terrible. I'm sure if people could change events they certainly would have. But they were out of the control of individuals and only one or two people could have changed it.

Mike: You were extremely close to both those people—we're talking about Wayne Carey and Anthony Stevens— weren't you? It left you in an invidious position didn't it?

Denis: Well, it did. I couldn't take sides with it. Anthony was at the club, he was the new captain, and we supported him. Wayne virtually went into hiding, and I spoke to him about it and there were things that occurred that shouldn't have. It's amazing, every time there's an indiscretion they always bring that up, and it must be terrible for Anthony to see that.

I just hoped that Anthony would get on to his life, and he's just proven what a great ambassador and a wonderful player he was to lead the Kangaroos.

Mike: It was almost a mortal blow for the footy club and you left 12 months later. Did that have any impact on your decision to leave North Melbourne?

Denis: No, my contract was up. I would have preferred to stay at North Melbourne. There's no doubt about that. My contract was up for renewal. They were making ridiculous offers at the stage: 'How many people come to the game? We'll pay you a dollar for every person that comes through.'

---

66 Carey and the wife of North Melbourne vice-captain Anthony Stevens, Kelli, were found together in the toilet during a party at Archer's house. It was subsequently revealed that they were having an affair.

Mike: Is that literally true?

Denis: Yes, I've still got the contract at home now, the offer at home now, and I started to think: 'This is funny.' Ron Joseph was no longer my manager at that stage, which was a mistake.

If Ron Joseph had have been my manager at that stage, I still would have been at North. I got the impression that people thought I was too autocratic; they needed to wrest a bit of the balance of power back. They did that and they made me an offer that I had to refuse. And at that stage Carlton were knocking at the right time. People said it was for money, but I think in the first year at Carlton my pay cheque was $25,000 less than it was at the Kangaroos the preceding year.

Mike: So the deal was a lower base fee and a commission on the number of people that turned up to watch North play?

Denis: Well, it was. I just thought: 'Oh, well, it's obvious that they don't want me here.'

Mike: It's my understanding from other people at North, and you know who that might be—Geoff Walsh and people like that—was that the offer was very significant?

Denis: Well, I don't want to beg to differ, but I've got it in black and white at home, and it wasn't. And the offer wasn't made until the season was over, virtually.

Mike: You had a 65-percent win rate at North. It just seemed incongruous that the two parties—you and the North Melbourne Football Club— would part company.

Denis: Well, at that stage there were people on the board and people in the football club who thought I had too much control over things. And you know, it was probably right, but we were having a lot of success in those days, and sometimes autocratic regimes are successful, and if they're successful, why would you want to change it? They changed it, and there hasn't been a lot of success since.

Mike: Denis, the move to Carlton in 2003 turned out to be a disaster, didn't it?

Denis: That's the biggest understatement of all time. It certainly did. From day one, I can remember my wife saying to me the next morning: 'Are you sure you've made the right decision here?'

Mike: Based on what?

Denis: Oh, just the way it ended at North Melbourne. That wasn't given any publicity in those days. It was more or less, 'Pagan's gone for money,' and I didn't. I didn't get up in the media and discount it or anything at that stage. I just moved on with it and from the moment I went to Carlton, losing your draft picks, and then those fines and sanctions[67], I think Carlton were the oldest list and the highest paid.

Mike: Did you not see that though when you took the decision? Weren't the warning bells ringing then?

Denis: Yes, but there weren't too many other people offering jobs, by the way. We lost Daniel Wells and Brendon Goddard, who would have been a handy pair to start with. We could have built from there. People were saying to me: 'Well, we've got to bring some professionalism back to the club.' The players had to take a pay cut and I delisted probably 15 blokes at the end of the first pre-season, and it wasn't a recipe for success. You can imagine the division and factions and disunity at a club like Carlton and the whole place was probably split into three or four sections.

It wouldn't have mattered what happened, you couldn't have been successful. It's probably 10 years now and it didn't work out. They never had any money.

I don't think people realise how close Carlton were to handing the keys back to the AFL and in my time there, I think they had three CEOs, and probably four presidents. There were a lot of changes. There wasn't any continuity and there was always going to be somebody who was appointed as coach who was going to do the donkey work.

Well, I was a dead man walking for a couple of years and I knew that. Having to tell so many footballers that their services are no longer required and having experienced some responses from players, from slamming the

---

67 Carlton was heavily fined and excluded from AFL drafts for salary cap breaches in years prior to
    Pagan's arrival.

door, to shaking your hand, to telling you to go and visit the taxidermist, all sorts of responses.

Mike: Did you take any positives at all out of your time at Carlton?
Denis: Yes, I accept and understand that life wasn't meant to be perfect, I can tell you that much. I'd like to catch up with that little invisible bloke who stood at the front gate with a sledgehammer every morning and hit you under the chin as you walked in. That's what it was like.

Mike: Well you were used to so much success and you had 100-odd games at Carlton for a 24-percent win rate.
Denis: For the first 25 years in coaching, everything turned to gold. In the last five years everything turned to cow manure.

Mike: On your relationship with Brendan Fevola; it looked like you should have treated him with kid gloves when you got to Carlton, and there was an instant response. Was that the way to handle him?
Denis: There are so many opinions on that. Brendan was a talent. When I went to Carlton there wasn't too much 'A-grade' talent around, and Brendan was. But he was a wayward talent and he had his moments and he was up and down. It was just like those little puppies that go for a walk on the lead: you give them a bit of leeway, they walk out three or four yards and you know when to pull them back, and that was basically coaching full stop, not just Brendan.

Mike: Where should he be? Should he be a great of the game, given his natural talent?
Denis: He's certainly talented and it was just so sad to see him in a situation where he got himself into issues that he couldn't say enough was enough.

Mike: Were you aware of his gambling problems when you were at Carlton?
Denis: I'm sure he had a punt and that sort of stuff, but not to the extent. There was an email going around with his betting sheet for one day at one stage there, and I was flabbergasted when I saw that. I think that was when he was up in Brisbane. I wasn't aware that he punted like that when he was at Carlton.

Mike: I always get scared when I ask you sensitive questions, and one's coming now. The year's 2000, your son Ryan is on the list, you give him three games; Mark Dawson, your long-time lieutenant, the chairman of selectors, leaves, apparently because you demanded games for Ryan. Is that story true?

Denis: He left, but the thing about it—and, look, it *is* a sensitive question—Ryan was getting 40 possessions in the reserves at that stage.

He deserved a chance. In retrospect, I would have loved Ryan to go somewhere else. That was the start of my demise at the Kangaroos. People thought that I had too much control and Mark was probably one of the ones who thought that.

Mike: Did you gift Ryan those games?

Denis: No, I certainly did not.

Mike: So the vote at the match committee was for him to be in the team?

Denis: Yes, I discussed it with my loyal lieutenants and that sort of stuff. If anyone was against it, why didn't they speak up at match committee? Was I that much of a tyrant I wouldn't allow anyone to talk?

Mark was the chairman of selectors. They came to the match committee; no one spoke about it. At the end of the day probably the coach has the final say anyway. I just wish the whole episode hadn't happened.

He ended up doing a pre-season at the Western Bulldogs when he was probably 22 and I can remember [coach] Terry Wallace ringing me and saying: 'Look, we'd like to put him on the list but he's too old now.'

Mike: You're one of the few that's had to coach his son. It must be a fierce pressure.

Denis: Well, it is. You're damned if you do and you're damned if you don't. And I always reckon leaders make tough decisions, and it was a tough decision, but I made a decision I thought was right. His form in the seconds was terrific.

He had the ball on a string for over 12 months. He deserved a chance. Okay, he played two or three games, he wasn't that far off the pace, but the pressure was enormous. It was just going to rip the club apart, and it probably did.

Mike: You and Geoff Walsh[68]**, in my view, are both great North Melbourne people. You had a falling out, didn't you?**

Denis: Well, that was all part of the last contract. He was CEO and he was Mark Dawson's brother-in-law. Look, these things happen when you work with people.

Mike: You haven't patched it up?

Denis: Well, I haven't been around to his place for dinner, and he hasn't been to mine.

Mike: I must say I've watched you closely through your playing career and particularly your coaching, I always had this impression that you were fuelled by the desire to prove yourself, and to prove people wrong. Is that a fair assessment or not?

Denis: Yes, it probably was. I was never gifted as a footballer and really had to fight to get an opportunity and to stay in the side each week, and I did that, and it was an obsession, coaching.

I wanted to be successful. It was a 10-year exercise, and plus another year at Essendon reserves. There couldn't have been too many people who thought I could coach or get a result with a group of players. You become obsessive at it, and you want to keep being successful.

Desire is probably the greatest motivating force there is. If you really want something badly enough, I think you can achieve it.

Mike: Are you optimistic about the future of your old footy club?

Denis: I have concerns, and I hope they're successful. There's only one thing that matters in the AFL—wins and losses.

I want to see them successful. I don't want to see any squabbling. I don't think it's a good thing when you see former North Melbourne presidents sparring with each other and having a go back. If you're a coach, if you're a player, if you hold a position in an AFL club you're going to be criticised. Just take it on the chin. If you argue with fools, soon people can't tell the difference.

---

68 Walsh was football manager and then chief executive of North Melbourne, later moving to Collingwood.

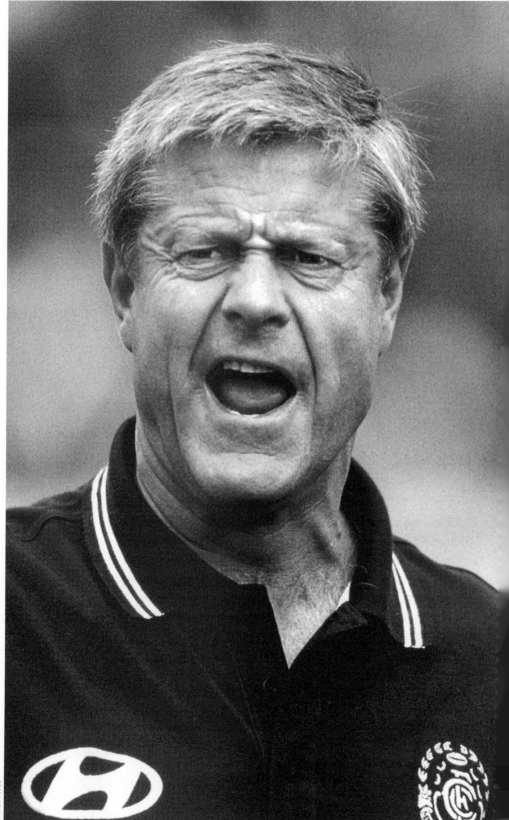

DAVID PARKIN

I t's one of the most over-used phrases in sport but David Parkin truly is
an 'ornament to the game' of football. His contribution to the sport as
player, coach, administrator and broadcaster is virtually without peer.

Recruited from Melbourne High School, Parkin played one game for
Hawthorn in 1961, and 10 in 1962, before become a regular in the 1963
season, playing in the losing Grand Final to Geelong. An uncompromising
back-pocket, he displayed a tremendous work ethic and his leadership
qualities saw him appointed Hawk skipper in 1969. He led Hawthorn to a
flag in 1971 and continued as captain until 1973.

Parkin bowed out as a player in 1974 and honed his coaching
skills in the WAFL with Subiaco in 1975, before returning to Hawthorn
as an assistant to coach John Kennedy in 1976. The Hawks won another
flag in that season and Kennedy then announced his retirement. Parkin
stepped into the senior role and took Hawthorn to a premiership in his
second year.

After a couple of relatively lean seasons with the Hawks, Parkin was
offered and accepted the coaching role at Carlton. The appointment
was an immediate success, with Parkin leading the Blues to successive
premierships in 1981-82.

Before the 1986 season, Parkin was involved in an unusual deal
that saw him become coach of Fitzroy, and Lions' coach Robert Walls
take the reins at Carlton. The swap paid dividends for both teams with
Fitzroy making the 1986 preliminary final, and Carlton the Grand Final.
The Blues went one better under Walls in 1987.

Taking a coaching sabbatical in 1989 and 1990, Parkin spent those years as Victorian football's director of coaching. He was coaxed back to Carlton in 1991 and rebuilt the team, taking the Blues to Grand Finals in 1993, 1995 and 1999; Carlton won the flag in 1995.

Retiring at the end of 2000, Parkin has remained heavily involved as a media commentator and a mentor to many others in the game. One of the sport's true greats, he was inducted into the Australian Football Hall of Fame in 2002.

JULY 2, 2012

Mike: I've got a feeling you don't want to be here.
David: I'm a reluctant participant.

Mike: Why is that?
David: I don't think that I'm the kind of person that has much to get excited about, what happened in the past and what's happening now, or what might happen in the future. So I'm a little reluctant. Ours has been, I guess, not so much a love-hate, but maybe a hate-love relationship, Mike.

Mike: That bad?
David: Well, you understand. The period when you were working hard at your previous job, and I was trying to work hard at mine, I didn't think either role was terribly compatible.

Mike: No, I accept that. I don't know if you've had time to notice, but you turned 70 recently. Isn't it about time you did something productive with your life? That's a joke.
David: Well, I know. But, yes, what has happened though, Mike, the decades go faster each decade. Thirty to 40 was moving steadily along, and then 40 to 50 started to gallop, 50 to 60, it went overnight, and I can't remember where 60 to 70 has gone.

I've been filling it as often and as hard as I possibly can in all elements of my life. And I'm one of those privileged people, Michael, who's been able to pursue the things that I love and have a passion for, and hopefully making a difference in, for the last 50 years.

Mike: You played 211 games for the Hawks, and you coached three clubs for a total of 518 games. That's the sixth-highest total ever.

Yet you're so self-effacing about your contribution to football. Why so?

David: I loved playing like most people, and without doubt, my most satisfying football moment was to captain a premiership in 1971. As a coach, I'm very honest about where I was. I took Hawthorn over in 1977 when John Kennedy could not continue, and I took over a premiership team that won in '76. We won again in '78 with the same talent that didn't I have to do too much.

Mike: It's been a lifelong love affair with the game for you, hasn't it? I know I was amazed, you were telling me recently about how many Grand Finals you've seen. It goes back to 1949.

David: My father was an MCC member. And I used to go, and the ladies' tickets allowed children to go in. And I went to every Grand Final. My dad had a great love of the game, too. Fortunately that was passed on to me, so we went every year. And I have had the privilege of not missing one, including the replays. So that would be a record that very few people could beat.

Mike: Now, I saw you play, and my memory of you was brave, always kept his eyes on the footy. I remember you as a back-pocket player. But you were concussed every second week. That's probably a slight exaggeration.

David: No, but I had 12. And I was concussed in my 50th, my 100th, my 150th and 200th. That's not bad, is it? That's pretty consistent.

Mike: So did you have a glass jaw?

CAREER

Born: September 12, 1942

THE PLAYER

Club: *Hawthorn*—211 games, 21 goals

THE COACH

Clubs: *Hawthorn*—94 games, 57 wins, 37 losses, 61 percent winning percentage, premiership 1978; *Carlton*—355 games, 219 wins, 134 losses, 2 draws, 62 percent winning percentage; *Fitzroy*—69 games, 30 wins, 39 losses, 44 percent winning percentage

Honours: Australian Football Hall of Fame inductee (2002); State representative (Victoria) 5 times; All-Australian coach 1995; Hawthorn premiership 1971; Hawthorn captain 1969-73; Hawthorn best and fairest 1965; Hawthorn Hall of Fame inductee 2003; Hawthorn premiership coach 1978; Carlton premiership coach 1981, 1982, 1995

David: Yes, I had a glass jaw. I remember going out the first time in the amateurs, the last one being when I coached Subiaco and I was knocked out at Claremont in the first five minutes. I woke up at four o'clock on Sunday morning, which was 26 hours later. And I retired on the back of that one.

Mike: You walk away from Hawthorn, Carlton has finished on top of the home-and-away ladder in 1980, and been eliminated with two losses in its two finals. What happened from there?

David: When I was offered the job, and it was difficult in those circumstances—I think Peter Jones[69] was pretty much offended, and it was a difficult and ongoing relationship with him. He never would talk to me as David; it was always 'The Hawthorn bloke'.

And for me, it was a godsend in that the team was talented. We made them work a bit harder defensively, I think. We put a few rules into place. We were in a pretty good place with resources, as Carlton were, when I compare where I'd come from. And we got every opportunity to do the job. And while we struggled the second year round, when I took my foot off the accelerator halfway through '82 and we lost our way a bit, the momentum we had—we were belted by Richmond in the second semi-final maybe by four or five goals—we were lucky to get up against Hawthorn at Waverley a week later. And then I think we had the advantage of knowing what Richmond were going to do, and how they were going to structure …

Mike: And then you belted Richmond, didn't you, in the '82 Grand Final? Literally.

David: Well, they physically got into us. I mean, that's a classical story of … and my probably most ashamed moment in football, that I had a sense when we were going down the race that it might be the Richmond mentality, as we called it. So I stopped the players on the way down to the ground.

Mike: So they're ready, they're assembled and ready to run at the race?

David: I said: 'Just a quick reminder: If one of our small blokes goes down, and there's every chance that will happen today...' So that wasn't a smart thing to say at all, the seven or eight little blokes running around, wondering where it was coming from. I said: 'When it happens, I want you to turn around and knock the bloke out standing next to you. And when he wakes

---

69 Parkin took over from Jones, having coached Hawthorn for the previous four seasons.

up and says, 'What was that for?' you say, 'That was for my little mate down on the ground'.

Mike: You said that?

David: I'm ashamed to admit it, but I did. And it happened. We kicked I think, three goals, one before Richmond even got the ball, so we're flying. And big Mark Lee knocked over Alex Marcou over there in bay 16. So I immediately looked to see who were the coachable people in the team. And I looked to the back half, because everybody ran to the blue, except the six back men who were locked at this end of the ground. Some great names, Bruce Doull, Ken Hunter and company. And it was Mario Bortolotto, and I'd buy him a meal every year on the base of it.

Mike: He was playing on David Cloke?

David: He was playing on David Cloke. He turned around and kinged him.

Mike: I can't believe ... and you're sitting here saying you're proud of that?

David: No, I'm not proud. I said I'm not.

Mike: You said you'd buy him a meal every year.

David: No, I'm thanking Mario because that's the most coachable act I've seen a player ... a disgraceful act, but it was coachable, because I asked him to do it. And he sat David Cloke down. David was big enough to take the punch and sit on the ground. Then while he was sitting on the ground, he spoke ... I couldn't see what he said, obviously. He spoke to Mario, and I saw Mario's hand go out to say: 'That's for my little mate down there.'

And look, I speak now, I speak about it openly now. It was a long while ago. But Neil Craig said: 'Have you ever cheated in a game?' And I told him that story. And he reacted as you just reacted then. So I'm not proud of it...

Mike: Because I know how important the essence of the game is to you, that you care about its welfare and its future.

David: I do.

Mike: Coaching does that to you.

David: Coaching does things to people and does things to players, as we're learning all the time. The white-line fever, the expectation of the moment, brings about behaviour, which you think might be a result of having too much to drink; you become the person that you really are. But under those extremes, you do and say things that you know you shouldn't, and that can cost you for the rest of your days.

Mike: You lasted five years before one of the most bizarre events that I can remember in football. Fitzroy and Carlton swapped coaches. Robert Walls went back to Carlton, Parkin went to Fitzroy. That couldn't have been by chance, was it?

David: Yes, totally by chance, in the sense that I was appointed to coach Carlton by Ian Collins and John Elliott on the Monday, might've been leading up to Grand Final week, I think it happened. And I went about my work, including working with the reserves, who I think were playing on that day, to be pulled in on Thursday night. It was on the back, I think, of Robert resigning from Fitzroy, and that was the first of the catalysts for it to happen. I think they were genuinely appointing me because Robert wasn't available. And the moment he became available, I was brought in and told by Ian and John that it was all over. And I actually took it more calmly than I can ever believe I did. And I looked at them, shrugged my shoulders and walked to the door. He let me get to the door, John, and he said: 'Parko, I wouldn't be worried about it too much.'

He said, 'I'll be ringing you up sometime down the track, because in the future you will be the right bloke to coach this club again.' I won't say what I said to him then, but it was similar to the words that he used. And it actually did happen, it came to pass. But then on the back of that, Fitzroy came to me to interview me. And I probably had enough at that stage, I really baulked.

Well, they came back and offered me the job, and I took it on. And to be truthful, Michael, it's 1986, and how lucky I was in a sense that I was on the back end of one of the best group of players I've ever had the privilege to work with.

Mike: You coached well at Fitzroy in 1986. The industry says that might have well been your best year of coaching.

David: I probably would agree with that. We had to win, Michael, I think three or four on the run home, to make it. And we won them all by less than two kicks. So we struggled to get there.

I think the first semi-final we went to, Waverley, and we'd played Essendon out there in the wet.

And Michael Conlan hadn't done anything for the day, he swung in off his right foot and kicked a goal , and we get home by a point. It was just a wonderful finish. And we're through that, and we're still alive, you know. We had to play Hawthorn in the preliminary final, and I will never forget this on the basis that Paul Roos was injured. He had a really bad ankle and couldn't play, he'd been ruled out.

When I got to the game probably an hour before, they were all sitting round in their civvies, almost resigned to the fact that, they couldn't do their job. They'd give it their best shot, it was all over. Very few people would know this, but 'Roosy' sensed and felt what I did as coach. He came over to me and he said: 'I'll go and see the doc; I think I might get filled with local, and I'll be right to play.'

Well he went in, had the injections, walked out of the medical room, nodded his head to me that he was all right—still with a limp—and the place realised he was going out to play. They were all hovering round the door and watching for the same result. I lifted in spirit, they all jumped into their gear, we went out. And you won't remember this, except Grant Lawrie, because he was the bloke who I had to go and tell wasn't playing. That was one of the more difficult things. But he still talks to me today.

Mike: So he was he dressed and ready to go?
David: Ready to play, and we made the change at the last minute. He missed out on the opportunity to play. I get emotional about that. That was one of the more difficult decisions that I'd made. But away we went ... and I think we kicked a bit like the start of the Grand Final in '82. I think we kicked three goals one before Hawthorn had touched the ball. But they kicked the next 13 goals, I think...

Mike: Your first year at Fitzroy was third place, and then it was two lowly finishes. There was a suggestion at the time that you had 'lost the players'.
David: I had. I put it on the players, and we lifted the expectation. I think we hardly won another game from that time. And the worse we got, the harder I went.

Mike: In a verbal sense.
David: In a verbal sense. And by the end of '87—and this is probably an interesting point—we totally lost the group. They rightfully were trying to

manipulate me out the door. On the back of that, very few people know I was given the job, offered and accepted the job, to coach West Coast at the end of '87. Few people would know, it was in my house at Templestowe. And even the family were reasonably happy to go at that stage. It was a done deal, and I slept on it over the night, and I woke up the next morning still with a year of my contract to run at Fitzroy. And the worst decision that I've made in football, I think, was to ring them up and say: 'I'm obligated to the contract, which I have with Fitzroy Football Club and I need to see it out.'

And that led to the worst year of my life, without doubt the worst year of my life. I went under as a person, I think mentally, socially, physically. It was a really tough time. It was a bad decision that I wasn't encouraged to go by the club, and a worse decision by me not to read the situation. And by the time we'd finished in '88, it was a basket case, the whole place.

Mike: Let's go to 1991. Two men named John Elliott and Ian Collins had sacked you from Carlton, but they came a-calling again and got you back to the Blues for 10 years. Did the pride in you make you a bit reluctant to take that job, or not?

David: No. He was true to his word, he did come back. And I can remember going to 2 Towers Avenue, Toorak, for the first meeting, when I went 'A over T' down the driveway in my shoes and cut my head open.

Mike: This is to John's place?

David: To John's place, yes. It took a while to get through the security, and I knocked myself out going down the driveway. The girl came out and gave me mouth-to-mouth, so I recovered pretty quickly. It was fascinating; walked through the door, and: 'What do you want to know?' was the first question. It's usually the last question in the interview. I said: 'How good are you?' They said: 'Well, we're not too good. That group of players that you coach, you'll have to get rid of all them, because they're all finished, and maybe start again.' I said: 'Oh, that's interesting. I'd really enjoy getting rid of all them.'

I said: 'That means it's a rebuild; we're talking about a rebuild here?' He said: 'Oh, we don't rebuild here, but it's a massive renovation.'

We actually got there in '93 and got cleaned up by Essendon, a really bad loss. It got worse the year after, when I probably should have lost my job because we lost to Geelong and Melbourne. I think I'm absolutely certain, I've never asked them straight out, but I think Gerard Healy, Dermott Brereton and Garry Lyon were the three that were given the opportunity to coach Carlton in '95. And for whatever reason—I've never had that conversation—the three knocked it back. So I actually held the job.

Mike: So you're saying that you would have lost that role pre-1995, had any one of those three said they wanted to coach Carlton?
David: That is my understanding. And I haven't had it confirmed by anybody other than a close person at Carlton, but I haven't spoken to those three players. So yeah, I think that was an absolute, real possibility.

Mike: You were famous for your animated addresses at quarter-time and half-time, and the anguish you showed in the coaches' box. Was that just spontaneous, or just occurred? Did you try not to do it?
David: I think that was me. People who know me … I have these dreadful highs and lows, in my communication with people. But when I am passionate about things, I want to deliver that as a meaningful way of expressing how I feel. And the players are on the end of some pretty vitriolic stuff. And once I'd set that pattern, I think if I'd spoken in very controlled ways, the message mightn't have got through with the same effect.

Mike: So are you saying that it was a little bit contrived?
David: A little bit contrived, yes.

Mike: The media saw it. You were responsible for the term 'the fifth quarter', which is when the coaches address the media after a game. You brought that same passion and anger at times to that.
David: I think the word you used was 'venom'.

Mike: Venom, yes.
David: Yes, look, and I didn't have much time for you or your mates. It got less and less receptive in a sense—I couldn't see what benefit the media were, and this was a stupidity, now I look back and I'm part of the media. I just couldn't see what benefit there was to anybody, me in particular, selfishly, or my team or club, by offering, you know, information post-match, pre-match, or whatever else. So you got little out of me except that I know they used to toss the coin outside the room to see who was

going to ask the first question and get the head bit off. I didn't know that until later.

Mike: Yes. That's true.
David: And I did take offence. I took offence at things that you wrote, too, and didn't have much time for you for a long time, until I actually got out of the business, could think a little more clearly, and actually get to know you. I've got four or five people now in the media who I would claim as my really good friends, that I enjoy their company, I understand what they're doing and the work, and I understand now from the other side how important it is to the game.

Mike: I tell you how serious it was from my perspective. I remember you and I go to a barbecue twice-a-year at Shane O'Sullivan's house, with assorted other people including Mark Maclure. And I remember ringing once, and Shane invited me, and I said: 'Is Parkin going?' He said: 'Yes.' And I found out later that you'd made the same phone call: 'Is Sheahan going?' Is that right?
David: And there were two empty...

Mike: Four empty seats. The women couldn't go. I think you almost sort of thought that we were parasites in the game.
David: I reckon that's ... I'd never use the word, but I think it was an appropriate way to define my thinking.

Mike: Yes. And yet the view we had was, we just have different roles in it.
David: And I know that now. I'm publically apologising. But it's the way I did it, and at the finish, I always come in, and we had a blue over that. Because one article you wrote really, really...

Mike: I probably think it did demean you, actually.
David: Well, it was an article ... you know what I mean, it was an article that suggested that I'd been sacked or was about to be rolled out the door. And I'd spent from 1998, '99, two years, I'd spent basically those three years trying to put in a well-thought-out succession plan. I appointed Ross Lyon.

I went into the football club late that afternoon as John Elliott and Stephen Gough[70] arrived from Perth, just to tell me that they've appointed

---

70 Gough was chief executive of Carlton at the time.

John Worsfold as my assistant for next year. So it turned out that we ended up having two coaches, and both have remained very good friends and I'm delighted they both are coaches.

Mike: In 1999, did you play your Grand Final in the preliminary final that year?

David: Oh, no doubt about it. We just played at the finish. Essendon didn't kick what they should have kicked in the third quarter, and left the door open. Anthony Koutoufides probably played the game of his life, and we were able to get over the line. And look, quite rightfully, the two best teams would have been Essendon and North Melbourne; we happened to be third-best, and we'd played it. But it's remembered by me, and it's remembered by Carlton people as much as any premiership they've ever won.

Mike: 'Parko', your anger is famous, and sometimes the final siren didn't bring an end to it. There's a mysterious incident, as bizarre as it sounds. Tens of thousands of people at the MCG, and you were in an altercation with a spectator. Are you prepared to tell us what actually happened that day?

David: It was an Essendon supporter; it was an Essendon game.

Mike: You were walking along the boundary?

David: Yes, I had my arm around Wayne Brittain[71]. I think we'd had a loss. And I was talking to him, going up the race. And a bloke came over the edge. I thought he was going to clock us or do something. And so my inclination was to throw a punch, which I did.

Mike: It landed, didn't it?

David: It did land, yes. And that was a bad moment, and I should have been—and I was, in fact—the man that night at Milgate. Thank goodness the person in charge at the police station was Michael Reeves, my ex-Fitzroy player. The man came and wanted to press charges for the assault. And Michael didn't know and hadn't heard, and convinced the man that he should go away and think about it, come back the next morning. He came back and I'm very thankful, he asked for an apology. So I was very happy to give that.

---

71 Brittain was an assistant coach at Carlton.

Mike: Which you delivered. So you did actually make contact with your fist to his mouth.

David: See, the word has got around there. I ended up with three stitches in my hand, yes.

Mike: Actually, you ran into that bloke later on, didn't you?

David: You got the story right. He was involved in footy, which is quite sad. He was a junior coach, and I was doing, as I so often do, a coaches course somewhere, and he came up and introduced himself to me.

Mike: No doubt you were the first coach to introduce detailed reviews of player games. Now, how extensive were they, and did they work?

David: Well I'm not sure. But I think no player ever played a game for me who didn't have one, and I've kept every one of those all the way through. In retrospect, they would've had a lot about the opposing team, would've had the statistical analysis and the stuff that we were delivering against them, but it also would have had a comment about their specific game, and a rating. It took my life away from me in a real sense, because I ended up working, you know, incredible hours, and sleeping four or five hours a day for about 20-odd years. And I don't think that helped me health-wise or relationship-wise. When you get so committed to that, the time you should be spending with family, and particularly children... I owe my kids gratitude and a real debt in a sense. I've actually got a relationship with my son and daughter for the first time in my life. And that's a sad thing to admit. I was a terrible father. But I'm trying to be a very good grandfather.

Mike: You are traditionally hard on yourself. Do you literally mean you've got a guilt burden about family?

David: I do, oh yeah, about family, and inability as a husband and father to do the things that I needed to do. So, yes, I have carried that; it's the one regret I guess I have.

Mike: More recently you came face-to-face with your mortality. In March 2009 your prostate gland was removed, after a diagnosis of prostate cancer. What effect did that have on your life?

David: A massive effect, Michael, because I'd had a father and grandfather who'd died of it, not with it, and I saw two very painful deaths. And I guess, it's like us all. You get old, and as you say, I'm nearly 70. And your own mortality looms up. There's a lot of unknowns in this area, which we're working very hard now to raise awareness, and certainly raise the money to do the research to find out.

It was one of the more difficult terms. But I've got a wonderful family and partner, and I was able to get through it. So I'm living a normal life now.

MARTIN PIKE

One of football's journeymen, Martin Pike's remarkable 247-game AFL career spanned four clubs across two states and included four premierships.

After showing great promise with Norwood in the SANFL, Pike was drafted with pick nine in the National Draft by Melbourne in 1992. He made his debut in the opening round of the following year but fell out of favour mid-season and did not play a game after Round 9. He did not return to the side until Round 7, 1994 and, although he was a solid contributor and played in all three of the Demons' finals that year, his off-field drinking excesses were a cause for concern and he was delisted at the end of that season.

Fitzroy drafted him and he had two good seasons with the Lions. Despite this, when the club merged with the Brisbane Bears to form the Brisbane Lions in 1996, Pike was overlooked. However, North Melbourne coach Denis Pagan saw an immensely talented player in Pike and he became a Kangaroo in 1997. Over the next four seasons Pike barely missed a game and was part of North Melbourne's 1999 premiership success.

Pike's reputation for excessive drinking sessions became an issue again after the 2000 season and he and the Kangaroos parted ways. After a meeting in Brisbane with Leigh Matthews, Pike found himself at his fourth AFL club. The move was successful beyond anyone's wildest dreams for both player and club as the Lions won flags in Pike's first three seasons at the club.

Pike played in another Grand Final with the Lions in 2004 before injury forced him into retirement late in the 2005 season. Despite his off-field reputation, Pike prided himself as a hard-working trainer and player, dedicated to the team's cause and his return of four flags bears testament to this attitude.

SEPTEMBER 3, 2012

Mike: Now it's an amazing record. It's 27 finals, nine years in preliminary finals, six Grand Finals, four flags. You've got to be mightily proud of that.
Martin: Yes. I suppose it happened really quickly because every year seemed to be finals and Grand Finals, so there wasn't time to sit back and reflect too often. Because the year after you're challenging again for another Grand Final.

Mike: And you played for four clubs, and yet had success at every one of them, including the best and fairest at Fitzroy.
Martin: You got to be at the right time at the right place, sort of thing. If the club is not ready to win flags, or the list isn't good enough to win flags, then you might go through your football life not achieving too much. But for me, I went to clubs that were ready to win Grand Finals, or that's what their list said. And I think I was a top-up to their list.

Mike: Melbourne took you with number nine pick in the 1992 National Draft, yet you only lasted two years at Melbourne. What happened?
Martin: I think we both know that.

Mike: I ask the questions, you give me the answers.
Martin: Look, I came over as a 20-year-old, and I wasn't ready for professional football, as simple as that. But it was hard, you know, you leave home, you're 20, there were no boundaries set for me. The guidance wasn't there. When you look at today's football, they've probably got probably five people working on development. Back then they pretty much give me a *Melway* and said: 'Away you go.'

Mike: Did that knock your confidence, or did you just sort of say: 'That's a step in life and I'll pick my life up elsewhere'?
Martin: The thing is that when you make mistakes, if you don't get over them… Look, I apologised every time. I manned up and said: 'Well, this is what I done wrong.' I took whatever punishment was given to me. A lot of times I was dropped or fined. But once that was over, then it was about trying to get a game again.

Mike: So were there any specifics at Melbourne that really hurt you?

Martin: No, not really. You missed a session on a Sunday morning. I wasn't a great Sunday morning trainer. But during the week, before games, I didn't have any problems with alcohol. A lot of people talk about alcohol-related incidents. All of them, were after games, not before or during.

Mike: Did you learn your lesson on the alcohol front?

Martin: It took a while. It took a long while. Look, I'm a sucker for good company. And I'm a person that doesn't know when it's time to go, as simple as that. If I left when everyone else went, I wouldn't have a problem.

> **CAREER**
> **Born:** November 14, 1972
> **Clubs:** *Melbourne—* 24 games, 25 goals; *Fitzroy—*36 games, 15 goals; *North Melbourne—*81 games, 19 goals; *Brisbane—* 106 games, 87 goals
> **Honours:** Mitchell Medal (Fitzroy best and fairest) 1996; North Melbourne premiership 1999; Brisbane premiership 2001, 2002, 2003. Brisbane Grand Final 2004

Mike: You're off to Fitzroy. You win the best and fairest in 1996. Yet you didn't excite a lot of interest when Fitzroy closed, did you? In the case of Brisbane, they had eight picks from the Fitzroy list, and ignored you.[72]

Martin: Yes, I didn't hear a thing from them, not even a phone call

Mike: So did that disappoint you? Frustrate you?

Martin: Not really. For some reason it should have, but I was walking out of Optus Oval one day, we'd played Essendon, and Kevin Sheedy was in his car, flicked his lights at me, so I walked over and had a chat to him. And I honestly thought I was going to get drafted to Essendon. We had a quick chat and he said that he was interested in recruiting me. But his recruiting managers didn't want it. But also Denis Pagan was at North Melbourne and he had made contact with me. I was pretty sure that I was going to get drafted anyway.

Mike: I saw Fitzroy's last couple of games, one on TV and one live. The second-last game at the MCG, and the last game Fitzroy played in Perth.

---

72 When the AFL set up the Brisbane Lions and Fitzroy closed, the Lions were given access to eight Fitzroy players in setting up their list. Pike was overlooked.

They were sad occasions, but you were on the field. What was it like to play in the last appearance of a foundation club in the AFL?

Martin: It wasn't built up that big. Like the last game at the MCG, I think there was nearly 70,000 people there, a lot of past players. But as players we didn't get told any of it. We didn't know there was a big parade beforehand. All we did was turn up and played the game. At least, you should have had past players walking through the change rooms all day, and maybe even speaking to us. But no one knew they were there. So we just went out and played another game, and it wasn't a good one.

Mike: You're the last best-and-fairest winner at Fitzroy. Does that mean anything to you?

Martin: Oh, it means a lot. It comes up. A lot of people still talk about it. A lot of people know me for it. A lot of Fitzroy people always come up and say they know that I won the last best and fairest, and you know it's a great thrill to have that associated with my name.

Mike: Fitzroy closes in 1996. North Melbourne is the premier team that year, and yet they were the ones that came looking for you. Did Denis Pagan say to you what he saw in you and why he was so keen to get you?

Martin: Not really, I don't think. He just liked the way I went about it and it was an opportunity.

Mike: So your first flag, the first of the four flags comes at North Melbourne in 1999. Twelve months later you're gone. Why?

Martin: It was what we talked about at Melbourne, behaviour. Behaviour, off-field. And I was stressed again, it wasn't during the week, it wasn't prior to a game. It was always after a game that you go out and let your hair down and it's something that I didn't learn quickly that this wasn't acceptable.

Mike: How disappointing was that, given that you were at a club that you thrived at, you had tasted the premiership experience and now it all turns sour?

Martin: I don't have any problems with Denis Pagan, or the decision he made. Denis made the right decision. He'd given me a couple of chances and I paid him back on the field, but off the field, I blew it. And it was sad to leave because they were a good bunch of blokes at North.

Mike: There was a family day at the zoo, Martin, do you remember it, for North Melbourne at the zoo, after a NAB Cup final. You turned up at the family day, you were late and probably overly refreshed. Is that fair?
Martin: That's fair. We played the NAB Cup Grand Final the night before. So it was a night game, you haven't left the MCG by 12. You go out. All the other boys are out, but I didn't go home. I went straight to the zoo. I think there was a jumper presentation, up on stage. I got pulled aside and said: 'Look, you better go home.'

Mike: Before you got your jumper?
Martin: Yes.

Mike: Who gave you that message?
Martin: It would have been Greg Miller and Geoff Walsh[73].

Mike: Did you think history sort of suggests that they stamped your papers that day.
Martin: Yes, well they did. I still did all right to play every game. Once your name has been stamped or a big cross goes through it, a lot of people struggle to get a game after that. I played every game that I was fit to play in and I played a preliminary final. That was my last game at Melbourne and North Melbourne, so that might say that I'm determined to keep playing no matter what the consequences.

Mike: Do you remember going to the casino one night after a North loss and, I think, playing blackjack or poker, for a long time, and doing quite well. Do you remember that night? When was that?
Martin: It was after the '97 preliminary final. I think I took out $300 with me that night. I blew $100 very quickly on the punt. I had another $100 to drink and then I had to decide what I did with the last $100. I threw it in to the blackjack dealer, and about four or five hours later I think I had 20 grand.

Mike: Johnny Blakey was looking after you that time, wasn't he?
Martin: Yes. The whole table was with North boys. I said to Johnny: 'I'll be out for a bit longer, Johnny, could you please take this home with you?' And he did. And his wife was petrified they'd get robbed, and two days later he said: 'I better give you that money back.'

---

73 Miller and Walsh were North's football manager and chief executive officer, respectively.

Mike: You once told a teammate if you had you been more spartan in your lifestyle, that your life might have been different. But your answer was, you wouldn't have been who you were and you didn't want to be a robot.

Martin: Well, that's true. That's true. I think some people will disguise who they really are just to get further in life. But, I am who I am and I'm not a closet person. I do things and it's out there for people to see and to be judged on. And I was judged harshly.

Mike: So, do you think you've been marked harshly or not?

Martin: Oh, absolutely. But I brought it on myself a lot of the time. When people talk, a lot of the time they don't talk about the premierships, they talk about the off-field stuff, and it's not easy to win a premiership.

Mike: You moved to Brisbane after the 2000 season for what was a dream run—four years in Grand Finals, three premierships. I want to take you back to your first meeting with Leigh Matthews. Now you realised the gravity of the situation. You needed another club. This was a club on the rise. Mathews was a tough task-master. How did that go?

Martin: Ron Joseph was my manager. He told me where to go and all that, but he told me the wrong hotel to start with. So I got there about half an hour early thinking I'd be prepared. The time goes past, and still no sign of Leigh. Probably a half-hour after the interview should have started, I found out I was at the wrong hotel. So I walked up to where they were staying. They were in shorts and T-shirts and thongs, and I had a suit on. It was 40 degrees. We spoke about football, and obviously what Leigh heard and saw in me meant I was good enough to be picked up.

Mike: I think they all knew you could play. That was a given. I know for a fact that Leigh was impressed that you actually thought enough about it to get dressed up properly and be in a suit. Did you think it was the last roll of the dice?

Martin: Oh, absolutely. Absolutely. Yes, I don't think a suit should really matter.

Mike: Well, why did you wear one then?

Martin: Well, that's a good question, too. I put one on and away I went. But, I actually went out to Ron's office first and we sat down and had a bit of a chat about what I'd like to get across. So I went into that meeting prepared for whatever they asked.

Mike: So what was the message? What was your sell to the Brisbane people?
Martin: Well, the sell was that I was keen as mustard to keep playing: 'I'm 28 years old. It's not going to cost you much to get me up there. I'm not going to come on big money. I'm happy to play on what you can fit into your salary cap.' But that didn't improve after five years. I didn't get a pay rise.

Mike: Do you remember what the fee was?
Martin: I think it was roughly about $80,000 base. So that's guaranteed, and then $3000 a game.

Mike: And you finished up a three-time premiership player on that money?
Martin: Yes.

Mike: So we're talking $80,000 base, and 25 times $3000 is $75,000.
Martin: About $150,000 I got.

Mike: In your last year?
Martin: Yes. After being a four-time premiership player, I didn't get a pay rise.

Mike: Was that one of the reasons that you were angry, or you expressed a large degree of anger towards Michael Bowers, the CEO of Brisbane?
Martin: No, not at all.

Mike: Now we're talking about an incident after the 2004 losing Grand Final, correct?
Martin: Yes. That's right.

Mike: It's a late night in Brisbane. Bowers is still there. You have an altercation with him.
Martin: That gets blown-up.

Mike: You didn't head-butt him?
Martin: I wouldn't have got a week in today's football.

Mike: Did you drop your head into his face?
Martin: I might have lent on him.

Mike: You lent on him?
Martin: But you wear glasses. If you get hit in the face with glasses on, it's going to make a bit of a mess.

Mike: It cut his nose, didn't it?
Martin: No. I saw him the next day and he was fine.

Mike: It was front-page story in Melbourne, do you remember that?
Martin: Yes, I know. I wonder how it got down here so quickly? I don't think I got home before that phone call was made by someone.

Mike: What's that implying, Martin?
Martin: Don't know. Some people, they work undercover, I suppose. The people that should have been there to protect that story were the first people to get it out. So, that was interesting.

Mike: I wrote that story.
Martin: Yes, I know. And you got that phone call. You know who rang, and I do.

Mike: I'm old now. My memory slips me.
Martin: Well, I do. I'm not that old.

Mike: Honest answer now, there was a collision of sorts, but it wasn't...
Martin: No, it was minimal. Minimal contact, and at the end of the day, we're both in the wrong.

Mike: What? Because he was out too late?
Martin: Well, no, not that. People don't have conflicts if there's not two of you going at it. I'll wear my share of blame, but at some point, Michael has to say he was in the wrong too.

Mike: So why was he in the wrong?
Martin: Well we were both having a discussion.

Mike: I'm not saying this to patronise you, but I'm amazed at that money for someone with that record. Do you think you paid for your reputation?
Martin: That's what it was. There is no doubt. There is no doubt that they saw me as a person that needed football, and I play for minimum.

Mike: And on one-year contracts.
Martin: On one-year contracts. If I was a lawyer, I'm sure I could have said: 'You can jam it. I'm going back to practice law.' Now I love football. I'll just play. If they'd paid me less, I would have still played.

Mike: Did you ark up about it on the way?
Martin: I went in there and asked for more, there's no doubt about that. But when they say you're only worth what people are prepared to pay, I walk out there and say: 'Oh, well, that's it.'

Mike: Do you remember the biggest, the most substantial amount of money that you earnt in any one year of football?
Martin: It was about $170,000.

Mike: Tell us about the Brisbane memories. That must have been the best four-year period of your life.
Martin: Amazing. When I first went in there, I think the first year in 2001 we were four-and-six after 10 games. We played a game at Optus Oval against Carlton, who beat us pretty well and it was embarrassing, and Leigh Matthews that day showed real disappointment in the team. You could see it in him, his body language, the way he spoke. He didn't point anyone out, but he was just very disappointed. And then from that day, I think every player walked out of that meeting thinking: 'Well, hang on a minute, the best, one of the best people in football, over 100 years, has been really disappointed with us.' I think that really sunk in. And then we got on a roll.

Mike: What was the strength of Matthews, the coach? Most people seem to think it's his man-management and his evenness. Is that fair?
Martin: Yes, I think having Leigh Matthews in our corner just gives us that much confidence, because at the time we had to beat Essendon, who had Kevin Sheedy, who could stir up the media. Eddie McGuire and Mick Malthouse at Collingwood always wanted to bring up the salary cap situation[74], so having Leigh always defending our group and our club was magnificent for the playing group.

Mike: In the preliminary final of 2003, you played the Swans, and you were in trouble at three-quarter time.
Martin: Yes, in the third quarter they probably kicked the last three or four goals. They had all the momentum going into the last quarter. Leigh had

---

74 The Lions had a salary cap allowance of 10 percent as part of the setting up a new club. It has since been removed.

spoken to us and then Michael Voss grabbed us also. We looked like we were about to go out and lose, that's the body language, and people were just dawdling back into 'Vossy', so I've given them a couple of swear words and everyone came in and then we went from there.

Mike: You kicked three of them?
Martin: I kicked two in the last quarter, and one in the first.

Mike: Okay, what was the gist of your message?
Martin: My message was to get the hell in here quick and Vossy talked about having a real crack in that last quarter. 'There's a massive reward if we do win it. There's a Grand Final next week.'

Mike: In 2004, you're going for four flags in a row, to equal the famous Collingwood record. The AFL programming came under criticism that year. You had to play a preliminary final in Melbourne, which reduced your stay at home. Did it affect you, do you think?
Martin: Absolutely.

Mike: The coach thinks that.
Martin: Oh, absolutely. We were an ageing list. A lot of us had played three premierships in a row, so you're playing the extra three or four games a season. We finished second; that should have guaranteed us a home final in the preliminary final. There was a rule in place saying the MCG had to be used. What should have really happened is if Port Adelaide played at home on the Friday night, we should have played Saturday afternoon, at least and got home on Saturday night.

Mike: So eight years on, that's the system in place now[75]. Do you think it cost you the flag?
Martin: Yes. You know what I would have said if I was running the Brisbane Lions? 'We won't see you at the parade. We're going to stay in Brisbane as long as we can, and we'll get down for the Grand Final.'

Mike: The Grand Final of 2004 finished with Alastair Lynch auditioning for Jimmy Sharman's boxing troop, throwing punches at Darryl Wakelin,

---

75 Under the system in 2004, the MCG had to host a preliminary final. Port Adelaide had finished first, so it played a home preliminary final and the Brisbane Lions had to travel to Melbourne to play Geelong. Although they won, the game was played on Saturday night and they did not return to Brisbane until the next day.

most of which missed. **Shane Wakelin criticised 'Lynchy' that night or the next day, and then you hoed into Shane Wakelin.**
Martin: Well, Shane was a player from Collingwood, and he wasn't involved in the game. I just thought I'd stick up for my teammate.

Mike: Well, you did, and it was quite colourful. I'll remind you about what you said, this is the quote: 'They both sleep with the lights on and in bunk beds and for them to have a crack at Alastair Lynch... everyone in football knows that they are weak pricks. If they want to have cheap shots at Lynch, well, come here and have cheap shots.' Now, that was in the *Herald Sun* of the day. My memory is that you rang for me and I wasn't there, and then you expressed these views to another reporter at the *Herald Sun*.
Martin: That's correct. It was halfway through Mad Monday. So I'm surprised my humour was so good.

Mike: So do you remember vividly what you did?
Martin: Yes. It wasn't on my phone. I don't know whose phone I borrowed. I just thought I'll make a phone call and have a chat.

Mike: Any regrets?
Martin: No, why?

Mike: It was just such a graphic response from a player that had played in the losing Grand Final team the day before. Now you said it was halfway through Mad Monday. Did you, or do you, have a drinking problem?
Martin: If a drinking problem is when you do have a drink you don't know when to go home, then I've got a problem. But, do I drink at home? Do I drink during the week? Not at all. Never have. You could come to my house after the show and there wouldn't be a beer in the fridge. So, a binge drinker? Probably, yes.

Mike: Did you drink during the week during your playing career?
Martin: Never. Not once.

Mike: What made you such a good player? Why do you think you were so competent and so creative at League level?
Martin: Well, the five or the six Grand Finals I played in, I played on every line. So, for a coach, I think I give him great flexibility with the way he set

up. If a spot wasn't filled with who he wanted to have there, I'd probably go there. I played centre half-forward when Jonathan Brown was out; I played back-pocket when they're resting 'talls'. I think I give the coach and my teammates a bit of flexibility. And I was determined. I loved winning.

Mike: Were you a sledger on the ground?
Martin: Big time.

Mike: Did you work on the principle that you could get into their head, and if you could, good luck?
Martin: Yes. And I had a lot of fun doing it, seeing blokes get upset by a few words, and it did throw people off their game.

Mike: Who's the best player you've played with?
Martin: It's a tough one. Wayne Carey, I think, has to take that crown. He was an absolute gun. But when you win premierships you've got so many good players. Wayne, he was a player that stood up on all occasions, you only had to kick it to his area, and he'd do the rest of the work. He played the hardest spot in the ground, and without him I don't think North would have won the premiership.

Mike: If you went out late, which the North blokes did a lot, could you match it beer for beer with 'The Duck'?
Martin: I think so. He could have a beer. But that was the thing that brought us so close, I think, at North Melbourne.

Mike: So the modern-day player wouldn't understand this, but my understanding was, Denis Pagan knew this happened, but Denis said it worked. I mean when work time came, you presented yourselves and you were very good at it. So he turned a blind eye to what happened Saturday night or Friday night. Fair?
Martin: Yes, fair. But you can achieve a fair bit over a beer too. I think with football today, they don't have to look anyone in the eye straight after a game if they've done something poorly, or they haven't worked hard enough as a team player.

Mike: Why don't they have to do that now?
Martin: Well, they get in their car and go home.

Mike: Don't the blokes socialise these days with each other?
Martin: Well, obviously they're not out having a beer. So I think a lot of things, a lot of issues got solved after a game.

Mike: So you think the rules are tough or fair these days about what players can and can't do in season?
Martin: I think they're hard, there's no doubt. Because they're young men. You take away a lot of their youth, so, I hope they're not doing things at 40 that they should have been doing when they're 20.

Mike: You have two children. Do they know the darker side of your football life or not?
Martin: I'm not really sure. I don't show them in anyway, the dark side. I'm a great family man, I think. Every opportunity I have, I go out and play with them. You know, I think they can look at their dad and say: 'Well, he's doing a good job with what he's trying to achieve with us kids.'

Mike: How do you want to be remembered for your time in footy?
Martin: Well, I have four premierships. And I'm sure that won't get lost in history. But, I was a likeable person, I think. I played it hard on and off the field, but everything that I achieved I had to work hard for, and I was prepared to do it.

MARK RICCIUTO

D espite an existence of not much more than two decades, the Adelaide Football Club has remarkably already produced four players who have played 300 or more games. The second of those to reach that milestone was Mark Ricciuto, unquestionably one of the club's greatest players. (The first was Ben Hart.)

Originally from Waikerie, 180km northeast of Adelaide, Ricciuto joined West Adelaide in the SANFL in 1992 and made such an impression that he was taken as a zone selection by Adelaide in 1993 and debuted for the Crows in Round 6 of that year, still not yet 18 years of age. He gathered 15 possessions and kicked a goal in that first match and played every other match in that season, including the heart-breaking preliminary final loss to Essendon.

Solidly built, Ricciuto was a strong, bullocking midfielder who could supplement those attributes with excellent kicking and handball skills. He also displayed the leadership skills that were to see him awarded the captaincy in 2001.

While Adelaide did not take part in the finals between 1994 and 1996, Ricciuto went from strength to strength as a player, establishing himself as one of the competition's premier on-ballers. The arrival of new coach Malcolm Blight in 1997 saw Ricciuto and the Crows rise to another level. But the year was to end in heartbreak for Ricciuto. In Round 22, having played every game for the season, he sustained a groin injury that forced him out the Crows' finals campaign, and he was forced to watch from the sidelines as Adelaide claimed its inaugural premiership.

Undeterred, Ricciuto had another fine season in 1998 and played an important role in that year's Grand Final as the Crows went back to back.

Ricciuto was a prolific ball-winner for most of the next decade. From a personal viewpoint, his career reached its zenith when he shared the 2003 Brownlow Medal with Nathan Buckley and Adam Goodes. He captained the Crows for the remainder of his career, which came to an end when the Crows lost a thrilling match to Hawthorn in the 2007 elimination final.

MAY 16, 2012

Mike: Now, your list of achievements is a mile long. I suspect that the 1998 premiership stands on a plane of its own.

Mark: Yes.

Mike: Which of personal achievements gives you the most pride?

Mark: Look, I'd be lying if I didn't say the Brownlow Medal. That was something that as a kid growing up, you always dreamed about. You never think you're ever going to win it. And it really didn't sit that comfortably with me for quite a while, when you get introduced as a Brownlow medallist, it doesn't feel right.

Mike: I must say as an observer, the fact that you played 300 games of AFL football in 13 years and 80-odd days, just staggers me. I mean, it's just the proof of your talent and your resilience. That's an average of 23 games a season.

Mark: Yes, I probably had a fair bit of luck with injury. I had a durable body. I only had the one real mishap in 1997. But apart from that, I could take a bit of punishment, and got through being able to play with injuries quite well.

Mike: So 1997 that was Adelaide's first premiership year, and you missed the Grand Final that year because of a groin problem, didn't you? That must have cut deeply. You were young, and it was just such a historic year for the footy club, and you missed it.

Mark: Yes, that was as hard as anything I'd had to deal with at the time. I mean, I'm very focused on team performance, and I come from a background of winning premierships at Waikerie. And when you build up and you miss your chance of winning a flag, it cuts deeper than anything can. I started getting issues halfway through the year with that, and it just gradually got worse and worse and worse, to the point where I tried to miss a game— I think it was Round 21 or 22—just so my groin would get better. But one day I couldn't get off the lounge-room floor, and I thought I'd better get an operation.

Mike: How difficult is it watching your team on the way to such a monumental occasion? Do you feel cheated, or is it that you're just happy that the boys are going to have a great moment?

Mark: One minute you're happy, next minute you're crying. And look, you don't feel part of it at all, and you can ask anyone who's been involved in that situation. You just don't feel part of it unless you play. With the celebrations that night, I went home early, and I was pretty annoyed for the whole summer, really. It wasn't just me; there was Tony Modra, there was Peter Vardy, there was Matthew Liptak, Simon Tregenza, there was quite a few other players that missed out that year, and I think that was one of the driving forces of helping us win it in '98.

> **CAREER**
> **Born:** June 8, 1975
> **Club:** *Adelaide*—312 games, 292 goals
> **Honours:** Brownlow Medal 2003; Australian Football Hall of Fame inductee (2011); VFL/ AFL Italian Team of the Century; All-Australian team 1994, 1997, 1998, 2000, 2002, 2003, 2004, 2005; AFPA Best Captain 2005, 2006; AFL Rising Star nominee 1993; South Australian Football Hall of Fame inductee (2012); Showdown Medal 2000, 2004, 2005; Adelaide premiership side1998; Adelaide best and fairest 1998, 2003, 2004; Adelaide captain 2001-07; Adelaide leading goalkicker 2006

Mike: You have eight All-Australian jumpers, which is fantastic achievement, the first of them at 19. Did you earn every one of them? I've got a suspicion that in 2002, your mate Neil Kerley, who used to sit on the All-Australian selection committee, might have got you over the line. You finished 12th in the Adelaide best and fairest that year.

Mark: Yes, maybe I did. I guess you get some things you don't deserve, and you miss out on others that you should. No, I was surprised. I'm happy to say that.

Mike: Now, you're an amiable guy, and everyone seems to love you, but you didn't line up any blokes on the footy field, did you?

Mark: I think that's part of footy. I think that's what everyone loves about footy, the contact side of things. So yes, if the opportunity presented itself…

Mike: Did the opportunity present itself one day when Dean Kemp was in your sights? He was almost out as soon as you hit him, and he landed like a log. And we know after his football career, he said he had problems with concussions and the effects of head knocks. Was that as heavy as you've ever hit anyone?

Mark: If it wasn't, it was close. I didn't line him up, and I only think I took a couple of steps, I think. And so I got him flush. And in those days, it didn't even give a free kick away, so I didn't get reported or anything.

Mike: You'd definitely get reported today.

Mark: That's four or six weeks these days. My shoulder did hit him in the head.

Mike: I know it's a tough arena and all that sort of stuff, but when those things happen and the consequences can be dramatic, as they've been in that case, would you bother to call him, or if you've seen him, do you have a talk about that?

Mark: I've never seen him. But on the footy field you hurt people as hard as you can, that's the way it was played. But you know, I wasn't aware for a while afterwards that he had any long-lasting effects, and I don't think it would have been just from my bump, if it did. Look, I don't like people suffering long-term effects from any sort of part of life. But if I knew I had an influence on it, I'd definitely contact him. I think if you looked at my medical file, you'd see that I've had quite a few concussions as well. So I know what it's like.

Mike: Okay, you're square. Now, you're extremely busy in retirement. You're a Fox Footy commentator, you've got a daily role on Triple M in Adelaide. You're a father of four. You own pubs dotted around South Australia.

Mark: Well, three pubs.

Mike: You're a keen fisherman, and you like to punt. Does coaching ever figure in your considerations about what you might do down the track?

Mark: Look, I always thought I was going into coaching, especially early in my career. Towards the end of my career, I was pretty tired mentally and physically—it was a pretty taxing footy career. And I had set myself up in the pub game from sort of early 2000s, so I was pretty entrenched in it. I had most of the money I'd made out of footy in pubs. I wasn't really in a position to either sell the pubs, or at the end of my career to go into coaching. So if I wasn't in pubs, I probably would've.

Mike: You've always been business-oriented, haven't you? I mean, reading your book, *Roo*[76], which came out in 2007, you bought a house at 19.
Mark: I started playing when I was 17. So the advice I got was: 'Buy a house and try and pay that off.' So I think it was pretty good advice. I grew up on a fruit property where it was pretty hard to make money, so the last thing I wanted to do was not capitalise on the position I was in with footy.

Mike: Does your Italian background influence your thinking about that?
Mark: Yes.

Mike: Your dad's parents can out from Italy, and made their way in the Riverland. Are you more conscious of that, because money's difficult to come by and you need to look after it?
Mark: Yes, absolutely. I've seen a lot of people struggle for a long time up in the Riverland, and that's the last thing I wanted to do. So I was always very conscious of making sure that I did the right thing with my money, so that our family didn't have to go through the same things that a lot of people are up there at the moment.

Mike: Tell us about life growing up. You were playing, and you obviously loved your lifestyle. You were playing with the men at Waikerie at 15 years of age.
Mark: Yes, that was a good experience. Waikerie's like any other country town, they're absolutely mad keen on their footy and sport, and they've grown up on the river, so there's the river sports as well, and fishing. But playing footy was sensational. Dad coached the under 10s, and I played all the under-age stuff, then the opportunity came to play A grade.

---

76 Mark Ricciuto with Shane Mensforth, *Roo: The Mark Ricciuto Story*, Macmillan, 2007.

Mike: Do you remember the day that Neil Kerley[77] went down to Waikerie to watch you play?

Mark: It's a good story. He'd organised with dad to come up and watch me play, and I didn't know anything about it. And my mate ran into the rooms and said he was there watching. I was only playing in the forward pocket that day, and 'Kerls' was pretty annoyed. My dad had saved the car park for him, and he'd rocked up with an Esky full of beer to watch the footy with my old man. And he wasn't happy I was playing in the forward pocket.

Mike: There's a post-script to that, though. You had a fair day in the forward pocket, didn't you?

Mark: I think I kicked 10.

Mike: Now, you've had a really interesting array of coaches. I mean, Kerls at West Adelaide, Graham Cornes, Robert Shaw, Malcolm Blight, Gary Ayres and Neil Craig, the full spectrum.

Mark: Absolutely. And I think I've learned a lot from all of those coaches, good and bad. That's important, I think. If you were to go into coaching, having experience from a number of different coaches gives me, I think, a pretty broad knowledge of what not to do and what to do. So you know, they all had their good points and bad points, and there are some very good coaches in there.

Mike: Your book clearly gives me the impression that 'Blighty' is on a plane of his own. He's someone who you learned from, and who was able to inspire the team.

Mark: Blighty was the best actual football coach I'd ever played with in terms of teaching you how to play footy, and he had some pretty basic rules in place about behaviour and on-field structure, and having a bit of fun off-field. So, I do think he was clearly the best football coach.

Neil Craig was also a very, very good coach. He probably didn't have the footy smarts of Malcolm Blight, but his professionalism, his structure, how he taught us how to be better people, was even better than Blighty. Graham Cornes was a good coach as well.

Mike: Didn't you have some run-ins with him?

---

77 Neil Kerley, a South Australian football legend, was on the staff of Adelaide Crows at the time.

Mark: Not really. I was only very young, about 17 or 18, while he was coaching. And you know, we could have easily won the flag in '93 if we'd kicked straight, but we didn't[78]. But he could've been a premiership coach for the AFL club within two years, so he would've been looked at pretty differently if that happened.

Mike: At half-time in the '98 Grand Final, you were in trouble. North Melbourne's 24 points in front. You blokes have got your heads down. They've dominated play, and they've kicked poorly. How did Blighty turn that around?

Mark: Well, for the previous six weeks, he'd absolutely flogged us on the track. We got beaten in the first week of the finals by Melbourne, played poorly. And then we trained really, really hard. We were super-fit. And he just was ultra-positive. He said: 'Throw it out the window, forget about what's happened. Back your fitness in, every time you get the ball, just play on.' Which was before sides were doing that. I think Leigh Matthews said in the commentary in the third quarter: 'It looks like they've changed jumpers.' And we did run over them, and won the game.

Mike: Now, one year later, in your book *Roo*, your view was that Blighty didn't even want to be at Adelaide at that point.

Mark: Well, there were rumours going around that after he—they—won the '97 flag, he'd ticked the box of being a premiership coach. He'd missed a few chances at Geelong. In '98, he coached fantastically, but the rumours were he didn't necessarily want to coach in '99 either. And we had a horrible '99 for a number of different reasons.

Mike: Could you detect that? Could the playing group detect that Blighty's heart wasn't in it?

Mark: No, not really. Blighty didn't do anything silly to suggest that. But a lot of things went wrong in '99, and Blighty said he would never coach again.

Mike: I want to take you to that. How did you feel when you woke up and read the news that Blighty had signed on to coach St Kilda in 2001?

---

78 The Crows kicked 8.20 in a losing semi-final against Carlton, then surrendered a two-goal lead from three-quarter time of the preliminary final against Essendon.

Mark: Well, he'd made it pretty clear he wasn't going to do it. But rumours again were saying that he got offered quite a bit of money and said no, quite a bit more, and said no. And then a million bucks, and he said: 'Well, I will probably have to take that.'

Mike: I get the impression that you weren't a huge fan of your two coaches from Victoria, Robert Shaw and Gary Ayres.

Mark: Not because they were from Victoria. I got on well with 'Ayresie', and 'Shawie', really. But I don't think Shawie's two years at Adelaide were his best couple of years, for a number of reasons. But I don't think he was a great head coach, Robert Shaw. He had some real good qualities, but the footy club went backwards those couple of years.

Mike: Did he try to turn you into an enforcer of sorts?

Mark: There was a little bit of that happening at the time. I think when he came over, he probably got some information to say they needed to toughen us up a little bit. But I didn't change my game too much. I didn't go forwards in my career. In fact, it was the first time I probably went backwards, so it wasn't great for me. But I hold nothing against Robert Shaw. I don't dislike him personally, but that just wasn't a good couple of years for the club.

Mike: Is it difficult, almost impossible, for someone to come from Victoria and go to Adelaide and be accepted?

Mark: I don't think so.

Mike: No?

Mark: No, not at all. Gary Ayres was a likeable bloke as well, and I played my best footy under Gary Ayres. So it had no effect on me. But Gary, as everyone would know, is a pretty tough bugger, he'll just ... he'll push you pretty hard, and he's got one way he does it, and that's probably the old school. It was fine by me, but he probably lost a few of the players towards the end. And we had some pretty good results under 'Ayresie'.[79] But they probably could've been better if a few things were done a little bit differently.

Mike: Did you seriously contemplate switching to rugby league, or is that a bit mythical?

---

79 Adelaide finished fourth and fifth in 2002-03 under Ayres.

Mark: I was a bit disillusioned for a while under Shawie, there's no doubt about that. But I was at that age where I was looking at life a lot differently. But, I'd never even played rugby; I just thought, I was that sick of what was going on there at that stage. But I wasn't the only one at the footy club that was a bit wayward.

Mike: Two of your most decorated teammates, Andrew McLeod and Tyson Edwards, had a major fallout[80]. You were the captain. What was the origin of the issue, and how did you handle it?
Mark: Well, it was a bit of a sticky one, really, because it was over another mate that we all knew, Lleyton Hewitt. And to be quite honest, we just thought it'd sort itself out pretty quickly, but it dragged on. And when we confronted it, it was a bit awkward, because they were both in the leadership group. Their families were involved as well, their partners or wives were involved as well. So, looking back on it, it would've been good for it just to sort itself out, and both of them front up and sort it out, but they both just didn't want to. They were both pretty stubborn lads, and weren't prepared to give an inch. And it made it a bit awkward. On the field, they were fine; off the field, they never spoke.

Mike: But you're an upfront individual. And in my view you would've said: 'Listen, you blokes, we need to sort this out.'
Mark: Well, they did do that to a degree. On-field, there wasn't an issue. But to say it didn't have an effect wouldn't be true. I mean, it always does. But they still don't talk, and I don't think they ever will, which is sad.

Mike: Did you side with either one of them?
Mark: No, absolutely not. But they're both great lads, and I love both of them.

Mike: Do you think the coaches and the administration of the Adelaide Football Club handled it as well as they could?
Mark: Yes, I think they did. It was a sticky one, Mike, when families are involved, and if they're not prepared to budge. I don't think it was far off one

---

80 The falling out stemmed from the release of a DVD by tennis player Lleyton Hewitt, which included footage of the duo at sacred Indigenous sites. McLeod launched legal action against Hewitt, but Edwards threw his support behind the tennis star. The feud later escalated to the point where Edwards' wife Mandy and McLeod's wife Rachel also became involved.

of them leaving the club, to be quite honest. It was really close to happening, I think. But that would've been a disaster as well.

Mike: Are you familiar with a place called Ramsgate? It's a hotel in Adelaide somewhere, isn't it?
Mark: Yes, it was one of mine.

Mike: You had an eventful afternoon there one Sunday, didn't you, back in about 2002?
Mark: Yeah. Was a little bit eventful, for all the wrong reasons, when you're captain. We were at Henley Square[81], and Simon Goodwin had just had his 100th game the day before against Port Adelaide, and we got beaten again, and they'd beaten us quite a few times. We just went down there for lunch, and lunch dragged on a bit longer than it probably should've on a Sunday. One of the lads went over to the bottle shop at the Ramsgate to get a couple of bottles of wine and said the Port boys were in there, and someone thought it was a good idea to go over there.

Mike: Did you go looking for Josh Carr?
Mark: Not in a bad sort of way.

Mike: Aren't you the bloke that spreadeagled him across the bonnet of a Mercedes?
Mark: A few things happened. But me and 'Carry' are good mates now. It was silly when you look back at it, a bit of fun.

Mike: He got under your skin, Josh Carr, didn't he?
Mark: Absolutely he did. At that time of the game, taggers were doing things that they probably shouldn't have been allowed to do, and I didn't like it.

Mike: Now, Johnny Reid was your football manager at the time and he pretended like there was a minor exchange of words. The true story is that there was a brawl, wasn't there, between a dozen or more?
Mark: I never threw a punch at Josh Carr. But I certainly let him know that I wasn't happy. A few other guys were throwing punches, and a few blokes got hit, there's no doubt about that. A few blokes were hiding under tables in gardens and things to get away from it, as well. But no, I was just annoyed,

---

81 A shopping precinct at Henley Beach in Adelaide.

and I'd had a few drinks, and it shouldn't have happened. But I was a pretty passionate guy, and I'd been dragged I think for giving away a couple of free kicks against Carry. And he was a lot smaller than me, and I didn't like losing to someone on the field.

Mike: The 'Showdowns' fascinate us, those of us who don't live in South Australia. I mean, the first showdown... the build-up to that was incredible, from this far. And Port Adelaide were playing their third or fourth game and they beat you, didn't they?
Mark: Yes, they did. And there was a huge rivalry for a long time. There still is, but early days it was out of control on-field and off-field. I mean, that's what footy's all about, isn't it. You either love or hate Port Adelaide, like you do with Collingwood or several other sides. So you know, it was full on, it was great; it was good to play them, and no one liked losing to them.

Mike: You've played with a host of champions at the Crows. I suppose most people's view is that you and Andrew McLeod are the two best. I mean, obviously leaving yourself out, is McLeod the best player you've played with?
Mark: Yes, look, there's plenty of good players. McLeod overall, with his whole record, I guess is unparalleled because of what he's done. To perform on Grand Final days like he did, to perform over 340 games, to play back, forward and midfield, his skills were sensational. He's special. So he's number one, he's up there. Darren Jarman for what he did on the Grand Finals and what he did on his best days was unbelievable. Some people would say he's the best player to watch. Tony Modra, I think, was the most exciting ever. His 1993, when he kicked 129 goals, that highlight reel would be better than anyone's.

Mike: Where is he?
Mark: He's living on a farm down south of Adelaide, and doing really well for himself. He's done all right money-wise, he's got a farm, he moves a few cattle around for a few farmers down around his area, he's had a couple of kids. He's just had a young boy, which has been fantastic. And he's got a little girl as well. So he's doing very well for himself.

Mike: It's interesting; 'Mods' didn't play in either of the premiership teams, did he? He was injured with you for the first one.

Mark: That was a very unfortunate part of history of the Adelaide Football Club. So he was injured in '97, and in '98 Blighty dropped him.

Mike: How late in the year was that?
Mark: In the finals. Yes, it was pretty tough. And the fact that actually Mods left and went to Fremantle was even tougher again. I mean, he's the most exciting player in Adelaide's history, and he thrilled the crowd more than anyone.

Mike: Mark, there's a moving account in your book *Roo* about you losing two of your mates. You were in your mid-20s. Matt and Joe both died in different sets of circumstances at about 30 years of age. That must have been very difficult for someone so young.
Mark: Yes, it was, when they were your best mates, your very best mates, and one was your cousin. So it had a big impact on my life, that's for sure. I guess that's why I enjoy the successes whenever they arise.

Mike: I was really moved by your story about Matt. You'd had a falling out with him. Yet when he died, you were moved to write a note to him and put it in his hand in the coffin. That must have been an extremely difficult thing to do.
Mark: Yes, it was. He died really quickly. When you see the mothers bury their sons, it's not a good thing. But everything that went wrong was forgiven straight away. He's still a great mate, I guess.

Mike: That must have weighed heavily on you, though, because you'd had this falling out and hadn't patched it up before he died.
Mark: Look, honestly, I patched it up pretty quickly, and we moved on. But yes, when you lose mates at that age until you experience it, you don't know what it's like. But to have that happen, and then have it happen three years later, was pretty tough. And when that happened in the week leading into a final, and I was captain, so I had to put on a pretty brave face.

Mike: How do you keep your focus?
Mark: You just block it out. You just block it out until you get the job done. And the day that Matt died, I did a triathlon straight after seeing him dead on the front porch. And then I broke down in the toilets after the triathlon. And when Joe died, you just steel yourself until after you play the game,

which we won against West Coast Eagles. And then same thing happened in the toilets; you just go and hide, and do what you got to do.

Mike: It makes you grow up in a hurry, doesn't it?

Mark: You pretty much realise what's important in your life after that.

Mike: The Brownlow. You were involved in the first triple dead heat we've had in the Brownlow, with Nathan Buckley and Adam Goodes. Does that make it more special or less special, because you're one of three?

Mark: Well, for me, probably some people would see it as a negative, but I always like doing things with other people. They're not too bad blokes to share it with, they can play a little bit. We've got a little connection, I think. And I think it was a great night. It was a fairytale, really.

Mike: So life's good, isn't it? I mean, your footy career's been great, you're enjoying your life. It's a bowl of cherries, isn't it?

Mark: Yes, I work very hard, and I'd like to think I've earned most things I've got. But I think a lesson for everyone is to enjoy successes. That was what made Blighty a good coach. If we had a good win, he'd say: 'Go out and have some fun.' I always did that; I'm not hiding away from that. I think it's an important trait, to have fun whenever you can.

MATTHEW RICHARDSON

A favourite son of Richmond and footy fans in general, Matthew Richardson's fine career encapsulated brilliance, frustration, triumph and despair. In his 282 games in the black and gold, 'Richo' never failed to give his heart and soul to the Tiger cause.

The son of former Tiger, Alan Richardson, Matthew was recruited to Richmond from Devonport in Tasmania as a father-son selection in the 1992 National Draft and made his debut the following year. In just his fourth match, he put in an eye-catching performance against Sydney, kicking six goals and giving notice that he was a star of the future.

Richardson opened 1994 in spectacular style, kicking eight and then seven goals in his first two matches. He kicked goals in all but two of his remaining games to establish himself as a bona-fide full-forward.

A good start to 1995 was soured in a match at the SCG when he slid into the boundary fence. A knee reconstruction was required and Richardson didn't play again until 1996. Rubbing salt into the wound, he missed Richmond's first finals campaign since 1982.

He marked his return with a six-goal haul against Essendon and went on to kick 91 goals in an outstanding season. Richardson continued to be a focal point in attack over the ensuing seasons, although a foot injury restricted him to just three games in 2000. He was back to his best in 2001, as Richmond made it through to a preliminary final.

When not hampered by injury, Richardson continued to play fine football as a key forward until 2008, when coach Terry Wallace decided to move him up the ground and play him on a wing. The move was an outstanding success, with Richardson relishing the opportunity to roam the ground. He still managed to kick 48 goals for the season and came within two votes of winning the Brownlow Medal.

Richardson succumbed to injury one last time in Round 6 of the 2009 season, his 17th. His 800 goals make him the 11th most prolific goalkicker in VFL/AFL history.

AUGUST 10, 2009—THIS INTERVIEW WAS RECORDED TOWARDS THE END OF RICHARDSON'S CAREER.

Mike: How does it feel to be the AFL's most popular player?
Matthew: I don't know if that's correct, but look, I reckon as my career's gone on I feel like I've harboured a bit more support off people.

Mike: I can remember periods when there was the normal sort of love 'Richo'/hate 'Richo', but it seems now you're sort of everyone's favourite.
Matthew: Well, I think once you get to be the oldest player in the AFL—as a lot of people have reminded me this year—I think people start feeling sorry for you...

Mike: I know on Brownlow Medal night they weren't feeling sorry for you; I mean, most of the people were willing you across the line. I actually felt sorry for [Western Bulldogs player] Adam Cooney; I mean, he's the bloke who's winning a Brownlow and knowing everyone in the room wanted someone else to win it. Tell us what the feeling was like.
Matthew: I think I just had a pretty fun night, and a fairly relaxed night because I knew the last two games I hadn't performed at all. I knew I wouldn't get votes and then I was 100 percent certain of that. I didn't have the nerves of thinking I was going to win. I was pretty relaxed and it was a good night and there was a lot of support in the room, and I was really appreciative.

Mike: Rate the year 2008 with the others you've played to that point.
Matthew: As far as playing I think it was one of the more consistent seasons. I think most weeks I got a pretty familiar result each week.

Mike: Seventeen seasons at one club, 'Matty', says a lot about your durability and your loyalty, but it produced only three finals. Cyril Rioli was 19 with three finals and a premiership to his name at the end of his first year.

Matthew: Thanks for pointing that out, Mike. I mean, that's disappointing obviously. Seventeen years—a lot of hard work went into it and you get your reward by playing in finals. So as far as that goes, I guess you look at it as a failure to play three finals in 17 years and it's very disappointing but, there have been some good players over the years who haven't played finals footy. I guess you've just got to be in the right place at the right time sometimes.

Mike: Do you ever regret spending your entire career at Richmond?

Matthew: No, not really. I'm proud to be a one club player and Richmond's been my life since I was a young kid. My father played there and I've supported the club my whole life; all my heroes were Richmond people so I certainly don't regret staying at Richmond. I certainly regret that I haven't played more finals football.

> **CAREER**
> **Born:** March 19, 1975
> **Club:** *Richmond*—282 games, 800 goals
> **Honours:** International Rules team 1999; All-Australian team 1996, 1999, 2008; Brownlow Medal—3rd, 2008; Alex Jesaulenko Medal (Mark of the Year) 1996; AFL Rising Star nominee 1993; Tasmanian Team of the Century; State of Origin representative, 1993, 2008; Richmond Team of the Century; Richmond best and fairest 2007; Richmond leading goalkicker 1994, 1996, 1998, 1999, 2001, 2002, 2003, 2004, 2005, 2006, 2007, 2008

Mike: Did you ever get close to leaving?

Matthew: No, not really. I think there were a couple of times where I was out of contract and I got to the point where I probably had a discussion with a couple of clubs but it never got to the point of sitting down and looking at numbers and really seriously contemplating it.

Mike: Matthew, it's a tough, demanding game on and off the field. Has it got worse as we've gone on?

Matthew: Tenfold, I think, but the players have got to accept that. There's a lot more money in the game now. As a young guy starting now the demands on them are pretty high. When I was 18 or 19 we could go out on a Saturday night and have a big night and you could get home and have a few hours sleep and then you'd be somewhere and have a Sunday session.

Everyone was doing it and it wasn't a big deal, but young guys now barely get the chance to go out and socialise with their mates, and when they do they probably drink too much because in between they've had six or seven weeks where they haven't been able to do anything. Just the constant pressure on them to never muck up, I would hate to have that as an 18-year-old, because you're going to make mistakes when you're that age.

Mike: Can they actually enjoy the game or has it become almost a chore?
Matthew: There's probably less enjoyment now because one game finishes and you feel almost like the next one's starting. When I first started you generally played Saturday afternoon; you didn't have to get up Sunday morning and go to recovery and you weren't required back at the club probably till five o'clock Monday, so you had a good 48 hours where you could actually have some down time and socialise with your friends.

Mike: What was the darkest period in your time at Richmond?
Matthew: I guess when you're inside a club you're probably a lot more optimistic than what people outside are, and every year you genuinely go through pre-season training and you genuinely think it's going to be a good year. I guess if you ever start thinking that it's not going to be at that stage, I reckon it's a pretty sure sign that you probably shouldn't be playing. So I don't think I've ever really had periods where I've been totally doom and gloom about the whole thing.

Mike: How did the club handle the coaching change from Terry Wallace to Damien Hardwick, did you think?
Matthew: Look, I think if you sat back, all things considered, I don't think they could've done a hell of a lot more. There was pressure on even before the end of last season, people were talking then. There were obviously huge expectations this year, everyone talking finals. Terry had said it, and the club had said if we didn't make finals then there probably wouldn't be a contract at the end of that year.

So the media from Round 1 built up every single week. Every time you turned up for training there were cameras there. There was another article every two days after every game and when it got to the point where finals were totally out of the equation, I think it was best for Terry and for the footy club. I don't think they could've done it much better really.

Mike: It's three decades since your footy club has won a premiership. Has there been one single fault in your mind that's stood out as to why this football club has been in the wilderness for so long?

Matthew: I think generally over the last 10 years they used to blame it on the coaches changing every two years. Well, two coaches have had five-year terms so I think they've been reasonably patient on the coaching front in the last 10 years. In hindsight you can look back at draft picks probably gone wrong and development of players, trading for senior players. I reckon in hindsight you probably would've just gone down the path of sticking to your draft picks and not trading and probably trying to develop your own. There probably have been some mistakes there, and I think everyone probably knows which ones they are.

Mike: What's been the highlight of the journey so far?

Matthew: I only played three finals so I definitely remember them; don't worry about that. Probably winning the game against Carlton at the MCG in 2001, a bit of an arch-enemy type of thing. Then we went up to Brisbane the next week; if that final had been in Melbourne, who knows?

Mike: What about personally? What's the favourite memory for you in an individual sense?

Matthew: I think 2008 was fairly satisfying individually. To change positions at the start of the year after three games, I would be lying if I said I wasn't a little bit worried about where I was at. I knew the club was looking to develop other forwards and obviously that needs to happen, so to get moved to a wing, I didn't know how it was going to go. Was I capable? I did have a few doubts there but it panned out fairly well so I guess at the age of 33 to change positions and actually have a solid year and All-Australian selection, if I look back that was a fairly satisfying year.

Mike: You had a massive engine. Is that something that you were born with, or is that a result of all the time you spent in training?

Matthew: At school I was always good at cross-country and long-distance running so I think you are born with a certain aerobic ability, but you then need to keep working on it and you also have to have the ability to keep pushing yourself. I know there are plenty of guys who have got a good tank if they do their max tests on the treadmill, but on game day you need to be able to dig deep and push yourself.

Mike: You've won just the one best and fairest when you were 32. Have you been harshly treated?
Matthew: Individual awards are generally won by midfielders and I think as a forward it's harder to have a consistent year, week-in week-out. You're going to have dry days just by the nature of the way the games are going.

Mike: But you must be pleased that your name's on the board?
Matthew: Look, I would be lying if I said I wasn't. I'll be honest by saying if I'd looked up at that board 15 years into my career and didn't see my name there, it would've been disappointing.

Mike: You were never captain. Was that disappointing?
Matthew: Yes, I'm disappointed I haven't been captain of Richmond. I just don't think that the timing's been right with the last two appointments. I think my chance was when Kane Johnson got the job. I put my hand up then and wanted the role but in saying that, Kane was an outstanding captain and he was voted in by his peers. One or two small faults can get in your way and I reckon sometimes you've just got to back people in a bit more.

Mike: What are the one or two small faults?
Matthew: Well, I reckon the reason I never got it was because of perceived body language issues and those type of things. That's my fault as well. I needed to straighten them out earlier than what I did.

Mike: I'm intrigued like a lot of people about that body language; I mean, everyone loves you and the Richmond faithful do, and yet there were periods where it would just surface, a pass would be misdirected or they'd ignore a lead and you would clearly be unhappy?
Matthew: As a person, I am fairly emotional in the way I express myself and playing footy is where I get my most enjoyment. A lot of the time people probably misconstrued it; a lot of the time I was more frustrated at myself than any teammates.

Mike: Matty, explain to us what happened that fateful night against Carlton at the MCG. You led, Matthew Knights miscued, you didn't seem to like it and you ended up back in the seconds the next week. Tell us what happened that night.

Matthew: 'Matty' Knights passed it to me and I was leading out, and on the footage I clearly slow up. I mouth some words at what everyone thought was 'Knighta' and it does look like that, but the whistle blew and I was reacting to the whistle blowing. I was more annoyed at what had happened, that the play had been pulled up for some reason. Everyone thought I'd blown up at Knighta and it did look like that, but it actually wasn't the case.

So it sounds like I'm making an excuse, and everyone will think I'm lying but I'm not but I actually did a few things that night and then Dave Rodan went to handball to me in the goal square, and I did react the wrong way to Dave, who was a young player. It was probably more over that incident that I went back to Coburg.

Mike: You kicked 91.49 in 1996. Why do people say that you couldn't kick for goal?

Matthew: I reckon you've had a few cracks too over the years, Mike. I think everyone has. Look, at the end of the day, I missed some real sitters, real shockers from two or three metres out and people really remember them. But if you actually have a look at the overall percentage it doesn't look too bad, but I reckon when I've had a miss I have had some really ordinary big misses and that always sticks in people's minds. Everyone went on about it, but I had a look at the percentages and I think at the time I was 60 percent and Bernie Quinlan was 56 percent and I thought: 'Hang on, wasn't he called 'Superboot'?' Perception's a big thing in football.

Mike: On those rare occasions when you missed a goal did you get any advice from the public?

Matthew: Yes, we've had plenty of advice over the years. I did kick well one year when Michael 'Disco' Roach took me. He was probably the best teacher I had. But the stupidest bit of advice I never tried, I got a letter from a gentleman one day and he wanted me to throw back to the early 1900s and bring back the place kick. It probably was not a bad idea if you look at it, because the ball is sitting still; there's no movement but can you imagine the flack I'd cop if I set up for a place kick and then mucked it up. I don't know how you guys would've reported on that.

Mike: You were 13 times leading goalkicker. It's a staggering achievement, I reckon; I mean, it's twice more than Skinny Titus[82] and he kicked 970 goals? It's a great reflection on your career to be consistent in that area of the game.

Matthew: I've never really been someone that's kicked massive bags of goals. I mean, 'Skinny' Titus was always kicking 80 or 90 goals every year, and then Michael Roach more than 80 probably four times in his 600 [goals]. But I was good for 50 or 60 goals a year, and I've been relatively consistent across the board for that, I guess.

Mike: Who have you most enjoyed playing with in yellow and black?

Matthew: I loved playing with [Brendon] 'Benny' Gale. When he went into the ruck later in his career some of the marks he used to take in the back 50, standing in front of full forwards and getting his back caved in and taking strong marks. You always knew he'd take them though. Matty Knights was a huge talent; I enjoyed playing with them and then obviously Wayne Campbell was consistent week-in, week-out. They're probably the three.

Mike: What about your toughest opponent?

Matthew: Toughest. There's been a lot of good players over the years. But probably the last 10 years, you know, I was never able to get a kick on Max Hudghton.

Mike: You know, Brendan Fevola says that.

Matthew: I would reckon he's hugely underrated in the overall scheme of things.

Mike: Is that because from the outside looking in his closing speed's good and he's got long arms?

Matthew: Max has got good closing speed. You think you've got him on the lead but he gets there and gets the fists in. He's strong, he's got a big

---

82 Jack 'Skinny' Titus kicked 970 goals for Richmond in the 1920s, '30s and '40s.

body and he's good at just getting you tangled up when you go on the lead. He'll put a hand in and you'll lose a bit of balance and it's very hard to get away from him.

Mike: You played your first game in Round 7 in 1993; tell us your memories?
Matthew: We played the Saints at the 'G'. We didn't have a good year, we only won four games but we won that one. I remember Danny Frawley told me he was going to belt me if I kept running. I don't think he enjoyed me running, the old 'Spud'. That made me run more.

Mike: Footy money's good money and you've been on footy money for 17 years. Have you used it?
Matthew: Yes, I reckon I've been fairly diligent with it. I try to tell the young players now: 'You don't know how long it's going to last, so while you're playing, put as much of it away as you can.'

PAUL ROOS

One of footy's 'Mr Nice Guys', Paul Roos did not find premiership success as a player, but achieved football immortality as coach of the Sydney Swans 2005 flag-winning side, a triumph that broke the longest drought in VFL/AFL history.

Appropriately for a future star, Roos was recruited from Beverley Hills, in suburban Melbourne, by Fitzroy and debuted for the Lions in 1982. He played much of his first season as a forward, kicking 26 goals in his 13 games, but was shifted more or less permanently into defence in the following season.

Roos became an integral part of the Lions for the next decade. Always capable of taking on, and usually beating, the opposition's best forward, he also had the happy knack of knowing the right moment to drift forward and kick a vital Fitzroy goal.

At the end of 1994, after 269 games, Roos was lured to Sydney, where he played a further four years. He came close to achieving the ultimate dream when he played in the Swans' losing 1996 Grand Final against North Melbourne.

Upon his retirement, Roos joined the Swans' coaching panel as an assistant to Rodney Eade. When Eade departed in mid-2002, Roos stepped up to take the senior post temporarily. Such was his effect on the players, that when the Sydney board moved to appoint Terry Wallace to the role, the support of the players and supporters held sway and Roos was appointed permanent coach.

It was a decision that would reap the ultimate award, as Roos led the Swans to a premiership in 2005, their first since 1933. The Swans made the Grand Final again the following year but fell one point short of back-to-back flags.

Roos continued to coach until 2010, when it was announced mid-season that he would hand the reins over to long-time assistant and friend, John Longmire, a move that was to take Sydney once more to a flag.

He continues in a media role but Roos will always be best remembered as a great player at Fitzroy and the man who broke the drought at Sydney.

APRIL 19, 2010

Mike: You're just 46 years of age and you've already flagged your intention to walk away from the Swans at the end of 2010. Why?

Paul: Well, it probably goes back to when I first took it on. I really felt at the time I was the right person to coach the club. And it was never a burning ambition to be a long-time senior coach, but I really wanted to coach the Sydney Football Club, because I knew the players well and I felt that we could do something special there. But, equally, at that time, I didn't think I'd be around for four, five, six years. I wasn't really sure how it was going to work out. And then, I just felt the timing was right to step away at the end of 2010.

Mike: Have you ever wondered what might have been had the Swans supporters not risen up in 2003 and thwarted the club's attempt to install Terry Wallace as coach?

Paul: Not really. It seems a long time ago, and I think I'm always the sort of person that sort of moves on reasonably quickly. I've spoken to Richard Colless[83] about it and, you know, he's adamant that nothing untoward happened. Andrew Ireland and I have got a great friendship, and Richard and I are great friends. So it's really not something I ever dwell on and look back on.

At the time I was coaching the team and the seconds were in the finals and it's sort of a bit of a blur. I think it was a good time for the footy club, in hindsight, because, people said that Sydney people didn't really have the passion. And it obviously kept on rolling on over the next six or seven years.

Mike: You've had a lot of success: the club's first premiership in 72 years, a 57 percent strike rate, finals in six of your seven full seasons. What is the greatest of those achievements?

---

83 Colless is longtime chairman of Sydney Swans. Ireland is chief executive of the Swans. Roos was appointed at the end of 2002 despite speculation that the Swans had already done a deal with Wallace.

Paul: The premiership, because I hadn't won one as a player and I played for 17 years. We played in '96 and lost, and it was so disappointing. I don't think you can ever top a Grand Final.

Mike: We don't see you excited all that often, certainly not in public. It must have been a magic moment when the siren sounded in 2005?

Paul: I think you go into a Grand Final and—not that I've ever spoken to any other Grand Final coaches about it—but you go in and you've almost rehearsed your victory speech and you've rehearsed your speech in terms of losing, as well. At that moment, thinking about how much had gone into it, I really took my time getting from the coaches' box to the field. Another coach would've probably done it differently, but I really wanted to embrace the whole moment. So in the coaches' box, I stayed for 30 seconds to a minute after the siren finished, and then walked down to the ground and saw people—obviously, my family—but people like Paul Kelly and Bobby Skilton and Barry Round and a lot of the guys that had put a hell of a lot of money in during those early years—and that really made me realise how big an effort it was, not just for the players on that day, and the coaching staff, but the football club as a whole.

CAREER
Born: June 27, 1963
THE PLAYER
Clubs: *Fitzroy*—269 games, 270 goals; *Sydney*—87 games, 19 goals
THE COACH
Club: *Sydney*—202 games, 116 wins, 84 losses, 2 draws, 57 percent winning percentage, premiership 2005
Honours: Australian Football Hall of Fame inductee (2005); All-Australian team 1985, 1987, 1988, 1991 (captain), 1992 (captain), 1996, 1997; All-Australian coach 2005; Sydney premiership coach 2005; Leigh Matthews Trophy (AFLPA Most Valuable Player award) 1986; Brownlow Medal—3rd 1985, 1986; E.J. Whitten Medal (Best player in a State of Origin game) 1985; 1988; 14 times Victorian state of origin representative; Fitzroy Team of the Century; Fitzroy captain 1988-90, 1992-94; Mitchell Medal (Fitzroy best and fairest) 1985, 1986, 1991, 1992, 1994; Fitzroy leading goalkicker 1990

Mike: You won a flag in 2005 and lost a flag in 2006, with a kick on both occasions. Were you lucky or unlucky?

Paul: That's a good question. I mean, I would've loved to have won two, and I would've hated to lose two. So, I guess in the course of history and the closeness of the games between the Eagles and Sydney and, if you look back now I think both John Worsfold and I might agree on one thing, that one and one is probably not a bad result.

Mike: Andrew Demetriou famously criticised your game style in the premiership year. You were angry about that, weren't you?

Paul: I thought it was probably unnecessary. But at the time, when you're in the midst of the season and you're playing and all those sorts of things, there's a lot of other things you worry about, the things you can control, really. One thing I've learnt over the years as a coach, there's so many things you've got to do, and if you waste a lot of time on things that are out of your control, it takes your focus off the things that you can control. So when I look back on it, I think it was unnecessary, but it happened. We've both moved on now, and we won the premiership.

Mike: You did boycott his visit to the footy club shortly after the premiership, didn't you?

Paul: I was supposed to be the guest, yes, and I just felt it was inappropriate for me to turn up at that particular stage given the comments.

Mike: You arrived in Sydney at the end of 1994 with a chap named Tony Lockett. The club had just won the wooden spoon. What were your expectations? Did you think you were just playing out time, or did you actually see a future there?

Paul: Oh, I saw a future, in a sense. You know, Ron Joseph[84] was responsible for me getting up there, and I think he's terrific. Ron Barassi was coach, Richard Colless is still there, obviously. But I did see a future. I think that was the big thing that probably sold me at the time. 'Plugger' going, I think, was huge, and I also had a lot of respect for some of the players that I'd seen play on television and played against—Paul Kelly, Andrew Dunkley, Mark Bayes, Daryn Cresswell. I felt they had the nucleus of a reasonable team. I didn't know whether we'd play finals. I originally signed for three years, '96, '97, '98; I ended up playing another year.

Mike: Tell us your memories of Fitzroy.

Paul: Really fond memories, going back. It's amazing the bond that exists

---

84 Joseph had been temporarily appointed by the AFL to run the Sydney Swans.

between that group of players, not that we spent a lot of time together, but it's amazing when a Mickey Conlan picks up the phone and rings you. You could talk for hours. I was fortunate to play with Bernie Quinlan and Garry Wilson and, in the history of footy, probably guys like Garry Wilson didn't get enough credit for how good a player they were. Bernie did because I think of his Brownlow Medal, but Garry Wilson was an absolute star. The disappointing thing from that era was that some of those guys, in the history of footy, haven't got the due recognition.

Mike: How difficult was it to actually walk away from Fitzroy when you knew, we knew, the club was in its death throes?

Paul: It was hard, but in a sense, because I felt it was crumbling so badly, I knew it was the right thing to do. It was hard because I really felt for the supporters, a great group of supporters. When you see supporters putting their money … putting their hand in their pocket over and over and over and over again—and that's what tended to happen at Fitzroy—you've got nothing but love for those people, because you're fully aware that they've funded the club. In '86, when we were going to go to Brisbane—so you're talking about a period of 1986, all the way through to when I left in 1995—I knew that people were tipping money in all the time, to keep the club afloat. But I just sensed… the biggest thing for me was the club was not the club I joined.

Mike: Were you committed to the move to Brisbane in '86?

Paul: Absolutely. Because the way it was put to us—I think it was Leon Weigard[85] at the time—was that, I think there was three options: We merge, we fold, or we go to Brisbane. I think it was on the tennis courts at Wesley College and I think pretty much unanimously we all said, 'Well, we don't want to fold. We'd prefer not to merge. And if we all agree to go, let's go as a group.' And I was very supportive of that.

Mike: Fact or fiction: you nearly followed your old mate, Gary Pert, to Collingwood before you went to Sydney, didn't you?

Paul: Before 'Perty' went, I got a phone call when I was in America, at the end of '90 from a manager—and he said: 'Fitzroy want you to take a 30 percent

---

85 Wiegard was president of Fitzroy at the time that a move to Brisbane was mooted. The players were in favour, but it never came to pass.

pay cut, or they'll trade you to the club of your choice, and Collingwood have already done a deal with Fitzroy, and I've already sat down and worked out the contracts.' Then a couple of people from Collingwood rang me. I flew back to actually sign with Collingwood. I still hadn't heard from anyone from Fitzroy at all, and they didn't trade me in the end, because I don't think they could get anyone from Collingwood to go to Fitzroy. And I rang them after the trade period, and went in and spoke to them, and they said: 'Ah, no, look, everything's okay. We're going to pay you now.' I resigned from the captaincy as a result of that, and ended up re-signing at the end of the following year.

Mike: So when you got on the plane in the States to come home, you thought you were coming home to be a Collingwood player?
Paul: Yes, absolutely.

Mike: Do you regret that it never happened?
Paul: Not necessarily, because when Dyson Hore-Lacy[86] took over I still enjoyed two or three years with Alastair Lynch, and I thought he'd developed into a terrific player, and Ross Lyon and I are really good mates, and Jimmy Wynd. I was really disappointed when I first got the phone call. I wanted to stay at Fitzroy and I was desperate to stay at Fitzroy, but I was pretty dirty when no one from Fitzroy had contacted me, and I actually had to ring them to find out—after the trade period—what had happened.

Mike: You were such a talented, adventurous player at Fitzroy, but as a coach, you are risk-averse, defensive first. Why the contrast?
Paul: No, I'm a student of sport, I think. I played a lot of basketball as a kid, growing up, and I'm a big fan of the NFL and the NBA and other sports. So I'm a student of sport. And I guess my philosophy's come from what wins. As far as I'm concerned, my only obligation to the board and to the fans, is to win, you know? And we implemented a game plan that we believed would win games of footy. And that's really where it stemmed from.

Mike: I understand your obligation to the board and to your footy club, but is there a responsibility for you coaches to concern yourself with the aesthetics of the game?

---

86 Dyson Hore-Lacy was president of Fitzroy at the time.

Paul: I don't believe so. Some coaches would say 'yes, no question', but I don't believe so, because I don't think there's ever been a coach that's been reappointed because the team looks pretty. And I say that in all seriousness. If you take that on as a responsibility, then you're in danger of actually not doing the job that you're paid to do.

Mike: Let's get specific on that. You were in the coaches' box in that infamous game at the Docklands—St Kilda and the Swans—a dozen goals for the afternoon. At the end of that, is it only the result that matters?

Paul: Well, the best way to answer that is the Grand Finals: How many goals were kicked in the two Grand Finals? How many goals were kicked in 2005?[87] And I think—correct me if I'm wrong—I think you were quoted as saying it's one of the best Grand Finals you ever went to see. Ironically, at the end of 2005, during the period of time where we copped the most criticism, I think one of the websites did a poll of the 10 best games for the year, and the Swans were in four or five of those. Have we played ugly footy? Absolutely. We've played some shocking games of football over eight years of football. We've played some terrible games of football. But is that a result of the game style? No, it's not. Clearly, we've been successful, and we've played games with that same game style that have been fantastic. What people sometimes fail to see is, there's an opposition, as well. You know, you come and watch us train; we're a bloody exciting team to train, because if we're 18 versus zero, we'll bring the ball down the corridor every time. Some games of football, I can completely understand where the fans would go: 'Gee, why would I come back?' But I don't think we're any different to any other team. If you look at an eight-year period, there wouldn't be a team in that eight-year period that couldn't say that they haven't been involved in some really bad games of footy.

Mike: You look so composed in the box. Is that real, or are you a bit like the duck? I mean, is it that the feet are paddling at a 100 miles an hour?

Paul: I think I'm naturally calm. But, I mean, you can't be a coach and not be emotional. I think that gets overplayed a little bit. If you asked the players, I think generally over a game … over a period of time, they would say I'm calm. But have I given them sprays? Absolutely. Would the coaches in the

---

87 Sydney won the 2005 Grand Final with eight goals.

box say at times that I've yelled and screamed? Absolutely. It's an emotional game. But I naturally operate better as a coach when I'm calmer.

Mike: I recall you telling me once that you never reviewed the players as a group immediately after the game, for fear of saying something that you might want to take back during the week. Is that still the case?

Paul: One of the things I wrote down before I started coaching was along those lines. I felt that—certainly, the coaches I'd had—that was the least productive time of the week. So I'm very, very careful to review the team after the game, and if I don't think I've got something constructive to say, I won't say it. And sometimes the players have said: 'Why didn't you speak after the game?' We've all seen it. It doesn't matter what level of footy it is, the coach that starts talking and can't be quiet, and then all of a sudden, he goes around and picks off 10 players in the room. I've seen more relationships broken—over my 17 years as a player—in that period of time, than any other period of the week.

Mike: Does meditation play a part in your coaching, or is that something reserved for the family and your private life?

Paul: I think both. Meditation sometimes get misconstrued as some spiritual thing where you sit in a cave for four hours a day. And you can do that. But, really, it's about focussing and clearing your mind, and just getting your day off to a good start, and that's the thing for me, is just trying to clear my mind. You know, be clear in what I'm doing at work, and whether it be the day of the game—and I always meditate the day of the game—just to try and make sure that I do clear my mind and get focused. So it's really a lifestyle thing, but it's certainly helped in my coaching.

Mike: Barry Hall was a premiership hero for Sydney and a co-captain on that day in 2005. Were you fair to him given his contribution to the club over the previous four or five years?

Paul: Well, he made the decision himself.

Mike: It was his decision, was it?

Paul: It was completely his decision. At some point, we would have to make a decision, but I think the way Barry handled it took that decision out of the club's hands, and took that decision out of my hands. So, in terms of the club, I'm more than happy with the way that the club handled it, and ultimately, I think the way Barry handled it was just super-professional, and that's why I'm really pleased that he's playing again.

Mike: Did you ever sympathise with the big bloke, in the way the ball came into his area? We'd see him so often lead, start another lead, and sort of clearly get frustrated with this, sort of, lack of direction.

Paul: I think there was a lot of things that frustrated 'Hally', I mean, there's another area of the game that frustrated him more than the way we carried the ball.

Mike: They're the umpires?

Paul: Clearly, that was a frustration. It was a discussion I'd had endlessly with Jeff Gieschen about Barry, so I completely understand his frustrations. We understand Barry more than anyone else. You know, as a club, we love Barry Hall, we absolutely love him. We saw week to week what he went through, what he did for the club. So you won't get a group of people that like Barry Hall any more than the Sydney players, the Sydney coaching staff, the Sydney fans.

Mike: Do the big full-forwards, do they get victimised?

Paul: That's just the history of the game, isn't it, really?

Mike: Paul, you saw 'Plugger' as an opponent and as a teammate. How good was he?

Paul: He was an exceptional player. And has done more for the game than any person. If you balance the ledger: what did Tony Lockett get out of the game and what did Tony Lockett give to the game? He gave to the game far more than what he got out of it. And so when he doesn't turn up at a function, or when people criticise him, I'm his greatest supporter, because he simply wants to be left alone.

Mike: You've played with an amazing array of champions, at both Fitzroy and Sydney. Do you want to elevate one to the top position?

Paul: One is very hard. There's four that stand out, Tony Lockett and Paul Kelly at Sydney, and Garry Wilson and Bernie Quinlan at Fitzroy. But I'd probably say ... 'Plugger'.

DON SCOTT

Don Scott is a true Hawthorn legend. Recruited from Box Hill, Scott made his debut in Round 5, 1967. He played nine games in that season but it wasn't until 1968 that he established himself as the Hawks' premier follower.

Capable of shouldering the ruck-load all day, Scott was also relentless in his attack on the ball and the player. He became a cornerstone of the team that was to win Hawthorn's second flag in 1971.

Scott was also amazingly durable and rarely missed more than one or two games in any season. Given the high-collision rate that is part and parcel of being a ruckman, it makes the achievement all the more remarkable.

As an aggressive player, Scott occasionally occurred the wrath of the umpires and the VFL tribunal, resulting in several suspensions during his career. In the main, however, his focus was the ball and when that was the case his rucking skills were among the best of his time.

Off the field Scott was renowned as a man who kept to himself, rarely socialising with his teammates. Fashion-wise, Scott also moved to the beat of his own drum, often wearing outfits that were seen by other footballers as belonging to the realms of high society.

Scott continued to give the Hawks sterling service until his retirement in 1981. He had a very brief and unsuccessful stint as coach of South Adelaide in the SANFL before taking up a special comments role with Channel 7.

When Hawthorn came close to merging with Melbourne in 1996, Scott famously and successfully campaigned to prevent the partnership eventuating (the campaign was known as Operation Payback). The image of Scott ripping a stylised Hawk from the proposed jumper of the merged team looms large in the memories of those who witnessed it, and that one action was seen as a pivotal moment in the campaign.

Although he now has little to do with the club, he is fondly remembered as one of Hawthorn's greatest servants.

SEPTEMBER 10, 2012

Mike: Don, you've fought and won a battle with prostate cancer? Your health, how is it?

Don: Yes, it's all right. I mean, it's frustrating; anybody who's been through it would know the difficulties, but that's part and parcel with it. I think there should be a little bit more support, not that I'm looking for it. I had terrific support through this from two football identities: John Newman was terrific, and David Parkin.

Mike: So it was obviously a big shock to you when you learned you had cancer?

Don: Well, it is, Michael. I mean, it's all done so very quickly. As soon as you get the word *cancer*, you go into panic mode. I certainly wasn't prepared.

Mike: Were you staring at your mortality for the first time?

Don: You do. Maybe you look at life a little differently.

Mike: More of that later, but I want to ask you about your footy club. They've had a pretty good five years. Are you proud of your contribution to the vibrant Hawthorn Football Club that we have these days?

Don: Well, I don't know about my contribution. You're only there for a certain time and you're used up at that particular time.

Mike: You're used up?

Don: You all are. I mean, there's not one football club that doesn't ask for emotional involvement, emotional attachment. You are never going to succeed in football unless you're emotionally involved; you cannot be a mercenary and just go out and play football. It takes something from inside to be able to commit your body, risk your body for the sake of getting team success. As soon as you're finished, the club just moves on and they sever that tie, and a lot of fellows don't realise, or have problems equating or readjusting their life because they're finished.

Mike: I was talking about the pride that you should have in the footy club. Apart from the fact that you were a dual premiership captain but then your role in that pivotal period when there was talk of a merger with Melbourne. It was aborted on the back of a campaign that you were seen to lead. I'm talking about where the footy club is from, where it might've been.

Don: Well, the reason I got involved in that, and I got players involved, was because we had the successful era and they were emotionally involved as well to this entity called the club. I also recognised the people who built Hawthorn up in the 1950s and they were still in the club. They stayed on for 20 years and there was tremendous history there, and also for the supporters. I just believe that those people weren't consulted at the time when Hawthorn and Melbourne were talking secretly and they were never given the opportunity of a say. Then

> **CAREER**
> **Born:** December 20, 1947
> **Club:** *Hawthorn*—302 games, 133 goals
> **Honours:** Australian Football Hall of Fame inductee (2001); Hawthorn premiership player 1971, 1976, 1978; Hawthorn premiership captain 1976, 1978; 4 times Victorian state representative; Victorian State of Origin captain 1978; Hawthorn Team of the Century; Hawthorn captain 1976-80; Peter Crimmins Medal (Hawthorn best and fairest) 1973

they were given the opportunity through Operation Payback[88] and had they not come on board the club would've folded. People were out in the cold; they hadn't been told what was going on. But the membership skyrocketed and Hawthorn took off from then.

Mike: So why, then, are you not closer to the footy club that you saved?
Don: Well, Hawthorn's not what it is...

Mike: What it was?
Don: Yes, not what it was, because when I was playing and involved there were people that had been there more than 20, 30 years. Trainers, I'm talking about, the people that make up a club, the officials who were there for a number of years, too. You could always walk back and I could see the

---

88 Operation Payback was the campaign to save Hawthorn as a single entity, run by Don Scott, after a failed attempt to merge with Melbourne in 1996.

past players and they were still recognised, acknowledged and they knew people still there.

Now, you walk back into Hawthorn and they wouldn't know. I mean, one coach goes in, he brings his lot of support staff, as soon as he's finished another lot come in. It's treated as a job; there's not too many people passionately involved in Hawthorn.

Mike: With due respect, how do you know that if you don't go back to the footy club?
Don: Because they go from one club to the other and it's a stepping stone in their career, and where I have a problem is the emotional side of it. A lot of people are there to get what they can get, not what they can give.

Mike: But do you still love the Hawthorn footy club?
Don: The football club is a different thing. I'm attached to the people that I went through with. I don't know anybody there now; I don't know the directors.

Mike: But the game changes, Donald, doesn't it?
Don: The basics in life do not change, Michael, and it doesn't matter. The basics of raising children haven't changed since Adam was a boy and the same with football clubs. They've lost something. They're unique businesses, and there's nowhere else in the world where football is like it is in Melbourne. But they've lost the uniqueness of what football was like. You know, I think it's still alive in suburban clubs and I get terrific enjoyment going and watching Sorrento, for example, because that feeling is still there. It's not at the AFL.

Mike: I know you coached Sorrento at under-18 level, but do you watch them in preference to watching Hawthorn?
Don: Oh my word, my word.

Mike: It's nothing to do with me emotionally but it would seem sad that someone who's had such a major contribution wouldn't still be involved with his footy club.
Don: Well, why should I? I mean, that's not my passion. My passion is my horses now, and I'll go and do that. The AFL has got no interest... I've got no interest in it.

Mike: Let's go back to the start. You were at Box Hill fourths, you go to Hawthorn and John Kennedy's the coach. Now, they give you John Peck's number 23. You must've been more talented than you would have us believe?

Don: John Peck retired after '66 and I was given his jumper and I remember that I used to hitchhike home. I used to live in Box Hill and I can remember walking from the post office in Box Hill on the corner of Station Street and Whitehorse Road to my place in Box Hill North, a mile and a half [2.4km], and I floated, because that night I'd been presented with John Peck's number. I actually slept with the jumper.

Mike: Well, the number's become even more famous; I mean, you wore it obviously for a long time, your whole career, then Dermott Brereton and now Lance 'Buddy' Franklin. Tell me what you think of 'Buddy'?

Don: Well, I think let's wait. He's the flavour of the month right now, but I like to judge players when they're finished. You know, we've had a photograph together, and I've found him a little bit shy; a bit introverted.

Mike: What are your excesses in life, Don?

Don: Horses.

Mike: That goes back a long way doesn't it? Did you win a horse riding award at 16?

Don: I rode as a kid; I started riding at seven and did all the shows. I was more or less forced to ride by my father. We had horses and they had to be exercised every night. I wanted a way out, and I was just so thankful that I had football, or that Hawthorn came along and invited me down there, because that allowed me to get away from the horses. My father was a bit of tyrant, and I was so sick of it after riding them every night from the age of seven.

Mike: You lost your mother when you were young. Did that have a profound impact on your life?

Don: Yep, just did then, too. You shouldn't have brought it up.

Mike: You don't want to talk about that?

Don: No.

Mike: No. What age were you?

Don: Ten.

Mike: Let's go back to the more comfortable part on the footy, your first game. It's 1967, and you're playing the Tigers who were to go on and win the flag. Any memories of that?

Don: Well, I was a protestant boy who went to Sunday school and I couldn't believe the swearing that went on. I really couldn't. It was unbelievable.

Mike: What about when Peter 'Crackers' Keenan punched you in the face in a final at the same ground—VFL Park? Then there was that farcical tribunal proceeding, where he cried, from memory?

Don: He did.

Mike: Any bad blood from your side about that?

Don: No, not at all. No, he's dined out on that.

Mike: John Kennedy took you to your first premiership in 1971. You were up against the fearsome Carl Ditterich and Brian Mynott. That was a brutal game, wasn't it, the '71 Grand Final?

Don: Yes, it was. Carl Ditterich was a ruck-rover, too, so that's how the game's changed. He was a huge man, he had a huge physique, they were horrible games to play in. You knew it was different to any other game and you just knew it was going to be a tough, horrible game and you just had to steel yourself. The team back in 1971 won 19 games and that team didn't make the finals the year before in 1970, yet in '71 they did that. It was a terrific example of just what mind can do over matter and it should be admired, that '71 team.

Mike: Now, fact or fiction? John Kennedy rang you a while ago and said: 'Don, I just want to congratulate you on the way you played in '71. I've just watched it for the first time.' Is that true?

Don: Well, that is true; it's a couple of years ago and it's about 40 years too late, I reckon.

Mike: So the phone rings and it's Big John on the phone. And he said what?

Don: First off, to get a call from him is very unusual. He never makes calls, never rings. And he said: 'I've just sat down and watched '71; you played all right.' I said 'Well, you're 40 years too late.' I did use a few expletives.

Mike: Well according to the *AFL Record Season Guide* you were among the best players in that game. Were you?

Don: They say.

Mike: What about your relationship with John? I know for a fact that he loved your endeavour and your commitment and your passion, so you obviously got on well with him?
Don: We never spoke.

Mike: You got on that well, did you?
Don: Well, I told the truth. I can only remember three conversations I had with him in my whole career. He has coached me more than any other player and in that time I recall three conversations, but they weren't really conversations. One was a statement, one was a question and one was a directive and so in total I'd say there'd be no more than 10 words spoken.

Mike: What do you take in your life... what do you take from Kennedy that would enrich your life?
Don: I think a lot of it is the way he approached football, and you can apply to life. Football is life in a microcosm; you're going to have ups and downs all the time but you've just got to weather it. It's pretty tough and football's pretty tough, too, and life is bloody tough sometimes as we all know.

Mike: You mentioned the minimal dialogue between you and the coach John Kennedy. What about the even more minimal dialogue between you and teammate Leigh Matthews at certain times during your careers?
Don: Well, we never spoke either.

Mike: Can you share the origin of that?
Don: There's no origin to it at all. I mean, there are a lot of diverse personalities that come into a football club, especially at the top level. The thing that you have in common is your ability to play football. It doesn't mean your personalities are the same, because when you finish you go back to what you were doing before, and it's only football that brings you together.

Mike: But did you have a falling out with Leigh?
Don: No, not at all.

Mike: Now, I might be missing something but it seems illogical that you would play and spend so much time with a person, not have a falling out, yet not have any dialogue with them at all.

Don: There's other guys ... not only me, who don't speak with one another either. You've got to understand that that's the only thing that brings you together. But I will say that the bond that you have with the guys when you achieve the ultimate, it's real. It's as close as a family, and I've seen them stripped bare and they've seen me stripped bare both emotionally and physically.

Mike: And you've shared that with Matthews, so why isn't it the same with him?

Don: I don't know. But why would you pick on Matthews? I could go through and give you a number of fellows that I haven't seen that I've played with for years and we never talked for years, so don't try and say that there's animosity when Matthews...

Mike: So there's no animosity?

Don: There's nothing. I don't think Leigh would be close to too many people that he played football with.

Mike: There's a story that when you're on your way through practice games and even training sessions, that you could have punch-ups with your teammates. Is that true?

Don: My word. I whacked Matthews one day.

Mike: Did you? That was pretty brave.

Don: Yes, he tried to even up and I just saw him coming. We had a practice game one night and 'whack', and then he thought he'd try and square up, but I just saw him coming.

Mike: You were one of the few that he missed.

Don: I was pretty quick.

Mike: So you had no problem with drawing blood?

Don: No, why? I mean, we're in there, they're going to do it exactly as it happened to me, you know, blokes went and hit. Norm Bussell[89] gave me one in a practice match. I mean, it went on all the time but that's the way we were trained. Kennedy delighted in that stuff and you had to win your stripes at Hawthorn.

---

89 Scott's Hawthorn teammate.

Mike: I want to take you to the year 1981, when you limped—and I'm using that figuratively—to 300 games. Allan Jeans was your coach and it was his first year there. It seemed to weigh really heavy on you that year. You stopped at 298 games, when you needed two more, and I presume you were injured?

Don: No, I wasn't out. I didn't play with any emotion that particular year. I didn't like what was going on with David Parkin[90]. I had offers to go elsewhere, but I just couldn't sever that emotional tie.

Mike: You tested Jeans' patience that year.

Don: Well, yes, and I told him, too. He tried me as well, so don't think it just went one way. I mean, I was given five minutes to perform. I mean, you would never say to a player: 'If you don't perform in the first five minutes, you're off the ground.'

Mike: Did you resent Allan Jeans because he took Parkin's job?

Don: No, I didn't, not at all. I just resented the process and I didn't like the way Hawthorn was governed. The way they did the Parkin thing was not Hawthorn-like, in my view.

Mike: But wasn't Ron Cook[91] the president at the time?

Don: Yes.

Mike: And he was as Hawthorn-like as anyone, was he not?

Don: Yes, but he also made the bullets but didn't fire them when Phil Ryan[92] was there. Phil Ryan would pick the bullets to fire.

Mike: Did you understand that Jeans was committed to getting you to 300 games; he told me that when I was working for *The Herald*, because he knew that we were friends. But it seemed like at different points that you were trying to make it difficult for him to get you to 300.

Don: No, in my mind I never made it difficult, I would turn up and I'd do my thing, and whatever else.

---

90 Parkin left Hawthorn at the end of 1980 to coach Carlton. He was replaced by Allan Jeans.
91 Cook was a player, recruiter, secretary and president of Hawthorn and is regarded as one of its father-figures.
92 Ryan is a former Hawthorn president and player, and member of the Hawthorn Hall of Fame.

Mike: Let's go to the merger in 1996. Take me to that night at the Camberwell town hall. You led the resistance movement, and the emotions that night were unbelievable weren't they?

Don: I can understand, and I'm not being trite or I don't want to be funny, but I can understand how dictators in this world can whip people into a frenzy. That was an unbelievable evening, to go out to the Camberwell Civic Centre and the line went up Camberwell Road, Burwood Road then turned left and came back down towards the tennis courts. The feeling in that room was ... seeing so-called educated, intellectual men lose it and become animals. People in respected positions, MPs, people who held positions in our society, that just went out the door.

Mike: It was eerie that night; I remember that night.

Don: It was scary, it was scary.

Mike: I think the masterstroke of that campaign—and I don't mean that to paint it as a strategic thing—was when you held that jumper up[93].

Don: There's a thing called faith that we don't understand, and in that campaign things were happening for a reason. Do you know that a man came to me the week before, and I was looking for something because I knew I had to address that auditorium? He said: 'I know what the jumper was.' Now, why would he come to me? I thought: 'It's fate, it happened for a reason.'

Mike: You were seen to be the hero of that—and I know you don't want that status afforded you. I asked you before about loving the footy club, and I think you said 'no'. But, I think you are frustrated by the club in its modern incarnation, is that right?

Don: No, I didn't have and I don't have a junior club. My club is Hawthorn. Others can go back to their local club that they played or grew up with and they may have that. The only club I played for is Hawthorn.

Mike: Why don't you go back then; why don't you reconcile?

Don: Because it's *not* the way it *was*.

Mike: Some people would say, Don, that communication wasn't your long suit.

Don: I can't... I don't tolerate fools.

---

93 In his speech at Camberwell town hall, Scott famously held up a Melbourne guernsey to the Hawthorn members and ripped a Velcro Hawk symbol away from the front—considered the most symbolic moment of the campaign.

Mike: Did you resent that Hawthorn was run by non-football people like Ian Dicker and Jeff Kennett?

Don: Exactly. Because no matter what business you go into, you've got to have product knowledge. You can then back it up, so don't get involved in football if you haven't got product knowledge. You've got to understand a bit about it.

Mike: Now, I know you've got a strong message about the prostate cancer; you don't think that awareness is as high as it should be, and the support system isn't as strong as it should be.

Don: I was told before I went in that only 40 percent of men get checked; I mean, that's just amazing. Women go and do it all the time for their various things.

Mike: Did you contemplate not having any corrective surgery?

Don: I did. Then Tony Costello, who was my surgeon, just got to David Parkin and told him: 'He's got an aggressive form of cancer; you better tell him to get it out.'

Mike: When you talk to 'Sam' Newman it would be unusual... a lot of people would think this is funny that Scott and Newman would talk about that...

Don: Yes, but I knew him when he was John. When I'm going through troubled times, I can ring John. He's terrific.

Mike: You played on him. Did you belt him?

Don: *He* belted me. He was dirty.

Mike: He was a good player Sam.

Don: Unbelievable player.

Mike: Who was the best and toughest player you played on? They can be two different people.

Don: I know, but he's always in the mirror when I have a shave.

Mike: You're doing humour now, Donald, are you?

Don: No, I'm not, it's just an attempt.

KEVIN SHEEDY

I t's difficult to imagine a discussion about Australian Rules Football in which the name Kevin Sheedy is not mentioned. As player, coach and ambassador, Sheedy looms large as one of the most influential characters in the history of the game.

Kevin Sheedy's VFL journey began when he crossed from VFA club Prahran after the 'Two Blues' had won the 1966 Second Division flag. He played six games in his first season for Richmond before cementing a regular place with the Tigers in 1968.

He went on to forge a magnificent playing career as a straight-ahead, no-holds-barred centreman and back pocket. A thinker and strategist even as a player, Sheedy is credited with developing the back-spinning handball, allowing it to become a more accurate means of disposal.

As a Tiger, Sheedy played in three premierships, won a best and fairest, and was captain in 1978. Injury forced his retirement in early 1979 and he spent 1980 as a *World of Sport* panellist before being appointed coach of Essendon for the 1981 season. His coaching tenure got off to a terrible start, with the Bombers winning just one of their first six matches. At that point nobody could have imagined that Sheedy would spend 27 seasons at the helm of the Dons.

The ignominious start was followed by a run of 15 straight wins. Essendon played finals in 1981 and 1982 but was eliminated in the first week in both years. Sheedy took the Bombers to the 1983 Grand Final, but they were trounced by a more experienced Hawthorn. Revenge was sweet for Sheedy and Essendon the following year as they came from behind to defeat the Hawks. They repeated the dose in 1985.

Sheedy took Essendon to two more flags (1993 and 2000) before parting ways with the Bombers after the 2007 season.

When Sydney's second AFL side, Greater Western Sydney, was formed, Sheedy became its inaugural coach, a position he will hold until passing the baton to Leon Cameron in 2014.

JULY 30, 2012

Mike: Take us back to that time you took that massive risk, crossing to Richmond from VFA club Prahran without a clearance after the 1966 season. You're an 18 year old turning 19 in the summer of '66-'67. The VFA had said: 'If you cross and leave Prahran without a clearance, you're banned for five years.' What convinced you to take that gamble?

Kevin: Well, the Prahran footy club were fantastic people, and they actually cleared me. My mother said: 'Take the risk.'

Mike: You and I first crossed paths in 1966 at Chirnside Park at Werribee, it was Prahran and Werribee in a VFA game. Now my memory at the time was that you were slow, not a penetrating kick, and not a huge amount of tricks. Is that a fair assessment?

Kevin: I probably had some tricks, but I was not fast. But I was a reasonable thinker. And you know, we played the premiership that year at Prahran.

Mike: An amazing thing about that Prahran premiership team of 1966, the ruckman in that team was Graeme McMahon, wasn't it? Who was later to become your president of Essendon.

Kevin: He was a terrific person, for a start. For him to end up president of Essendon after leaving Ansett, it was a bonus for me. In the end I might not have even been around Essendon if he hadn't got there back in around about '97, I think it was.

Mike: A thousand games, Kevin, as a player, coach, State of Origin level, international rules, pre-season competition. It's amazing. It is unprecedented in football and perhaps in world sport. You must be really proud of that.

Kevin: Oh, I am. And I mean, they accumulate. But I love the game, and I'll never change.

Mike: That plumbing apprenticeship was a waste of time, wasn't it?

Kevin: No, it wasn't. I learnt to actually understand how this country ticks. I was very lucky to do plumbing. I had five years as an apprentice and then moved into the Army, into National Service, after we won the '69 premiership—I won it on a Saturday and you're in the army on the Monday. And that sort of upbringing was a really earthy one for me, not that I necessarily needed it, because you had Tom Hafey and Graeme Richmond and Alan Schwab knocking on your brain. But it was good, really good. The Tigers were a fantastic club, and I thought the defence forces really made me look at the serious discipline, about people going to Vietnam and coming back. And that's probably how the Anzac Day game ended up with the Bombers and the Magpies, to be honest.

Mike: Kevin, '67 was your first year at Richmond. You played a half-a-dozen games. You couldn't get into the centre, because Billy Barrott was there. Then you went back to the seconds and had a major knee injury. What were your thoughts then, given the background of crossing over from Prahran?

Kevin: I nearly ended up going to Central Districts. Dennis Jones, who ended up coaching me at Prahran, was the coach of Central Districts in Adelaide. I thought my career might have been over then, but Tommy was terrific.

CAREER
Born: December 24, 1947
THE PLAYER
Club: *Richmond*—251 games, 91 goals
Honours: Australian Football Hall of Fame inductee (2008); State representative (Victoria) 8 times; Richmond premierships 1967, 1973, 1974; Richmond captain 1978; Jack Dyer Medal (Richmond best and fairest) 1976; Richmond Team of the Century; Richmond Hall of Fame inductee 2002
THE COACH
Clubs: *Essendon*—634 games, 386 wins, 242 losses, 6 draws, 61 percent winning percentage, premierships 1984, 1985, 1993, 2000; *Greater Western Sydney*—22 games, 2 wins, 20 losses, 9 percent winning percentage
Honours: All-Australian coach 1993, 2000; 4 times International Rules coach (Australia); 4 times state coach (Victoria); Essendon Team of the Century (coach); Essendon premiership coach 1984, 1985, 1993, 2000

Mike: How serious was the knee injury?

Kevin: Well, I was out for the year. I needed my cartilage out. Then I had a knee reconstruction also later, and a couple of broken legs and so forth. But in the end, you pursue whatever you really want to do.

Mike: What was the highlight of your playing career?

Kevin: Probably in a Grand Final, maybe kicking the first three goals in '73. I mean, I didn't kick a lot of goals in my life, but I kicked a few in the Grand Final.

Mike: Tommy Hafey remains a strong friend of yours. He must have been a major influence in your life when you were young.

Kevin: My father's name was Tom. When dad died, you meet another guy called Tom. That's quite strange. And I thought to myself, this guy was totally different. My dad didn't really know a lot about football, and Tom was fanatical, absolutely fanatical. He was about in his mid-30s, and a super-freak athlete for a guy that age. I mean, no player at Richmond could catch him.

Mike: Why did he take to you, do you think? I know that you had this application and this want to be a successful footballer. But was there a personal bond between you two?

Kevin: No, not really. I mean, a lot of the boys felt he favoured a bit non-drinkers. The boys that had a beer might have felt that. But I just did everything that was asked.

Mike: Did he ever ask you to do anything, what we would call untoward, on the football field?

Kevin: No, no. That was more Graeme. Graeme Richmond was ruthless.[94]

Mike: Because you were pretty tough on the field, weren't you? You had the view from the outside that there were no-holds barred out there.

Kevin: No. You're there to win. And we did stretch the rules, and we broke the rules. And you look back, some of my kids have watched the games, Sam and Renee and Chelsea and Jessica, and they'll see an old replay and they see you do something, and they just nod their head and they can't believe you've done that.

---

94 Graeme Richmond was secretary of Richmond in the '60s, and a committee-member and powerbroker.

After you get hit in the head yourself and spat on yourself, you give it back. That's what we did. And that's what we did in the '60s and '70s, you know. I know it sounds awful, but you gave as good as you got, and Graeme expected you to. He's a different guy. He was challenging. He'd drain the energy out of you, make sure that you didn't fail.

Mike: Do you remember any specific assignments that Graeme gave you under the context of looking after your teammates and flying the flag?
Kevin: You actually would make sure you tackled blokes really hard. And if you were going for a mark, you'd take them out as well as taking the mark. I mean, I never got outed.

Mike: No, you were never suspended. You had a ritual for finals. You would take yourself off to the MCG on the day before the game, sit in the Great Southern Stand, as it was then, and play the game in your head. True?
Kevin: Yes.

Mike: Played over the duration? Was it a 10-minute exercise, or would you stay for a couple of hours?
Kevin: No, I wouldn't stay any longer than an hour.

Mike: Because your finals record is outstanding.
Kevin: Well, that's what the deal's about.

Mike: I understand that, but it's easier said than done. I mean, this visualisation was you being good, was it? I mean, you doing things for the team...
Kevin: It's all about the team. And if you can do that, then you become a very powerful, mentally strong person in your mindset. Even to leave Richmond to go to Essendon and stay there 27 years, that is in itself a mindset. And to come back into football and coach a brand-new club, and get them into the trenches and then build them out of the trenches with a group of people up in west Sydney with the Giants, that's a mindset in itself. And so you don't let anyone interfere with that in mind.

Mike: Now, Carlton was probably Richmond's strongest opponent in that period. Robert Walls played forward for the Blues, you played back for

Richmond. You and 'Wallsy' have had a couple of celebrated exchanges on TV and on radio, where I've been a close observer. What's your relationship with 'Wallsy' like?

Kevin: It's getting better.

Mike: You did call him a sniper, didn't you?

Kevin: No. I said: 'Not all snipers are in Vietnam.'

Mike: Correct. Yes, and that was looking him in the eye with those blue eyes of yours.

Kevin: He took offence to that.

Mike: Did you and he have baggage?

Kevin: No, we sniped at each other, so don't even worry about that. But I mean, I never actually said it was Robert.

Mike: You didn't need powers of deduction to work out who you were referring to.

Kevin: That's okay.

Mike: But I want to take you back: Was there on-field baggage between you and 'Wallsy'?

Kevin: Yes, a little bit. I used to play on him. Six foot four or five[95], he was and I'm not exactly six feet. But my job was to make sure that I could beat him any way I could, that was the deal. He was a fantastic player, by the way. A hell of a player. And he was cunning.

Mike: Dirty?

Kevin: Oh, yes. We were both dirty, yes.

Mike: After Richmond, the Bombers came a-courting. They took a big risk, didn't they, for a conservative club like Essendon to come to you? You'd only been out of the game 18 months as a player. You didn't seem like, at the time, an Essendon type, yet the Colin Stubbs administration was prepared to entrust the club's future to you.

Kevin: I mean, the people at Essendon were desperate and wanted to get somewhere.

---

95 Six foot five inches is about 195cm; Walls is 193cm tall.

Mike: Allan Jeans was in that field, wasn't he?

Kevin: Oh, yes. John Nicholls, too, I think. I think it was about eight, through a series of very good coaches. But Essendon do pick young coaches. And they went through a period where they didn't, and then they tried Barry Davis, and then myself, and then Matthew Knights, and now James Hird. So they picked first-year coaches. They go that way. They've found that that was better than a coach that might have been tried.

Mike: There's a famous photo of you, Kevin, training at Essendon, in your first year as coach. I think the Bombers were one-five from memory. You've got the footy boots on. And the word was that because of the team's plight at that time, you were going to come out of retirement and play. Was that ever serious?

Kevin: No. Brian Donohue, the chairman of selectors, wouldn't allow that.

Mike: Did you contemplate that?

Kevin: I would have thought so, and I put it to him. We discussed it, and he said: 'Don't do it, because you're here to coach.'

Mike: Do you remember the last game of the '81 season at Waverley Park? Neale Daniher hurt his knee, and after the game, it was reported that he had a bruised knee. It ended his career, didn't it?

Kevin: It did. He'd torn a cruciate.

Mike: Now, you made Neale captain for the following year, and he wasn't able to complete those duties because of his knee. How good would he have been? I know Leigh Matthews named Neale Daniher on a half-back flank in his best team, and Daniher had only played 60-odd games. How good was he?

Kevin: He's in my best team. He was as good as his brother Terry. You remember, Terry had been sacked by South Melbourne at the same age, and Neale Daniher had won the best and fairest at the same age that Terry got released by the Swans. So I think that Neale was as good as Terry, and very, very unlucky. And for him to actually come back after about three knee reconstructions and play, probably 10 years later—that's a great effort.

Mike: Kevin, you coached, I suspect, about 400 players in your time at Essendon.

Kevin: I have no idea.

Mike: I think that's a reasonable guess. You can't be close friends with all of them, I understand that. Are there any of those in that group that you wish you had have done things differently? I'm talking about perhaps Derek Kickett, when you didn't tell him that he was going to miss out in the Grand Final team. Maybe Ron Andrews, when you left him out. Merv Neagle, who you had a fight with.

Kevin: First of all, in Derek's case, somebody told him before I did.[96]

Mike: In Derek's case?

Kevin: Yes.

Mike: It was Danny Corcoran, wasn't it?

Kevin: Yes. But that's ...

Mike: Didn't you send Danny Corcoran to tell him?[97]

Kevin: No, no, no, no, no.

Mike: Didn't Danny Corcoran go to his house?

Kevin: No, no, that's okay, that's up to him. But it's up to me to make that call.

Mike: You wanted to make the call?

Kevin: Of course I will. But I'll do it in my time, not in any other person's time. It's as simple as that.

Mike: But you still haven't spoken to Derek Kickett, have you?

Kevin: I have.

Mike: Have you squared it up with him?

Kevin: No. I always say to Derek when I meet him: 'I'm ready to talk when you are.' And he said: 'I haven't made up my mind yet.' I always say 'hello' first, and always will.

Mike: There's a finite number of players that can play in a premiership, I understand that. But can you understand the pain of this bloke, to play

---

96 Kickett was dropped after the 1993 preliminary final and missed a premiership.
97 Danny Corcoran was running football at Essendon in 1993.

the entire year and then to miss out on what would have been the biggest moment of his life?

Kevin: Well, you go and ask Tony Buhagiar.

Mike: So he copped it better?

Kevin: Go and ask Ron Andrews. Go and ask David Flood, who was in better form, or Michael Symons. They were both in better form than Derek. I can tell you now, Michael Symons and David Flood turned up to the Grand Final, and Derek didn't. So maybe we got it right. And we won the game by eight goals. And we weren't a great side.

Mike: Ron Andrews, how difficult was that?[98]

Kevin: Yes, hard.

Mike: Given that you loved the way Ron Andrews played.

Kevin: If I had my time again, he probably would play. What our club needed at the time was sorting out. And in the end, Ron probably took the bullet. Look, I'd only been there at Essendon two or three years, and the place was not being dedicated. They all thought they were dedicated. I'd just come out of a club that had been to five premierships, and we knew what dedication was.

By the time that we got to the 1983 Grand Final, I think I cleared about 70 percent of the list, and kept maybe 12 players. And that's not easy. A lot of people mightn't like me, but it's quite simple. In the end, when we did that, we won two premierships against a great club in Hawthorn. And Hawthorn were just marvellous, absolutely. I mean, I always mark Hawthorn as *the* club.

Mike: Yet Hawthorn and you particularly had a strained relationship for quite a long time. What was the origin of that? Was it just because you were the two best teams?

Kevin: It'd be no different than America and Russia in the Olympics in those days.

Mike: What about when you blew the whistle on the Hawks with what you thought was this weird concoction that they used to sniff at the breaks at quarter-time? That was a mistake, wasn't it?

---

98 Andrews, a tough centre half-back, was left out of the 1983 Grand Final team.

Kevin: No, it wasn't.

Mike: Did you initiate proceedings that led to the police getting involved in that?
Kevin: I didn't. I just asked the person, and it was Iain Findlay, what could that be?[99] All I did was ask the question. In the end, it was headlines.

Mike: It was very provocative, though, wasn't it?
Kevin: Yes, it was.

Mike: And it was something that Hawthorn's coach Allan Jeans didn't forgive you for.
Kevin: No. And that's fair enough. But I wanted to make sure.

Mike: What did you think was in that stuff?
Kevin: I have no idea. That's why I asked the question.

Mike: Did you think it was illegal?
Kevin: I don't know. But should have I asked, or do we run away from what is happening in our game and in sport in general? Look what's happened in the last 25 years in sport.

Mike: By that, what are you referring to? You mean, about the drugs?
Kevin: Yes. All through sport.

Mike: Could you have been more discreet?
Kevin: No. Bang. Put it on the table, and don't hide.

Mike: They took offence at it, Hawthorn.
Kevin: Look, bad luck.

Mike: Did you ever make your peace with Allan Jeans?
Kevin: No.

Mike: Do you regret that?
Kevin: No. I liked him, I've always liked Allan Jeans. But we never went and sat down and spoke about it and put it on the table to each other. So maybe in one way, I might've been trying to protect something that was going on that nobody knows. Sometimes the last person that knows is the damn coach.

---

99 Findlay, a senior policeman, was working at Essendon at the time.

Mike: In the 1990 Grand Final, the brawl at quarter-time in that game. Did you whack Graeme 'Gubby' Allan?

Kevin: Yes. I didn't know it was Gubby.

Mike: You just saw a Collingwood official?

Kevin: It was a Collingwood jacket, a Magpie. I've turned around, and this guy's—whoever it is— just dropped my runner, Peter Power. And I've belted him right over the ear-hole.

Mike: Because 'Gubby' is a friend of yours, isn't he?

Kevin: Yes. I couldn't believe it was Gubby when he got up. And it was on, you know. And of course, big John Synan, that's our trainer, he was fantastic. But he actually took the rap for everyone.

Mike: Were you embarrassed by what happened that day? I'm not talking about the result, because it didn't go the way you would have liked, but just that. It was a bad image for footy, was it not?

Kevin: Yes. But I was there in '74 at the Windy Hill brawl.[100]

Mike: Did you throw one in '74?

Kevin: No.

Mike: What was your function in that?

Kevin: Stay out of the road.

Mike: But it was wild, it was raw, wasn't it?

Kevin: Yes, it was. I had not seen that happen. And Graeme Richmond just pulverised Jim Bradley.[101]

Mike: Jimmy Bradley, yes. But that wasn't the only one; there were a lot of punches thrown there.

Kevin: Yes, but that stood out then. Jimmy Bradley was in street clothes, and you'd think the person had jumped the fence. They'd have no idea, and that's the problem. When people jump the fence, they can be in real trouble, I'm telling you.

---

100 Just after the half-time siren sounded in a Round 7 match between Essendon and Richmond, a clash between Tiger Mal Brown and Bomber Graeme Jenkin escalated into a brawl that involved almost every player, as well as trainers, fans and police. A fan and an Essendon trainer were both knocked unconscious during the brawl. The fall-out saw several players and officials suspended, with Richmond team manager Graeme Richmond ousted for the remainder of the year.

101 Bradley was Essendon's fitness coach. He had his jaw broken.

Mike: You once nominated Graham Teasdale as the worst-ever Brownlow medallist. In fact, I think I wrote that story. And Teasdale was mortally wounded by that. Did you ever square it up with him?
Kevin: I don't think so.

Mike: Did you ever feel the need to?
Kevin: Look, did I say 'worst', or 'there are Brownlow medallists that I didn't think were great players'?

Mike: No. You said 'worst'.
Kevin: No, no, no, and I can name another half a dozen.

Mike: Yes, well, Graham Teasdale came to see me about that, and wondered of the origin of it and why you would do it.
Kevin: Yes. My concerns are for blokes like Kevin Bartlett and Leigh Matthews.

Mike: That they didn't win them?
Kevin: That's correct. So take out of the picture what I'm saying any way you like—a lot of blokes won Brownlows with no one on them, because they just took a mark behind the play. And tactically, our coaches were not up to scratch in that period. That's all.

Mike: The Mitchell White throat-slashing gesture. Now, I think you were fined $7500, were you not? My memory was that you were really, really offended that the AFL imposed that sanction on you, not so much because of the money but because of the statement that you had done something to bring the game into disrepute.
Kevin: Look, I'm not worried about it.

Mike: You were though, were you not, at the time?
Kevin: No, I wasn't over the top. I mean, I was guilty, so how can you actually defend it? I thought it was probably foolish taking me to the tribunal and just fining me. What were you getting a tribunal for— to say you didn't do it? I can't believe that. So I went along there and you're sitting in the dock as if you murdered someone.

Mike: The other one that we love, the jacket-waving. That was a game against West Coast. Your Bombers won. You were really excited. I might

be reading too much into this, but was it a statement directed at Mick Malthouse, who was coaching the West Coast at the time?

Kevin: No, not overly.

Mike: Partly?

Kevin: No. People made it out to be, because we're two competitive Richmond back-pocket players. But really, if you look at the game, it was the catalyst for the whole year to swing our way. And West Coast had to then come to Melbourne for the first final, and we stayed.

We'd come from a long way back with a bunch of kids each week, just nearly getting there and then we got there, and then all of a sudden we were a chance. Paul Salmon finally kicking a goal after six points, and then the siren went. Would you be happy, Mike?

Mike: Of course I'd be happy. It was a very emotional reaction from you, though, wasn't it?

Kevin: Well, can't help it. How do you plan waving your jacket? You don't.

Mike: Salmon's an interesting one. You let him go[102]. He had a sad finish, I think.

Kevin: Our fans were cruel.

Mike: They were. I sat at Waverley the day that they jeered him and mocked him, and he deserved better than that.

Kevin: I just said to Paul: 'Where do you want to go?' He initiated it. But in due respect to the club, my comment would be: 'Well, where do you want to go?' I don't think the club should be telling him what to do after his fine performance as a player. He selected Hawthorn, and I said: 'Well can you just let us work out the negotiations, and not you and your manager? Otherwise the club will get stroppy.' And in the end, it worked out.

Mike: I want to ask you about two Essendon losses. One was to Sydney in a preliminary final at the SCG in 1996. Now, those who were in that team said that you have never berated them before that or after that, as you did that night.

Kevin: Yes. Correct.

---

102 Salmon left Essendon after 1995 and went to Hawthorn. He retired after 2000 but came back for one final season with Essendon in 2002.

Mike: Did you say things that you regret, or was this just sort of talking about the wasted opportunity?

Kevin: Well, both. First of all, it was my worst performance.

Mike: What do you mean by that?

Kevin: Well, in letting my players know about the displeasure of the performance. My reaction afterwards, I was very disappointed in that. But at least they got the message.

Mike: Were you personal?

Kevin: On one or two occasions, yes, because I think their egos got ahead of themselves, and sometimes you have to do that. You can't blame that bloke, when it's actually you.

Mike: Who did you label?

Kevin: It doesn't matter about the names. No names. Probably in the end it was the greatest win for Swans ever.

Mike: You should have won the 1999 flag, shouldn't you?

Kevin: Well, we never got there.

Mike: No, I know you didn't. But weren't you complacent against the Blues in the preliminary final?

Kevin: You think I'd be complacent against the Blues? There's no love between Carlton and Essendon.

Mike: Okay. So it wasn't a lost opportunity?

Kevin: You had no James Hird, no Scott Lucas, right, Jason Johnson who won two best and fairests, Lucas two, Hird five. There's nine. So I don't think anybody ever understood that this team had performed unbelievably well without three of their absolute stars.

Mike: In '99 you lost the preliminary final that most of us thought you couldn't lose. You then ordered the players to go the Grand Final as a group. You then ordered them to leave the ground 15 minutes before the final siren, went to a restaurant, gave them a dossier, and said: 'We're now starting our 2000 campaign.'

Kevin: Absolutely. Look, mate, I've been in trouble at Essendon over hardline stuff. But I just think, sometimes, you get a bee in the bonnet about something. You don't want to waste opportunities, like we had wasted a couple. I mean even in 1990, we had to wait three weeks to play Collingwood. I mean, that's another premiership we could have...

Mike: That was just a quirk of fate. I mean, that was a draw, yes.
Kevin: No, that's okay, but it happened. So how many times do you actually keep leaving one behind? I mean, you're here to win premierships, and that's the deal.

Mike: In the year 2000, you won 24 of 25 games. You lost one game to Western Bulldogs all year. Would you have liked to have been the only coach to sweep a season?[103]
Kevin: No. That ball ricocheted off Dustin Fletcher's shin out of bounds [in that game] and Chris Grant kicks a left-foot snapshot goal, and that is probably the reason behind us winning the Grand Final. Because all I did was pound the players: 'That's how simple it is to lose a Grand Final. If you think you've won it, you're in trouble'. So I'm telling you boys now, we just edit it out, and it was subliminally added into every edit right throughout the next month.

Mike: So it worked in your favour?
Kevin: Absolutely. You had to make it work in your favour.

Mike: Kevin, did you stay too long at Essendon?
Kevin: Probably. Yes.

Mike: By how many years?
Kevin: Only a couple, yes. I think our club tapered down in the footy department. And you know, we went down to the bottom four in the AFL of spending. So when Mark Harvey left early, he said: 'Mate, I'm going. We're not going to spend the money that we need to.' So he went. And he probably read the play. I mean, there were things that happened in contracts with players that were probably not right.

Mike: Like?
Kevin: No comments. But I'm just letting you know.

---

103 In Round 21, 2000, the Bombers lost their only game of the season to the Bulldogs, with Chris Grant kicking the winning goal from a free kick awarded after Dustin Fletcher kicked the ball out on the full.

Mike: What are you saying?

Kevin: We lost four premiership players. And then we signed our first-ever player on a five-year contract, Mark Mercuri. So they're the sort of things that happen that a coach should have control over, but you don't. That's life.

Mike: Who did?

Kevin: Doesn't matter. It was the club.

Mike: Was it Peter Jackson, the chief executive?

Kevin: No, the club. It's a board decision as well. Peter Jackson's the best CEO I ever had. I'll put that on the table right now.

Mike: Okay. But he actually moved you on?

Kevin: That's okay. That's not a problem.

Mike: So there's no lingering resentment about that?

Kevin: No. I've been fortunate to have 27 years at one club. That's just beautiful. But he was the best, and he told you the truth. I can't say any more about that.

Mike: In retrospect, Kevin, are you happy with the answer that you think you may have only stayed two years too long?

Kevin: About two.

Mike: The broad view is that it could have been eight or 10 too long.

Kevin: Well, it could have been.

Mike: Could have been?

Kevin: Well, it doesn't matter.

Mike: Did you get lazy?

Kevin: Oh, look, yes, I'd probably say I was tired.

Mike: Tired?

Kevin: When opinion comes that people might have thought that you lost your edge, I've got to agree with that, yes. But when you know that the club's not really going to go hard again, that's when I say, two years, maybe.

Mike: Did you get distracted? Did your focus go?

Kevin: If I get bored, I'm in trouble.

Mike: Yes. And were you bored?
Kevin: In the end, if you are not going to recruit, if you're not going to be ruthless, you're telling me, the club sends a message to coaches. They send it in different drums.

Mike: But you remember that you were supposedly spending so much time in the corporate sector, and speaking...
Kevin: Well, it's the best thing I've done. Getting to know Australia.

Mike: But when you're the coach, when your fundamental role is to coach, can you spend so much of your time?
Kevin: I normally spend time with our corporate area, to build the Essendon footy club. And I'm doing the same thing in Sydney now. If you don't have off the field correct, you're in real trouble. Go and ask some of the clubs in Melbourne. You understand that?

Mike: Yes. But weren't you pursuing things that suited you, like speaking at engagements that were just a personal thing.
Kevin: Of course. That's my business, that's my own company.

Mike: Isn't your business to coach the footy team?
Kevin: No, no, no. Because we had one day a week that you can do that stuff. That's why the coaches' association brought it in. Because otherwise, what was happening to the coaches, they're burnt out by not having time off during the week. And the club would just keep asking for you to do more and more and more and more. So in the end, that's when we started the coaches' association with Neale Daniher, which everybody thought would be a failure, but it's been a success.

Mike: I remember writing an article that you took offence to, and the implication was that perhaps your drinking was a problem. Did you ever compromise your job?
Kevin: Oh, look, I relax when I have a wine. I don't worry about that.

Mike: You never turned up to training having had too many?
Kevin: No. No.

Mike: That's honest?
Kevin: Yes.

Mike: You never turned up to training having had...
Kevin: Maybe once. But that was in the '90s.

Mike: I know when you went to Greater Western Sydney, though, it was a new Kevin Sheedy. You were rejuvenated. You and Geraldine were riding bikes, you were in the gym.
Kevin: Well, you're not bored.

Mike: Your four premierships as a coach were spread over 17 years. Which is your favourite of those four premiership teams?
Kevin: You've got a bunch of kids in '93, and you've got a team that got beaten in one game in 2000. I can't split them. I mean, they're very enjoyable. We didn't have the right to win '93. West Coast were the best team in it, and we probably snuck one in between their two premierships. But look, when we got Tim Watson back out of retirement, you've got to thank Roger Hampson[104] for that and David Shaw, because I don't think I could've done it.

Tim had retired, and we made an error; we delisted him. We never had the capacity as a club to give him a six-month break, send him and Susie overseas. He started footy at 15, you know, and it wasn't just a professional era at that period.

Mike: How's your relationship with Tim? I don't know why this happened, but there was always this sort of innuendo that you aren't as close as you would expect of two people, given their common history.
Kevin: Look, I don't and never have got all that close to the players. I was coach of the club. We lost a lot of players at times. Somebody walks along, very wealthy people, and takes them off your club. So I just probably took a backward step, not only with Tim, but most of them.

Mike: Do you think your relationship with Tim was harmed a little bit by what was seen to be your harsh treatment of young Jobe?
Kevin: I was hard on Jobe, yes. It may have, yes.

Mike: You might well take the view that Jobe is the player he is now because of the way you treated him early.

---

104 Hampson, the Essendon CEO, and Shaw, the president, were instrumental in talking Watson into returning after he missed the 1992 season.

Kevin: Well, you've got to come to an AFL club, and any of the under-18 boys out there in the TAC Cup, just come prepared. And Jobe probably wasn't prepared at that time, and it might've taken him a few years. So I didn't play him in Hirdy's and my last game.

Mike: That was deliberate, wasn't it?

Kevin: Yes. Well, it sent a message: If you want to be really, really good, you get your act together, and the rest is history. He's been a damn fantastic player.

Mike: Did you tell him that?

Kevin: I've always told the players, absolutely.

Mike: But did you say to Jobe: 'You need to become more committed to this game and work harder'?

Kevin: Absolutely. He's done very, very well. He's actually a beautiful young man, there's no doubt about that, from a quality family. But you've still got to be hard. And if I copped the blame for that, well, I can cop that. I don't have any worries with that at all.

Mike: Kevin, the great players at Essendon, there's lots of them. You mentioned Simon Madden, who was probably the most accomplished ruckman that I saw over a long period.

Kevin: No doubt about that.

Mike: Watson, we talked about, Daniher, so many of them. Are you prepared to rate them for us? Who's your favourite all-time Bomber player?

Kevin: I think Kevin Walsh and Dean Wallis were two of my favourites.

Mike: I know you've invested so much time and emotional energy into Kevin Walsh...

Kevin: You've got to find a person who can run with Dermott Brereton and not worry about getting smashed. I mean, he was just like a Titan.

Mike: The Melbourne coaching job. You were a contender when Melbourne went for Dean Bailey, who was an assistant coach at Port Adelaide and a former Essendon player under you. Did you feel slighted by that?

Kevin: It was quite amazing, really. Because probably 15, 20 minutes into the interview, you immediately know you're in the wrong place.

And look, let's be honest, I hadn't had an interview for 27 years. Basically, you know, that was with Essendon with Colin Stubbs. So it wasn't as if it was a common practice for me.

Mike: Were you unprepared, are you saying?
Kevin: No, no. I was pretty prepared for the interview, but…

Mike: So was it the tone of the questions that threw you, was it?
Kevin: I don't know what they were really looking for. I thought Melbourne needed a head coach that's going to take them to another dimension, but I may be wrong.

Mike: But did you feel just a tad humiliated?
Kevin: No.

Mike: You wanted the job, though, didn't you?
Kevin: Well if you actually like them, you might. But if you don't go, you don't know. So actually, I went to investigate them. They'd only still be thinking that they're investigating me as a coach. So they don't think that way, people.

Mike: So when you walked out of that interview did you want the job?
Kevin: I would have thought, no.

Mike: Okay. How close did you get, Kevin, to going to what most people thought was home to Punt Road? Was it ever a reality?
Kevin: Well, there's only one president there that I liked, where I might have gone.

Mike: Leon Daphne?
Kevin: He's the best. I like Leon. I think Leon was the soul of Richmond, and his wife and family.

Mike: Did he nearly get you over the line?
Kevin: Yes, look, I could work for that guy.

Mike: Yes, but did he nearly get you back to Richmond at any specific point?
Kevin: Yes.

Mike: When?
Kevin: In the late-'90s.

Mike: And what made you baulk at that?
Kevin: Well, I thought Essendon were about a year or two off a premiership.

Mike: And you were. Kevin, you've been described various ways: quirky, innovative, from left field, eccentric, crazy. Which one is the most accurate?
Kevin: I don't think I'm much of any of those. I mean, there's a little bit there, here and now.

Mike: A lot of the things that are in the game now, and are entrenched in the game and are positives, come out of your mind. I think the game owes you a debt for the rookie list. I think that's a great innovation. One that I'm not sure about, is the introduction of the 50-metre penalty, which was brought in because of a tactic of yours.
Kevin: Yes.

Mike: Now, you had this great Essendon side, you wanted to hold up play, so you told your blokes to concede the 15-metre penalty at the time, and then you could get your blokes back. And it was a tactic of yours. Do you regret that, given that it's given us the 50-metre penalty, which so many people are so frustrated about?
Kevin: No. You don't have to have the 50-metre penalty. Have a 25-metre penalty. Have them both. If it's bad, give them 50.

Mike: I think perhaps your greatest legacy to football is your faith in Australia's indigenous players, and the way you've encouraged them and cultivated them and given them confidence. What's the origin of all that?
Kevin: Look, I've been moving around Australia since 1970. And you know, I didn't realise there was another part of Australia out there, being brought up in Chapel Street, South Yarra, and Prahran and Armadale and Richmond for 25 years of my life. And not many people travelled in the early days. I just couldn't believe that we didn't see indigenous people the way we should have.

Mike: But what swung you, what changed your thinking, because many of us grew up the same way. We knew there were Aboriginal people, but we didn't have a lot to do with them. You seemed to actually make a conscious decision to go and find out.

Kevin: Look, probably growing up a Catholic and a Christian made me think a bit about it. To me, just go and do some good things in your life. It's not just about footy. Can you understand that we have a nation of people that were here first; they're 30,000 years in existence, and there's only half a million left? And can we actually get it right after 200 years of not having it right? So if you're going to stand for anything, put it on the table.

Mike: You've described your wife Geraldine as probably the perfect football coach's wife.
Kevin: Is this going to go to air? She's actually been very good. Very good.

Mike: What toll does such a total commitment to football take on a man and his relationship with his family?
Kevin: Oh, enormous.

Mike: You've got four kids.
Kevin: My kids know I love them. I spent a lot of time with them, as much as I can.

Mike: Do you think that the Sheedy name—and it is a famous name in that country—do you think it weighed heavily on your kids?
Kevin: It's a solid, awkward position to be in. To be honest, I don't know.

Mike: Is it true that you used to go and watch Sam play his junior footy, and watch from behind a tree so you wouldn't be noticed?
Kevin: Sometimes I would. But I copped a barrage of criticism and terrible things when they saw me there.

Mike: But you love the interaction with the public.
Kevin: Yes, but they were awful.

Mike: Any regrets, Kevin, about the journey?
Kevin: No. None at all.

Mike: Not one moment or day in your football life?
Kevin: No, no. I mean, I've really stretched everything you could in regard to Tigers and footy and the mighty Bombers. I love both the clubs, and I'm a life member of both the clubs. I probably look more at the game now,

more than where we're going over the next 25 years, and hopefully play a game for four points in China, that sort of thing. I think we've got to move the game into the next dimension. And I think that could be successful, if we had the courage to do that.

JIM STYNES

T he tragic loss of Jim Stynes to cancer in March 2012 at just 46 years of age serves only to magnify the remarkable achievements, on and off the field, of an unlikely legend of the game.

Born and raised in Dublin, Ireland, Stynes knew nothing of the Australian game growing up. His sporting world was dominated by the Gaelic version of football, but at 18, Stynes was spotted by Melbourne talent scouts at a training camp set up as part of Melbourne's famous 'Irish experiment'.

Stynes struggled to adapt to the game upon his arrival but a season with VFA side Prahran enabled him to hone his skills and adjust to the aggression of the game. He debuted for the Demons in 1987 and went on to play in that year's finals series, the first for Melbourne since its 1964 premiership year.

Heartbreakingly for Stynes and the Demons he gave away a 15-metre penalty after the final siren of that season's preliminary final, allowing Hawthorn's Gary Buckenara to kick a relatively comfortable goal, leaving Melbourne an agonising two points short of a Grand Final berth.

Stynes put that behind him to become an incredibly durable and athletic follower. His ability to absorb pain and carry serious injury enabled him to play in a VFL/AFL record of 204 consecutive games. Although he was a great player for his entire career, the pinnacle came in 1991 when he was awarded the Brownlow Medal. Stynes famously had his father as his 'partner' at the award ceremony that night.

Stynes retired after Melbourne bowed out of contention in the 1998 preliminary final. Sadly, he did not taste premiership success but he achieved almost everything else there is to achieve in football.

Stynes co-founded The Reach Foundation in 1994, a youth support organisation, and he remained heavily involved in its running until his death.

Soon after becoming Melbourne's chairman in 2008, Stynes was diagnosed with cancer. Although he went to great lengths try to find a cure to his illness, he died in 2012.

His death was marked by a state funeral at St Paul's Cathedral in Melbourne, with mourners filling the church and spilling over into Federation Square. Channel 9 commentator and former teammate Garry Lyon delivered a moving eulogy to his longtime friend. Stynes died less than 12 months after the death of Sean Wight, the Irish youngster who accompanied him to Australia on one of the great adventures of world sport.

MARCH 29, 2010

Mike: The nation knows you're fighting cancer. Tell us how you're feeling both physically and mentally?
Jim: Yes, look, I'm actually feeling really good at the moment. It's bizarre as people would know who have had it before, you go through periods where you feel sick or nauseous, or you feel really good or lethargic and often there's no reason.

Mike: When I first saw you in the mid-'80s running around for Melbourne in the number 37 guernsey I thought: 'This guy's not going to make it.' You went on to play 264 games and win a Brownlow Medal; I'm officially sorry.
Jim: Well, I would have to say that every year in my career I reckon you were telling me I wasn't going to make it at some point; as I said, you got me eventually.

Mike: Now, Jimmy, there can't be an interview with you without reference to the 1987 preliminary final, Waverley Park, Hawthorn and Melbourne and an Irishman unfamiliar with the rules ran through the mark and cost the Demons the game. What's your relationship like with coach John Northey?

Jim: Yes, good, really good. We had him at one of our games this year and they had a team of past players and corporate teams and he came along.

Mike: You would vividly remember the day I know, but the fiercest look on any coach's face, Ron Barassi included, was the look that John Northey gave you with his finger pointed at you in the rooms after the game. Did you feel like going home to Dublin then?

Jim: Yes, he was devastated, he was gutted and back then it was fire and brimstone. That was the era. We were coming towards the end of it and he was lost in the moment. For me, I was used to it—my old man was just as bad—and I just went: 'Oh well, that's life; you just cop it; you sit down and you just hope it all goes away.'

As it turned out when we left the dressing room we ended up in the same lift and I couldn't believe it. He just looked at me and kind of half-smiled and didn't say a word and look, he's never apologised for what he said but he doesn't need to. We got on with the business of playing footy, but he did leave me with one piece of advice, and I'm not sure if it was before then or after that. I'm pretty sure it was after it where he said: 'Jim, you don't ever want to have any regrets with your footy career, just don't have any regrets because there's a lot of players that I played with and they just didn't train enough or they retired too early or whatever it may be, and they never got a second chance.'

Mike: Take us back to the mid-'80s. You were a young man from Ireland in a foreign country trying to conquer a foreign game. Did you ever lose the faith?

Jim: Look, it's interesting because I did. In the second year of my career I was let go by Melbourne and I went to Prahran, but there was something

---

CAREER
Born: April 23, 1966
Died: March 20, 2012
Club: *Melbourne*—264 games, 130 goals
Honours: Australian Football Hall of Fame inductee (2003); Brownlow Medal 1991; Leigh Matthews Medal (AFLPA Most Valuable Player) 1991; All-Australian team 1991, 1993; International Rules representative (Australia and Ireland) 8 times; State representative (Victoria) 10 times; Melbourne Grand Final side1988; Melbourne best and fairest 1991, 1995, 1996, 1997; Melbourne Team of the Century

in me that just knew that I was good enough to make it, and I suppose I had a few people around me that had a bit of faith in me. I remember Chris Connolly and Shane Zantuck, they would take me for a run. I remember at that time in the middle of the season they said: 'Hang in there, it will come, it's just the opportunities out there at the moment.'

You either believe that or you don't and I really believed it, so I went down to Prahran and I really enjoyed my footy there, and so when I came back for pre-season I was just much more prepared. I was young, I was immature, I had a light frame, and there were a lot of big guys around the club at the time.

Mike: You played an average of 22 games a year for 12 years; that suggests an extraordinary strength of both body and mind and they're two qualities that are being sorely tested at the moment, aren't they?

Jim: I think the mind thing is really important for me. I say: 'Look, I'm really lucky I've got it because I don't have to work as hard on that, whereas other people do.' But it's like footy, I wasn't as talented as some people so I had to work much harder than the people that had the talent but didn't work as hard. It balanced out but you still doubt yourself though. It doesn't matter how good or not good you are, there's still times where you are challenged and you have to remind yourself and it's like motivation, you've just got to keep going back to the source and remind yourself that you can do it.

Mike: Can you share with us how you felt when you first got the news mid-2009 that you had melanoma?

Jim: I was shocked. It was just like: 'That doesn't happen to me.' The ego kicks in and goes: 'You'll be able to say you had cancer but you get on with it and you beat it.' But then the doc did the test and came back and said: 'No, we've got some more tumours lying around the body.' Then I was like: 'This is really serious.'

Mike: You were on the front pages the following day. Has it been a negative or a positive to be fighting this battle in the public arena?

Jim: It doesn't really faze me. I've played a game that's under the spotlight for 14 years and I've never really had a problem with the media in any serious way. The media have a job to do and I just figured you're better off having some sort of control over it, rather than trying to hide away.

Mike: Tell us about that day when you announced your plight at a media conference... a packed media conference and suddenly your illness became a public event?

Jim: Look, I was really shocked at the support and the attention I got from it. I just thought it was the usual five or 10 media people coming and it would be somewhere on the back page, but when I walked in there this room's packed. The support I got from people and letters and cards and everything else was just awesome, a lot of people live a very lonely existence when they're sick and particularly people when they get old. Whereas I've got people supporting me all the time and I know it makes a difference, that thought and prayer and all that, those make a difference.

Mike: Are you a man of faith?
Jim: Yes. Look, I am.

Mike: You haven't got your scapular on, have you?
Jim: Yes, I actually do. You remember that.

Mike: I do from a long time ago, yes.
Jim: I've got this green one here and obviously people wouldn't know but a lot of people have given me little things.

Mike: And do you find yourself praying more these days?
Jim: Yes, I do now. I did for a long time and then it just waned away and now I'm sort of bringing it back.

Mike: Do you ever ask the big fellow 'Why me?'
Jim: Not so much 'why me?' Part of me goes: 'This is ridiculous, like how could this be?' I know it's just part of nature, it's just going to happen, we're all susceptible to different things and when you get the balance out, then things are going to happen and an illness will come your way. I'm not blaming anyone; don't blame the big fellow. It's not payback; it's just these things happen and then it's how you respond to it.

Mike: What many of us find amazing is your ability to cope with your problems, undergo your treatment, be a husband and a father and still run the Melbourne footy club. You've got an amazing appetite for work.

Jim: One of the things that I probably learned from it all is I've got to slow down and it's been the best thing in my life because I've slowed down. I'm more present, I spend more time with my kids, my wife. We're a lot closer, you know, I don't sweat the small things like I used to, like I was getting out of control I was getting worse and worse, not better and better. My relationship with my wife is amazing. It was easy to take those things for granted.

Mike: You mentioned purpose. Right now what's the overriding purpose in your life?

Jim: Well, my main purpose is my kids, my wife. The other things are just small, they're on the periphery, really. But I love making a difference; I love the work I do at Reach, I love what I'm doing with the footy club, I enjoy what I do in the business world. But the main thing is my family.

Mike: When the children talk to you about your illness, what do you say to them?

Jim: They're pretty good about it. I took my boy. I had to do a blood test at a clinic and there was about 10 people sitting around, and he sat up next to me and he looked at me and he said: 'Have all these people got cancer, daddy?'

Mike: But they saw your hair fall out. For kids that's a visible sign that something's wrong with daddy.

Jim: Yes, but it didn't have to fall out for them to know. It didn't fall out, we shaved it out and then my little boy wanted to shave his head: 'I want to be like daddy.'

Mike: Let's talk about Reach and your involvement with young Australians who may have lost their way. How did you become involved with that?

Jim: Probably going back to when I used to go away in the summertime in Ireland. I'd go to these summer camps. They were actually sort of boarding schools and we learnt about Ireland and all Irish culture, our language, we had to speak in our language and you learnt about your song, your dance and so on. When I went down there I didn't have any love of the language and all that; I didn't see any purpose in it because we spoke English. But the guy who set it up wanted us to become great leaders and passionate about our country and understand if we ever left our country we understood what we were all about.

And I was amazed by that. I really looked up to him as a figure and also he was so passionate about the cause. We were all wanting to get better grades but he didn't really care about the grades; he wanted something much bigger than that. After going back year after year, something was happening in me. I was becoming very passionate about life and going after the things that I wanted, so it made it easier to go to Australia and go after what I wanted.

When I came here and started getting the opportunities to hang out with kids through footy and so on, it was always the bit near the end where we get to talk, sit around and then ask questions and I'd always say to them: 'Don't ask me the questions that are in the footy records and how many goals you've kicked and all that, tell me things that can help you as a kid or help you on your journey, your career, your football, whatever.'

And I used to love it and then it happened, it just morphed into this I'd love to set up a camp where kids could take this passion they have for sport and take it into life and we did. We took away 100 kids from all walks of life, you know, primary school, public school and I actually remember Gary Ablett senior coming down as one of the sports guys to come and talk to the kids, and he brought Gary junior with him and that was the first time I got to know them.

I could see that there was things missing in these kids' lives and we needed to unlock it. I had a guy come down one night; he was a drama coach and he ran this workshop and it just blew the kids away. They were just amazed and so when they woke up the next morning they just were changed kids. They were talking to kids they wouldn't normally hang out with, instead of picking on each other and being in their little cliques and all that sort of stuff they just stopped all that. They stopped hanging it on each other, the judgement just went out the window; it was great.

Then I knew 'this is where the kids need to work from', they needed to then work on their paths and work on their faults and their imperfections and not be afraid to explore that side of themselves. So with Paul[105] we started running workshops during the evening, and Reach was born.

Mike: Does it ever strike you that it's incongruous that we've got an Irishman who's the president of Australia's oldest footy club?

Jim: It is the weirdest thing ever because I never thought I'd get involved in the politics of footy or the management of football. In the previous four years I'd stepped right back. I was involved in supporting Neile Daniher in the supporting coach role and then I made a decision to get away from it all in the middle of the footy season so I could be with the kids. It wasn't until I saw that we had a really sick club that someone needed to get in there and do something.

Mike: You told the reporters from the *Herald Sun* at Christmas time just gone that your wish was that you would see Christmas 2010; is that still the focus?

Jim: Yes, well, he asked me what my New Year's resolution would be and I said: 'Well, to still be here next year.' Very simple. Life is very simple now and when I'm wondering: 'Should I do this, shouldn't I do this.' I don't do it. I don't have to any more whereas I used to feel obliged all the time, and then I'd feel bad if I didn't. I suppose it's time that I can be selfish now or I can be non-committal. But also what I've noticed is people have really taken a step up and I've actually allowed them to take a step.

Like at Reach—I've allowed people to really own the organisation whereas I was getting in the way. I was owning it too much if you know what I mean, so now the young people who have come up the ranks are running so much of it.

Mike: You won four best and fairests, which is a joint record at Melbourne, you won a Brownlow Medal, you were Victorian of the Year and you're in the Hall of Fame. Does one of those achievements stand above the rest?

Jim: Obviously, because I didn't win a premiership, the Brownlow was clearly the highlight of my footy career. It was totally unexpected, not something I ever thought would ever happen. I was still understanding

---

105 Paul Currie, a film director, helped Jim Stynes start the Reach Foundation in 1994.

the game and here I was in the middle of a room with all these people that I admired since I'd been here, and I'm looking out at them, not the other way around. It was a surreal moment, absolutely surreal and then you feel a real part of the game. You get it because you realise that you're part of history now and you have responsibility.

You don't just come into the game, play and then you disappear like many players do, but when you achieve something like that, you become part of the game, part of the club, the competition.

ROBERT WALLS

Robert Walls made his debut for Carlton in 1967 while a 16-year-old student at Coburg High School. He had an immediate impact at full-forward, kicking goals in his first three matches. His form tapered after that but he was back in the side as a permanent selection by Round 1 of 1968.

In just his 28th match, Walls became a premiership player, as back-pocket in Carlton's 1968 premiership win over Essendon. In 1969 Walls switched back to the forward line and became one of the League's premier centre half-forwards. He kicked two goals in the Blues' famous flag win over Collingwood in 1970 and six goals as Carlton kicked the highest Grand Final score in history to defeat Richmond in 1972.

Although lightly built, Walls was a strong mark and a courageous player who was never reluctant to throw himself into the fray. He captained the Blues in 1974, 1977 and 1978.

Walls fell out with Carlton early in 1978 and moved to Fitzroy. He was a fine contributor for the Lions over the following two-and-a-half seasons before knee problems forced him to retire. He took over as coach and immediately led Fitzroy into the 1981 finals. After falling just short of September action in 1982, Walls again took the Lions to the finals in 1983 and 1984.

Fitzroy slipped to ninth in 1985 and Walls moved to Carlton, coaching them to a Grand Final in 1986 and then going one better as the Blues defeated Hawthorn in the 1987 Grand Final.

Sacked by the Blues in mid-1989, Walls re-emerged as coach of the Brisbane Bears in 1991. He took them to their first finals campaign in 1995, before Richmond took him on board in 1996. His time at Tigerland was less than successful and he was replaced halfway through his second season.

Walls then went on to forge a successful media career as a forthright commentator. Although his opinions in this capacity were not always shared, he continued to command great respect among his peers

AUGUST 27, 2012

Mike: Interesting ride?
Robert: Well, it has been and who would've thought that 47 years ago when I went down to Carlton as a kid, that I'd still be part of AFL footy.

Mike: Have you got 50 in you?
Robert: No, Mike, next year will be the last year.

Mike: And what prompted that decision?
Robert: There are other things that I'd like to do. My partner, Julie, and I are looking to live overseas in 2014. We're going to live in France, that's something that we've wanted to do for a while and the opportunity's there to do it, so we will.

Mike: Let's go all the way back to 1967. You were 16, you were at Coburg High School and you travelled to Carlton to Princes Park to train via the tram. Ron Barassi is your coach and you barrack for Essendon. Now, I know people won't believe that last bit.
Robert: I was a mad Essendon supporter as a kid. My mother was an Essendon supporter and I used to go to the footy with her and we'd pick up a few mates and we'd go out to Windy Hill. We did it for years and players like Jack Clarke and Ken Fraser and Alec Epis, they were heroes of mine.

Mike: Why are you so hostile towards Essendon these days?
Robert: Look, a lot of it's made up, but I guess part of it was that Kevin Sheedy was there for a long while and we were pretty fierce rivals as players and coaches. I also played my last game of AFL football at Windy Hill and I buckled my knees, got carried off and as they did in those days, they gave me a bit of abuse and a bit of spit as I went up the race.

Mike: You had a super career at Carlton, there's no doubt about that. You played 218 games, won three flags before you turned 23 and ended

up being captain. That's where your heart lies, isn't it?

Robert: Absolutely. The Carlton Football Club was so good to me in so many ways and Ron Barassi, in particular, and John Nicholls who succeeded him as coach. They were my first two coaches for the first 10 years that I played, and obviously had a massive impact on me and I played with some terrific players. We played in premierships and we celebrate those premierships today.

Mike: The year 1972 is my favourite memory of you. In the Grand Final against the Tigers, there's 50 goals kicked in that match and you kicked six of them. Is that your personal highlight?

Robert: It would be. I think to play in a premiership and to play well in the game, I don't think you can do much better than that. As a youngster I can remember going to Norm Smith's home; and Ron Barassi took us there, and the thing that Norm Smith said to the Carlton players was that the biggest stage was an MCG final, and to play well in finals was the true test of a footballer. And I guess, you know, for us to have won that premiership and to have played well made me feel pretty good.

CAREER
Born: July 21, 1950
THE PLAYER
Clubs: *Carlton*—218 games, 367 goals; *Fitzroy*— 41 games, 77 goals
Honours: Australian Football Hall of Fame inductee (2006); 4 times state representative (Victoria); Carlton premierships 1968, 1970, 1972; Carlton captain 1974, 1977-78; Carlton Team of the Century
THE COACH
Clubs: *Fitzroy*—115 games, 60 wins, 54 losses, 1 draw, winning percentage 53 percent; *Carlton*—84 games, 55 wins, 19 losses, winning percentage 89 percent; *Brisbane*—109 games, 30 wins, 78 losses, 1 draw, winning percentage 28 percent; *Richmond*—39 games, 17 wins, 22 losses, winning percentage 44 percent
Honours: Carlton premiership 1987

Mike: Were you a dirty player, Wallsy?
Robert: Yes.

Mike: There are no conditions on that; you were just dirty?
Robert: Well, look, it was a pretty tough era and I played under John Nicholls and he was the protector and the leader at Carlton. When John

finished, I looked around and there wasn't too much there as far as doing that role. Don't get me wrong, there were players like Peter Jones and Trevor Keogh who would back you to the hilt, but as far as squaring up—and in those days square-ups needed to be done—I sort of carried a bit of that.

Mike: What was the biggest hit that you laid?
Robert: Look, I knocked Jimmy O'Dea out once.

Mike: I get scared when I hear this story.
Robert: And I got squared-up upon. The St Kilda boys got me and that's fine. I've got no problem with that.

Mike: Is that the day that you heard the message among the St Kilda players that: 'Walls isn't to leave the ground on his feet'?
Robert: Yes, and I didn't.

Mike: I remember a famous case involving you and Francis Bourke. I think it was at Princes Park, the Richmond champion was reported for kicking you, correct?
Robert: Yes.

Mike: He beat the charge, didn't he?
Robert: He did.

Mike: How did he beat it?
Robert: Well, they got that many character witnesses, they got everybody from the Catholic Church bar the Pope, and the character evidence was so outstanding I felt I needed to apologise for being part of it. There wasn't too much in it, and I'm glad he got off it, yes.

Mike: Did you ever get reported for kicking?
Robert: No.

Mike: Did you ever kick anyone?
Robert: Yes. Not a vicious kick, but an ankle tap or two. I actually gave an ankle tap to a North Melbourne player when I was very young and I thought no one noticed it. Ron Barassi was captain-coach, and as we came up the race at Princes Park and we got in the rooms, the door was slammed and he grabbed me by the throat and slammed me into the wall. He said: 'I saw what you did; don't do it again.'

Mike: Was there a similar incident involving Peter Knights?
Robert: There probably was, Mike, yes, and I regret that. Again, it was an ankle tap but he didn't deserve it; some people do deserve it.

Mike: Did anything come of the Knights incident?
Robert: No, it played on my mind a bit and I felt I should apologise, but I never have.

Mike: You left Carlton on a sour note. The year's 1978, Ian Stewart is appointed coach. I reckon a month or two into the season Stewart wants to relieve you of the captaincy?
Robert: No, it was earlier than that. It was after the first game. We played Richmond and we got beaten by about 10 goals and immediately after the game he cancelled the social function, which was with wives and girlfriends having a dinner. That's okay, then on the Monday night I went to training, did my warm-up laps and he called me into the middle of the ground, just the two of us, and he said to me: 'You didn't try.' And I told him: 'You've been here five minutes, I've been here 15 years. Don't you tell me that I didn't try.'

Mike: How did it end?
Robert: Well, he said: 'I don't want you as captain. I don't want you to come to match committee.' And I sensed that he didn't want me.

Mike: Off to Fitzroy for five years and then you returned to Carlton in '86 as coach in, what was seen to be at the time, a bizarre swap with Walls going back to Carlton and David Parkin leaving Carlton for Fitzroy. How did that all eventuate?
Robert: Well, let me say this. I went to Fitzroy and played there for three years, not very well. I coached there for five years and just loved it, so I had eight years at Fitzroy that I still cherish. How did I go back to Carlton? I coached Fitzroy for five years, and at the end of the fourth year I got a phone call from John Elliott, who I'd never met because when I played at Carlton he wasn't about. I think he was mainly in America and he said: 'I'd like to meet you at the Jam Factory.' That's where his offices were.

So I went to meet him and he said to me: 'I want you to coach Carlton next year.' I said: 'I can't do that, because I'm contracted to Fitzroy.' And he said: 'Well, don't worry about that, we can sort that out.' I said: 'Well, no, I've got a fifth year at Fitzroy and I'm going to coach there.' And I can remember driving away thinking: 'I've just knocked back the Carlton coaching job.'

I didn't know whether Fitzroy wanted me to continue on as coach and I put it to them: 'Do you want me to coach next year?' And I was told: 'You can throw your hat in the ring.' It didn't please me, because I'd been there for five years and it had been Fitzroy's most successful five years in its last 50 years[106]. I was disappointed in that.

And anyway with a bit of pressure in the media, Fitzroy came to me and said they would like me to go on as coach, and I said 'okay'. Well, about five days after that, Carlton got knocked out in the finals and I got another phone call. This time it was Ian Collins and he said: 'I want to meet with you and John Elliott.' I met them and they wanted me to coach Carlton. I was in a bit of a quandary, because I'd agreed to coach Fitzroy, but I also thought: 'Well, I'd love to be coach of a premiership team.' Fitzroy didn't afford you that opportunity—Carlton did just with pure finance—so I took the Carlton job.

Mike: And did you leave bad-blooded with Fitzroy?
Robert: There were people at Fitzroy who were really disappointed in me, and they had good reason to feel that way, but it was a tough decision that I had to make. I couldn't have given Fitzroy any more in the five years that I coached them.

Mike: You introduced the 'huddle', which is where the players congregate at centre half-back at a kick-in and then they all spread. Now, was that your idea or what was the origin of it?
Robert: The origin of it was from my two fitness guys at Fitzroy, Chris Jones and Tony Knights; both of them had experience with overseas sport, particularly basketball, and in England with rugby, so they would question AFL. They would say to me: 'Why do you do this? Why when the ball's kicked in at full-back, why do they kick it to a pack of players and point to where they're going to kick it?' The game was played the same way for 100 years. If you had the ball the opposition would follow you, so if your teammate had the ball, wherever you moved your opponent would follow you because that's what he's been told. Well, we can take some advantage

---

106 Fitzroy made the finals in three of Walls' five years.

of that, because if we put all of our boys on that side well, they're going to follow us. You create space on the other side.

Mike: You go to Carlton 1986 and the Blues play in a Grand Final. You win the flag in '87, finish top three in '88 and you've gone halfway through '89. From memory you were playing the Brisbane Bears at Princes Park, and Warwick Capper kicks a late goal. Brisbane beats Carlton; Robert Walls gets the sack. It's a dramatic fall from grace wasn't it?

Robert: Yes, it was. It was three-and-a-half years and, as you mentioned, two Grand Finals, a loss, a win, a third placing and then the sack halfway through that fourth year. I deserved to get the sack.

Mike: Did you?

Robert: I did, because I was very negative, demanding, looking for fault and the players would've had a gutful of me by then. Having said that, I felt I was left to my own devices a bit, but in those days the coach was expected to know all and be all. Looking back, it would've been nice to have got a little bit more support to sort of say: 'Well, maybe you need to change your ways a little bit.'

Mike: Did you have a lieutenant there?

Robert: Not really, no. That was my fault, because I didn't delegate too much, and probably they were too afraid to say: 'Well, Wallsy, try this.'

Mike: I think to be fair, and this is not meant to be harsh, but you were seen to be blunt, demanding, uncompromising and occasionally brutal in the way you treated your players particularly in training sessions. There were some notorious programs that you had at training, weren't there?

Robert: Solid sessions, absolutely. Having said that, I reckon if you speak to 95 percent of the players I coached at Fitzroy, Carlton and Brisbane, they will say: 'We're really glad he coached us that way.'

Mike: After Carlton, it's off to Brisbane for five years with the Bears and very tough times. It was a new club, the AFL didn't service it properly. You were the spruiker, the coach, all things. How difficult was that up there?

Robert: I could write a book about it, and I *might* write a book about it. How difficult was it? It was tough, because no one had much interest in you up there. The membership when I got to Brisbane was 1800. The crowds were five, six and maybe seven or 8000 at Carrara if you played Collingwood, Carlton, Essendon. Having said that, they were five of the most satisfying years of my footy career.

Mike: Why?

Robert: Because when I went there no one wanted the job, and when I left, they were lining up for the job. When I went there, we were based at Carrara with nothing solid around us. Everything was portable. When I left they were at the Gabba and they were putting in plans for a really good stadium. When I went there, you had one of the oldest lists in the AFL and when I left it was one of the youngest. So many of them went on to be triple premiership players and when I went there you had a group, some of them weren't fair dinkum, and you had others like Roger Merrett and Michael McLean and Scotty McIvor and Johnny Gastev and Martin Leslie, who were absolutely fair dinkum.

Halfway through the first year we hadn't won a game and there were a few players that I had cut, and Roger Merrett, who was captain, came up to me. He hadn't said much to me in this first year, and he said: 'I can see you're fair dinkum. I'll give you 100 percent of what I've got left.' And that meant a lot to me.

Mike: In Brisbane there's a notorious story about you, where a player called Shane Strempel has driven you to distraction. You don't know how to handle him, and in the end you circle him with the players and they take turns at sparring with him, true?

Robert: True. Truer to the extent that we did a lot of sparring, the boxing gloves were at Brisbane when I got there, and that was part of their summer training. They enjoyed it, so the gloves came out at training quite often. And Strempel had let himself down and his teammates with a lack of discipline, and on this particular night I felt he needed to have a chance to earn a bit of respect within the group. So sure, he was put in the ring... we didn't have a ring as such, it was on the ground and he went a bit longer than the average player would've.

Mike: But didn't you rotate players against him.

Robert: He had two or three go out and spar with him.

Mike: Is that all, two or three?

Robert: Might've been three or four. Let me tell you this, I never lost a second of sleep over that. I went home that night, slept without even thinking about it and for the next 10 years didn't even think about it. Then a documentary was made and they had a re-enactment of that, and it was dramatic and it was eerie.

Mike: Was it faithful?

Robert: No, I don't think it was. I believe I was set up, and so too do a lot of the players who were there that night, because once they saw it they contacted me and said: 'The wrong thing's been done by you.'

Mike: Your relationship with Kevin Sheedy... it had its origins when you were playing for Carlton and he was playing for Richmond. How hostile was it on the field?

Robert: We didn't like each other at all.

Mike: I remember sitting on the 3AW panel with you one Saturday, and we talked to Kevin Sheedy and from memory Kevin Sheedy raised the 'sniper' tag: 'Not all snipers were in Vietnam.' You, I think rightly, believed that he was referring to you. That issue erupted soon after on *Talking Footy* on Channel 7. It was some of the most dramatic footy television I've seen.

Robert: I took exception to him not being direct and saying: 'Well, you were a sniper.' Because I would've accepted that. It didn't worry me at all but he just beat around the bush. He was being very general and I challenged him to be specific: 'If you believe I'm a sniper, tell me I'm one. Don't just go on with your games.' But he wasn't prepared to do that. The other thing that annoyed me was that he had a shot at my coaching of Brisbane and said: 'You went up to Brisbane and hid.'

I went up to Brisbane and I know the effort that was put in by a lot of people there, so I regarded that as an insult to the Brisbane Bears, the players, people like Scott Clayton, Andrew Ireland, and don't forget that some of those young players a few years down the track beat Essendon for a premiership.

Mike: Do you like him?

Robert: I can't say I like him because I don't know him well enough, but I wouldn't say I disliked him.

Mike: He says he's growing on you... that you're growing on him.

Robert: Like a wart.

Mike: In 1987, Wallsy, it was a big year for you... then you take off to London for an event called the Battle of Britain. Tell us your memories of that. Carlton are playing North Melbourne at The Oval.

Robert: I didn't want to go to London, and I've told Ian Collins and I've told John Elliott I don't want to go, because it's a junket. 'The boys have won the premiership, let them enjoy the premiership.' And somehow or other they said: 'Well, the sponsorship we get for this game goes to pay your contract.' I said: 'Well, why doesn't it go to pay Stephen Kernahan's contract or Craig Bradley's contract or whoever? Why is it my contract?' So we play the game, they punch us up and I'm just thinking: 'Two weeks ago we were at the MCG doing what footy is all about, and here we are in this ridiculous game.'

So Alastair Clarkson did what he did to Ian Aitken[107] and it had to be squared-up upon, and I didn't have to look for volunteers because they just said: 'Well, we'll make sure that he gets squared up.'

Mike: On the coach's instructions?

Robert: Well, I was happy for it to happen.

Mike: Did you ask for it to happen?

Robert: I said: 'He's got to be squared up upon.' And they knew that, Alastair Clarkson knew that, John Kennedy, who was coaching North at the time, knew that because John Kennedy could've taken him off the ground. John Kennedy knew that what he'd done was beyond the pale and knew that it needed to be rectified, and it was.

Mike: When Clarkson hit Aitken did you pick up the phone and dispatch it in the direction of John Kennedy?

Robert: I did. I was up in the little stand, and he was down at ground level. I didn't try to hit him with the phone, I wanted it to land near him just to get his attention and just say: 'This is bullshit, John, we should call the game off because this is just rubbish.' The phone smashed behind him and he didn't flinch. After that game my players were spread on the floor in the change

---

107 Clarkson, playing for North Melbourne, king hit Carlton's Aitken, breaking his jaw.

room at The Oval and Aitken's got the broken jaw, Kernahan's got what he's got and God knows what else. And that was, in a way, the beginning of my end at Carlton because Elliott was there with a few of his Fosters mates and I said to him: 'I hope you're satisfied, this is the cost of the junket. I hope you're satisfied.'

Ian Collins was filthy with me for saying that, and the next day he said he wanted to meet me at 7am. I met him and he virtually said: 'How dare you speak to a Carlton president like that.' And I just said: 'Well, I don't care. It needed to be said.' I knew they wouldn't sack me, because we'd won the premiership two weeks before.

I remember going back to my hotel room and my wife Erin was there and she said: 'How did it go?' And I told her, and I said: 'They won't sack me. But when the wheels start to wobble, I'll be in trouble down the track.' And it's funny, winning a premiership is the greatest, and I enjoy it today more than ever with that group of Carlton players, the bond's there 25 years on. But two weeks after we got it, I was as flat as a tack.

Mike: You're coaching Brisbane in 1993, and Nathan Buckley arrives. What was your understanding of his tenure with the Brisbane Bears?
Robert: I knew he'd come for one year only and I was sort of responsible for that, because when I got up there that many players who'd been signed by Brisbane refused to come. I even had players ... their managers or the player themselves would say: 'Don't draft us because we won't come. We don't want to go up there.' And before my time too many players like the Jarman brothers and Chris McDermott just turned their back on Brisbane and got away with it. So I felt that a stand needed to be taken.

Now, Nathan Buckley was on Brisbane's list. Collingwood desperately wanted him, and I for one said: 'No way known does he go to Collingwood without first playing for Brisbane.' So by him coming to Brisbane we at least got him for a year, got some credibility that we stood firm and okay, I knew he was going to go to Collingwood, but we got their first choice in the draft, which was Chris Scott. We got Craig Starcevich and Troy Lehmann who were handy and there might've been a few other things.

Mike: Like?
Robert: I suggest there might've been some cash.

Mike: Are you suggesting any figures?
Robert: I've got no idea.

Mike: The Richmond coaching experience in 1996-97, Wallsy, it didn't end well. It was short-lived, probably should never have happened. I remember my own view was that you were finished with coaching and they talked you into it.
Robert: Yes, that's right. I left Brisbane for a couple of reasons. I'd had five years there, my mother was ill, Erin's mother was ill and David, our eldest son, was going to be taken by Carlton under the father-son rule, so there were reasons to come back to Melbourne. That was decided halfway through that fifth year up there as coach. *The Age* had offered me a job to be a full-time football writer and I'd accepted it, so I was more than happy to come back and do that.

Well, as it turned out the Brisbane job was taken by John Northey; he had a year of contract to run at Richmond, he jumped out and took the Brisbane job. Richmond was after a coach and they spoke to me. Looking back on it I shouldn't have taken the job.

Mike: Was Ross Lyon one of your assistants at Richmond?
Robert: Yes.

Mike: This is my statement here, my assertion to you. You single-handedly got him the job at St Kilda?[108]
Robert: I don't think that's right.

Mike: Well, he wasn't in the applications as I understand it. You'd gone through the first and maybe even second round of interviews and then the grapevine says: 'Walls says there's a bloke up in Sydney that we should have a look at. I think we should interview him.'
Robert: When I was on that committee to help appoint the St Kilda coach we probably started with a list of 30, which is ridiculous. You immediately say 20 and it was 10, and then Ross's name came up as one to be considered.

Mike: What did you see in Ross that made you so keen for him to at least have a crack at this?

---

108 Walls was on the panel asked by St Kilda to appoint a head coach in 2007 after the sacking of Grant Thomas.

Robert: He's smart and he's tough and he's got respect for the sort of person that he is and the life that he leads, and I reckon he thinks on his feet far better than most.

Mike: Wallsy, your relationship with the media wasn't healthy when you were a player and probably as a coach. I think you mellowed a bit when you went north to Brisbane because it was a bigger job, but you've spent the past 15 years working in the media and you seem like you've enjoyed it?

Robert: I've loved it; I'm very grateful and thankful that I had the chance to do that. It gave me a chance to enjoy football. I never really enjoyed coaching, I didn't allow myself the chance to enjoy it. It was always the stress, the pressure, the strain of coaching, so I didn't give myself a chance to relax and I regret that. I felt I could work the media and give my opinion because I don't reckon there's many in the media who've seen football from all the angles that I have. I never felt too bad about being critical of a player or a team, because I've been there and I know what it's like. It's not like I'm talking from a position where I wouldn't know.

GREG WILLIAMS

Carlton might have been apprehensive about the ability of Greg Williams to make the grade when he attempted to break into League football but the man himself never had any such doubts. The conventional wisdom at Princes Park said that Williams would be too slow for the game at the top level, but the man they call 'Diesel' set about proving them wrong.

After being sent home to Bendigo by the Blues, Williams joined Geelong, then coached by Tom Hafey. Making his debut in Round 1 of the 1984 season, Williams immediately impressed Hafey with his ability to run all day and his lightning fast and accurate disposal by hand. It was these skills that enabled Williams to counter his lack of pace and forge a 250-game career that encompassed two Brownlow Medals and a premiership win capped off by a Norm Smith Medal.

He played every game in his first season until injuring his knee, and all 22 games in 1985. Before the 1986 season, the Swans lured Hafey north to take on the Swans coaching role and Hafey brought several of his charges, including Williams, with him.

Williams had a stellar first year at Sydney, one that saw him share a Brownlow Medal with Hawk Robert DiPierdomenico and the Swans make the finals for the first time in nine years. He went from strength to strength until after the 1991 season, when the club that had originally rejected him—Carlton—offered him a lucrative contract to play out his career with the Blues.

Accepting the offer, Williams turned out another six years of exquisite football, winning the 1994 Brownlow Medal and the 1995 Norm Smith Medal as Carlton powered away from Geelong to win its 16th premiership.

By the time his career ended in late 1997, no one at Princes Park was left in any doubt that Williams was an elite performer at the top level.

JUNE 27, 2011

Mike: How can a bloke of 175cm, who can't run and can't jump, be so good?

Greg: Yes, well that was a big problem in the early days, Mick. The recruiters thought that and Carlton did as well. Obviously, they gave me the arse a couple of times and I just had to fight back from there.

Mike: So in 1983 you went to Carlton, was that the first time?

Greg: I actually played when I was 17. I played a seconds game for Carlton and I kicked four points that day on the half-forward flank and had 25 possessions. I actually remember it. I don't remember a lot well, but I remember that well, and I just think if I'd kicked four goals then maybe I would've stayed there, you know?

Mike: So what was the verdict? Did they come to you and say that they didn't think you were up to it?

Greg: No, not so much. They were happy with what I did that day. I was only a young bloke. But I went back to Bendigo and did pre-season with the Carlton group up there, and that's where it started with Carlton.

Mike: Now, let's fast-track to the end of it. We review the career, 250 games, two Brownlow Medals, two best and fairests, a Norm Smith Medal and six All-Australian jumpers. It's a staggering return for someone who took a while to get into the system?

Greg: It was, exactly and, you know, that's the great thing I think about my story. I didn't give up; I fought hard and trained hard. I ended up writing a letter to Tom Hafey in the '83 pre-season when he was at Geelong, and he said: 'Come down and train.' I was lucky enough to get really fit and I got the first game for Geelong in '84.

Mike: So when Carlton said 'No', you went back to Golden Square in Bendigo and played. Was your self-belief as strong as it had been before that?

Greg: I had doubts, don't worry. That's where the old man really was the biggest supporter, and mum, of course. Dad said all the time: 'You're as good as them.' He had so much confidence in my ability but I went home crying a couple of times from Carlton, don't worry.

Mike: Did you?

Greg: Oh yes. I was very upset but even saying that, Carlton had their 'mosquito fleet' in those days and played in premierships. They weren't really looking for a small slug.

Mike: So, did you actually think that the chance had gone? Or you obviously were renewed when you decided to sit down and pen a letter to Tom Hafey. Who put you up to that?

Greg: I was playing with Golden Square. And Tony Southcombe was coach, he played with Carlton, he's a great player. Ron Best was playing as well.[109] 'Besty' is a good friend of mine as well, and he helped me write the letter to Geelong. He was a bit the same: 'Keep going, have another go.' So, that's what I did.

Mike: So why did you pick Geelong?

Greg: Good question. I think we just hoped that Tommy would like the idea and, yes, he wrote straight back to us and said: 'Come down and do pre-season.' We didn't want any promises or anything. We just asked to do pre-season, there were a lot of country kids who tried that, most senior clubs would have four or five country kids who would come down and do pre-season.

CAREER
Born: September 30, 1963
Clubs: *Geelong*—34 games, 10 goals; *Sydney*—107 games, 118 goals; *Carlton*—109 games, 89 goals
Honours: Australian Football Hall of Fame inductee (2001); AFL Team of the Century; Brownlow Medal 1986, 1994; VFL/AFLPA Most Valuable Player award 1985, 1994; All-Australian 1986, 1987, 1993 (vice-captain), 1994 (captain); State representative (Victoria) 9 times (one as captain); Carlton premiership 1995; Norm Smith Medal (best player in Grand Final) 1995; Geelong best and fairest 1984; Carlton best and fairest 1994; South Melbourne/Sydney Team of the Century; Carlton Team of the Century

Mike: Let's stay with Golden Square for a minute. You played with your brother, John. He used to ride shotgun for you.

Greg: That's right, yes.

---

109 Best is a legendary Bendigo player, who kicked more than 100 goals in 13 different seasons of country football.

Mike: He was pretty rugged, wasn't he?

Greg: Yes, he's 15 months older than me, a bigger man than me. He was six foot two inches [187cm] and I think there's a lot of trainers say he had the biggest legs they'd ever rubbed. He's a real big man, and he was tough. John was the toughest person I've ever played with or seen, really. There's no doubt about it.

Mike: So you would've had a fair bit of confidence, knowing that your brother was in the vicinity?

Greg: I did. I had the dream run through school. I went to Kangaroo Flat Tech and John was the best fighter in the school when I got there.

Mike: What about your father, Leigh, he was a Bendigo identity? He was pretty keen dishing out some advice to you, wasn't he?

Greg: Oh yes. Dad was an expert on football and sport. He's a good sportsman in his own right; he's a fantastic squash player, played for Victoria. I'd talk to him after every game and he'd always tell me if I was hanging out and not going in hard enough.

Mike: Did that ever occur?

Greg: Oh yes. All the time. If he wasn't happy with the way I was going, he'd certainly tell me and it was pretty simple, the game and the way I played it. He'd say: 'You're not going in hard enough.' Pretty much, that was the difference between a good game and a bad game.

Mike: Any golden pieces of advice from him?

Greg: There's a lot of advice. Even early days I was getting a lot of attention from taggers and opposition. Everyone was trying to stop me getting the ball really, and I put up with a lot. Dad always said: 'Make sure that you don't let them keep getting away with too much or they'll keep doing it.' So, I didn't let blokes hang on and that sort of stuff, as much.

Mike: So did you whack them then?

Greg: Yes definitely and I think I sent that message early days and I think it stood me in pretty good stead. There was obviously a couple of games—probably more than a couple—where I got into a bit of trouble. But no, I think most people knew that if they did hang on or do things against the rules, well I wouldn't put up with it.

Mike: Your first game at Geelong, you play Fitzroy. Fitzroy has come off a final series. The Geelong centre-line in that first game in 1984 read: 'Michael Turner on a wing, this slow bloke from Bendigo in the middle called Greg Williams, a chap called G. Ablett on the other side.' The Fitzroy boys were in for a surprise, weren't they?

Greg: They really were. I think Mark Jackson was full-forward. I'd often say: 'That's the best day of my life.' It was that hard to get there; it took me years to get there. I was really fit. Tommy trained me like no one else and I was really fit and I was ready. I'd had three years of training to get to that game and I really made the most of it when I got there.

Mike: Do you remember your numbers that day?

Greg: Thirty-eight possessions, I had.

Mike: Thirty-eight, did you? You think.

Greg: I know I did. I remember it well.

Mike: What about the handball? You came into League football handballing like we grew to acknowledge later on in your career. What made you so keen on using handball as a weapon?

Greg: Speed was obviously an issue and my strength, obviously, was getting the ball. Handball was just part of my game in the juniors and all the way through, and obviously it didn't change.

I relied on my teammates so much as well. I remember even the first practice game I played for Geelong where Mick Turner was captain and I told Mick, I reckon it was the first boundary throw in: 'Mick, just stand over there.' So I'm telling the captain what to do in the first game—and I got it of course—and handballed and he wasn't there. I blew up at him and said: 'Just stand there.' I always liked to know what I was going to do with it before I got it, you know. And it was always handy to know a bloke was going to be there. I always had a couple of blokes set up to make sure they're there when I got it.

Mike: But you admitted it yourself, that's pretty cheeky for a bloke who finally gets his chance at an AFL club and he's playing his first game and he's telling the captain where to stand?

Greg: Very cheeky. But Mick stood there every time since. Don't worry, he loved it and he was really good at it. He just got in the good position all the time.

Mike: The pace you talked about before, you wore calipers as a kid, was there a relationship between that

Greg: I'm not sure about that. I'm really not. All our kids are slow, so I don't think it was the calipers. John was slow, my younger brother's six feet four inches [193cm] and he's nearly the slowest person I've ever seen.

Mike: So what were your calipers for?

Greg: Well, my legs were crooked. That's what they did in those days.

Mike: In your second year, 1985, you played in the infamous Geelong-Hawthorn game at Princes Park, the day made famous by the Leigh Matthews-Neville Bruns incident. What are your memories of that?

Greg: It was a pretty electric day that day. It was a bad finish, a very bad finish. I remember Jacko was being Jacko, and I think I ran through Michael Tuck, myself, early in the game.

Mike: You *think* you did, you *know* you did.

Greg: Oh, I know I did. It just grew from there. Then, there was the Bruns incident and it even looked like the whole crowd was going to get involved that day. It was really a sad day.

Mike: Have you ever been on a football field with an atmosphere like that it was that day?

Greg: No, it was a dangerous sort of an atmosphere at the end. It was really like the crowd was going to come on to the ground, sometimes unfortunately those sorts of things happen.

Mike: You damaged your knee in your first year at Geelong, won the best and fairest in your second year, and then you're off to Sydney. That seems incomprehensible these days. Apparently it was over five grand, is that right?

Greg: Yes, that's a true story. I wanted half of what Sydney offered me.

Mike: So what did Sydney offer you?

Greg: It was $100K. There were a few benefits as well, and incentives and stuff like that. But it was a lot of money back then, it really was. And I said to Geelong: 'Pay half and I'll stay,' and they offered me $45K and that was it.

Mike: Yes, but what were you playing on initially at Geelong?
Greg: Oh, it was about $30K or so. I was on a pretty good wicket the first year or so for a new bloke.

Mike: Who blocked it, do you know?
Greg: I think I know.

Mike: You *think* you know?
Greg: I do know.

Mike: Billy Goggin?[110]
Greg: Yes, I think it was Bill.

Mike: For any good reason?
Greg: No, not sure. But I think there was like a sleepy hollow sort of thing where they thought: 'Greg won't go. He loves Ocean Grove and loves Geelong.' And he mucked it up.

Mike: You could've played at Geelong, they played in four Grand Finals during your playing career. You could've spent your entire career with Gary Ablett senior. Any regrets?
Greg: Well it would've been great to have stayed there and played, and who knows what would have happened? I decided to go and I was a professional footballer. I had that chance to make money as well and I took the chance.

Mike: Now, you went to Sydney with several big names. Who targeted you? Geoffrey Edelsten was the man that was seen to be trying to amass these big names and create a football team there, but who was doing the recruiting?
Greg: Tom Hafey was the main one. He was coaching.

Mike: I remember you saying about the way you planned your career. Your preparation was faultless and when you ran out on the ground every week you had a target, did you not?
Greg: Yes, I did. I had a game plan, definitely.

Mike: Which was?
Greg: It was to get 40 possessions every game.

---

110 Goggin, the Geelong playing legend, was football manager at Geelong at the time.

Mike: And broke them down to 10 a quarter?

Greg: That's all I did… possessions, possessions, possessions. I trained to do that and it got to the stage where the bloke would tell me what I had at half-time. I always wanted to know what I had at half-time. I never counted my stats like some blokes did because I was concentrating on other things.

Mike: You topped 50 once, is that right?

Greg: Yes I did. For the Swans I got up to 53 or so. So…

Mike: Fifty-three or so?

Greg: Yes. That was St Kilda at my favourite ground—the SCG. I kicked six goals as well, Mike.

Mike: Now you went to war with several players over your career, didn't you? Lots of them actually. A couple of famous ones, a couple of names that spring to mind, Sean Denham and Tony Shaw.

Greg: Yes, that's right.

Mike: You didn't like taggers, did you?

Greg: No I didn't. I didn't like people trying to stop me doing what I did. Like, that was their job, but I just didn't like it and I made it as hard for them as they made it hard for me.

Mike: You were happy to administer your own form of justice? I mean, if they hung on, they copped one, is that right?

Greg: Yes, I did. And also, I got whacked a few times as well. You know, so if I got hit I most often retaliated. Maybe not straight away, but maybe a year later or two years later.

Mike: Wasn't that one of your dad's pieces of advice, always get square?

Greg: Yes it was.

Mike: Tell me about 'Shawy'. Carlton and Collingwood are always massive games, obviously, because they're such powerful clubs. He went to you most times, I'm suspecting he probably played on you a dozen times, didn't he?

Greg: He's a similar sort of a player. You know, same size and about the same pace as me. We're a good match-up. So I really respected that guy and we played on each other a lot.

Mike: You respected him. Not enough to stop smacking him right in the nose one day.

Greg: I split his nose really badly one day. But that was a bit of a retaliation from when he got reported for something that was probably a year or two before that. And like I said, I had a long memory and his nose presented itself and I hit it, you know? I didn't even go out there trying to do it or meaning to do it, it just happened like that. So, I'm sorry 'Shawy'.

Mike: So, sometimes there are blokes who play on each other regularly and they almost call an unofficial truce. Did that happen with you and 'Shawy'?

Greg: Actually that did. I think it was the week after I broke his nose badly. He came up to me before the game and said: 'Look, no fighting today, let's just play footy.' And actually it was a good thing that he did. It needed to be done and it was good that he said it, because I would never have said it.

Mike: Sean Denham, who I really reckon got under your skin, you smacked him in a final probably about 15 metres off the ball. Is that a fair account of what happened?

Greg: Yes, that was in the 1993 Grand Final.

Mike: You didn't like him, did you?

Greg: No I didn't, but he got five weeks for hitting me the same day. The first quarter he belted me at a throw-in. He was right next to me later and I belted him back and, yes, he went off. I broke his nose. But he had the last laugh. Unfortunately, the Bombers beat us.

Mike: Which regular opponent gave you the most grief?

Greg: Shane Heard from Essendon was tough. Dwayne Lamb from West Coast, he's a big strong man, a bit bigger than me and strong. Like, they're hard to get around. You know, they really are.

Mike: You didn't actually care much about your opponents, though, did you? I mean, if you were pitted against someone, you did your thing and they did theirs? You backed yourself against them, correct?

Greg: I did. I had a pretty simple game plan; just get to all the stoppages and try and wear out the bloke I'm on.

Mike: You play with lots of big names at the clubs you're at. Probably the biggest of all is Gary Ablett senior. You had two years with him. Where does he sit among the blokes, in terms of pure talent?

Greg: Gary's the best player I've ever played with. I always say that. I was in awe of his ability and he just had the best highlights tape of any player I've ever seen. I remember running beside him at training, he was just like a powerhouse. His shins nearly hit himself in the mouth, and he just had so much strength and power and, he was a skilful champion player, he was.

Mike: You wouldn't have known much about him when you got to Geelong, when he played half-a-dozen games with Hawthorn. He would've been in his athletic prime then. He was probably 21 or 22, and he could do anything couldn't he?

Greg: Yes, he could do anything. He didn't train much either. Tommy handled him well. He just had that good rapport with him. He was a bit of a different bloke, Gary, there's no doubt. But he's a nice guy, a bit of a loner type of guy. I reckon it was '85 pre-season, we had a training camp at Anglesea and he hadn't been training before Christmas.

He'd been pig-shooting or whatever he does, and he came down there and the first session we did 100 metres sprint and 200. He won both of those. He didn't go in the 400 or 800 because that was too hard for him. He kicked left foot 60 metres, right foot 65-metre drop punt. He told me he had this massive medicine ball and I remember Darren Flanagan threw it about a metre further than anyone—all the team—and then Gary threw it four metres further than him.

Mike: I know they're different players, G. Ablett senior and G. Ablett junior, but I think it's valid to compare them over their career.

Greg: Gary junior's a serious, serious player. Like, right up there in the best players in the League now.

Mike: Is he the best player in the League now?

Greg: Oh well, he's in there with Jobe Watson and those guys. There's no doubt he's a superstar and, you've got to hand it to him. It's not easy for young blokes to have a father like he had and be in the limelight and to come through and to be good as young junior.

Mike: You played just over 100 games at both Sydney and Carlton. Was there any difference between your output at either?

Greg: Look, I played some really good footy at both clubs. I loved the SCG as well, I really loved that … the Swans days there and I love that ground, it just suited me.

Mike: Your mate from Sydney—your teammate and mate—Gerard Healy. He was a serious player, wasn't he? I mean, you were at your peak in Sydney playing in the centre and alongside Gerard. Gerard won three best and fairests and you were runner-up three times in a row.

Greg: Thanks for bringing that up. No, Gerard was a star, there's no doubt. And we had a great rapport on the ground and he knew what I did and I knew what he did.

Mike: When I was working at the AFL in the '80s, you came into my office and you were in a tizz, you needed to find Warwick Capper. The talk was that he was going to go to Brisbane and I had this feeling that you thought things were falling apart in Sydney. You needed to get Capper and try to talk him into staying.

Greg: Yes, I was. I don't think it was a good move for Warwick going there. It was a terrible move. He was that sort of guy that fitted well with us and our team, but a new team, Warwick didn't suit and it proved right as well.

Mike: When you left Sydney, did you think that the club was going to go down? I don't mean down the ladder, I mean just go down and out?

Greg: I wanted to come back to Melbourne when I did—to Carlton—and I was lucky enough that I got back to Carlton. But, the AFL were giving up on us up there. I really did feel that it was true. They just gave up on the club and there was no direction whatsoever. And it got to the stage, I didn't really want to spend the next five or six years just up there on our own again. The club was in serious trouble.

Mike: So, did you think that they felt it was a problem they were never going to solve?

Greg: Well, that's what it felt like to us up there. And it felt like it to me. We were just getting no feedback of what they were going to do to help us and I just decided to leave and that was one of the main reasons. I remember trying to get the Swans to get the New South Wales zone for a start. But the AFL weren't interested.

Mike: Who sparked the interest from Carlton?

Greg: Peter Jess was my manager then and—it was three months out from the year, that's how bad we were going. I think we finished last that year, we were just in rock bottom and Jessie said Ian Collins was very keen to get us back, and we did a deal. But it was hard to get back, it really was. The AFL didn't want me to go, of course. I had to go to court.

Mike: They rubbed you out, didn't they?

Greg: Yes, I got de-registered for six weeks by the AFL, which was great. I got fined 25 grand.

Mike: But that was over contracts that didn't match up?

Greg: Yes, but it was just a whack over the knuckles, I reckon.

Mike: Was it?

Greg: Yes.

Mike: Because you were 'abandoning the ship'?

Greg: Yes, they didn't want me to go, and technically they were probably right.

Mike: You love playing in the middle, I know, you saw that as your domain. How did you feel in 1995 at Carlton when the edict came that you were going to go to a forward pocket?

Greg: Well I didn't feel very good about it, I didn't. But it just worked out like that. David Parkin talks a lot, but he didn't talk much about that.

Mike: To you?

Greg: No, he didn't. He might say he did, but I can't remember it. It just worked out that I was going to play forward and ended up playing up there.

Mike: So when did you learn that? Match day or during the week or when?

Greg: I can't really remember exactly when, I can't. But it worked out that I went up there more, and I liked it up there, so I stayed.

Mike: Well, you kicked five goals in that premiership win. But early on it didn't look like that you were going to be making the most of your chances.

Greg: No, that's true. And I didn't go out there looking at kicking goals either, I just went out there with the same plan I always had, which was to play in the centre. People get the perception that AFL players don't get nervous or they just look like they're calm and cool and collected, but I remember that. The first kick went out of bounds, and it went out of bounds just near the point post. It was a shocking kick because I was just that nervous. I was fine after that. Nerves of the day and the big occasion, of course.

Mike: So, fact or fiction—the runner comes out to you in a final at Waverley and says: 'Diesel, go to half-forward, Fraser Brown's going to the middle.' And you said: 'I play in the centre here'?
Greg: I can't honestly remember.

Mike: You're fibbing 'Diesel'.
Greg: I can't honestly remember that. And that's not to say it didn't happen, but…

Mike: You think it may have?
Greg: I know the runner went out to Bruce Doull one day and Bruce said: 'The runner doesn't come out to me.' That's a true story.

Mike: Don't take this the wrong way, but the way you played your footy— when you're talking about the 40 possessions per game and doing the things on your terms, were you selfish?
Greg: I think I was committed and I went about it a different way, I was focused. But whether you call that selfish or not… I did go out there to get 40, you could probably say 'that's greedy', but that's the standard I set. I don't know what else to say I didn't go around telling everybody this, either. I just went out there every game to be best on ground.

That was my mentality, that I wanted to make sure on Monday that I was the best on the ground. That's what I wanted to do every Monday, to read that. And I was pissed off if I wasn't, you know. I'd just build myself up for the next week if I wasn't, and try and get back to being the best player on the ground again. That's what I did for 14 years.

Mike: Did you ever get stitched? You know, just had a shocker? The bloke on you played well, you couldn't find it, it just didn't work, did you ever have a really bad day?
Greg: Yes, I think, Gary Buckenara did it, it was shocking. They were on fire, the Hawks, and the whole team struggled.

Mike: Any on-field incidents that you regret? There's been lots of them I know, but are there any that sit uncomfortably with you now?

Greg: Yes, I'd like to take them all out.

Mike: No you wouldn't.

Greg: No look, most of them.

Mike: I think you thought that you were justified in the Tony Shaw case and the Denham case.

Greg: Yes, I honestly believe they were retaliations, I really do. Even David Rhys-Jones, that one was a retaliation. I think that's the way it was then. But they shouldn't have hit me first. I'm sure there's a few of them that weren't justified either. Nowadays there's hardly any punches thrown there.

There was punches thrown in those days and you just had to protect yourself and try and get through. You know, I really came through a whole career of a lot of players trying to get me from off the square. Every centre bounce I had players trying to line me up. I had a tagger on me. You know, it's not an easy situation for a star player, which I was at that stage. You might think that's arrogant or selfish, but that's that way it was Mick. I had to put up with that every week and, you know, sometimes I got frustrated and retaliated.

Mike: I know there's one incident you regret. There was a photo in *The Herald*, I think at the time, of you chesting a bloke called Tony Lockett.

Greg: That was definitely a mistake going anywhere near 'Plugger'.

Mike: Now the black spot clearly was the incident involving umpire Andrew Coates, wasn't it? You got nine weeks' suspension. How does that sit with you?

Greg: No, I wasn't very happy for the nine weeks, I can tell you. I didn't think it was justified, it wasn't a deliberate action. I reckon I was crucified. Blokes now run over umpires and push them over and…

Mike: Well, not quite.

Greg: Well, they run into them. They knock 'em harder than I touched them.

Mike: So, can you take us through that? I mean, you appeared to be looking somewhere else.

Greg: Yes, that was Denham again. He wouldn't shake my hand after the game and I was a bit pissed off with him, and I was focused on him, and the umpire sort of came across my space, really. I just pushed him out of my space, that's all. It wasn't an aggressive action.

Mike: You knew it was the umpire though?
Greg: No, I don't reckon I did.

Mike: You've got the best vision of any bloke I've ever seen, and you didn't know that it was the umpire in your face?
Greg: No, you're correct, I did have the best vision. No, I didn't see him.

Mike: Didn't see him?
Greg: And there was an eye expert at the tribunal who said that you can be focused on someone else and not see someone in your vision.

Mike: I remember the time and I was pretty harsh on you in print...
Greg: Yes you were.

Mike: I wouldn't have been so harsh now, but you were bitterly disappointed with the decision and the reaction of lots of people in the media, too, weren't you?
Greg: Yes, I got railroaded, I reckon.

Mike: You got what?
Greg: Railroaded, they made a point of making sure it didn't happen again which is fair enough. But also, the guy who cost me that time was Neil Busse, the tribunal chairman. He was away on holidays and they bought in... I know the guy's name, I don't have to name him.

Mike: Well, it was Shane McGuire.
Greg: Yes and I reckon he had a shocker. First time on the tribunal and I reckon he got it wrong.

Mike: What should the penalty have been, given the same circumstances again?
Greg: Well now it's a $900 fine.

Mike: But the irony is, the umpires really liked you, didn't they? Or they loved the way you played your footy. Only 12 blokes in history have polled more Brownlow votes than you, did you know that?

Greg: No I didn't, I didn't know that. I actually polled better as more umpires came in. I actually polled better when there was three.

Mike: Should you have won three Brownlow Medals?
Greg: Look, I think I should've yes, I really do.

Mike: You were beaten by a vote by Gavin Wanganeen in 1993. You should've won the medal that year?
Greg: Well, it's not so much 'I should've'. I think there's a heap of players that haven't won one. You know, I'm lucky enough to have won two and I'm very happy with two. I'm not trying to say that three's the be-all and end-all, but it was the way I lost it that disappointed me. That was all.[111]

Mike: Tell us?
Greg: Well, I'd had 44 possessions and kicked a couple of goals and I got named best in every paper. I was best on ground by every journalist in Australia and I didn't get a vote in the Brownlow that day. Now why didn't I get a vote that day? I could tell you that day, I never swore at an umpire or gave an umpire an issue, because it's not easy when you're getting 44 possessions to be talking to anyone. You're flat out.

So I was really focused on the game and I played well. I reckon I deserved to get a vote and I got none.

Mike: Was there bad blood between you and umpire John Russo?
Greg: Yes, there definitely was. He never gave me a free kick in his life. You might argue that, but he never did. He didn't like me and I didn't like him. That was just … he got me back and that's where he got me back.

Mike: So you reckon he deliberately decided not to give you a vote that day because he didn't like you?
Greg: Well, a few years ago at the Brownlow, an umpire came up to me and said: 'Look Greg, I want to talk to you for a minute.' It was the other umpire that day and his name was Murray Bird. He said to me: 'Look, I just want to apologise for that day.' And I said: 'Oh yeah, what happened?' The gist of it was, they sat down after the game, and Russo asked him because Russo was a lot more senior umpire.

---

111 The game was against Melbourne in 1993.

So, Russo asked Murray: 'Who do you think was best?' He said: 'Oh, Greg Williams was best, no problem, easily best on ground.' And then Russo said, 'Nah,' and he put Mil Hanna down, right? Mil had 19 possessions and Russo asked Murray again: 'Who do you think was second best?' And he said: 'Obviously, I think Greg was best, he deserves two votes.' And he said, 'Nah,' and he put Steve Silvagni and 'SOS' had 12 possessions. I've done my homework on it. And he said, 'Well, who do you think for one?' Because I only needed one vote to draw the Brownlow. Anyway, 'Justin Madden, one vote.' It's not the Russo Medal. It's the umpire's...

Mike: I'm glad you've moved on, Diesel.
Greg: You asked me what happened, I'm telling you.

Mike: No, I appreciate it.
Greg: So, he apologised for ... he didn't stick up for me.

Mike: Do you know what the Carlton voting was for that game?
Greg: No I don't.

Mike: Peter Dean got three that day.
Greg: From who?

Mike: In the Carlton award.
Greg: What, the best and fairest?

Mike: Yes.
Greg: I thought it was Mil who got the Brownlow votes.

Mike: Check that one out. But there's pretty substantial evidence there. I'm on your side mate.
Greg: I'm just saying, I reckon it was unfair.

Mike: From memory, you were very angry at the Brownlow Medal count that year, is that fair?
Greg: No, I don't reckon that's fair. I was disappointed that I didn't get a vote in that game, there's no doubt. But I didn't go around telling everyone I was pissed off or anything. I didn't.

Mike: How many weeks did you get for whacking David Rhys-Jones in 1989?
Greg: I got five weeks, three suspended.

Mike: That was crazy that night. I remember, that was an SCG game wasn't it? Rhys whacked you and broke a bone or the back of your shoulder?

Greg: Yes he did.

Mike: Okay, pick up the story from there?

Greg: Well, I was wrestling. There was a bit of an all-in on the ground and I was wrestling, with Craig Bradley actually, and we were on the ground and next I got kneed from behind and it was Rhys. And he actually broke my shoulder blade, which is not easy to break. But he did, he kneed me in the back, from behind and about a minute later there was a ball-up in the centre and, unluckily for Rhys, he grabbed the ball and I belted him back.

Mike: Broke his jaw?

Greg: Yes I did.

Mike: So it's just an-eye-for-an-eye?

Greg: I just think it is. Like I'm sorry, but I did.

Mike: Now, someone badly advised Rhys after that, didn't they? Instead of going off...

Greg: I went down to the goal square and actually he followed me down there, which was a bad move again. It was a bad move.

Mike: Did you hit him again?

Greg: He came at me again in the goal square, he did. And I hit him in the jaw again. He went down again because he was in a lot of pain of course. He was in a lot of pain.

Mike: And, oddly enough, you end up going to Carlton and playing with Rhys. Did that relationship... was that ever healthy again?

Greg: No, it wasn't. Rhys was really upset with it and that's fair enough. But I think I had a reason to hit him back and I did. I just think... I see Rhys now and then, I talk to him and it's okay, you know?

Mike: I remember you going to Carlton in 2009, and thinking what a smart move it was to get you to come and do some coaching—I think we can see some of your imprimatur on Marc Murphy. What about Chris Judd? Was there any part of 'Juddy's' game that needed any attention?

Greg: I've taken them for a one-on-one … ball-handling's my domain really. I take it seriously—ball-handling and the skills—and I just try and pass on to the players what I did.

I had a really good technique when I played. I hardly ever fumbled, I just had a really good technique where you could attack the ball as fast as you could and it works for everybody.

Mike: What would you say to 'Juddy' when he put one down?
Greg: I just said he's not as good a ball-handler as he thinks he is, that's all.

Mike: Can you say that to a dual-Brownlow medallist?
Greg: I think you can. I think that's the good thing about him as well. He's a fantastic ball-handler, he's a superstar player as well. But I think the stars also need help, you know? I really believe that. I've spoken to 'Juddy' about a few things, between him and me, and I think they're starting to come through, they really are.

Mike: Like?
Greg: Oh, just his focus. Like, I don't know how to say it, he's so unselfish, you know? I'm the opposite, probably. I remember saying to him three years ago when he got to Carlton that he can do a lot of things that no other players can do, which is to win another Brownlow and then maybe win another one and another one. It's a lot to put on a bloke and I probably shouldn't be saying it in public either, but he's the type of player that can. He's won two already and I think there's a serious chance that he could win three. But if he says that doesn't mean anything to him, well that's fine. But I think he can set the standard again and be the best player of all time.

Mike: So, I want to ask you about that, where he sits. I mean, you've played with Stephen Kernahan and Craig Bradley and Stephen Silvagni and some great names with Carlton. Where does Judd sit in that group?
Greg: He's right up there, there's no question. But I think as he continues on with his career, he's probably got five or six years to go, and who knows what he can end up with in regards to hopefully premierships and Brownlows, best and fairests. He's on track to be the best player of his time, no doubt. He's an amazing athlete. Like, you talk about speed, I don't think I've ever

seen a bloke who can pick the ball up as fast as him and run it as fast. And I don't know how he does it. He just bends over and scoops it up like no one else.

Mike: Where does the 'Diesel' come from? Who christened you 'Diesel'?
Greg: That was in Geelong. Mick Turner actually did that. He was a really good captain and I had a lot of respect for him as soon as I got there. He had team meetings in those days, well before his time and he actually had a motivational tape as well, which was a gridiron tape. It was John Riggins, I'm not sure if you've ever heard of him?

Mike: No.
Greg: He was a great running back in America at that time, and he still holds the world record for yardage. His name was Diesel and for some reason that was where it came from.

Mike: Now we talked before about Brownlows. In your first Brownlow, there might have been an element of luck attached to that Diesel? In the last game against Fitzroy you smacked Scotty Clayton.
Greg: Yes, I was very concerned at that stage. I thought I would've got rubbed out. But he did the right thing at the tribunal and said...

Mike: And lied?
Greg: Probably did, yes. But I always hit my taggers in the chest. I did it all the time and it was a bit like that with Scotty, but I just went a bit low, got him in the guts.

Mike: You went on after football and went into a printing business and did very well out of it. So well that you don't have to work from your mid-40s. Is the story true that you sat next to a woman on a plane and accommodated her with an autograph and she then said to you, 'Look, you're a printer, why don't you put a tender in for this printing job?'
Greg: Yes, that's true. It wasn't on a plane, but it was a lady who asked me to do a birthday card for her mother and she was a purchasing officer at Kmart. I did the signature and everything, she said: 'Well, why don't you come in on Monday and have a chat about the printing?' I ended up with a Kmart account and...

Mike: And it was worth millions, wasn't it?
Greg: Yes it was. We did a good price though, Mick, it was no funny business or anything.

Mike: Is there any one thing in your footy career that you'd like a second crack at?
Greg: The biggest disappointment for me was when I went to Carlton and I was injured. I had a really bad knee then, my right knee, which is still … it's buggered now. If I'd stayed as fit as I could've then and trained as well as I had at Sydney I reckon I would've been a lot better even at Carlton.

ACKNOWLEDGEMENTS

To all those who have made my professional life so exciting, so rewarding, so inspiring, by virtue of their skill, courage, athleticism, application and daring—the players.

All of us immersed in football in our various ways are blessed to have been born into such an engrossing way of life, or to have been seduced by its vast array of attractions along the way.

My thanks to Geoff Slattery and the entire Slattery Media Group for taking the program into book form; to Fox Footy, particularly Rod Law, Bill Cannon and Joel Starcevic, for their faith in the concept (for indulging me), and to my family for their understanding and support—most of the time!

And to Andrew Denton for the inspiration.

Finally, to all those who agreed to sit down with me and share their experiences, good and bad.